Luis de León
The Names of Christ

TRANSLATION AND INTRODUCTION BY
MANUEL DURÁN AND WILLIAM KLUBACK

PREFACE BY
J. FERRATER MORA

PAULIST PRESS
NEW YORK • RAMSEY • TORONTO

GLORIA DURÁN is an artist, writer, and teacher of Spanish literature at Yale University.

Library of Congress
Catalog Card Number 83-62992

ISBN: 0-8091-2561-7 (paper)
0-8091-0346-X (cloth)

Published by Paulist Press
545 Island Road, Ramsey, N.J. 07446

Printed and bound in the
United States of America

Contents

THE NAMES OF CHRIST

Editors and Translators of this Volume

MANUEL DURÁN was born in Barcelona, Spain, in 1925. He studied in Spain, France, Mexico and the United States, obtaining an MA degree in Philosophy from the University of Mexico and a Ph.D. in Romance Languages and Literatures at Princeton University. He is Professor of Spanish Literature and Chairman of the Department of Spanish and Portuguese at Yale University and the author of numerous books, including *Cervantes, Luis de León, and Ambiguity in Don Quixote*. He edited anthologies of Ortega y Gasset, Lorca, and others.

WILLIAM KLUBACK is Professor of Philosophy at Kingsborough Community College of the City University of New York. His two most recent books are concerned with the Neo-Kantian philosopher Hermann Cohen. The books will be published by Brown University Press and Mercer University Press. He is now completing a study of the humanism of Paul Valéry. He has published in *Idealistic Studies, Revue Internationale de Philosophie, Midstream, Tydschrift voor Filosofie, Judaism*, and other journals.

Author of the Preface

JOSE FERRATER MORA was born in Barcelona, Spain, in 1912. He graduated from the University of Barcelona in 1936. After teaching Philosophy in Cuba (1941–1942) and Chile (1942–1947), he came to the United States with a Guggenheim Fellowship. He was a member of the Bryn Mawr College faculty until 1981, when he retired as Professor of Philosophy and Fairbank Professor in the Humanities. He has taught in various American universities, including Temple, Johns Hopkins, and Princeton. He is the author of some twenty-five books, in Spanish and English, including *Man at the Crossroads* and *Being and Death*. His four-volume *Diccionario de Filosofia* is known all over the world.

Preface

Spaniards have been presented much too often under inquisitional garb: an army of Torquemadas trying to purify the world from heretics and dissenters. This view of Spaniards and Spain, the so-called Black Legend, has some historical support, but misses two points. One is that inquisitional minds are not scarce in other countries, including some that seem to enjoy an inexhaustible supply of good conscience. The other is that although a number of Spaniards have sympathized with the spirit of Torquemada, others have been its victims. Among the latter was Fray Luis de León.

Fray Luis was the perfect target for inquisitional rage. Inquisitors are not too worried by people who maintain extreme views, even if such views are opposed to their own. They known that extremists, always striving for some dogma, are easily converted. On the other hand, inquisitors are bothered by people like Fray Luis, who are permeated by the spirit of humanism. Humanism—the love of beauty and truth is all cultural traditions—is the greatest threat to narrow dogmatism, so brashly promoted by inquisitors. The true humanist is ready to accept everything that is valuable regardless of origin, for as the famous line says, "I am human and nothing human is alien to me." Here, among other things, "human" means, of course, "civilized." This celebrated line hides a system of values that are implicit in the ordinary meaning of the term "humane." To be a humanist means, therefore, to be sensitive to everything that a truly humane person cherishes: kindness, generosity, friendship, peace, beauty, truth; and to be, as it were, allergic to everything that perverts human nature: wickedness, greediness, hostility, violence, ugliness, falsehood. Humanism in this sense is an exaltation of all that is best in mankind.

Fray Luis showed his humanistic leanings in many ways: in his reverence for the great literary and religious traditions known to him—Greek, Latin, Christian, Hebrew, in his fondness for music, his profound religiosity, his attitude in front of all his fellow beings. Humanism seems somewhat suspicious today, because it is believed that the insistence on human nature, even on its most noble features, is detrimental to the rest of the cosmos. Such a belief does not find support in the works of Fray Luis. To be sure, he viewed God as the supreme Good, and man as the creation of God, but he never disengaged man from the context of nature, whose beauty he proclaimed in some of the most profound and delicate lyrical poetry ever written. Fray Luis's humanism is, therefore, never confined to the narrow limits of human nature: he projects it to God and to the entire world. It is even possible, albeit mistaken, to view Fray Luis as a pantheist, or perhaps as a "panentheist"—the term that Spanish Krausists used to emphasize the idea that God, nature, and man are, at bottom, one. Fray Luis was not a pantheist: He was too close to the Christian, and to the Hebrew, traditions to eschew the notion of God as a person, and of the world as a creation of God. But his lyrical feeling for nature makes a humanist with a vengenance. Since nothing human is alien to man, and since man lives in nature as a creature of God, nothing that is truly human—his natural being no less than the divine spark of his soul—should be neglected.

The editors of this book, William Kluback and Manuel Durán, have presented with utmost clarity the most important features of Fray Luis de León's work, emphasizing its religious and literary aspects. Their essays can serve not only as an introduction to the translation of Fray Luis's *Los nombres de Cristo*, but also to the work of Fray Luis as a whole. For the *Nombres de Cristo* is only one side, albeit a very significant one, of the many-sided Fray Luis, a scholar and a poet in the great tradition of Spanish Renaissance humanism. Years ago a book was published under the provocative title *Spanien. Das Land ohne Renaissance (Spain: The Country without a Renaissance)*. The work of Fray Luis is a refutation of the title, as well as the contents, of such a book.

Foreword

To read Fray Luis de León's *The Names of Christ* is to be introduced to a world in which God's love and man's devotion were not rare incidents and moments to unique individuals. Faith was not a peculiar experience and God's reality not a flickering glimmer or a rare and quickly disappearing light. Men took seriously divine revelation; they read the Bible with imagination. They saw and heard only what was immediate. The Bible was a continuous source of meaning that needed exploration, insight, and the construction and transformation of language. In the simple but devastating question, What does it mean? the endless dialogue of love, trust, and search found no ground for rest and comfort. God's majesty exhausted and overcame all human effort, however profound and devoted. The enchanting conversations that build *The Names of Christ* should be read with the appreciation that belongs to every human achievement—to every attempt to draw the divine into the human and to explore the human through the divine.

The work of Fray Luis can be characterized as a *Heilsgeschichte*, a history of salvation, which we can perceive as the realization of God's presence in history. This necessitates a comprehension of the relationship between what Mircea Eliade has designated the sacred and the profane: "The manifestation of the sacred in space has cosmological valence; every spatial hierophany or consecration of a space is equivalent to a cosmogony."[1] What is fundamental is the fact that there has been a *Heilsgeschenk*, a theophany, a revelation of the sacred in profane reality, and it is this *Kairos* that founds sacred history. It gives purpose and orientation to what is profane and chaotic. The religious man comprehends sacred history to be the only meaningful order of events.

---

1. Mircea Eliade, *The Sacred and the Profane* (New York, 1959), pp. 63–64. This book is fundamental for any reader who is concerned with the difference between sacred and profane time and space—in other words, between sacred and world history. See also Karl Lowith, *Meaning in History* (Chicago, 1949).

Profane history is for him without purpose. It has no beginning and no end; in other words; it is devoid of the theophany that creates sacred history, that is, sacred time and space. Every image of Fray Luis speaks a theophany. The names of God are the theophonic revelations of His manifestations. Whether we call God shepherd or path, we are engaged in an attempt to grasp an aspect of revelation and make it more realizable and graspable in time and space.

What we grasp is a two-leveled reality. The divine reality has been revealed and has founded sacred history, a history that remains for man as yet veiled and that man struggles to unveil in the course of his attempt to comprehend the distinctions between the sacred and the profane. Standing between the sacred and profane, man reaches out to the sacred as the "wholly other." He can never leave the profane as long as he remains man, the creature who grasps and is grasped by the sacred, but who remains tied to the profane by the fact that, in freedom, he can turn again to the unreal, to a history, in which he attempts to see his own activity and values as true reality. "In other words the more religious he is, the more does he enter into the *real* and the less is he in danger of becoming lost in actions that, being nonparadigmatic, 'subjective,' are, finally, aberrant."[2] From Fray Luis's review we could say that history and theophany are one. *The Names of Christ* is a sacred history. The names are an unfolding of Christ's sacred purpose: the salvation of humanity. It is this theophany that makes it possible for Fray Luis to construct his theology of history. Each name is a new sign. Each makes possible the path of the redemption.

A theology of history begins with the *Kairos*, the divine or sacred breakthrough into history from which and by which history is now given a sacred purpose, toward which it moves. The movement of history is the constant revelation of the divine presence. This presence creates sacred time and place. The mystical body, the heavenly Jerusalem, are the transcendent models of the sacred indwelling of the divine in the profane. These sacred places embody the movement of sacred time; they are witness to the hope of redemption toward which sacred history moves, founding those spiritual paths that are the sacred names. The

---

2. Eliade, *The Sacred and the Profane*, p. 96.

sacred place that we call also a spatial hierophany is the center of communication in which the profane is consecrated and the sacred is revealed as the space in which and through which the new world is founded. It is within this structure that we can begin to make sense of Fray Luis's vision and cosmological conception of sacred history. *The Names of Christ* is a cosmology. It also provides the threads that makes this cosmology comprehensible. As we move from name to name, we encompass more meaningfully the purpose of God.

There is in the religious man something that can be designated the "ontological thirst." To understand the nature and quality of this thirst requires a comprehension of the chaos and violence that threaten the religious man at every moment of existence and that we can call the confrontation with nothingness. The ontological thirst or the thirst for Being, permeates the soul in search of God's presence, the soul that attempts to understand that theogonic process, that process of divine life by which God manifests Himself both in Himself and outside Himself. The realization that the process is incomplete both in God and in His manifestation is coupled with the realization that the human is fallible and forever condemned to incompleteness. There is an unfinished quality about all divine speculation, and every theology of history reveals and unveils its own incompleteness and inadequacy.

The work of man is infinite. The mystery of the sacred remains forever veiled. There is a dialectic between the veiling and unveiling of the profane and sacred interrelationship that challenges the creative imagination and makes it the source of communication between the sacred moving toward the profane, and the need and longing within the profane to be impregnated by the sacred. Is not the profane the negation of the sacred embodying in itself the source of its redemption, being the other of the sacred, related to and only estranged from it? The sacred and profane do not exclude each other; rather, we should say that in their estrangement they reveal their relationship.

The comprehension of these religious realms presupposes a highly complex religious development. What is significant is the exploration of these realms in those religious souls whose works form the heritage of ideas that unveil to us the nature of religion. It is our purpose to speak of a few of these figures and movements both in Spain and elsewhere and delineate what we believe to be some of the rarer contributions to religious life and to be fundamental for a comprehension of Fray Luis. *The Names of Christ*, we believe, belongs to the tradition of literature that has attempted to comprehend the divine-human dialogue, and that we grasp more sympathetically when we read several masters of its art.

One of the grandest theological creations of Muslim Spain is the theosophy of Ibn al-Arabi (1165–1240) of Murcia.[3] There is a cosmic *sympatheia*, a passion among things, that we call the metaphysics of love, a movement that liberates potentiality from actuality, a movement toward openness, efficacious in a love that dwells both within the passivity of potentiality and in the activity of liberation. There is a need that ties the love of the lover to the love of the beloved and unites them in mutual dependency.

> "But this sympathy, precisely, does not signify acceptance of their limits; it signifies rather that in opening ourselves to them we open them to the expansion that the primordial divine *sympathesis* demands of them; that we increase their divine light to the maximum; that we "emancipate" them—as the divine Compassion did in preeternity—that is, emancipate them from the verticality and the ignorance which still confine them in this narrow intransigence."[4]

Sympathy is the source of accessibility to the lights of theophanies. There is deeply embedded in Ibn al-Arabi's faith the realization that God yearns to be revealed to what is other to Him, that the divine names seek incarnation, and that there is in the inscrutable depth of the divine a longing sadness that seeks redemption in the sympathy of the faith and love of the believer. Here is so deeply and abundantly expressed that interrelationship between the theomorphic and anthropomorphic dimensions of man and God. Each seeks the other in love, each is dependent on the other

---

3. Henry Corbin, *Creative Imagination in the Sufism of Ibn Arabi* (Princeton, 1969). Ibn Arabi's *The Bezels of Wisdom* is now available in English in the Classics of Western Spirituality (New York: Paulist Press, 1980). See also Miguel Asin Palacios, *The Mystical Philosophy of Ibn Masarra and His Followers* (Leiden, 1978); and *Sufis of Andalusia*, trans. with introd. R. W. J. Austin.

4. Corbin, *Creative Imagination*, p. 118.

for fulfillment and realization. What deeper pathos than this cosmic mutual dependence of the divine and the human, the sacred and the profane?

The pathetic God of Iban al-Arabi "is a suffering and passionate God, a notion which has at all times been a dreaded stumbling block to the rational theology and philosophy of Christianity, Islam, and Judaism alike. The notion of a God who is affected by human events and feelings and reacts to them in a very personal way, in short, the idea that there is a divine *pathos* in every sense of the word (affection, emotion, passion),"[5] allowed Ibn al-Arabi to conceive of *pathos* as a turning, either the turning of God to man, anthropotropism, or that turning of man to God, theotropism.

The noble Neo-Platonic philosopher Proclus, who gave us such profound insights into the *hieratic science*, embodies in his visions of the longing of the soul to return to God and the mystic bonds uniting all beings, the animals, the plants, and the minerals to their source, the touching prayer of the heliotrope that Henry Corbin, the scholar of Persian thought, so fittingly quotes at the beginning of his chapter on divine passion and compassion.

> What other reason can we give for the fact that the heliotrope follows in its movement the movement of the sun and the celentrope the movement of the moon, forming a procession within the limits of their power, behind the torches of the universe? For, in truth, each thing prays according to the rank it occupies in nature, and sings the praise of the leader of the divine series of things to which it belongs, a spiritual or rational or physical or sensuous praise; for the heliotrope moves to the extent that it is free to move, and in its rotation . . . we should be aware that it is a hymn to its king, such as it is within the power of a plant to sing.[6]

It is the metaphysics of love to which we return again and again in Ibn al-Arabi's thought. We are speaking of love as the power that awakens in the beloved the love with which he is

---

5. Ibid., p. 108.
6. Ibid., p. 106.

loved. Love is that circle in which the lover understands that he is
both lover and beloved. The love for God that man finds awakened in him is already the love of God that is in him. He loves the
love that is vibrating in him. The love that comes upon him does
not incite a strange, but only an estranged, love. What vibrates in
him is the love that is receptive to a love that is both that of lover
and beloved.

We experience in Ibn al-Arabi the force and power of the
active and creative imagination forging the links of a theophanic
union between the sacred and the profane, the spiritual and the
physical. The powers of love surpass sharp and precise distinctions and categories; the imagination of love is a mediating power
with a distinct dignity whose limits and projections transcend
every attempt of limitation and clarification. We experience a
divine-human mediation whose presence proclaims divinity and
humanity linked in a dialogue of confrontation and realization.
Here in the *Book of Theophanies* Ibn al-Arabi speaks the poem of
love:

> Love me, love me alone.
> Love yourself in me, in me alone.
> Attach yourself to me.
> No one is more inward than I.
> Others love you for their own sakes,
> I love you for yourself.
> And you, you flee from me.
> Dearly beloved!
> You cannot treat me fairly,
> For if you approach me,
>   It is because I have approached you.
> I am nearer to you than yourself,
> Than your soul, than your breath.
> Who among your creatures
> Would treat you as I do?
> I am jealous of you over you,
> I want you to belong to no other,
> Not even to yourself.
> Be mine, be for me as you are in me,
> Though you are not even aware of it.

FOREWORD

A similar cosmogonic and theogonic drama is put forth in the world of Jewish Kabbalah.[7] The struggle of the imaginative religious soul is constant against the rational, the polemical, and the pedagogical; in the realm of myth, which situates him on the divine plane, he believes he becomes truly man interpreting and conforming to the myths that lie at the ground of the divine. "Thus at the heart of the Kabbalah we have a myth of the one God as a conjunction of all the primordial powers of being and a myth of the Torah as an infinite symbol, in which all images and all names point to a process in which God communicates Himself."[8] The Torah becomes the *corpus mysticum*, that mystical body in and through which the drama of Israel's redemption is made possible. There is a grand myth among the rabbis of Kabbalah that speaks of "exile as an element in God Himself." These thoughts cannot be easily confined to the limits and confines of rational thought, but here we have the symbols that stir and seduce the minds of men for whom the imagination is the living reality of all human creativity. This cosmic drama of exile and redemption in the divine is perhaps one of the boldest visions ever brought forth of the interrelationship between man and God, the profane and the sacred. The living quality of divinity, its anthropological reality, brings forth that theomorphic dimension of man which makes possible the divine-human dialogue. The drama bears within itself a close connection to the expulsion of the Jews from Spain, "an event which more than any other in Jewish history down to the catastrophe of our own times gave urgency to the question: Why the exile of the Jews and what is their vocation in the world?"[9] The attempt to answer this question becomes the challenge of a theology of history. The Kabbalistic myth speaks of vessels that "were designed to receive the mighty light of the *sefirot*," of Adam

---

7. Gershom Scholem, "On Sin and Punishment: Some Remarks concerning Biblical and Rabbinical Ethics," in *Myth and Symbols: Studies in Honor of Mircea Eliade* (Chicago, 1971); idem, *On the Kabbalah and Its Symbolism* (New York, 1969); idem, *Major Trends in Jewish Mysticism* (New York, 1972); idem, *Von der mystischen Gestalt der Gottheit* (Zurich, 1962); *Le Commentaire d'Ezra de Gérone sur le cantique des cantiques*, trans. George Vajda (Paris, 1969); S. Shahar, "Ecrits cathares et commentaires d'Abraham Abulafia sur le 'Livre de la Création': Images et idées communes," in *Juifs et Judaisme de Languedoc* (Toulouse, 1977); René Nelli, *La Philosophie du catharisme* (Paris, 1975).

8. Scholem, *On the Kabbalah*, p. 95.

9. Ibid., p. 110.

Kadmon, "from his eyes, and to serve as vessels and instruments of creation and which shattered under its impact. This is the decisive crisis of all divine and created being."[10] Here we are confronted with cosmic disorder, or what we can describe as the terror of existence. Order has become disorder, things have lost their place and time, the harmony and sympathy of the cosmos are interrupted. "Everything is somewhere else. But a being that is not in its proper place is in exile. Thus, since that primordial act, all being has a being in exile, in need of being led back and redeemed. The breaking of the vessels continues into all the further stages of emanation and creation; everything is in some way broken, everything has a flaw; everything is unfinished."[11] What adds vast dimensions to this drama of sin and redemption that belongs so deeply to the soul of the exiled Israel is that exile is also a dimension of divinity. Rare are the moments of the religious imagination that are bold and audacious enough to create that sympathy between God and man to such a degree that the *pathos* of human suffering and the exilic nature of Israel's history become dimensions of the divine life.

In the soul of man this battle is fought out, this struggle to redeem the profane and to bring forth the *pax aeterna.* The pain and joy that accompany this struggle in behalf of God's will and love create the communion that brings us to the likeness of God. Nowhere is this struggle sharper or more acute than in the *Confessions.* Augustine struggles not only with a faith he knows is dependent on God's mercy, but also with a love that can only be the creation of the divine love. Where do we find the anguish and struggle more beautifully expressed than in these words of Augustine:

> "I cast myself down under a certain fig-tree somehow and gave free rein to my tears and the floods of mine eyes gushed forth, an acceptable sacrifice to Thee, and I besought Thee at length, not indeed in these words but to this effect, "and thou, O Lord, how long? How long wilt Thou be angry, forever? Remember not our iniquities of old times," for I felt that I was held by them. I continued

---

10. Ibid., p. 112.
11. Ibid., pp. 112–13.

to utter my sorrowful cries, "How long, how long, tomorrow and tomorrow? Why not now? Why not an end
to my uncleanness this very hour?"[12]

The decision is God's, the effort is man's. Each man is given
anew the struggle, but little do we know of success or failure; it is
our trust in God's mercy that determines the outcome.

Nothing was clearer to Augustine than the reality of evil, the
experience of the erring soul; error was not the consequence of
ignorance; it had meaning and without an immersion in its meaning there was no good, no salvation. This radical break with
ancient philosophy was the ground of the theology of history.
Nature was no longer "whatever has persisted in accordance with
the divine will but rather whatever has become depraved contrary
to the divine will."[13]

The dimension of sin was radical. Dualism was fundamental;
it had both a cosmic and an existential realm. The struggle between good and evil was played out in each man's soul; it is on the
cosmic level the supreme meaning of Christ's coming, for in Him
the two cities were separated from eternity, the city of God and
that earthly city of man.

The Christian lives in obedience to this cosmogonic reality.
He seeks no logical justification or rational explanation. He knows
sacred history and myth, and he is aware that only through the
will can he grasp the fact that before this world came into being
there was the will and the word of God, and it is to this will and
word that he must cling if he wants to avoid falling into the chaos
and terror of profane history. Nothing else matters for Christian
ethics than the primacy of the will over knowledge. We have
previously stated that Fray Luis gave us more than a scriptural
commentary to the names of God, but that each name is another
dimension of the nature of the divine presence in history. The
historical-theological drama of Augustine has made possible every
Christian reflection on history. We believe that only with this
Augustinian structure in mind is it possible to begin reading *The
Names of Christ.*

---

12. *The Confessions of St. Augustine,* trans. C. S. C. Williams (Oxford: Basil Black-
well, 1953), pp. 38–39.
13. Ibid., p. 187.

FOREWORD

A word should be said about the mystical significance of the names of God. Every thinker worthy of the designation has known the differences between what is revealed and the source of revelation. These mysteries have given wide fields of speculation to those who have sought meanings behind meanings, and those who felt the magic and efficacious relationship between the hidden and the revealed. Scholem tells us of one text, the *Theurgic Uses of the Torah*, that was known to the Kabbalists in both Provence and Spain about the year 1200. Nahmanides, one of the great rabbinic thinkers of the age, refers in his preface to this Torah commentary:[14]

> "The statement in the Aggadah to the effect that the Torah was originally written with black fire on white fire obviously confirms our opinion that the writing was continuous without division into words which made it possible to read it either as a sequence of esoteric names or in the traditional way as history and commandments."[15]

We read similar statements by Ezra ben Solomon, a member of the famous circle of Kabbalists in the Catalonian town of Gerona. He states that "the five books of the Torah are the *Name* of the Holy One, blessed be He"; he further affirms the older doctrine, already declared in the *Midrash Genesis Rabbah*, to the effect that the mystical light shining in the Torah is the great name of God. "The same thesis is to be found in the writings of several members of the Gerona group of Kabbalists, and was finally taken over by the author of the *Zohar*, the classical book of Spanish Kabbalism."[16] What we comprehend here is the experience of the mystical power and efficacy of the name, the realization that there lies behind what is revealed a noumenal harmony of laws that governs the visible world but to which the mind of man has little access, and to which he unceasingly strives to

---

14. Scholem, *Kabbalah and Its Symbolism*, esp. chap. 2, "The Meaning of the Torah."

15. Ibid., p. 38.

16. Ibid., p. 39. George Vajda has now made available in French translation the commentary of Ezra ben Solonon on the Song of Songs: *Le Commentaire d'Ezra de Gérone sur le cantique des cantiques* (Paris, 1969).

penetrate. This preexisting, eternal world, of which we have only glimmers, stimulates and stirs the creative imagination of every great mind to find the vehicle by which the infinite is mediated in the finite and the finite in the infinite.

In the fifth century there appeared a work, *The Divine Names*, of a Dionysius the Areopagite that had a profound influence on the theological speculations of the Schools.[17] Dionysius puts the question in the following manner:

> "Furthermore, if It [Divinity] transcends all reason and the whole of knowledge, and is established above intellect and essence, and embraces and unites and comprehends and foreknows all things, while Itself is altogether beyond their grasp and beyond the reach of any sense-perception, observation, imagination, opinion, name, word or touch, how can our treatise thoroughly examine the Divine Names, when the super-essential Godhead has been proved to be nameless and above all names?"[18]

The transcendent Divinity is the cause of all that is, but, at the same time, transcends being. Whatever we say of Divinity, we deny at the same time. Divinity is the Nothingness, beyond everything, and is yet the source of all things. Dionysius leads us to the *via negativa*, making us aware that the approach to the Divine is possible only to the degree that we are aware that whatever we say of Divinity is dependent on the reality of negation. The insight of Dionysius that negation and privation are the paths to Divinity was already grasped by Plato. Privation and negation lie at the ground of infinite judgment, link the finite to the infinite, and deny any judgment the possibility of becoming one with divine reality. Dionysius makes this very clear when he states:

> "And even the Name of Goodness is not given to It as being appropriate, but desiring to think and speak about Its Ineffable Nature, we consecrate, as the most highly appropriate to It, the most revered of Names. And al-

---

17. Dionysius the Areopagite, *The Divine Names*, trans. The Editors of the Shrine of Wisdom (Surrey, 1957).
18. Ibid., p. 13.

though in this matter we are in agreement with the theologians, the truth about this is very far beyond us. Therefore they have chosen the negative way, since by this the soul is lifted above things akin to itself and travels throughout the conceptions of God which are transcended by That which is above all names and all reason and knowledge."[19]

The names of God given in the Scriptures reveal to us not only what we can say about Him, but that God in His infinity surpasses whatever it is possible for us to say of Him.[20] We are obliged by our faith and our reason to speak of God and are guided by the Scriptures in our attempts to comprehend the ways and the names that make Him meaningful to us; but we know at the same time that whatever we say of Him is surpassed by Him in the hiddenness of His Majesty. With the realization that the positive is rooted in the negative and that privation is the source of all genuine thought, we approach that divine-human dialectic which is revealed in the never-ending search to mediate the visible in the invisible and the invisible in the visible. *The Names of Christ* is one more example of the undeniable strength of the religious soul to find in the sacred the meaning and coherence that are denied him in the profane, to develop those myths that link the light of Theophanies into a meaningful theology of history. The names of God are the signposts along that path which Divine Presence has from eternity revealed in glimmers to the believers and the lover.

---

19. Ibid., p. 90. See the excellent editions *Sources chrétiennes: Denys l'aréopagite, La Hiérarchie céleste* (Paris, 1976). There is a good introduction by R. Roques.

20. F. Ruello, "Le Commentaire de Denys par Albert," in *Archives de philosphie: VII centenaire d'Albert le Grand*, Oct.–Dec. 1980. "De ce point de vue, l'"art de nommer' Dieu qu'enseigne l'Ecriture est de proclamer qu'il est en lui-même et non seulement à titre de cause, ce que ses noms signifient. Mais il est, également de proclamer, à l'aide de negations, que, par son infinité, Dieu dépasse notre compréhension de chacune de ses 'raisons' auxquelles cependant, avec l'Ecriture, nous donnons un nom" (p. 613).

Introduction

There can be no doubt that *The Names of Christ* is one of the greatest masterpieces of Renaissance philosophical and spiritual thought. In its pages Christianity comes to terms with many other sources of wisdom: As a river nourished by powerful affluents, the biblical exegesis that constitutes the essence of this book is enriched by the Greek tradition of Plato and Aristotle; by the Hebraic sources of interpretation, including the Kabbalah; by the Arabic religious thought, including most specifically the Sufi mystical experience; and finally by the ecumenical spirit of Italian, Spanish, indeed Western European Renaissance. Many of its pages, paragraphs, sentences, seem to hold in their middle, as a precious seed, the message by which the past endures today and makes it possible to affirm that we are the proud heirs of this great tradition.

A life-giving, powerful river: There is nothing small or mediocre in Luis de León's thought and expression. The book was conceived from beginning to end as a masterpiece, a human work worthy of its lofty subject, which is no less than an attempt to come closer to God by defining and understanding the meanings of the words with which the Son of God, Christ, is named in the Bible. It is, if you wish, a roundabout way, since the naming of God had proved too hard and dangerous a task: There is often wisdom in an oblique step-by-step approach when a frontal assault has failed.

Luis de León was born in Belmonte, a little Castilian town, either in 1527 or in 1528.[1] One of his biographers, Aubrey Bell, writes about León's birthplace, which is situated in La Mancha.

---

1. We know he was baptized in Belmonte, but the records for the period are missing. Aubrey Bell (*Luis de León* [Oxford, Oxford U. Press, 1925]) gives 1527 as a

1

INTRODUCTION

The inhabitants of the town, hospitable, courteous and independent, have a strongly marked character. La Mancha, to the east of New Castile, produces a keen, energetic, tenacious race ... of which Don Quixote himself was so chivalrous an example. They can combine a Castilian chivalry towards the weak with a hatred of injustice and a vehemence which is almost Valencian. A foreigner well acquainted with Spain, when asked how he would distinguish the inhabitants of Cuenca (the provincial capital) from those of other Castilians, answered without hesitation that he considered them "a little fiercer."[2]

His family was well-to-do, cultured, influential, with friends at the Court. His father, a lawyer, was to become a judge at Granada. There was Jewish blood on the maternal side. Young Luis went to school in Madrid and Valladolid. In 1543 he entered the Convent of St. Augustine in Salamanca as a novice, and professed in 1544. The Augustinian Order had been recently reorganized. The order was originally devoted to meditation, contemplation, and prayer, and its best writers had been preoccupied for generations with the possibility of reconciling Plato's philosophy and the gospels. The new trend was to enlarge the order's interest in theology in general, as well as in all humanistic studies, and to establish strong links between the order and the universities. The young Luis de León would mature intellectually in a climate that recognized the humanistic disciplines as the firm foundation of all religious speculation and the right path toward theology, dogma, Scripture, ethics, asceticism, and mysticism.

During his life León would play many roles: university professor, poet, essay writer, "executive" of his Augustinian Order, theologian—even the role of victim of fanaticism, his role as a Renaissance scholar persecuted by the Inquisition, jailed and interrogated at length, is an important one in his total experience as a man and as an intellectual. There is no doubt that he always felt at home in the university, where he had many friends, many disciples who admired his teaching, his integrity, his wisdom.

---

probable birth date. A French biographer, Adolphe de Coster, proposes June 1528 as an equally possible date. Most modern critics have accepted Bell's date.

2. Bell, *Luis de León*, p. 86.

INTRODUCTION

Also, and at the same time, he felt the sense of belonging to his Augustinian Order, which had reached a high plateau of achievement, which had created an intellectual climate open to every new trend, which in many ways was among the most modern centers of thought in sixteenth-century Spain.

Let us observe in passing that ever since in the Forties and Fifties the great Spanish scholar Americo Castro started publishing a series of books and articles dealing with the presence of Jewish and Arabic elements in Spanish Medieval and Renaissance culture (see the item *The Spaniards: An Introduction to Their History*, in our Select Bibliography), a bitter and seemingly endless controversy has raged among Spanish scholars and Hispanists: Did Castro exaggerate such a presence? With respect to the Spanish Humanists the answer is simple. Out of the *three* greatest Spanish Humanists, León, Luis Vives, and Antonio de Nebrija, *two* of them, Vives and León, had Jewish ancestors. We can find no parallel in Italy, France, England, etc. Of the three, León was perhaps the most dedicated Humanist in his attempt (so typical of all Humanists since Valla's generation) of *going back to the sources*— and since the sources in his case were often the Biblical texts, he had to come in conflict, unavoidably, with a religious and academic bureaucracy intent upon preserving the current texts and deeply worried about the consequences of going back to the sources of the sacred texts.

Salamanca, where León lived and taught, was basically conservative. Looking for more contemporary lines of thought, he traveled to a younger university, Alcalá, near Madrid, in search of guidance. He found it in a great teacher, Cipriano de la Huerga, who taught him the Hebrew language and much more: Hebrew and humanistic wisdom. This took place in 1556. Our young scholar was aware that his excursion to Alcalá was mainly an intellectual and spiritual vacation: His career as a theologian and as a teacher had to be integrated with the University of Salamanca, to which he returned shortly and where in 1558 he was awarded the degree of Master (what we would now call Ph.D). in Theology. At the age of thirty-two he was competing for a chair. At that time in Salamanca there was a strange custom: University chairs were not appointive but rather elective. Students, colleagues, university officials could all vote, after hearing lectures from various candidates; the result decided who would become the professor in charge of a specific chair. León was elected in 1561 to the then vacant chair of St. Thomas Aquinas's philosophical and theological thought—an advanced course taught, as most other courses at the time, entirely in Latin. He was elected by 108 votes to 55. No corruption of any kind was involved. Luis's talent and erudition were overwhelming.

A few years later, during a difficult period for our scholar, who had been indicted and was being tried by an Inquisition court, a distinguished scholar and composer, Francisco de Salinas, one of the great organ players and composers of the century, who also knew much about theology and humanistic studies, testified in court as a character witness and explained that many of León's admirers were convinced that he could carry any university chair against all competition, in other words, that he was a "super-teacher," a genius who could teach successfully all subjects being taught in the university of his time.[3]

Luis de León soon came to be known as a gifted poet and a great theologian. Poetry has been revered in all ages; theology is appreciated and admired only in certain times and places. Spain at that time was a country in which theologians were revered. One could even say that within the complex political system of six-teenth-century Spain the best theologians could occasionally mus-ter enough influence and power to change official and socially accepted attitudes, much as the U.S. Supreme Court has on occa-sion changed legal and ethical trends in this country. After all, it was left to theologians to interpret the divine law, the Scriptures. Thus a theologian, Father Las Casas, could argue forcefully and with some success in favor of the rights of Indians conquered by the Spaniards in the New World.

Of course knowledge of Scriptures could be a two-edged sword. Already in 1566 rumors were spreading among his col-leagues and students at the University of Salamanca that León had more than once claimed to have found errors in the text of the Vulgate, the Latin text accepted all over the Catholic world, and also had affirmed that many passages could have been made clear-er and more full of meaning if the Hebrew text had been translat-ed with greater precision. This was a dangerous subject since it

---

3. On this subject see Bell, *Luis de León*, p. 111, and also Manuel Durán, *Luis de León* (New York: Twayne Publishers, Inc., 1971), esp. chapters 1–3.

was precisely the interpretation and translation of the Bible that was at the origin of several Protestant heresies, and of course had been the mainspring of other more ancient heresies during the first centuries of Christianity. Luis de León was an excellent Hebraist. This only served to irritate most of his colleagues, who knew little or no Hebrew and felt inferior every time they debated him. On top of all of this his colleagues, at least some of them, found León contentious, arrogant, short-tempered: Briefly, he was a better scholar than diplomat and did not suffer fools gladly.

Hostility against him crystallized after he clashed time and time again with one of his colleagues, León de Castro, during the committee meetings in which a French version of the Bible was being revised. Soon all of León's bitterest enemies got together and wrote to the Inquisition, mentioning unrest at the university and claiming seventeen heretical propositions were being taught there, by León and other professors. In March 1572 León was arrested and imprisoned in the secret cells of the Valladolid Inquisition. For five long years he would be confined to a small room almost without light and air, with little to eat, deeply anguished and depressed, not knowing for a long time who his accusers were and what he was accused of. The orders were that he was to be tortured "softly," because of his "delicate health." Apparently he was not tortured, except mentally—the long interrogations and the uncertainty about the future were indeed a form of torture. He was also accused of having translated into Spanish the Song of Songs, which was indeed true. The Sacraments were denied him.

Despite moments of despair he found a way to hold firm, to disprove every accusation, and he was finally freed in December 1576, the Inquisition having found him innocent. He came back to the university in triumph, to the applause of students and colleagues, and was restored to his position of professor, receiving a new chair.

A great writer knows how to transform his experiences into literature. This is what he did: Both during his years in prison and after them he turned his suffering into some of his most poignant poems and intense prose. Several of the most personal, autobiographical fragments of *The Names of Christ* could not have been written without his bitter experience as a prisoner. For instance, in the anecdote at the end of the chapter dealing with the name "Son of God," the three companions whose conversation consti-

INTRODUCTION

tutes the essence of *The Names of Christ* have just had an extensive discussion in a garden, near a river. On the shore opposite the spot where they are seated, perched on a tree, a little bird is singing. While Juliano speaks, as if listening to his voice, the bird remains silent. At times the bird's song soars into space. It is a song of such sweetness and harmony that Marcelo and his friends cannot help but pay attention to the little bird. Suddenly a noise is heard: Two huge, ugly crows appear; they attack the little bird with their beaks and claws. The bird is trapped. At last the crows force the bird to fall into the river where it cries as if begging for help. The crows rush to the water and continue their vicious attack. At last the bird disappears in the swift current without a trace. One of the friends, Sabino, laments such a sad fate: The poor little bird has drowned before their eyes. The friends become sad and silent. Suddenly, near Marcelo, almost at his feet, the little bird's head emerges from the river. Soon the bird is on the bank, wet and tired. Shaking off the drops of water from its feathers it spreads its wings and rises on the air singing even more sweetly than before. Other birds like it come out, fly around it, and seem to congratulate it on surviving the attack of its enemies. Then all together they make three or four wide circles in the air and fly on until they disappear from sight.

This fable is a clear depiction of the enemies and accusers of Luis de León, that is, León de Castro and Bartolomé de Medina, the two wicked crows. The sufferings of the little bird symbolize León's anguish during his trial, the birds who accompany him in his final victorious flight are León's friends and allies. Yet this allegory has been projected to a universal level that transcends the concrete sufferings of one man: We are told in it about injustice and cruelty everywhere, and about the survival and vindication of the innocent who dare fight for their rights and who are protected by Jesus' love.

The rest of León's life was a long series of intellectual and social victories. After his triumphant return to Salamanca he plunged into research, teaching, writing—and, of course, polemics with his colleagues. His five years in jail seem to have made him more stubborn, more convinced than ever of his principles and his approach to theology and the Holy Texts. Some of these debates with his colleagues seem to have motivated a second trial by the Inquisition, from 1582 to 1584, less dangerous than the first, during which he remained free, and after which he was also declared innocent. In 1578 he had obtained, for life, the chair of Moral Philosophy. In 1579 he won the chair of Holy Scriptures. In 1580 he published his comments to Psalm 26 and the Song of Songs. In 1583 he published the first edition of *The Perfect Wife*, a guidebook for married women, and the first part of *The Names of Christ*. During these years he also wrote and rewrote original poems and translations of poems from many languages, including Latin and Greek. His fame had spread throughout Spain.

The painter Francisco Pacheco has left us a portrait of the mature Luis de León, and also a written portrait, a description of his face and body that is expanded into psychological insights and observations:

> He was not tall, but well proportioned; his head was large and shapely, his complexion dark; his most noticeable features were the broad forehead, surmounted by thick and curly hair, and his piercing green eyes. His temperament was quiet, subdued, he loved silence, yet could be sharp and witty. Most moderate and abstemious in everything, food, beverages, sleep; punctual and faithful in words and deeds. A grave simplicity and humility were apparent in his face, which rarely relaxed into a smile . . . in spite of his choleric nature he could be most considerate towards his fellow men.[4]

As time went by León, who had so often longed for the peace and serenity of the countryside, became a busy ecclesiastical executive whose advice was sought by his peers and his colleagues, a man plunged in the complex politics of the university and of his order, burdened by a vast correspondence, having to travel near and far on business either academic or ecclesiastical. In 1591 he attained the highest rank among Augustinian friars, having been elected Provincial (that is, head) of his order in Castile. Exhausted by his work, his travels, his worries, he died shortly afterward in the Castilian town of Madrigal de las Altas Torres.

During his whole life Luis de León was prey to conflict and

---

4. Francisco Pacheco, *Libro de retratos verdaderos* (1599). Quoted by Bell, *Luis de León*, p. 216, note.

tension. He could not refuse the call of spirituality, of lofty ideas, of holy texts, of poetry and philosophy, and at the same time it was impossible to ignore the thousand urgent tasks imposed upon him by his religious order and by academic life. The university could have been a refuge, an ivory tower, yet was the opposite, a battlefield of rancor, envy, opposing groups. The convent could also have become a refuge, and yet it was the fact that he belonged to the Augustinian Order that made him almost automatically the enemy of several other orders, most especially the Dominicans. Such rivalries were not always of an intellectual nature, but rather were often related to a competition for prestige, a desire to amass more and more academic chairs to the detriment of another order, and so forth. Controversies opposed constantly the traditionalist groups and the scholars favoring a renewal of thought. Scholasticists fought specialists in Scripture, scholars favoring a literal interpretation of the Bible abhorred those who interpreted many biblical passages as allegorical—and were repaid in kind. Many of these debates appear artificial and even childish to the modern spectator; yet this was not the case, since most were born out of a basic struggle between thinkers, scholars, and theologians who wanted to accept the ideas brought to light by the Renaissance, those who wanted to consolidate and Christianize the humanistic revolution, on the one hand, and, on the other, the superconservative scholars who tended to reject *in toto* the new ideas and met with suspicion anything that was not sanctioned by tradition. Needless to say, León belonged to the first group. His character, his ideas, even his family and educational background, were to turn him occasionally into a moralist and a social critic.

Born during a period of expansion, international exchange, hope, optimism, Luis de León was educated in a Spain that reached the most remote corners of the planet through her explorers and conquerors, a Spain that received a steady stream of books, works of art, visitors, from the very core of Europe, from Flanders, Italy, France, Germany. Gradually this interaction between Spain and the rest of the world was to slow down. The new monarch, Philip II, would try to curtail intellectual exchanges between Spain and those European countries where Protestant doctrines seemed to prosper. Spanish students were forbidden, by a royal decree given in 1559, to study in foreign universities, save the sole exceptions of Bologne, Rome, Naples, and the Portuguese

INTRODUCTION

Univeristy of Coimbra. The Spanish Empire was preparing for a long siege.

The main aim of Philip II was to preserve, insofar as possible, and to expand on occasion, the vast dominions assembled by Charles V. Hampered by continuous troubles in his lines of communication and his supply of money, the young king had to improvise and soon withdrew behind a barrier of committees, bureaucrats, paper-shufflers, having contributed perhaps more than any Renaissance leader to the creation of modern bureaucracy. His father had led his armies into battle; Philip preferred to lead endless committees in the intricacies of preparing lengthy reports. Caution, not courage, was the key word. With caution came intellectual timidity, and in the long run a disinclination to deal with any controversial problem that might bring the thinker into conflict with the state and the Inquisition.

As we have witnessed in our century, every totalitarian regime, whether Hitler's Germany or Stalin's Soviet Union, to give only two notorious examples, would like to make use of a few chosen intellectuals, scientists primarily, occasionally writers, for its own purposes, yet the realm of intelligence and reason is more unified than totalitarian leaders believe: The whole atmosphere degenerates and ultimately the intellectuals that assent to becoming the tools of the totalitarian state turn out to be mediocre and incapable of advancing its goals. The Spanish intellectuals, under pressure, either gave up their efforts or went abroad (let us note in passing that some of those who went abroad fared badly at the hands of Spain's enemies, just as fanatic in their beliefs as the most fanatic Spanish Inquisitors: It was in Calvin's Geneva that the great Spanish scientist and theologian Miguel Servet, otherwise known as Michael Servetus, was executed). All over Europe people who dared to think for themselves were being imprisoned, tortured, executed. England, France, Germany, bear a heavy burden of guilt during this troubled period. Tolerance was slowly and painfully being discovered by a few enlightened Dutch thinkers, partially under the inspiration of Erasmus's writings. In Spain the situation was bound to deteriorate, given the inner and outer pressures acting on both king and society. The Spanish intellectuals, especially those of Jewish origin, felt besieged. Many of them gave up their efforts and ceased to publish, or else they went abroad. In any case freedom of thought was ebbing when the

INTRODUCTION

great Spanish historian Juan de Mariana wrote his famous comment to Luis de León's imprisonment and trial:

> A sad condition that of a man of virtue. As a reward for having made a great effort he is compelled to suffer the animosity and the accusations of the very same men who should have applauded and defended him. With that example [Luis de León's] in mind it was unavoidable that the zeal of many distinguished men should become blunt, that their strength should debilitate and vanish. This affair depressed the courage of those who witnessed such dangers and such storms menacing those who maintained the integrity of their thought and beliefs. Thus many were those who went over to the other side or were molded by the pressures of this situation. And what was to be done? The greatest folly is to struggle in vain, to exhaust one's energies in order to reap only hatred.[5]

This text underlines clearly the anguish and frustrations of Luis de León's "fellow travelers." Their enemies were simply too powerful. The kings of Castile, and later the kings of Spain, had fully realized long ago the value of the support the Inquisition would give to the unifying and centralizing tendencies of the Spanish Crown. And an alliance had been struck among the Crown, the Inquisition, and the lowly hungry masses: It was to crush with iron pincers a group caught in the middle, made up of intellectuals, the middle classes or rising bourgeoisie, and even the nobility. Jews and Conversos would be the main victims. Their rise to power and wealth had lasted over a century and had been nothing short of miraculous. They were to be plundered, exploited, subdued, slowly replaced by a new generation of Old Christians. Naturally this process was to subject Spanish society to innumerable tensions and distortions. The secret religious police, the Holy Inquisition, once in power, would crush under its heels not only its intended victims but any other segment of the population that might represent a hope for individual and free thought. Slowly the whole social body would become poisoned and the possibility of creating a middle class of professionals, bureaucrats, and intel-

---

5. Quoted in Americo Castro, *De la edad conflictiva*, pp. 169–170.

lectuals would recede ever more. While great writers such as Lope de Vega and Calderón depicted mainly the noble and elegant aspects of Spanish society in their plays, where wit, humor, a complex plot, and a poetic style combined to produce a picture of refinement and to put on a pedestal the human models and the socially accepted ideas that inspired their period, other writers, such as Cervantes, subtly satirized a social system in which irrational values had usurped the place of honor.

Needless to say the situation was not noticeably better in the rest of Europe. Religious persecution was widespread in France and England, among other countries. What the Inquisition accomplished piecemeal in Spain was achieved in a matter of days or hours in France during the massacres of St. Bartholomew. The killings of witches in Germany during the sixteenth and especially the seventeenth century have almost no parallel anywhere. Yet in the European political scene Spain's position was paramount, and Spain felt besieged, which gave rise to further tension, to the will to win, resist, and conquer through repression, then as always a close ally of a siege mentality. The Spanish Empire was attacked not only by foreign enemies, it was felt, but also by internal dissidents. The Inquisition was to be reinforced and would become an instrument of state policies, and at the same time Spanish politics would be coordinated with the conclusions of the Council of Trent and the Counter-Reformation would become a national goal. We must never forget, the French scholar Marcel Bataillon wrote in his preface to the Spanish edition of Erasmus's *Enchiridion*, that *The Names of Christ* was written by a man who was twice denounced to the Inquisition. Luis de León, born and educated in a Spain where freedom of thought was taken for granted, did not know how to conform to the new times, or if he knew how to adjust chose not to do so, for reasons of pride and integrity, the basic reasons that move any true intellectual to do battle against a totalitarian regime.

As a humanist and an intellectual León was outraged by the increasing intolerance in Spanish society. As a man with Jewish ancestors on his mother's side he may have felt menaced, vulnerable. Yet he could not remain silent: He had to criticize and castigate a system of values that was cruel, unfair, and especially prone to prey on the most distinguished, the wealthiest, best-educated Spaniards. The Conversos, who had changed their religion from Judaism to Christianity, often in good faith, often contributing deep and creative ideas to their new religion (we should not forget, for instance, that one of the great Spanish mystics and writers of that period, St. Teresa of Avila, was a member of the Converso group), were singled out for persecution and annihilation. The Inquisitors were rewarded with the property of the victims they condemned, an easy way to ensure zeal in prosecutions and severity in judgment. As Stephen Gilman explains:

> We must realize that the Inquisition operated in the way Fortune had been traditionally thought to behave— which is to say its malevolence was attracted by wealth and high honor ... a typical trial was initiated by greed and terminated in the gratification of the masses at the fall of the mighty in a public "auto de fe." In the Inquisitors the goddess Fortuna had found willing and efficient human agents for her labor on Earth.'[6]

As the pluralistic society of the thirteenth and fourteenth centuries became more and more a society "for Old Christians only," the Conversos had nowhere to turn. Some tried to influence the emperor's attitude toward the Church, hoping that a strong lay government, holding the Church and the Inquisition in check, would allow the Conversos, who at the beginning of the sixteenth century made up the bulk of the incipient middle classes, to breathe freely. As J. F. Montesinos puts it, "the hope that it would be the emperor, the secular power, not the ecclesiastic power, the one in charge of giving the Catholic world its definitive shape and structure"[7] animated both humanists like Juan de Valdés and political figures such as Charles V's agents in Italy. The Spanish Jews had found their best protectors among the high

---

6. "The 'Conversos' and the Fall of Fortune," in *Collected Studies in Honour of Americo Castro's 80th Year* pp. 129–130.

7. See J. F. Montesinos's introduction to Alfonso de Valdés's *Diálogo de las cosas ocurridas en Roma* (Madrid, pub 1928), p. 53; and also Manuel Durán, "Américo Castro, Luis de León, and the Inner Tensions of Spain's Golden Age" in *Collected Studies in Honour of Américo Castro's 80th Year*, ed. Marcel P. Hornik (Oxford: Lincombe Lodge Research Library, 1965), pp. 83–90.

nobility and the kings, who clearly saw that it was in the public interest that all their subjects should prosper, and especially a group that had played such a significant role in banking, administration, and intellectual pursuits. But the uncompromising attitude of Ferdinand and Isabella, first, then the waverings of Charles V, finally the sternness of Philip II, had put an end to such hopes. When Luis de León wrote his *The Names of Christ,* his attitude toward Spain's government and toward the external values of Spanish society was made up of a mixture of contempt and despair. No wonder that the Spanish essayist and historian Joaquín Costa should see in Luis de León a social critic and even a forerunner of modern anarchism: "Luis de León's ideal is a stateless society, or rather a 'Libertarian' State, as we would say today, in which God's grace, by illuminating men's souls from the inside, would replace law, and where the ruler's role would be akin to that of a shepherd."[8]

Luis de León is but one of the many Spaniards of that time who felt anguished and oppressed. We cannot understand his individual problems without linking them to those of other Spaniards who felt trapped by the hopeless, bitter quality of Spanish life for all those who could not prove that they were Old Christians. Some of the most distinguished Conversos, like the Valdés brothers and the great humanist Luis Vives, took refuge abroad. Others took part in the antistate revolts of the Comuneros. St. Teresa and Luis de León are but two of the Spaniards of Jewish descent who came to despise self-censorship. Luis de León, quite aware of the crisis, refused to take precautions: He defied the system repeatedly, paid a dear price for his defiance, and yet went on defying the system and ultimately succeeded in being vindicated personally and—also worth noting—was rewarded by his peers and his society, and became the highest authority in his monastic order, the provincial of the Augustinian Order, shortly before his death.

León had noticed that in the midst of all the social and political changes that were taking place in Western societies one fact emerged as paramount: It was the princes, the kings, that were increasing their power at the expense of all the other social

---

8. *Historia política social patria,* Aguilar edition, p. 250.

13

centers of power. It was certainly true that in Spain as elsewhere the royal house had to strike alliances with other social centers of power in order to subdue the unruly feudal lords. Yet in Spain the victory of the kings was swift, since Ferdinand and Isabella were able to accomplish in a short time what in France Louis XIV would achieve only much later, in the seventeenth century, after years of careful plotting. León, aware of the crucial role of Spanish royalty in the deepening social crisis—expulsion of Jews, persecution of converted Jews, curtailment of links between Spain and other countries—had to register his firm protest. He was, let us add, one of the very few intellectuals, whether in Spain or in any other Western European country, to realize clearly what was happening and to denounce in no uncertain terms those responsible for the deepening crisis.

A target for his criticism is the arrogance of our earthly princes, especially when compared with the meekness, sweetness, and humility of Jesus, Prince of Princes. In his chapter "King of God," León concludes that when God chose Jesus above everybody else He also decided that the most essential quality of a ruler was to be humble and kind. Just as in the music of a madrigal we hear several voices singing in harmony, the humility and meekness in Christ's soul harmonized with the lofty ideas, the universality of wisdom and power, that were also part of His being. We do not understand this clearly because our princes have acted most of the time in a haughty and proud fashion, and therefore we no longer expect our rulers to be humble. We have been perverted by history—and the behavior of our princes has been influential in creating such a perversion. The rulers who are alive today, León states, have not followed Christ's example. They have become self-centered and arrogant. Christ accepted all kinds of suffering, but today's princes have as a main goal to avoid all suffering, and of course to gain advantages for themselves: They care little for their subjects, selfishly taking advantage of them and even harming them when they think they can gain by it, and this very fact prevents them from reaching true greatness: "Why do you think, Sabino, that they burden their subjects with such heavy yokes, establishing cruel laws and executing them without pity, if not because they have never experienced in themselves the pains of affliction and poverty?" This is partly the fault of a wrong education: Those who educate our rulers do not want them to lower their eyes and look with kindness at their subjects. Moreover, the rulers are in part captives of a system that isolates them, for those who surround the kings not only make many mistakes but often try to deceive their rulers in order to further their own private purposes. The kings, incapable of breaking through the invisible barriers created by their courtiers, seldom find out the truth about the real condition of their subjects.

Up to this point León's words can apply to dozens of European rulers. What follows in this same chapter, however, seems specifically directed to the Spanish royalty. In contrast with Christ's goal, which is to ennoble and dignify each human being, to turn him or her into a king and a Christ, there are rulers, León states, who despise and debase a group of their subjects. "What can we say about Kings and Princes who not only lower and despise some of their subjects but think that this is the only way they themselves can feel important, and try their best so that the groups they have lowered and despised will be held down and despised generation after generation?" This can apply to Spanish society, where the Conversos were subject to constant persecution, humiliation, and exclusion, where the "Statutes of Blood" barred them from numerous professions and activities, turning them in practice into second-class citizens. There is vehemence, anger, passion, in León's words. "And besides the King who debases his subjects debases himself. If the King is the head, what honor is there in being the head of a deformed and vile body? If the King is like a shepherd, why should a shepherd want to care for a sickly herd? Seneca was right when he wrote, 'It is beautiful to lead illustrious people.' "

Luis de León clearly understood that theology was not merely a series of theoretical propositions about God. On the contrary, it dealt as well with everyday life, with the fabric of our experience and our actions, since the essence of God required, to be properly understood, a definition of the relationship between God and the creation, between God and the cosmos, God and history, God and mankind. The sorry condition of mankind, of the states in which it had organized itself, of its awareness of God's presence and purpose, could be seen most clearly from the vantage point of theology. And yet the first and most urgent task was to approach

INTRODUCTION

God through the complex, step-by-step way of a definition and explanation of God's biblical names. This approach was to take place in a book of noble and serene proportions, one that could be compared in structure to a building by Vitruvius or Palladio, or to the Monastery of El Escorial, or to Solomon's temple. It is clear that *The Names of Christ* was conceived and carried out in an expansive frame of mind. It was not going to be a chance masterpiece: It was planned to be one of the most ambitious and powerful books ever conceived and written by man.

As is often the case with long books, *The Names* grew by stages. The first edition (1583) is made up of only two books, the first one embracing five names (the name "shepherd" is missing) and the second four more names. The second edition (1585) offers one more book, Book III, which includes four new names and adds the name "shepherd" to the first book. Finally, the posthumous edition of 1595 includes one extra name, "lamb," which according to León should be placed between "Son of God" and "beloved," which is what we have done in our version.[9] Each book ends in a lyrical meditation expressed in a poem. Sabino, the poet, is always in charge of lyrical interludes, which, together with landscape and nature descriptions, play an important role, both as respite from the arduous theological discussions and expositions and as a clear expression and symbol of the beauty of the world—which is a mirror of God's beauty. For we should not forget that, as a genre, *The Names* draws its structure and its style not only from the Platonic dialogue but also from the pastoral novel. Its three books form a sort of triptych, a slightly asymmetrical one since the first book is somewhat longer than the other books, and the number three appears again in the number of its characters: three Augustinian friars, Marcelo, Sabino, and Juliano, each with his clear and well-defined personality—Sabino, as we have said, is the poet, full of wonder and always sensitive; Marcelo is the seasoned theologian to whom the other two turn when the time comes to elucidate the meaning of an idea or a name; while Juliano

---

9. See also about this point the modern Spanish edition by Cristóbal Cuevas (Madrid: Ediciones Cátedra, S.A., 1977), especially his Introduction, pp. 121–124.

by his questions and his prodding keeps the conversation running smoothly toward its lofty goal.

We are dealing therefore with a Renaissance dialogue, one in which the ideas of beauty, order, purpose, love, are analyzed within a double framework, the physical framework of a harmonious landscape—orchard, grove, hills, river, brook, sky, clouds, singing birds, trellised vines and their cool shade—and the spiritual framework of biblical quotations, the framework of the idea of God as developed in the Old and New Testaments. Each name of God, each definition and explanation of this name, is like a facet of a huge diamond: It is impossible to understand the diamond as such unless we lovingly study, contemplate, caress, each facet in turn, after which we may try to comprehend the whole. León has discovered, with the force of revelation, that words open worlds.

Who are the three characters? According to some critics, Marcelo, Sabino, and Juliano are totally fictitious characters, and hence it is useless to try to identify them with flesh-and-blood contemporaries of our author. According to other critics Marcelo *is* Luis de León and his two companions are two friends with whom he may have had several conversations dealing with theological subjects. Finally, and this may be the most plausible interpretation, it may well be that the three speakers represent three different aspects of León's personality: León as a student of Holy Scripture (Marcelo), León as a scholastic critic and commentator (Juliano), León as a poet (Sabino). The lines that separate each personality are not always unbroken—each is capable of thinking and speaking as the others do, each complements the others without opposing them. These Three Musketeers, all for one and one for all, are engaged in a long and arduous quest: how to define and understand God.

A remarkable achievement of Luis de León as a writer is that he managed to formulate a message that is at the same time universal, addressed to all human beings of all countries and all centuries, and yet deeply Spanish, rooted in Spanish traditions

INTRODUCTION

and attitudes. There is a facet in his works that is clearly related to the Italian Renaissance, to the Florence of Ficino, to Plato and Neoplatonism. Yet another facet, to be found in his poems as well as in his prose works, is uniquely Spanish. The universal facet is perhaps easier to define. As Edward J. Schuster points out:

> During the sixteenth century the Italian Renaissance accelerated the dissemination of Platonic and Neo-Platonic thought in Spain. Earlier, at the new Platonic Academy of Lorenzo the Magnificent in Florence, scholars like George Gemistos Plethon had expounded the Platonic doctrines which Cardinal Bessarion and others attempted to interpret in moderate tones. In a dazzling assembly of sophisticated intellectuals, which included the magnetic Medici princes, the Bishop of Fiesole, Marco Antonio degli Agli, and Christopher Marsupini, perhaps the most outstanding contributions came from Marsilio Ficino. The doctrine of love formulated by these intellectuals later influenced the last great Spanish-Hebraic interpreter of Plato, León Hebreo who, in his *Dialogues of Love,* presented a complete philosophy of love based on Old Testament as well as Platonic sources.[10]

León Hebreo is of course not the only link between the Spanish mystics and the Neo-Platonic tradition, but his influence can be found in many instances: He seems to have made many

---

10. In his Introduction (p. xxvi) to *The Names of Christ,* tr. Edward J. Schuster (St. Louis & London: B. Herder Book Co., 1955). We should like to point out that this book is by no means a complete text. To make this perfectly clear we need only quote Jordan Aumann, O.P., who writes, in the Editor's Preface, as follows: "The present volume is not the complete treatise on the names of Christ nor is it a literal translation. From the complete translation made by Dr. Edward J. Schuster a selection has been made with a view to the inspiration and instruction of English readers. Nevertheless, the doctrine that is here offered is the doctrine of Fray Louis of León. The literary editor assumes full responsibility for all deletions and adaptations that have been made in the editing of this work." (p. x). We should further point out that our present edition is, indeed, a complete one, including as it does every word Luis de León wrote under the title *The Names of Christ,* and furthermore is based on the best available Spanish text, the critical edition by Cristóbal Cuevas published by the Madrid publisher, Ediciones Cátedra, S.A., and having compared this text with other editions, such as the one by F. de Onís, and the recent translation into French by Robert Ricard.

18

INTRODUCTION

Spanish writers aware of the need to define love in its different aspects. His own definition of love is as follows:

> The voluntary affective act of enjoying union with the thing esteemed as good. . . . Men whose will is directed toward the useful never satisfy their diverse and intimate desires. Not so the man who feeds his soul with speculative exercises and contemplation, in which happiness resides. The love of pure truth is superior to either of the foregoing, since it affects neither the senses alone, like delights, nor calculating, prudent thought, as in the case of things which possess utility. Instead, the love of truth captivates the intellectual soul which, of all man's faculties and powers, is closest to the divine light.[11]

It is quite possible that the interaction between Plato, the Bible, the Sufi tradition, and the medieval mystical tradition is the only way to explain historically and rationally a phenomenon that is hard to understand: More than three thousand religious books of deep significance, both literary and spiritual, appeared in Spain during the Golden Age, that is to say, the period between 1492 and 1681. Prose and poetry of the highest quality were written during this period, some of the best authors—St. Teresa, St. John of the Cross, Luis de León, among others—having turned to both poetry and prose in order to express a message that was so subtle, intense, and overpowering as to be almost ineffable. All of which means that although Luis de León is among the half-dozen first-rank mystical and spiritual authors of Golden Age Spain, and although his *The Names of Christ* is the highest, most sustained, most coherent effort in his religious writings, it would be a mistake to think of the man and of the present book as isolated phenomena: On the contrary, it was because the spiritual climate was perfect, because León knew he was going to be understood and therefore influential, that he undertook with optimism and joy the vast effort of writing such a long and difficult book. The twin and in many cases parallel phenomena of Italian Renaissance

---

11. Marcelino Menéndez y Pelayo quotes this passage in his *Historia de las ideas estéticas en España* (Madrid, 1883), vol. 2, p. 15 of the mod. ed. (Madrid: C.S.I.C., 1940).

INTRODUCTION

and German Reformation had brought together—in what we would nowadays be tempted to call a "critical mass,"—an explosive mixture infinitely powerful: the wisdom of the ancient world, both Greek and Roman; the wisdom of the Bible and medieval religious traditions, both Christian and Jewish; and the keen modern thought of sixteenth-century commentators, scholars, humanists. This mixture was of course bound to differ from country to country, the Spanish ingredients being stronger in their Oriental and Jewish components. The great Spanish nineteenth-century scholar Marcelino Menéndez y Pelayo underlines both what so many religious writers had in common and, what is perhaps equally important and useful, how and why each one of them differed from the others:

> The basis of their speculations being common to all our mystics, an unending wealth of variety resides in the forms or accidents of their expression, because no author or book and no system of theology can comprehend all the ways in which the divine manifests itself to the soul of man, nor can anyone enclose in dry aphorisms and categories all the dazzling brilliance of that everlasting, transcendent wisdom which the soul acquires on its mystical journey in order to illuminate the way. Furthermore, since mysticism, while it is the science of love, is still, in the final analysis a science, that is, a speculative activity of the mind, without which it would degenerate into the fanatical doctrine of the Illuminists, it is clear that the manner of presenting and understanding mysticism will reflect for each individual student of this phenomenon those dispositions and tendencies which are most characteristic of himself and his race, even though all who thus interpret and expound it be Christians who acknowledge that the chief element of their speculation is revealed doctrine and recognize—all of them—the ineffable power of divine grace. Consequently, some will be ontological mystics while others will be psychological mystics; some will be analytical and others will be synthetic and integrating. All this will be in accordance with the understanding which God has given them, the nation

to which they belong, and the education they have received.[12]

At this moment it would be wise to remember that of all the religious writers of that era, that is to say, the sixteenth and seventeenth centuries, the Spaniards are often more intense, more passionate, almost anguished in their search for wisdom, light, God's presence, because many of them are doubly motivated by the love of wisdom and God and by the disdain, irritation, hatred of a society in which the Inquisition had made life on earth especially unpleasant for religious and racial minorities. It was truly and literally, for the Spanish Conversos, a valley of tears. As a first-rate Spanish scholar of our century, perhaps the historian who has contributed most to our understanding of the anguish of such a group, puts it:

> It is quite logical, from the viewpoint of history, that Spaniards should not be interested in finding theoretical, rational, objective explanations to God's works, such as those sought by Descartes, Galileo or Kepler. For the Spaniards the existence and reality of God and Nature did not become a problem. They became interested instead in the ways in which man's existence is reflected in the mirror of man's own consciousness. Luis Vives, anchored in the tradition of his Spanish-Jewish origins, asked himself the following question: "Who may be capable of explaining all the whims and fancies of man, that *difficult animal*, who is sometimes so hard to bear, and can himself not bear other men?" Two centuries earlier Sem Tov of Carrión had written: "Nothing in the world is as dangerous and *restless* as man...." Animals calm down once they have had their fill, but man "can never be satiated, not with a thousand cords of gold." According to Sem Tov, man does not judge the world in a rational and objective frame of mind, but rather "according to his pleasant or unpleasant experience of it." Reali-

---

12. Ibid., pp. 78–79.

21

ty, therefore, is fleeting, restless, for it depends on what man has to fashion out of it, not on the logical rigor of man's thought.[13]

In other words, man was the problem, man in society oppressing other men, and the solution had to be found either in the inner life of the mind and the spirit, a life to be expressed in works of art, or in the meditation that would bring the individual closer to a God who was the only salvation out of a wretched existence on earth.

In this way the subjective Spanish approach, rooted in the medieval tradition, was to flower in a period during which, in other countries, the objective scientific tradition was slowly emerging. Great works of art would be produced in this subjective mood, the works, for instance, of Lope de Vega, Cervantes, and Velasquez. Luis de León occupies a special role in this vast array of religious writers since basically he had a double personality: on the one hand a rational self, steeped in Aristotelian and Thomist principles, logic and theology, well acquainted with the reasoning and reasonable principles of scholastic philosophy; on the other hand, an intuitive and artistic self, in love with poetry, passionately admiring beauty and music. Perhaps because this duality caused tension and turmoil Luis de León turned his admiration more than once toward another great writer of that era, St. Teresa. He may have admired in her the absence of inner conflict since from the beginning her intuitive poetic self had gained precedence over her rational self. When she wrote a treatise of religious instruction, for instance, she did not follow in the rational and systematic footsteps of St. Thomas's *Summa Theologica*. She built her book from the beginning around a poetic metaphor, the soul as a home, a dwelling place, a castle, with many rooms and even a secret inner chamber: Her whole book then becomes an extended metaphor. León felt deeply about Teresa's writings: As a fellow artist and as a committed religious writer he could appreciate better than others the importance of her message. Hence it is not among the least of León's merits that he contributed more than anybody else to making her message clear and available to future readers.

---

13. A. Castro, "En el cincuentenario de nuestra asociación," *Hispania* L, no. 4 (Dec. 1967): 920–921. Emphasis in original.

INTRODUCTION

In a way her ideas became part of his outlook. Hence the importance of this statement by Luis de León:

> I never knew nor saw Mother Teresa de Jesús while she was on earth, [writes Luis de León in his dedicatory letter addressed to the nuns Ana de Jesús and the other barefoot Carmelite nuns of the Madrid convent] but now that she lives in Heaven I know and see her almost constantly in two vivid images which she has left of herself, and these are her spiritual daughters and her books. Which in my judgment are also faithful witnesses . . . they bear witness to her great virtue. For the features of her face, if I were to see them, would show me merely her earthly face. And her words, if I were to hear them, would show me only one aspect of her soul's virtue. And her face was like any other face; and her words might be misinterpreted. Which is not so in the two images in which I see her now. For as King Solomon says, one knows a man by his children: because the fruits that each one of us leaves after him when he departs are the true witnesses of his life. . . .
>
> The second image, that of her books and writings, is no less clear nor less miraculous. In these, without doubt, the Holy Spirit wished that Mother Teresa should become a rare example. For in the loftiness of the subjects she deals with and in the delicacy and clarity with which she treats them, she excels many men of great talent. And in her style, in the purity and fluency of her language, and the grace and splendid organization of her words, in an informal elegance that delights us to the utmost, I doubt that we could find in our language another work that may be said to be their equal. And so every time I read her books I am again full of admiration and in many parts of them it seems to me that it is not the genius of a human being that I hear; and I doubt not but that it was the Holy Spirit that was speaking through her in many places and that prompted her pen and her hand; and this is shown by the light that she sheds on obscure matters and by the fire that ignites through her words the heart of her readers. For, leaving aside other great advantages

which will be found by those that read her books, there are two, in my opinion, which are most useful. One is to render accessible in the soul of those who read her the path to virtue. And the other is to ignite in them the love of virtue and of God. For in the first instance it is a marvelous thing to see how her texts place God before the very eyes of the soul, and how they show Him so easy to find, so sweet and friendly for those who do find Him. And in the second instance, not only in all of her words in general, but in each one of them, we shall find that they communicate to our souls the Heavens' fire, a fire that burns and transforms our souls, and, removing from our eyes and senses all the difficulties that exist, manages not to conceal them but rather helps us to overcome them. Our soul then becomes disabused from all the traps that imagination had plotted, lightened from burdens and from its own coolness. And so encouraged, it becomes so desirous of the good that it soon wants to fly towards it, moved by a burning desire. It is as if the great love which dwelt in that saintly bosom leapt out, entwined in her words in such a way that it kindles a flame wherever they reach.[14]

León's endorsement of Teresa's work had been preceded by a labor of love: the arduous task of collating her manuscripts, checking references and notes, preparing a definitive text. Without León's edition of 1588 it is quite possible that we would not have received one of the most important messages from the Golden Age Spanish spiritual vision. Mysticism had to be rescued against its numerous enemies, so powerful in the official Church, the ecclesiastical Establishment. Teresa's works could have suffered partial destruction, neglect, or both without León's all-out effort. As one of León's critics, Father Félix García, points out:

León's pages dealing with St. Teresa are among the most admirable and penetrating which he ever penned. Today we tremble to think what might have become of St.

---

14. In *Obras completas en prosa*, ed. P. Félix García (Madrid: Blblioteca de Autores Christianos, 1957), pp. 1349–1350.

Teresa's works, the essence of heavenly milk and honey, if they had not luckily fallen into the devout and careful hands of Fray Luis de León. Some had already begun to treat them with clumsiness and obvious lack of understanding. There were many people still incapable of understanding the light and the beauty in the life and works of the Saint when Luis de León, with the valiant attitude of one who has been dazzled by the brilliance of Teresa's writing, became her greatest apologist, the most lyrical and warm critic that she ever had. . . . Luis fully understood the greatness and holy nature of Teresa's life and works. What he said in words that are enduring and heartfelt was said for all time. His opinion is definitive, and we are amazed to see the clarity and depth of the perception which he had of the works of the Saint at a time when her reputation was still far from secure.[15]

Just as he sought to integrate the thought of St. Teresa within the mainstream of Spanish and Western European orthodox thought, León tried and often succeeded in blending and harmonizing different aspects of differing traditions. Parallel lines do meet, he seems to say, provided their meeting point is infinity, that is, God. Schuster explains León's harmonizing spirit in the following manner:

Fray Luis accommodates elements which are to all appearances antithetical, but it is no mere psychological sublimation which he applies to the opposition between flesh and spirit, emotions and intellect, human aspirations and the divine will, the ravishing beauty of this world and the ineffable beauty of God, immediate rewards and everlasting happiness. In the background of this struggle echo the words of his spiritual father, St. Augustine: "Our hearts were made for Thee, O God, and we are restless until we rest in Thee."

Specifically, the reader can discern here the skillful blending of several doctrinal aspects or certain schools within the Church, which at first glance appear antago-

---

15. Ibid., pp. 1329–1330.

nistic. Fray Luis was seeking that higher unity which would reconcile them. Consequently, instead of stressing the differences between the Platonic-Augustinian and the Aristotelian-Thomistic schools, he saw them as differences of emphasis or separate facets of immutable truth. Accordingly, he did not denounce those within the Church who held differing views, provided they did not depart from orthodox teachings. If the Franciscans seemed to stress love and the will while the Dominicans generally appeared as champions of the intellect and truth, Fray Luis did not on that account denounce either the one or the other. Instead, he sought the ultimate integration of truth itself.[16]

Perhaps because any intelligent reader of León's works could sense that one of the main goals of his life was to increase and enrich the spiritual and humanistic tradition, to harmonize its inner tensions, to make it available to a select public, the respect for him as a man and as a writer has always been paramount in the Spanish-speaking world, and, we hope, will become similarly high in the rest of the world as well. In the seventeenth century he was highly praised by the great poet Francisco de Quevedo, who prepared an edition of León's poems. In the eighteenth century he was a source of inspiration to several of the best Neoclassical poets of that era. The nineteenth and the twentieth centuries have witnessed many editions and numerous scholarly studies devoted to the elucidation of his texts and their meaning. No cultured person in the Spanish-speaking world ignores his name and no one among the educated could be found that could not quote a few lines of his writings or an anecdote from his life. What he did for St. Teresa others did for him, since indeed a cultural tradition is a fabric, a continuum, a series of links, a network of roads and bridges. One of his modern critics writes:

> As an editor and a critic ... León's work became invaluable to students of Teresa's works. Since it is acknowledged that these works are masterpieces of Spanish prose and offer deep insight into human psychology, León's

---

16. In his Introduction to the Herder edition, p. xviii.

contribution to their preservation and enduring fame ranks as a major victory in Golden Age criticism. Protecting a work of art, preserving it, calling attention to its merits, have always been among the major functions of criticism. What he did for Teresa, another great Spanish writer, Francisco de Quevedo, would in turn do for Luis de León. The chain of intelligent criticism was not about to be broken: in fact, it was about to be established, and its links would be prolonged into our own times.[17]

It is conceivable that the day in which León's spiritual texts will be understood and accepted has not arrived yet. This gloomy assessment can be explained by the fact that the peak of Western spiritual thought took place in the Medieval and early Renaissance periods, just when the scientific and rational approach was also developing, and as we all know it was the rational and scientific approach to our relationship with the cosmos that attained dramatic and almost immediate successes. The long-range prospect could of course be vastly different—and it was.

We understand León much better from the vantage point of our twentieth century since we live in an era that is beginning to have doubts about the rational and scientific approach, not because we doubt reason and science but because we see them misapplied every day. Our era is one in which rationalism coexists precariously with occultism and astrology. We send rockets to the moon, build giant computers, and then ask casually the very scientists who did these deeds, during a cocktail party, what their astrological symbols and horoscope may be. Luis de León was both a rationalist thinker and a sensitive poet, a lofty philosopher and a pragmatist who could deal with organization charts and academic politics. His message is more accessible to most of us than the purely spiritual message of a St. John of the Cross or a Jacob Boehme. His wisdom, both spiritual and down-to-earth, makes him a man for all ages.

And if indeed we are beginning to understand León's thought today, we can also hope that tomorrow our understanding will be

---

17. Durán, *Luis de León*, p. 153.

much more thorough. Sooner or later we shall come to terms with the dichotomy between reason and the irrational aspect of our life. Only writers like him may lead our way toward this long-due integration. Only when poets become philosophers (and perhaps rulers), when philosophers—that is to say, nowadays, scientists—become both rulers and poets, will the different aspects of our psyche become fully integrated in one single and well-balanced view of our cosmos. When this takes place León's writings will be fully understood and enjoyed; only then will the link between his prose and his poetry become fully evident.

Sometimes it is useful to complement the world of ideas, texts, written statements, with the world created by art, the world of sculptors, architects, engravers, painters. The Spanish painter Francisco Pacheco has left us a beautiful portrait of Luis de León, one that is realistic enough so that we can believe that it conveys some truth about the physical aspect of our writer. If we observe it carefully we may come to understand some of the inner tensions, complexities, and contradictions of our writer. When we concentrate on the upper half of this portrait we see the spacious and serene brow of a thinker, an intellectual, a dreamer. Yet the lower half of this same face is the portrait of a man of action, with a firm energetic jaw and with the hard lines of someone used to action and power. A mixture of melancholy and willpower, yearning for serenity and impatience with the world as it is.

His works reflect the inner man unveiled in this portrait: a synthesis of all the trends around him, the Classical heritage, the Italian Renaissance values, the traditional Spanish religious values, the new freedom of thought and intellectual curiosity. Plato and the Bible, Saint Augustine and Virgil, Horace and the mystics—plus, of course, Cicero, his great master of polished prose, and Petrarch, together with the Spanish Garcilaso, to guide him into the enclosed garden of poetry.

In *The Names of Christ*, and also in a handful of perfect poems, he attained the serene balance, the harmonious unity, the elegant beauty, the loftiness of thought that everyday life had too often denied him. He could thus become the master of his own destiny. He never doubted that a synthesis of the Old Testament and the gospels, of Plato and Aristotle, of St. Augustine and St. Thomas Aquinas, and of all these elements joined to the Jewish and Arabic mystical and numerologic traditions, was both possible and desirable, and never ceased to work toward this goal.

Finally, he left us the legend of his life, the life of a courageous man willing to fight for his principles. To be an intellectual and a poet is good: To be a brave intellectual, a brave philosopher, a brave poet, is even better. It is above all in the present book, *The Names of Christ*, that he attained his goal of conciliation, harmony, serene contemplation of divine power and beauty: freedom and happiness, at last, for him and for any reader who would share his views, freedom and serenity through intuition, sensitivity, wisdom, learning, thought, and art.

_____

Luis de León
The Names of Christ

Book I

DEDICATION

TO DON PEDRO PORTOCARRERO, COUNSELOR TO
HIS MAJESTY AND TO THE HOLY AND UNIVERSAL
INQUISITION

Among all the calamities of our age, which are numerous and grave, as you know, illustrious Lord, the least is not the state to which men have come and which makes poisonous what usually was their medicine and remedy. We must also see the certain sign that the end approaches and the world is near death since it finds this sign in its life. We know the Scriptures which we call holy have been inspired by God in the prophets who were the authors of them in order that they bring us consolation in the pain of this life and a luminous and faithful clarity in its darkness and errors, so that each of the wounds inflicted on our souls by passion and sin finds the universal therapeutic, the salutary remedy which is suitable for it. Since God wrote them for this purpose, which is general, it is manifest that He wished that their usage be common to us all and it is thus that He acts with everything that depends upon Him. In fact, He composed them with very simple words and in a language that was common to those who received it. Then when the treasure passed from them to the Gentiles and was transmitted to them at the same time as the true knowledge of Jesus Christ, He made them translate it into several languages, in all those that were then known and common so that they all would profit. Thus, at the beginning of the Church and for a number of years afterward it was regarded among the faithful as a grave error not to study diligently the holy books. It is because ecclesiastics, and those we call seculars, as well as doctors as those who did not study, dedicated themselves to this knowledge that the interest shown by the vulgar caused those whose office is to teach, I mean the superiors and the bishops, to work harder in this field. They were accustomed to explaining in their churches, almost every day, Holy Scripture to their people so that the particular reading which each made alone, clarified by the light of this public teaching and directed by the teacher's voice, avoided error and brought about considerable advantage. What was also great was that the system was good and the harvest responded to the seeds, as those know, who are acquainted with some of the history of the period. But, as I said, this thing which in itself is so good and was then so useful, the sad character of our age and the experience of our profound misfortune, shows us that for us it is the experience of a mount of evils. Thus those who govern the Church, after mature reflection, and as if constrained by necessity, introduced in this domain the limit which came about by prohibiting the Holy Scriptures in a vulgar tongue, preventing the ignorant from coming to read these books. Since we are dealing with gross and brutal people, incapable of comprehending these riches or making good use of them, if they comprehended them, they are taken away from the vulgar.

If someone is surprised, because it is something worthy of surprise, that among men who profess the same religion it can happen that something which was profitable previously is now harmful and if one desires to penetrate to the origins of this evil and discover its source, I will reply that, by what I can see, there are two causes for this situation: ignorance and pride and pride more than ignorance. Such are the evils into which the Christian people have slowly fallen from its first virtue. Ignorance has been the fate of those to whom it has fallen to know and explain these books, and pride also has been their fate and the fate of others but in different ways. The first know pride as the presumptuous concern for their honor; and the title of master which they assume without merit blinds them from recognizing their faults and realizing that it is better for them to apply themselves with diligence to learning what they do not know and yet they pretend to know; for the others this disposition not only takes away their desire to be learned in these books and letters, but persuades them that they can know and comprehend them by themselves. Thus ignorant people presume to be masters, and as those who are and must be cannot be as it is fitting for them, the light becomes darkness and the reading of Scriptures by the vulgar become for the latter a chance to conceive numerous and very pernicious errors which arise and are manifested at each moment.

But if the higher ecclesiastics, in the way that they can take Scriptures from the ignorant, could also put and establish them in the will, understanding, and knowledge of those who must teach them, this misery would bring forth less tears. In fact, since the

BOOK I

latter are like the heavens, being rich possessors of this treasure and of its virtue, there could flow from them great benefits for the poor who are the terrain upon whom they act. However, very often things are so reversed that they not only do not know Holy Scriptures, but misrepresent them; they show little appreciation and judge unfavorably those who know them. They exaggerate with satisfaction small pleasures which they derive from certain disputes, and they hold the title of master of theology, when they know no theology. We can understand that the disputes of the Schools are only the beginning of theology. Its growth is the doctrine which the saints expose: Its summit, its perfection, and its loftiness are the Holy Scriptures. To understand them is indeed the necessary end, and everything which we have just said is ordained to that purpose.

Leaving them aside and returning to what is common to the people, this evil which is their fault and caused by their pride has made the people incapable of reading Holy Scripture, and has been followed by an even worse evil: They are given to the reading of thousands of vain and harmful works which can be seen as the handiwork of the Devil, and in absence of good ones multiply more in our age than in any other. What happened to us happens to the field. When it does not produce wheat it produces thorns, and I say that to a certain degree the second evil is still greater than the first because the first causes men to lose the possibility of being good and the second offers them instead the way to be bad. In the former, virtue is deprived of a rule; in the latter, we nourish vice. If, as St. Paul says, "evil communications corrupt good manners" (1 Cor. 15:33*), the indecent and poisoned book which speaks at every moment with those who read it; how much harm will it not do? How is it possible for him who eats thorns and venom not to produce vicious and unhealthy blood?

In truth, if we wish to look at things attentively and as just judges, then we cannot fail to think that these pernicious and licentious books and their reading engender the ruin and the perdition of our morals. The feelings of paganism and infidelity which zealous men in the service of God feel in them (and I don't know of any epoch of Christianity where they were more deeply felt) find, in my view, in these books, their very principle, root,

---

*Bible quotations are taken from the Authorized King James Version.

and origin. We have great sorrow seeing so many simple and pure people being lost by this evil use before even becoming aware of it. Without knowing the where or the what, they find themselves poisoned and they are broken, in a pitiful way, on this hidden reef. Many of these evil writings are ordinarily found in the hands of young people, and their parents don't take care, and from this results most often that their other precautions are fruitless and useless.

This is the reason it has always been praiseworthy and advantageous to expose in writing the salutary doctrines which excite or lead the soul to virtue. This task is always so necessary, from my point of view; all of the good men upon whom God has bestowed qualities and talent for such a mission have the obligation to dedicate themselves to it and to compose in our language for the use of everyone texts which either are born from sacred letters or are related and conform to them, so that they supplement them, to the degree that the common occupations of men allow, and at the same time, they take from them books which are only harmful vanity and replace them with salutary ones.

If it is true that some learned and very religious persons have worked very happily in this domain and have given us many writings where utility is joined to purity, the others can apply themselves to the same enterprise and must not refrain from it nor believe themselves obligated to abandon, for this reason, the pen. In fact, even if all those who can write would write, the number would be insufficient for what has to be written for similar material; but this is true even for what we must write for our needs, because the tastes and the inclinations of men are so different and because the bad writings which good men must combat are already so numerous and widespread. In war when one attacks and lays siege to a fortified place, we begin by testing all its sides with all the procedures which military arts teach. Indeed, all good and learned men must do the same today, without depending upon any other, against the equally strong and powerful habit of which we have spoken.

This is what I think and have always thought. In fact, I regard myself as the last of those who can serve the Church with the material of which I have just spoken; yet I have always desired to serve it in this regard to the extent that it was possible for me. My poor health and excessive concerns had not permitted me up

BOOK I

to now to do it. Since in the past these preoccupations and my work have prevented me from carrying out this resolution and desire, it seems to me that I must not let this opportunity for leisure go by which the injustice and maliciousness of some people have caused. In fact, the experiences which have besieged me have been numerous, and yet the long favor of heaven which God, father of the persecuted, granted me without my merit and the testimony of my conscience in the midst of all of them have brought me so much serenity and peace not only in the improvement of my life but even in the search and knowledge of truth I see now, so that I can do what I could not do previously. This experience the Lord has transformed for me into light and health, and from the hands of those who intended to do me harm He has drawn my good. I would not reply with just gratitude to this excellent and divine favor, if now when I can do it with my humble talent and powers and in my own way, I did not apply myself to the task which seems so necessary for the good of the faithful.*

In reference to this subject some thoughts are brought to mind: Three of my friends who also belong to my order exchanged, during these last years, ideas on the names of Jesus Christ given in Holy Scripture. I was told of it shortly afterward by one of them, and its significance caused me not to forget it. Desiring today to write something for the people of Christ, I thought of beginning by studying the names given to Christ in the Bible, and believed that this was the happiest and the best sign for the most profitable use of the readers; and for my particular pleasure it was the sweetest and most agreeable material. As Christ is a source or rather is an ocean which holds in itself all that is sweet and meaningful that belongs to man, in the same way the study of His person, the revelation of the treasure, is the most meaningful and dearest of all knowledge. With good logic this knowledge is at the base of all other notions and knowledge because it is the foundation and the goal at which all the actions and thoughts of the Christian aim. The first thing which we must establish in our soul is to desire much knowledge and for this reason to possess it, because from it desire is born, inspired, and increased. Wisdom for man is in the knowledge of Christ and in

---

*These pages were written from the prison of the Inquisition of Valladolid.

truth it is the highest and most divine of all wisdoms. To comprehend Christ is to comprehend all the treasures of divine wisdom which are in Him as St. Paul says (Col. 2:2–3). It is to comprehend all the love of God for man, the majesty of His grandeur, the abyss of His counsel, the immense power of His invincible force, together with the other grandeurs and perfections which are in God and which show with brightness, more than anywhere else, in the mystery that is Christ. All these perfections or a great part of them can be understood if we grasp the force and significance of the names which the Holy Spirit gives Him in God's Scripture. These names are abbreviations of God in which He has marvelously enclosed all that human understanding can grasp and is suitable to its grasp.

Thus what was said on this matter I will subsequently recollect in the form that the conversations were related to me and in a manner most in conformity to the truth or to its similitude. I have put it in writing and am now sending it to Your Grace, whose service inspired all my actions.

INTRODUCTION

It was the month of June, about the time of the fiesta of St. John, and at the time of the end of the academic year at the University of Salamanca. Marcelo—I want to use a fictitious name for certain reasons and I will do the same for the others—after a long course which lasts a year, retired to the solitude of a farmhouse which my monastery, as Your Grace knows, owns along the banks of the River Tormes. He was joined there by two others who wished to keep him company for similar reasons. After a few days, one morning—it was the feast of St. Peter—after mass the three left the house and went into the garden.

It is a vast garden filled with trees that seemed to be planted without any order but which nevertheless lent charm to the view, the hour, and the occasion. After having entered and for some brief moments walked about and enjoyed the coolness, they then sat down in the shade of grapevines and close to a small spring. The spring came from a slope behind the house, from there it entered the vineyard; its running and its stumbling gave the impression that it was laughing. Close by there was a high and beautiful poplar grove. Not far was the Tormes, which at this time filled its banks and went twisting its way through the fertile plains. The day was peaceful, pure, and very cool. They sat down and had a moment of silence. Then Sabino—this was the name I was pleased to give the youngest of the three—looking toward Marcelo began to smile and then spoke:

"There are people who become silent by the view of the countryside and they must be those of profound understanding. But, as for me, I am like the birds, as soon as I see green I want to sing and speak."

"I understand why you say that," Marcelo immediately replied, "yet it is not the depth of spirit as you imply in order to flatter or comfort me, it is the difference of age and attitude which control us and which, when looking at this, excite the blood in you and melancholy in me. But let us know," he said of Juliano (this will be the name of the third), "if he also is a bird or if he is made of a different mettle."

"I am not always in the same mood," replied Juliano, "although at this moment I lean a little more toward the mettle of Sabino. Since he cannot now converse with himself, seeing the beauty of the fields and the grandeur of the heavens, it will be good if he tells us what conversation would suit us now."

Then Sabino drew out a small paper where he had written something:

"Here," he said, "is my desire and hope."

Marcelo, who recognized at once the paper because it was in his handwriting, turned to him and said with a smile:

"Desire, at least, will not torment you much, Sabino, since you already have your hope in your hands. Neither one nor the other must be very full if they are on such a small piece of paper."

"If they are meager," Sabino said, "that will deprive you of any cause to refuse me so meager a thing."

"In what way," replied Marcelo, "or how can I satisfy your desire, or of what desire do you speak?"

Then Sabino, unfolding the paper, read to him the title, which was on The Names of Christ. He read no more and then said:

"By chance yesterday I found this paper which is Marcelo's and where he noted, it seems, some names which Christ received in Holy Scriptures and the passages where these names are indicated. As soon as I saw it I wanted this subject to be discussed. For this reason I said that my desire was enclosed in this paper. My hope is there also because since it comes from him it is a subject which Marcelo has studied carefully and it is a subject which he knows on the tips of his fingers. He will not tell us this time what he usually says to excuse himself when we press him to speak, and he argues we take him unprepared. Since, this time, he doesn't have this excuse, since time belongs to us, the day is holy and the moment propitious for such conversation, it will not be difficult to make Marcelo give in, if you, Juliano, come to my support."

"Never will you find me more at your side, Sabino," replied Juliano.

There were statements and replies concerning this proposition. Marcelo pretended many excuses or asked Juliano at least to play a role and speak equally as much. They agreed that Juliano would do so when the occasion arose and it seemed opportune. Then Marcelo turned toward Sabino and said:

"Since the paper has been the point of departure of our conversation it will be proper for it to serve as a guide. Read it, Sabino. We will speak of what it contains in the order that it follows; at least, this seems the best course to follow."

"Yes, indeed, it is also our idea," replied Sabino and Juliano together.

Sabino glanced at the wording, read in a clear and moderate voice:

ON NAMES IN GENERAL

"The names which Scriptures give to Christ are numerous, like His virtues and attributes. But the main ones are ten. The others are included and recognized in these ten. These ten names are the following."

"Before dealing with this," Marcelo said, extending his hand toward Sabino to interrupt him, "it will be fitting to say something about our presuppositions and it would be good for us to leap backward and follow the water from its source, so that we can define what a name means, what is its function, for what purpose it is introduced, and in what manner it is to be used. Before we consider all this there is another preliminary.

BOOK I

"What other preliminary," asked Juliano, "before we discuss the essence of what we are speaking of, and a short explanation of it, which the Scholastics call 'definition.'"

"Like those who wish to build a ship," replied Marcelo, "and put out to sea and before unfurling the sails, turn toward the heavens and ask the favor of a safe journey; so now at the beginning of a similar journey, I, for myself, or rather all of us, let us ask the One we are going to discuss to grant us thoughts and words which are fitting for the subject. Because if in minor things we cannot bring forth their fullness nor even hope to begin without God's particular favor, who can then speak of Christ and of such elevated things as those which concern the Names of Christ if he is not inspired by Christ's spirit?

"Mistrusting ourselves and confessing the inadequacy of our knowledge, as if being in a state of utter worthlessness, we must fling aside the afflictions and plead with humility for this divine light which dawns upon us, so that it sends down to my soul the rays of its splendor and illuminates it in order that what we want to say of Him be worthy of Him, and that what is felt in this way may be said in the form that it must.

"Because, Lord, without your help who can speak of you as you deserve? or who will not be lost placed in the immense ocean of your perfection if you do not lead him to safe haven? Shine in my soul, you who are the sole true light, and shine with such abundance that your rays enflame my will so that it loves you, enlighten my intelligence so that it may see you and enrich my mouth so that it may speak of you, if not how you truly are, at least how you can be understood by us, with the single end of glorifying and exalting you forever."

And after a pause he said, "the name, to designate it with a few words, is a brief word that replaces the one of which we speak and substitutes for the same. The name is the same as that which is named, not in the real and true being that it has, but in the being which our mouth and understanding give to it.

"We must understand this: The perfection of all things and in particular those capable of understanding and reason is that each bears in itself all the others and is in its turn all the others because in this it has its affinity to God, who contains in Himself all. The more it grows in this the more it will be pleasing to Him and resemble Him. This similarity, if we can use this expression, is the universal aspiration and desire of all things and the goal and aim toward which all creatures move their desires. The perfection of all things is that each one of us strives to be a perfect world so that in this way, I being in everything and everything being in me, and I having being from all things and things having my being, we all embrace and link this whole universal mechanism and reduce the multitude of differences to a unity, and so without being mixed we touch each other, converse, harmonize; and being many we are not, showing and displaying before us variety and diversity so that unity may conquer, rule, and place its domination in all. This gives man a dwelling with God from whom flows a single perfect and simple excellence which in the three persons is a single essence and an infinite number of noncomprehensible excellences.

"If our perfection is what I have said and that each one naturally desires his perfection, nature not being parsimonious with means to satisfy our necessary desires has provided in this, like in all other things, admirable contrivances. Since it was impossible that coarse material things be in each other, it gives to them, besides the real being that they have in themselves, another being similar to the first but more delicate and which is born from it and which each is and makes it possible for them to live in the spirit of their neighbor, each in all, all in each. It ordained that they come forth from the understanding so that they could through the word attain the mouth. Nature disposed of it in such a way that in its material existence as had for its particular place, each thing could in its spiritual existence be reunited in great numbers in the same place without hindering each other, and what is still more astonishing is that the same thing is found at the same time in several places.

"A mirror can be used as an example. If we put many mirrors together and place them before our eyes, the image of the face, which is one, is reflected in each thing as the same and at the same time, and from all these images, without confusion, they return to the eyes, and from the eyes to the soul of the person who looks in the mirrors. To conclude from what has been said: All things live and have being in our understanding when we understand and name them with our mouths and tongues. What they are in themselves, they preserve in us this same existence, if our mouth and our understanding are true and veritable.

"I say "the same" by reason of similarity although the quality, the mode is different, according to what has been said, because the being they have in themselves is bulk and corporeality, a stable being which endures. In the understanding which grasps them they adapt themselves to its nature and become spiritual and subtle. Precisely, in themselves they are truth, but in the mind and in the mouth they are images of the truth, that is, of themselves and of the images which are substituted for the things themselves and take their place. In themselves they are themselves; in our mouths and minds they are names. Thus it remains clear what we said at the beginning, that the name is like an image of the thing we discussed or the same thing dressed in another way; the substitution and replacement take place for purpose and design of perfection and union.

"Similarly, it is also known that there are two different forms and manners of names: those which are in the soul and those which are in our lips. The first are beings that things possess in the spirit of the one who comprehends them; the second, the being that they possess in the lips of the one who expresses them and enunciates them with words so as to comprehend them. Between the two exists this conformity that both are images and as I have said many times a way of replacing them for what they are with names. There is however this difference: Some are images by nature and others by art. I mean that the image and form which are in the soul replace things whose representations they are. As we apply to each thing the chosen name which we have forged, words replace things. When we use the term "name" we usually speak of the latter although the former are principally names. We will speak of both."

Marcelo was ready to continue when Juliano said to him:

"It seems to me that you have sought the water at its source as is necessary to do in everything we discuss in order that it be perfectly understood. If I have heard you well, of the three points which you mentioned at the beginning you have already treated two of them: What is the name and what is its function. The third point remains to be examined, that is, the form which must be observed and to what we must be attentive when we choose it."

"Before that," replied Marcelo, "let us add a word to what has been said. In the same way that we comprehend things, we form at times an image of them in our mind which is the image of many objects, that is, it is an image in which many different things harmonize and appear; at other times the image which we sketch is a picture of one thing and a proper picture of it which says nothing else. In the same way there are words and names which apply broadly and are called common names and others which are fitting for one object. We are now speaking of these last ones. For the latter when they intentionally are given, their meaning and nature require that we follow the following rule: Since they are proper names, they must designate a particularity and express something proper in reference to what they are speaking; they must come forth, as if born and arising from a source which belongs in particular ways to it. Because if the name, as we have said, is given for what is named and if its purpose is to make what is absent and what is designated become present to our mind, and close and near what is distant, it is fitting that in the sound, in the form or truly in the origin and significance from which it is born, it should approach and become similar to what it is, as much as it is possible to approach the sound of a word to a material being.

"The truth is that this is not always realized in language. Yet if we want to tell the truth in the first of all languages, Hebrew, it is almost always observed.* God, at least, preserved the "names" which He had given as is seen in the Bible. If this is not so, why is it said in Genesis (2:19) that Adam, inspired by God, gave its name to each thing and what he named them that is the name of each? That is, that to each one that name came as if born with it, and that it was its for some particular and secret reason, that if it were given to another thing it would neither be fitting nor would it adjust well. But, as has been said, this similarity and conformity are attained in three ways: in the figure or form, in the sound, and especially in the origin of its derivation and meaning. Let us speak of each, beginning with the last.

"Pay heed then to this similarity in origin and meaning from which it is born, which is to say that when the name is given to something that is deduced from another word or name, that from which it is deduced must signify a thing which approaches a trait which is proper to the named object in order that the name coming from it, and as soon as it is pronounced, brings forth in the mind of the person who comprehends the image this particu-

---

*This refers to Hebrew, which Fray Luis considered to be the source of all other languages [editor's footnote].

lar property, that is, in order that the name contains in its signific
cation something of what the thing contains in its essence. For
example, in our language the name given to those who carry the
emblem of authority of justice in a city is *corregidores*, which is the
name born and taken from the verb to correct, *corregir*, because to
correct evil is their function or the essential fact of their office.
Thus whoever hears the name, upon hearing it understands what
it is and what he must do who bears it. Similarly, those who
regulate marriages are called in Castilian *casamenteros*, which
comes from one who makes mention or brings into question,
because those who make mention of marrying intervene in it, by
speaking of it and dealing with it.

"In the Bible this is preserved in all those names which God
gave to someone or which through his inspiration were given to
others. In this manner God not only adapted the names which he
gives to the proper element which the named things possess in
themselves but also every time that he conferred upon an object a
remarkable quality by adding it to those that it possessed by
nature, he gave it also a new name which was fitting for it. This is
seen in the new name which he gave to Abraham and to Sara, his
wife, and to Jacob, whom he called Israel, to Joshua,* the captain
who brought the Jews their own land, and many other names.

"Not long ago," Sabino said, "we heard a particular example
and upon hearing it I harbored some doubts."

"What example," replied Marcelo.

"The name Peter," said Sabino, "which Christ gave him
which we now read in the mass."

"It is true," Marcelo said, "and it is a good example. What are
your doubts?"

"The reason that Christ gave," replied Sabino, "is the cause of
my doubt, because it seems to me that it must have within it some
great mystery."

"Doubtless," Marcelo said, "a very great one, because Christ
giving Peter this new public name was a sure sign that it was a gift
of invincible strength infused into his soul, more than to any of
his other companions."

---

*Abram, extolled father, becomes Abraham, father of the multitude. Sarai, mock-
ery, becomes Sarah, princess. Jacob, supplanter, becomes Israel, he who struggles with
God. Joshua means health and rescuer.

"That," replied Sabino, "makes me doubtful because how did he more than the other apostles have either more inspired or self-possessed strength when he alone denied Christ on so important an occasion? Is it strength to promise audaciously and not to carry out resolutely?"

"It is not so," replied Marcelo, "and we cannot doubt that this glorious prince excelled the others for his gift of strength in his love and faith to Christ. Clearest proof is in his zeal and haste which he always had in advancing whatever seemed to touch either his Master's honor or trust. Not only after he received the fire of the Holy Spirit, but even before, when Christ asked him three times if he loved Him more than the others and he replied that he loved Him and Jesus said, "Feed my sheep" (John 21:15–17), and with this act Christ bore witness to the truth of Peter's reply and He held his love with the firmest and strongest love. If he denied him at some time, it can be believed that any one of his companions, fearing the same question and in the same situation, would have done the same. Not having faced it, they are not therefore stronger.

"If God wished that God's support be offered to Peter alone there was reason for it. One reason is that henceforth he would trust less in himself, after having found too much confidence in the force of love which he had in himself. Another is that in order to be shepherd and like a father to all the faithful, with the experience of his frailty, he would be sympathetic with the weaknesses of his followers and would know how to bear them. Finally with the bitter tears which he shed for his fault he would deserve the added strength. Thus it was that after giving himself, and many others, strength in himself, I mean, all those who are successors to his apostolic chair, the true doctrine and confession of faith has remained firm and whole and will remain so until the end.

"Turning again to what was said, this remains certain: All the names which are bestowed by God's command bear in them the meaning of some particular secret that the thing named contains in itself and in this meaning the name becomes similar to the thing, which is the first of all the elements to which this similarity refers, as we have said. The second refers to the sound, that is, that the name which is given must be of such a nature that when it is pronounced it has the same sound as the usual sound of what it signifies either when it is spoken or in some other accident that survives it. The third is the form which is made by the letters with which we write the name, their number and disposition, and what they habitually cause in us when we pronounce them. In the divine books, in the original language, there are infinite examples of these last two methods, because from the sound there is no word among the names which signify something which, if it were well pronounced either by the voice or by the sound which it emits from itself, does not evoke either the same sound or some other very similar one.

"What concerns form, if we regard it carefully, is a marvelous thing: the secrets and mysteries that are in the holy letters. Because in them, in some names letters are added to signify an increase in good fortune and the removal of certain others shows poverty and calamity. Certain names, if what they designate is male, undergo some accident which makes them feminine and soft and borrow letters from those which in this language are of feminine softness. Others, on the other hand, which signify feminine things for themselves, borrow virile letters to make comprehensible a virile accident. Among others the letters modify their own form, the open ones close and the closed ones open, and they change places, they are transposed and disguised with different faces and gestures like the chameleon. They all become accidents with those with whom they form names. I give an example of this because they are the details that are well known to those who, like you, Sabino and Juliano, know this language and in particular because these are things which belong to the eyes and are hard to understand in the spoken language.

"If you wish, let's limit ourselves to the form and value of the letters with which in that language the proper name of God is written which the Hebrews call the Ineffable because they did not believe it lawful to bear the name on their lips and the Greeks call it the "name in four letters"* because four are the letters with which it is composed. If we regard the sound with which it is pronounced, it is all vowels like what it signifies, that all is being, life, and spirit without any mixture of matter, and if we consider the nature of the Hebrew letters which are used for writing, they possess the characteristic that each can be put in the place of the

---

*The Greek word *tetragrammaton* corresponds to the four-lettered name of God, the word that is unexpressible.

others and this is often done in this language. Thus each of them is all of them and all is in each one; it is like the image of simplicity that, on the one hand, there is in God, and, on the other, He has an infinite multitude of perfections, because He is altogether a great perfection and His simplicity encompasses all His perfections. If we speak with propriety God's wisdom is not different from His infinite justice, nor His justice from His greatness, nor His greatness from His mercy and His power, and in Him power, love, and knowledge are one. In each one of these perfections, however they may drift apart from each other, they are all together and from whatever part one regards it, they are all one and the same thing. With this course of reasoning the nature of the letters conform. It is not only in the nature of the letters but also in their form and disposition that the name represents Him in some way."

Marcelo, while saying this, leaned toward the ground and with a small stick formed these three sevens in the sand and said:

"Why is this holy name so figured in these Chaldaic letters? As you see, they are the image of the number of the divine Persons and the equality and unity which they have in one essence as these letters are of one figure and of one name. Let's leave it thus."

Marcelo was going to say something else, but Sabino and Juliano interrupted and said it in this way:

"Before you continue, Marcelo, you must tell us how you reconcile with what you have just said the fact that God has a proper name. From the beginning I wanted to ask you and I failed to do so because I didn't want to break the thread of the conversation. But now, before you leave it, tell us, if the name is the image which replaces what it represents, tell us, what name or word or what idea conceived by the imagination can come to be an image of God, or if it cannot attain it, in what manner is it a proper name? There is still another difficulty. If the purpose of names is to make us penetrate into the things which they represent, it is, as you said, useless to give God a name, because He is present in all things, rooted in their entrails, and is as profoundly intimate in them as their being itself."

"You have opened the door, Juliano," replied Marcelo, "to great and profound considerations, yet we must discuss first the much that there is to be said in Sabino's proposal. I will not reply with more than is adequate to untie and resolve your difficulties. I will begin with the last and say that it is a great truth that God is present in us as so close and so within our being as He is in His own. In Him we not only move and breathe but live and have our being as St. Paul preaches (Acts 17:28) and confesses. In this way He is so present to us that, paradoxically, in this life His presence never appears to us.

"I mean that He is present in us and close to our being but very far from our view and the clear knowledge which our understanding desires. Whence, it was suitable, or better, necessary that "so long as we are in the body, we are exiles from the Lord" (2 Cor. 5:6) in the valley of tears, while His face does not show itself to us nor close to our soul, we should have upon our lips some name and some word and in the spirit some imperfect and obscure figure of Him as St. Paul enigmatically said (1 Cor. 13:12). When we manage to escape from this earthly prison in which now our captive soul toils and labors it will be like coming forth into the clarity and purity of this light which is now united to our being and will be united to our spirit and by itself, and without the help of a third image, God will be in the eyes of the soul. His name will not be other than Himself, in the manner and form that He will be seen, and each will name Him as He will be seen and known by him, according to his fullness, in the manner that he will know Him. It is for this reason that St. John says in Revelation (7:17) that in this happy moment God will not be content "to wipe all tears from their eyes" and the past sorrows from their memory; "I will also give a white stone, and on the stone it will be written a new name, known to none but him that receives it" (2:17). It is no other thing, if not the sum of Himself and His essence, that God will communicate to the spirit of each of the blessed, being one in everything, with each one however at a different level and with a different feeling that will be singular and certain for each. And this secret name which St. John speaks of and the name with which we will then name God will be everything which then will be divine in our souls, for as St. Paul said (1 Cor. 15:18), God "will be all in all." Thus, in the heavens, where we will see clearly, there will be no need for another name than that of God Himself. But in the present obscurity, where we all possess God and yet have not noticed Him, we are obliged to give him a name. We have not given Him one ourselves. He through His great mercy gave it to us when He saw cause and need for it.

"It is wise to consider the secret teaching of the Holy Spirit

which the holy Moses followed in the book of creation, also called
Genesis. Treating here the history of creation in all its aspects and
having named God often, never did he name Him with His own
name until God created man and Moses could write of this creation. It seems that he wished to have understood that before this
moment God had no need of a name and that with the birth of
man, who could comprehend Him without seeing Him in this life,
it was necessary that He be named. And as God had decided that
He would become man afterward, as soon as man appeared He
wanted to become more human by naming Himself.

"The other point that you propose, Juliano, that God being
an abyss of being and of infinite perfection, and since the name
must be an image of what is named, how could it be understood
that a limited word comes to be the image of what has no limitations? Some say that this name, like a name God gave to Himself,
declares all that God understands about Himself, which is the
concept and divine word which it will engender from itself and
that this word which speaks to us and sounds in our ears is a sign
which explains to us the eternal and incomprehensible word that
is born and lives in God's womb, as the words of our mouth
declare the secret of the heart. However this may be, when we say
that God has proper names or that this one is God's proper name,
we do not mean that it is a perfect name, or a name which
embraces and declares to us all that there is in Him. To be proper
is one thing; to be equal or perfect is another. For a name to be
proper it is sufficient that it speaks of the things that are proper to
that or to whom it says something; that name is partially adequate,
but it does not declare them entirely and perfectly because what
the mouth says is the expression of what the soul comprehends.
Thus words cannot attain what the understanding has not attained, and thus we could never give God a complete and adequate
name.

"Let us approach the subject proper of our undertaking and
what Sabino read from the paper and see why Christ is given so
many names. This is so because of His limitless greatness and the
treasury of His very rich perfections and with them the host of
functions and other benefits which are born in Him and spread
over us. Just as they cannot be embraced by the soul's vision, so
much less can a single word name them. It is as he who spills
water into some glass with a narrow and long neck, and distrib-

BOOK I

utes it drop by drop, so the Holy Spirit which knows the narrow-
ness and poverty of our understanding does not give us that
greatness all at once but offers it to us in drops, telling us, at times,
something under one name, and some other thing, at other times,
under another name. Thus, the innumerable names which divine
Scriptures give to Christ come into existence, they call Him: Lion,
lamb, door, path, pastor, priest, offering, spouse, vine, bud, king,
face of God, stone, star, source, father, prince of peace, salvation,
life, and truth, and numerous other names. From these the paper
chose ten as being more substantial. The others can be reduced to
the chosen ten.

"Before proceeding it must be remarked that Christ is God,
that He has names which are fitting for His divinity, some related
to His person and others common to the Trinity, but our discourse does not speak of these because only the former belong
appropriately to the names of God. The names of Christ which
concern us belong to Christ as a man, conforming to the rich
treasures of righteousness which encompass His humaneness and
to the works which God operates and has operated in us.

"Now, Sabino, if you have nothing else to propose, proceed."
And Sabino read:

BUD

"The first name given to Christ in Castilian will be 'bud,'
which in the original language is *cemah* and the Latin text trans-
lates it by *germen* and at times by *oriens*. Thus in the fourth chapter
of Isaiah the Holy Spirit said: 'In that day the Bud of the Lord
shall be in magnificence and glory, and the fruit of the earth shall
be high.' In Jeremiah (33:15), 'In those days and at that time, I will
make the Bud of justice to spring forth unto David, and He shall
do judgment and justice in the earth.' In Zachariah (3:18), 'I will
bring my servant the Orient,' consoling the Jewish people recently departed from Babylonian captivity, and in (6:12), 'Behold the
man whose name is Bud.' "

Sabino stopped here and Marcelo began.

"Let this be the first name since this is the order of discourse.
There is reason that this be the first because, as we will see, it
touches in a certain way the quality and order of Christ's birth

53

and His new and marvelous generation which from the point of good method is the first that is usually spoken of.

"Before we explain what bud means and what this name signifies and the reason Christ is called bud, it is fitting that we see if it is true that this is a name of Christ and if it is so in divine Scripture. We will see if the indicated passages speak properly of Christ because there are some people who, from ignorance or lack of faith, want to deny this fact.

"Referring to the text of Isaiah, it is clear that it speaks of Christ. The Chaldean text whose authority in antiquity was very great, in the passages where we read 'In that day shall be the Bud of the Lord,' says, 'In that day he shall be the Messiah of the Lord.' This passage cannot be understood in any other way. Because those who say that it refers to Zerubbabel and of the happy state which the Jewish people enjoyed under his rule seem to think that he was the bud of the Lord of whom Isaiah spoke, 'In that day the Bud of the Lord shall be glorious in its sublimity.' They speak without knowing what they say because whoever reads what is related in the books of Nehemiah and Esdras of the state of the people will see much toil, poverty, and contradiction, and no marked felicity either in temporal goods or in the goods of the soul—the felicity which Isaiah speaks of when he writes, 'In that day the Bud of the Lord shall be in greatness and in glory.'

"Although the age of Zerubbabel and the state of the Jews might have been happy, it is certain that was not the heights of happiness marked by the prophet. What word is there in the passage which does not note a very rare divine good? It speaks 'of the Lord,' which is a word added to everything in that language and which increases its excellence. It says, 'glory, greatness, magnificence,' which is all that one can say to exalt Him. To eliminate all doubt the Prophet points to the time and day of the Lord expressing himself thus, 'in that day.' But what day? Doubtless, no other but that same day of which was said:

> Therefore the Lord will smite with a scab the crown of the head of the daughters of Zion, and the Lord will discover their secret parts. In that day the Lord will take away the bravery of their tinkling ornaments about their feet, and their cauls and their round tires like the moon. The chains and the bracelets, and the mufflers, the bon-

nets and the ornaments of the legs, and the headbands and the tablets and the earrings, the rings and the nose jewels, the changeable suits of apparel, and the mantles and the wimples and the crisping pens, the glasses and the fine linen, and the hoods and the veils. And it shall come to pass that instead of sweet smell there shall be stink, and instead of a girdle a rent; and instead of well-set hair baldness, instead of a stomacher a girding of sackcloth, and burning instead of beauty. Thy men shall fall by the sword and thy mighty in war." (Isa. 3:17–25)

"Then in that day when God destroyed Jerusalem's greatness with Roman arms which burned the city, put its citizens to the sword and brought them into captivity, the fruit and the bud of the Lord was revealed and came forth and grows in glory and great honor. At the time of the destruction of Jerusalem by the Chaldeans, if someone pretends the Prophet was talking of it, it cannot be truthfully said that 'the fruit of the Lord increased,' nor that 'he fructified gloriously the earth' at the same time that the city was lost. It is well known that in that calamity there was no moment or mixture of happiness neither in those who were captives in Babylonia, nor in those whom the Chaldean conqueror left in Judea and in Jerusalem to cultivate the land because the former were in miserable servitude and the latter were in fear in their abandonment. We read this all in Jeremiah (39:5).

"On the other hand, it is clear that the light of the name of Christ is linked to this other catastrophe of the Jewish people and the Church began to rise when Jerusalem fell. He who a short while before had been condemned and suffered an ignominious death by those who wished to ruin and obscure His name began to emit rays of light through the world and show Himself to be the living Lord, so powerful that He chastised His murderers with a severe scourge and deprived the Devil of his control over the earth and destroyed slowly the cult of idols by which the Gentiles served the Devil, and comparable to the sun which triumphs over the clouds and disperses them, Christ alone fills the whole earth with His shining splendor.

"What I have said of this passage is seen clearly also in Jeremiah (33:15) with the same words. To say to David and to promise him that the fruit and bud of justice would be born of him was to indicate exactly that the fruit was Jesus Christ, adding that this fruit would bring justice and reason on the earth, because it is the proper work of Christ and one of the reasons that He came. It is the work which He alone and no other could accomplish. For this reason in numerous passages of Scriptures where we find mention of Him, we hasten to attribute to Him this work and to present it as His essential work and glory. We observe this in Psalm 72: 'Give the King thy judgment, O God, and thy righteousness unto the king's son. He shall judge thy people with righteousness, and thy poor with judgment. The mountains shall bring peace to the people, and the little hills, by righteousness he shall judge the poor, he shall save the children of the needy, and shall break in pieces the oppressor.'

"The third passage, which is from Zachariah (3:8), the Jews themselves confess, and the Chaldean text which I spoke of confirms, that it applies to Christ. Similarly, we understand the fourth testimony of the same Prophet. We are not hindered by a tract where some see a difficulty which forces them to interpret the passage in another way, for it says that 'this bud shall grow out of his place and he shall build the temple of the Lord' (6:12). They believe that this refers to Zerubbabel, who built the temple, and it bore true fruit for many centuries before Christ. This does not impede but rather reinforces and favors our design. Because to fructify in oneself or as the original exactly says, about oneself, is proper to Christ alone and to no other. It is what He says of Himself, 'I am the vine, ye are the branches (John 15:5). In the recently cited Psalm where whatever is said belongs essentially to Christ, does it not say, 'In his days shall the righteous flourish' (Psalm 72:7)? Oh, if we desire to confess the truth, who engendered in lost men, just and holy men, what fruit has there ever been which has been better than Christ? Doubtless, this is the same thing that the Prophet tells us because he gave to Christ the name 'fruit' and because he said in showing Him to be the unique fruit: 'You see here a man whose name is fruit.' And so that we did not believe that His fruit ends in Him, that He was simply a fruit and not a tree capable of producing fruits, he added immediately: 'He will fructify about himself,' that is, in a more detailed way: It is a fruit which gives much fruit, because about Him, that is, in Him and from Him throughout the earth limitless and noble and divine fruits will be born and this bud will enrich the world with still unknown buds.

"Thus is this a name of Christ, and in our order, the first, without their being doubt or dispute about it. Several other names are like neighbors and relatives which are given Him in Scriptures, even though in sound they are different but when clearly seen all are reduced to the same design and agree in the same meaning. In Ezekiel (34) He is called 'plant of renown.' In Isaiah (11) sometimes He is called 'branch' and at others 'flower,' in the fifty-third chapter, a 'tender plant and root,' and all this to tell us what the name 'bud' or 'fruit' indicates. It is what we have already said, because the first point concerning the attribution of this name of Christ is adequately proven, if nothing else is suggested by you."

"Nothing else," Juliano said, "on the contrary, the name and hope of this fruit have awakened in us a sweetness for it."

"It deserves the sweetness and desire," replied Marcelo, "because it is the sweetest fruit and no less beneficial than sweet, although it may be spoiled by the poverty of my language and talent. But answer me, Sabino, because I want to agree with you. This beauty of sky and world which we see and the greater beauty which we understand, and which is still hidden from us in the invisible world, was it always as now, or did it make itself or did God make it and bring it forth?"

"It is certain," said Sabino, "that God created the world, with all that there is in it, without presupposing any previous matter, but only with the strength of His infinite power with which He made come forth from where there was nothing before this beauty which you speak of. But is there doubt on this point?"

"There is none," replied Marcelo in turn. "But let us go on. Tell me: Is the world born of God in such a way that He took no notice of it, as a kind of natural consequence, or did God make it because He wished and it was His free will to do so?"

"It is also proved," Sabino then replied, "that He did it with design and freedom."

"Well said," Marcelo remarked, "and since you recognize that, you will also recognize that God intended some great purpose."

"Doubtlessly great," replied Sabino, "because as soon as one works with judgment and freedom it is always in view of a purpose."

"Did God intend in this way," said Marcelo, "some growth of Himself?"

"Not at all," replied Sabino.

"Why," said Marcelo.

And Sabino replied:

"Because God, who already has all goodness in Himself, cannot wish to attain the least growth or the least progress in what He would do outside of Himself."

"Thus God being the infinite and perfect good," said Marcelo, "when He created the world did not seek to receive any good from it, as it has been said, but intended some purpose. Then if He didn't intend to receive, doubtless, He intended to give, and if He didn't create to add something to Himself, He created it to communicate Himself to Himself and to spread His goodness among His creatures. Certainly, this alone is the purpose worthy of God's grandeur and fitting for the one whose nature is goodness. Because what is good induces the doing of the good through its own inclination. If God's intent in the creation and construction of the world was to do good to what was created, spreading His good in it, then what good or communication was God's purpose in the carrying out of His work?"

"The same purposes," replied Sabino, "as those He assigned to the creatures, to each in particular and to all in general."

"Exactly," said Marcelo, "but you have not replied to the question I asked you."

"How is that?" Sabino replied.

"Because," said Marcelo, "as these goods are of different degrees and do not have the same value, the question which I pose is this: What good, what degree of goodness, is the principal aim of God?"

"Of what degree are we speaking?" replied Sabino.

"There are many," said Marcelo, "in their different parts, but the Scholastic usually reduces them to three: nature, grace, and personal union. To nature belong the goods which we are born with, to grace belongs that which after birth God add to us, and the good of personal union is to have God join in Jesus Christ His person with our nature. There is a great difference among these goods.

BOOK I

"To begin with, every good which lives and is manifest in the creature is the good which God put in it. But God put in the creature goods proper and natural for it. Its being consists in this and what flows from it. These goods, we say, come from nature because God planted them in nature and we are made of them: being, life, understanding, and other similar things. There are other goods which God didn't put in the nature of the creature nor in the virtue of His natural principles in order that they be born there, but rather He added them Himself to nature and thus they are not fixed nor set in nature like the others, but they are inconstant goods like grace and charity and the other gifts of God, and these we call the supernatural gifts of grace. It is given as a truth that all this communicated good is a mirror of God because it is God's work and God can do nothing which doesn't reflect Him because insofar as He creates He takes Himself for the model. But although this is so, there are many different ways of imitating Him. In nature creatures imitate the being of God, but in the goods of grace they imitate, in addition to His being, His character, style, and to some degree His manner of living and His beatitude, and thus the creature which possesses grace approaches and joins God even more intimately. How much more is this resemblance than the first! In the personal union the creatures do not imitate nor approach God but come to be God because they unite with Him in the same person."

Here Juliano interrupted and said: "Do all the creatures join in one person with God?"

Marcelo replied laughing:

"Until now we were not concerned with number but were concerned with manner. I mean, I did not count which and how many creatures unite with God and imitate Him, but I was concerned with the way they unite and imitate Him whether through nature, grace, or personal union. As for the numbers of those who unite with Him, it is clear that in the goods of nature all creatures approach God, but in the goods of grace, not all, but only some of those who possess intelligence. In personal union only the humanity of our Lord Jesus Christ is of similar nature to God's. However, although the personal union, properly speaking, is only achieved with the singular human nature in a particular way, that is, when God is united with it, it seems to unite with all creatures because man is an intermediary between the spiritual and corporeal and contains in himself the one and the other. He is, as the Ancients said, a small or an abbreviated world."

"I am waiting," said Sabino, "to see to what end your discourse leads."

"We are close to it," replied Marcelo. I ask you if the end for which God created all things was only to communicate Himself to them and if this gift and communication occurs in different ways and if some of these ways are more perfect than others. Does not reason seem to assume that such a great Creator, in such a great work, had as purpose to establish the largest and most perfect communication that was possible for Himself?"

"It seems so," said Sabino.

"And the greatest," continued Marcelo, "of those that are made and can be made is the personal union that is produced between the divine Word and the human nature of Christ, by which God became one with man."

"There is no doubt," replied Sabino, "that it is the greatest."

"Then it is necessary," added Marcelo, "that God in order to produce this blessed and marvelous union created everything that is seen and unseen. The end for which everything was created, all the variety and beauty of the world, was to bring forth this mixture of God and man or the one who is both God and man: Jesus Christ."

"It is a necessary consequence," replied Sabino.

"Well," Marcelo then said, "it is thus that Christ is a fruit. When Scriptures give Him this name, it makes us understand that Christ is the purpose of all things and that His birth was the purpose of creation. In the tree the root is not made for itself and even less the trunk which is born from it and is supported upon it, but both together, with the branches, flowers, and leaves and everything which the tree produces, have their purpose in the fruit which comes from them and which is its purpose and its achievement. These wide heavens which we see and the stars in them, this fount of clarity and light that illuminates everything, which is sound and so beautiful, the earth painted with flowers, and waters filled with fish, animals and men, this whole universe, how great and beautiful it is! God made it for the purpose of making man His Son, to give birth to this unique and divine fruit which is Christ and which, in truth, we are able to call the common parturition of all things.

BOOK I

In the tree the solidness of the trunk, the beauty of the flowers, and the freshness of the green of the leaves were made for the birth of the fruit which has in itself all that belongs to it from the tree, or we may say, it contains the tree entirely. Similarly, God—who created at first the strong and deep roots of the elements, established upon them this greatness of the world, and this variety of branches and leaves—was planning the birth of Christ. Christ contains and embraces everything in Himself as St. Paul says, 'For by him were all things created that are in heaven and that are in the earth visible and invisible' (Col. 1:16). That Christ has been called fruit makes us understand that the whole creation has been organized around Him, and if we are attached to what has been ordained we can understand the inestimable value of the fruit in relation to which such great things have been arranged. From the greatness, beauty, and quality of the means we infer the immeasurable excellence of the purpose.

"If someone enters into some palace or a rich and sumptuous royal house and sees at first the strength and firmness of the wide walls and towers and the array of sculptured windows, and the narrow and covered bridges, the spires which dazzle the sight, and after the high entrance, adorned with rich ornamentation; he sees the vestibules and the great and vast patios, the marble columns, the large halls and rich wardrobes and the diversity, the multitude and arrangement of apartments, all embellished with rare and selected paintings, and with jasper, porphyry, ivory, and gold which shines in the floors, walls, and ceilings; he sees together with all this the multitude of those who serve, the good looks and rich finery of their person, and the order with which each carries out his service and ministry, the harmony they all preserve among themselves; he hears the minstrel players and the sweetness of their music, he sees the beauty and luxury of their beds and the priceless richness of their cupboard; then he knows that the one for whom all this service is ordained is incomparably great. Thus we must understand that if this spectacle of earth and heaven is of admirable beauty, the one for whom it has been created is beauty without comparison and even more astounding.

"There is no doubt of the greatness and majesty of this universal temple which we call the world. Christ, for whose birth it was ordained from the beginning and to whose service it will be subjected and whom now it serves and obeys and forever will obey, is incomparably the greatest, the most glorious, and the most perfect being, much more than anyone can comprehend or exalt. Being so, St. Paul, inspired by the power of the Holy Spirit, wrote to the Colossians (1:15–19):

> Who is the image of the invisible God, the firstborn of every creature? For by him were all things created, that are in heaven, and that are in earth, visible and invisible, whether they are the thrones or dominions or principalities or powers: all things were created by him and for him: and he is before all things, and by him all things consist. And he is the head of the body, the church: who is the beginning, the firstborn from the dead, that in all things he might have predominance. For it pleased the Father that in him should all fullness dwell.

"Then Christ is called fruit because He is the fruit of the world, because He is the fruit for whose production the world is ordered and created. Thus Isaiah, desiring his birth and knowing that the heavens and all living nature possessed their being from His parturition, writes, 'Drop down, ye heavens, from above, and let the skies pour down righteousness, let the earth open, and let them bring forth salvation and let righteousness spring up together' (45:8).

It is not only for this reason that we have said that Christ is called fruit, but also because all that which is true fruit in men, that is, that merits appearing before God and entering into heaven, is not born only in them by virtue of the fruit which is Jesus Christ, but is also Jesus Christ Himself in a certain way. The justice and sanctity which pass into the souls of His faithful as well as the other goods and holy works which are born from it, and being born from it then increase, are like an image and live painting of Jesus Christ and so alive they are called Christ in Scriptures, as can be seen in passages where St. Paul admonishes us to take Christ upon ourselves because a holy and just life is the image of Christ. It is through His spirit that Christ communicates to the just and is infused into their soul, gives to each the name of Christ, so that all united, they form one Christ.

"St. Paul testifies to this, saying: 'For as many of you as have

BOOK I

been baptized into Christ have put on Christ. There is neither Jew nor Greek, there is neither bond nor free, there is neither male nor female, for ye are all one in Christ Jesus' (Gal. 3:27–28). And elsewhere he said (Gal. 4:19), 'My little children, of whom I travail in birth again until Christ be formed in you.' And admonishing the Romans to good words, 'The night is far spent, the day is at hand: let us therefore cast off the works of darkness, and let us put on the armor of light. Let us walk honestly, as in the day; not in rioting and drunkenness, not in chambering and wantonness, not in strife and envying. But put ye on Lord Jesus Christ and make no provision for the flesh, to fulfill the lust thereof' (13:12–14). And all these Christians are one Christ, he says it to the Corinthians, 'For as the body is one and both many members, and all the members of that one body, being many, are one body: so also *is* Christ' (1 Cor. 12:12).

"As St. Augustine remarks, he does not say, concluding the similitude, 'this is Christ and his members,' but *'this is Christ' (De peccatorum meritis et remissione* 1. 31, 60; PL 44, 135). He wants to show us that Christ, our head, is in His members, and that the members and the head are one Christ, as will be said more fully later on. What we say now, and the result of all that has been said, is to know how deservingly Christ is called fruit. All the good and valuable fruit that lives and is fructified in man is Christ and comes from Him. It is born from Him and it resembles and imitates Him. For the moment we have spoken enough of this. Continue, Sabino, the reading of your paper."

"Let us stop," said Juliano, extending his hand toward Sabino, "because, if I have not lost my memory, it will be necessary for you, Marcelo, to explain what you told us at the beginning concerning the new marvelous concept of Christ which, as you said, this name signifies."

"It is true and you did well, Juliano, in refreshing my memory," Marcelo immediately replied, "and what you are now asking is this: This name that we often call 'bud' and at other times 'fruit' is not in the original word any sort of fruit but is properly the fruit which is born spontaneously without cultivation or industry. Concerning Christ to whom it is now applied, we indicate two things: (1) there was neither knowledge, nor courage, nor merit, nor industry in the world which might lead God to become man,

THE NAMES OF CHRIST

that is, to produce this fruit; (2) that in the purest and holiest womb from which this fruit was born, only God's virtue and work were operative and without man's intervention."

When he heard this Juliano pretended to move his seat a little and he leaned toward Marcelo, then he looked at him with a happy face and said:

"Now I am even more content, Marcelo, having called to your mind what you forgot, because I am delighted to hear you say that the principle of virginal purity and integrity in our common Mother and Lady is specified in ancient letters and prophecy. Reason demands it. When they said and wrote so many things of less importance, it was not possible to silence such a great mystery. If other references appear which belong to it, and they surely will present themselves, I would be very happy if you state them, if it does not bore you."

"In no way," Marcelo replied, "does it bore me to say something in praise of my unique advocate and Lady. Although she belongs to everyone, I dare call her my Lady and my particular advocate because from childhood I put myself completely under her protection. You were not deceived, Juliano, in thinking that the books and writings of the Old Testament did not pass over in silence the wonderment so new and remarkable. In fact, in many places they speak in terms which are clear to the faith, although somewhat obscure to hearts that are blinded by infidelity, in the same way with many other things which relate to Christ. St. Paul says that this is a mystery which has been hidden (Col. 1:26), a mystery which God wanted both to say and conceal for very just ends, one of them being to afflict this ungrateful people with the punishment of blindness and ignorance of such necessary things; this is a punishment which such enormous sins merited.

"Now, coming to what you asked, there is the clearest testimony, in my judgment, in favor of your proposition in that passage of Isaiah which we cited previously: 'Drop down, ye heavens, from above, and let the skies pour down righteousness.' Although he there speaks of Christ since you see Him as a plant which is born in fields, he mentions neither plow nor hoe, nor agriculture, but only sky and clouds and earth to which he attributes the whole birth.

"In fact, if we compare Isaiah's words with those of the Archangel Gabriel concerning the very holy Virgin (Luke 1:35)

BOOK I

we will see that they are almost the same. The Archangel is concerned with a contemporary event and Isaiah expresses himself metaphorically and figuratively, which is the prophet's style. The Angel for his part says, 'The Holy Ghost shall come upon thee.' Isaiah says, 'You shall send, oh heavens, your dew.' The Angel says that the virtue of the All High shall cover her in shadows. Isaiah prays that the clouds will envelop. The Angel says: 'That holy being who shall be born of thee shall be called the Son of God,' and Isaiah says, 'Let the earth open and let it bring forth salvation' (Isa. 45:8). To be free of all doubt this is what he adds: And let righteousness spring up together, I the Lord have created him.' He does not say, and I, the Lord, it is righteousness which I have created and which should flourish at the same time. He says, 'It is he whom I have created,' and he points to the Savior, Jesus, because Jesus is the name the original text gives. He says, 'I created him' and attributes to Himself the creation and birth of the blessed salvation and glories in it as a unique and admirable fact and says, 'I, I,' as if to say, 'I alone and no other with me.'

"There is another, no less efficacious proof of this same truth, and it is in the manner that the same prophet speaks of Christ in chapter 4 when he uses the same figure of plants, fruits, and things of the countryside which for their birth show no other cause than God and the earth, that is, the Virgin and the Holy Spirit. He says, 'In that day shall the bud of God be beautiful and glorious and the fruit of the earth shall be excellent and comely' (Isa. 4:2).

"Among the other passages there is one in particular, Psalm 110, doubtlessly somewhat obscure in the Latin version but very clear in the original text. The clarity caused ancient authors who lived before the coming of Christ to conclude from it, and they wrote it, that the mother of the Messiah would conceive although she would remain a virgin by the sole virtue of God and without man's activity. If we translate literally, the passage says, 'In the beauties of holiness from the womb of the morning thou hast the dew of thy youth' (Ps. 110:3). These words, not single ones, but all speak and reveal the mystery of which I was speaking. In the first place, it is certain that in these Psalms the prophet speaks of Christ; in the second, it is equally clear that in the verse he speaks of his conception and birth, and the words 'womb' and 'birth' which follow the original can be called also 'generation.' This is clearly demonstrated.

"That God alone, without human intervention, was the creator of this divine and new work in the virginal and purest womb of our Lady, this is apparent from the words 'in the beauties of holiness.' Which is to say that Christ was conceived not in the lustful ardors of flesh and blood but in the holy splendor of the heavens, not in sensual impurity, but in the spiritual beauty of holiness. What then follows about the dawn and the dew expresses the same thing in an elegant form because it is a hidden comparison which when analyzed sounds like this: In the womb (it is implied, in your mother's womb) you will be engendered like the dawn, that is, as what in this season is engendered in the countryside, affected by the dew which descends from heaven and not as the result of irrigation and human sweat. Finally, to explain it totally, he added, 'Thou hast the dew of thy youth.' As he had compared the dawn to the womb of the mother and because it is in the dawn that the dew falls and fructifies the earth, he continues this comparison and called the dew the virtue of generation.

"Truthfully, it is this name which in many other passages of Holy Scriptures bears this virtue, produces the life by which God engendered from the beginning the body of Christ, through which after His death He again engendered and resurrected Him and through which in the general resurrection He will give life to our dissolved bodies as we see in chapter 26 of Isaiah. David said to Christ that this dew and virtue which formed His body and which gave Him life in the virginal entrails—they were given to Him and were placed in the sacred womb not by someone from without, but He possessed them in His own right and carried them with Him. For it is certain that the holy Word that became man in the sacred womb of the holy Virgin formed the body and the human nature with which it clothed itself. In order that we understand this, David says that Christ possesses with Him the dew of His birth. Although in this place we say birth we could also say childhood, because if the word has the same meaning as birth, it is nevertheless a term which designates the new and corporeal being which Christ assumed in the Virgin and where He was first child, then young man, and then perfect man. In the other eternal birth which is in God, Christ is born God, eternal, perfect, and equal to His Father.

"Concerning this truth I could discuss many other things, but in order that we don't lack the time for what still remains, let us limit ourselves to but one thing: It is what is said of Christ in Isaiah 53:2, 'For he shall grow up before him as a tender plant (bud) and as a root out of dry ground.' Truthfully, although the Prophet uses figurative and obscure words, he could not say it in clearer terms than the ones he has used. He calls Christ 'plant' and follows this with 'ground,' that is, His holy Mother, as is proper. After having called her this, that is, that she conceived without man, there was no better or comprehensible way to express it than 'rich soil.' Do you wish, Juliano, that Sabino continue?"

"Yes, that he continue," replied Juliano. And Sabino then read:

FACE OF GOD

"Christ is called also face of God, as we see in Psalm 81:14, which says, 'mercy and truth shall go before thy face.' And it is said that with Christ truth, justice, and mercy were born, as Isaiah affirms when he says, 'and let righteousness spring up together.' And David says the same when in Psalm 85 (10–13), which is concerned entirely with the advent of Christ, 'Mercy and truth have met together, righteousness and peace have kissed each other. Truth shall spring out of the earth, and righteousness shall look down from heaven. Yea, the lord shall give that is good, and our land shall yield her increase. Righteousness shall go before him, and shall set us in the way of his steps.' Christ is given the same name in Psalm 95 where David, inviting men to receive the good news of the gospel, says to them, 'Let us come before his presence with thanksgiving'; and more clearly in Psalm 80, 'Turn us again, O God, and cause thy face to shine, and we shall be saved.' Also, Isaiah 64:1 speaks of His name and says, 'that thou wouldst come down, that the mountains might flow down at thy presence.' He speaks clearly of the coming of Christ; this is shown in this passage."

"In addition to the passages which Sabino has read," Marcelo then said, "there is another very remarkable one which was not mentioned which deserves to be recalled. But before speaking of it, I want to say that in Psalm 80 the words which we have just read, 'Turn us again, O God,' are repeated three times, at the beginning, in the middle, and at the end of the Psalm. This is not without its mystery. I believe it is done for one or another of two reasons: the first, to make us know that to achieve and perfect man, God puts His hand three times upon him; the first time creating him from dust, drawing him from nonbeing to give him being in paradise; the second, in restoring him after the corruption of sin and by making Himself man for this purpose; the third, by resurrecting him after death, so as to spare him eternally from death and change. It is to mark this that in the book of Genesis and in the history of the creation of man we find repeated three times the word 'create.' The text says, 'So God created man in His own image, in the image of God created He him; male and female created He them' (Gen. 1:27).

"The second reason and the one which I consider to be the most certain is that in the aforementioned Psalm, the Prophet requests of God in three places to convert His people to Himself and to reveal to them His face, which is Christ, as we have already said. Three times the divine Word was shown and will be shown, particularly to the world and to the Jewish people, to bring them light and salvation. Once He showed Himself to them on the mountain where He gave them the law and where He showed them His love and His desires, and surrounded and covered with fire and other visible signs, He spoke to them in a clear and loud way, so that the whole people heard Him speak. He began then to become man to them; like someone who has decided to be man among them as He was to do later. The second came about when He was born with our flesh and conversed with us and procured our welfare in His living and dying.

"The third will come about when He will return at the end of time for the salvation of his Church. And even if I am not mistaken these three comings of the Word, one in appearances and in audible words, the other two already made truly man, the Word itself had predicted and announced them in the bush, when Moses asked Him for signs of who He was and said these words, 'Who I will be, I will be, I will be' (Gen. 1:27). He repeated the verb three times in the future as if to say: I am who I promised your fathers, to come to liberate you from Egypt, to be born among you, to redeem you from sin and to return finally in the same form of man to destroy death and to perfect all. I am who will be your guide in the desert, who will be your salvation when I will be man, and your perfect glory when I will be judge."

Here Juliano interrupted and said:

"The sacred text does not say, 'I will be,' but 'I am' in the present tense. However, if the original word in reference to its sound is indeed 'I will be' in reference to its meaning, it signifies 'I am' if we want to take into account the character of this language."

"It is true," replied Marcelo, "that in this language the proper words for future time are at times put in the place of present time, and in this case, we can indeed admit that we have put them there, as at first St. Jerome and then the Greek translators understood the words. What I say for the moment is that without taking the meaning from the words, but by giving them their first sound and signification, we explain the mystery which I stated. And since it is a mystery whose design Moses wanted to know, what has been said fits very well.

"I ask you, Juliano, is it not certain that God communicated the secret to Abraham that He would become man and be born from his lineage?"

"It is a truth," he replied, "and He attested to it Himself in the gospel, saying, 'Your father Abraham rejoiced to see my day, and he saw it, and was glad' " (John 8:56).

"Then, is it not also certain," continued Marcelo, "that this same mystery God kept hidden until it had come to pass, not only from the demons but also from a great number of angels?"

"So it is understood," replied Juliano, "from what is written in St. Paul" (Col. 1:26).

"And so," said Marcelo, "it was a hidden affair and something that passed between God and Abraham and some of his successors, that is, between the principal successors and the heads of the lineage to whom this promise of God had been communicated from one to the other as from hand to hand."

"So it seems," replied Juliano.

"If it is so," added Marcelo, "and if it is equally manifest that Moses in the passage of which we are speaking (Ex. 3:13) says to God, 'Behold when I come unto the children of Israel, and shall say unto them, the God of your fathers hath sent me unto you; and they shall say unto me, What is His name: and what shall I say unto them?' it is manifest that Moses by these words, which I have stated, asks of God for a sure sign of Himself. This sign was to assure Moses and the notables of Israel, who were to receive this message, that He was their God who had appeared to them and who had sent a message, and not some perfidious spirit and deceiver. If, when Moses asks God for a sign like this and if God gives it to him in these terms, 'I say to you, that I will be who I will be, who I will be,' then the same reasons obligate us to think that what God says in these terms is a secret and hidden thing for every spirit, that it is a sign which uniquely God, and those to whom it was to be communicated, know, and that it is comparable to a military password or secret watchword, to what in war is the password which remains a secret between the captain and the soldiers who are on guard. This same reason makes us conclude that what God said to Moses in these terms is the mystery of which I have spoken. This mystery is the one which was known by God, Abraham, and his successors and which was a secret among them.

"The other things which God announced and revealed from Himself to Moses in this place, that is, His infinite perfection, the fact that He was the same being in His essence, was known not only by the angels but also by the demons. It is equally clear for learned men and scholars that God is being through essence, that He is thus infinite being. It is something which the natural light teaches. Thus every other spirit which would want to deceive Moses and pass before him as his true God would have been able to say it of himself deceptively and in listening to this sign Moses would not have had sufficiently adequate reason to free himself of doubt, nor a sure enough sign to extricate from this doubt the notables of his people.

"But the passage which I spoke of in the beginning, and which the paper forgot, is at the beginning of book 6 of Numbers (25–26) where God orders the priest to say over the people when He blesses them: 'The Lord makes his face shine upon thee, and be gracious unto thee. The Lord lift up his countenance upon thee, and give thee peace.' We cannot doubt that Christ and His birth among us is this face which the priest asks God to show to his people, which the holy and ancient doctors, Saint Cyril and Theodoret, affirm (Theodoret of Cyr. *Quaestiones in Numeros XI*, PG 80, 363; Cyril of Alexandria, in *Ioann. Evang.* book IX, ch. 40). In addition to their testimony, which is of great authority, we are led to the same conviction by the fact that in Psalm 66 where, as we all agree, David asks God to send Christ into the world. The Prophet begins with the words of this benediction and shows it with his finger and proclaims it, and he is no longer hesitant to express to God, more or less, the following idea: 'The benediction which the priest gives the people on your command, that is what I beg you to do in it: show us your Son our Lord, as you are requested by the public voice of your people.' He says the following: 'God be merciful unto us, and bless us, and cause his face to shine upon us' (Ps. 67:1).

"In Ecclesiasticus when the Sage asks God with numerous and ardent words for the salvation of his people and the destruction of the arrogance of sin, freedom for the oppressed, the reunion of the dispersed, the vengeance of his honor, the desired judgment, and the manifestation of his exultation over all the nations, which is asking God for the first and second coming of Christ, he concludes and says, 'Lord, act toward your people according to Aaron's benediction and direct us in the path of your justice' (Ecclesiasticus 36:19). It is known that the path of divine justice is Christ, as He Himself says, 'I am the way, the truth and the life' (John 14:6). St. Paul says in his letter to the Ephesians, 'Blessed be the God and Father of our Lord Jesus Christ, who hath blessed us with all spiritual blessings in heavenly places in Christ.' It is completely marvelous that in the benediction that was given the people before the coming of Christ, nothing was asked of God but the Christ, that is, the source and origin of every joyful benediction. The two testaments harmonize and respond in the same way. Christ is the 'face of God' who was asked for in this passage, of this there is no doubt.

"What agrees with this is that it was asked for twice, to show that there are two comings. In this it is proper to consider the justness and propriety of the words which the Holy Spirit uses for each thing. For the first coming He says, in effect, 'to show': 'Let God show His face.' It is then that Christ began to be visible in the world. For the second, He says 'to turn': 'Let God turn his face,' because then He will be seen for the second time. For the first, according to another text, He says 'to shine' because the effect of this coming was to chase from the world darkness and error, and as St. John says (1:5), to make the light shine in the darkness. It is for this reason that Christ is called light and sun of justice. For the second, he says 'to exalt,' because who comes first in humility will then come surrounded by glory, and He will no longer come to bring a new teaching, but to distribute punishment and glory. For the first he still says, 'May he have pity upon you,' as if he knew and announced that the Jews recognized and proclaimed in some way that they would behave toward Christ in a cruel and unpleasant way, and that their blindness and their ingratitude would merit their being consumed by Him. For this reason it is asked that God have pity upon them, that He not consume them. In the second he wishes that God grant them peace, that is, that He put an end to the long test, that He lead them to the harbor of rest after so violent a storm, that He put them peacefully in the shelter of His Church, in the peace of the spirit which is His in all His spiritual riches. Or he says the first thing because then the Christ came only to pardon the committed sins and to seek for what was lost as He Himself says in Matthew 18:11, and the second thing because He must come to bring peace and rest to those who have acted saintly and compensate those who acted well.

"Since Christ bears this name we must know why He bears it. Here must be remarked that if Christ is called and is the face of God from whatever side we regard him, it is because He is the same insofar as He is man, insofar as He is God, and insofar as He is the Word; He always is properly and perfectly the image of His Father as St. Paul says of Him in another passage (Heb. 1:3). Nevertheless, what we are concerned with at this moment is His humanity, and what we seek to comprehend is the title by which the human nature of the Christ merits to be called 'face.' Let us say briefly that the Christ is the face and visage of God, because in the way that each of us is recognized by his face, God, in the same way, is shown to us in it and is revealed in a very clear and perfect way to us. This is true because no creature or assemblage of creatures causes the rays of the divine qualities to shine in our eyes more clearly or abundantly than Christ's soul, His body, all His gifts, deeds, and words, together with everything that belongs to His mission.

"Let us first begin with the body; it is the most apparent. Without seeing it, but through the relationship which we have with it, we expect the blessed day when, thanks to His infinite goodness, we hope to see Him gather us joyfully. Without seeing Him we can with the eyes of our faith contemplate this divine face and these features fashioned by the Holy Spirit, see His beautiful face, His grave and sweet posture, His eyes and His mouth, the latter bathed in sweetness, the former with an even more resplendent brightness than that of the sun; let us look also at the whole harmony of the body, its aspect, its movement, its members conceived in the same purity and endowed with incomparable beauty. . . .

"But why spoil this good with my poor words when we have those of the Holy Spirit itself who formed Him in the womb of the very holy Virgin? They depict Him for us in the book of Canticles (5:10–16) through the mouth of the loving shepherdess saying:

> My beloved is white and ruddy, the chiefest among ten thousand. His head is as the most fine gold, his locks are busy, and black as a raven. His eyes are the eyes of doves by the rivers of waters, washed with milk, and fitly set. His cheeks are as a bed of spices, as sweet flowers, his lips like lillies, dropping sweet-smelling myrrh. His hands are as gold rings set with the beryl, his belly is as bright ivory overlaid with sapphires. His legs are of pillars of marble, set upon sockets of fine gold, his countenance is as Lebanon, excellent as the cedars. His mouth is most sweet, yea, he is altogether lovely.

"Let us rest our eyes upon this perfect beauty and contemplate it. We will then see that everything that a body can embrace of divinity, every part that it can possess of God, all the traits by which it can recall Him, reproduce Him and resemble Him, all that, and at the highest level, shines in this body among all the others, and we affirm that in kind and nature He is the living and perfect portrait of God. In fact, what in the body is color—and I wish to compare in detail each thing with another and show in this its picture which God, in fact, formed, having depicted it in words many years before, how it responds entirely to its truth, although, not to be too long, I intend to say little of each thing and to limit myself to mere reference—what is color in the body, which results from a mixture of qualities and moods in the body and which is the first thing that is seen. It responds to the union or in some way to the mixture and fabric which are woven by

God's perfections. In fact, we say that a color is made up of red and white; in the same way this secret mixture of His soul is colored with simplicity and love. What our eyes at first see when we raise them to God is a pure truth and a totally simple and loving perfection.

"Similarly, the head in the body responds to what is in God the summit of knowledge. The head of Christ is of the gold of Tibar and the latter is a treasure of wisdom. The hair which grows on the head is curled and black, the thoughts and decisions proceeding from God's knowledge are lofty and obscure. The eyes of God's Providence and the eyes of His body are similar; the latter see the waters as pigeons who bathe themselves in milk, the former wait upon the universality of things and provide for their needs with extreme sweetness and gentleness, giving to each his food, and in some way its milk.

'What shall I say of the cheeks which are odorous garden beds of plants and which in God are His justice and His mercy which are revealed and shown more particularly, as we might say, on one and the other side of the face and which spread their sweet aroma through all things? In fact, as it is written (Ps. 24:10), 'all the paths of God are mercy and truth.'

"The mouth and the lips which in God are the advice which He gives us and the Holy Scriptures where He speaks to us, similarly as in this body they are violets and myrrh, they are in God powerfully bitter and burning, so that they incite virtue and render vice bitter and weaken it. Similarly, what in God forms the hands, that is, His power to act and the works made by Him, are similar to those of this body, made like the rings of gold from the stones of Taris, and they are of perfect beauty and are all excellent as the scriptures say (Gen. 1:31), 'And God saw everything that he had made and behold it was very good.'

"For the entrails of God and the fecundity of His power is there a better image than this white abdomen made of ivory and made ornate with sapphires?

"His legs, which are beautiful and strong as if of marble on a base of gold, are truly a clear picture of divine force which is immutable, as everything upon which God rests. His countenance is comparable to that of the Lebanon mountains, which is like the summit of divine nature full of majesty and beauty.

"And finally His palate is only sweetness and the whole

inspires only desires so that we will understand how this body deserves to be called 'image, face and image of God.' Because in all things it is very sweet and lovable, thus it is written, 'Taste, then, and see that the Lord is good' (Ps. 34:8) and 'Oh, how great is thy goodness, which thou has laid up for them that fear (love) thee' (Ps. 31:19).

"Well, if in the body of Christ is revealed and shines forth the divine figure, how will we not see an image still more perfect in His very holy soul since the latter truly, through the perfection of its nature as through the supernatural riches which God gathered there, resembles God and reproduces Him in a closer and more perfect way than any other creature? After the original world, which is the Word, the vastness and the closest universe to the original is this divine soul, and the visible world in comparison is only poor and small, because God knows and has present before the eyes of His knowledge everything which is and can be. And the soul of Christ sees through everything that is, has been, and will be. In God's knowledge are the ideas and the reasons for all things, and in Christ's soul the knowledge of all the arts and sciences. God is the source of all being, and the soul of Christ is the source of everything that has goodness, that is, of all the goods of grace and justice, through which what is becomes just, good, and perfect, because all grace flows from what is in Him. It is not only for Himself, but also for us that He possesses grace in the eyes of God, because He possesses justice which makes Him appear before God more lovable than all other creatures, and He possesses a justice so powerful as to render all of them lovable, pouring into the receptacle of each of them some effect of this great virtue of which He is endowed, as it is written, 'And of his fullness have all we received, and grace for grace' (John 1:16). This means that from a grace has come another grace, that from this grace which is source is born another which is like the stream which flows from it; and this model of grace which is in Him has produced a reproduction of grace or another grace which reproduces itself and which dwells among the just.

"Finally, God creates and sustains the entire universe, guides and leads it toward its good, while Christ's soul re-creates, restores, and defends, and without interruption animates and excites the whole human species toward goodness and justice, as far as it can. God loves Himself and knows Himself infinitely, and

Christ's soul loves and knows Him with an infinite love and knowledge. God is powerful and Christ's soul is powerful beyond all natural power. If we place several mirrors at different distances from a beautiful face, its form and traits will appear better in the mirror which is closest. It is the same with Christ's soul: Through personal union closest to the divine Word, and so to speak, totally attached to it, this very holy soul receives its splendor and reproduces it more strongly than any other face.

"But it is necessary to go on. Since we have spoken separately of Christ's body and soul, let us speak of the union which they form and seek in His gifts, in His character and manners, this face and image of God. He says of Himself that He is sweet and humble, and He invites us to learn from Him to be so (Matt. 11:29). A long time before, seeing Him in spirit, the prophet Isaiah painted Him for us similarly and he tells us (Isa. 42:2–4): 'He shall not cry, nor lift up, nor cause his voice to be heard in the street. A bruised reed he shall not break, and the smoking flax shall he not quench; he shall bring forth judgment unto truth. He shall not fail or be discouraged, till he has set judgment in the earth; and the isles shall wait for his law.' We must understand that the Christ is not only sweet and humble by virtue of the grace which He possesses; similarly as a natural inclination carries some men toward one virtue, others toward another, Christ's humanity, by its natural constitution, is full of sweetness and simplicity.

"As much by the grace which He possesses as by the disposition of His nature, Christ is a perfect model of humility. But, on the other hand, He has so much loftiness and grandeur of soul that it belongs to Him, without any vanity, to be the king of men, lord of the angels, head and ruler of all things, and the adored being of all of them, to be placed at the right of God united and fused with Him in a single person. Well, what is this if not to be the face itself of God? The latter has been as sweet as the enormity of our sins show and attest; and the grandeur of His pardons, and not only of His pardons, but even of the procedures which He employed to pardon us, is similar to the height and greatness which the name of God demands and as Job says elegantly (11:8–9): 'It is as high as heaven; what canst thou do? deeper than hell; what canst thou know? The measure thereof is longer than the earth, and broader than the sea.' But with all this immensity and grandeur of elevation, we can say that He humiliates Himself so by placing Himself on the level of His creatures that He is concerned with little birds, nourishes the ants, and descends to the lowest of terrestrial life and to the vilest. This is the clearest proof of His unadorned goodness; He sustains and comforts sinners and enlightens them with this magnificent light which we see. So elevated by Himself, He lowers Himself by placing Himself near His creatures as the Psalm says (Ps. 103:19): 'The Lord hath prepared his throne in the heavens; and his kingdom ruleth over all.'

"What will I say of the love which God has for us and of the charity which burns for us in Christ's soul?—of what God does for men and what the humanity of Christ has suffered for us? How will I be able to compare them or be able to say, seeing them alongside each other, something which may be truer than to call this face and image of that? Christ loved us to the point of giving us His life, and God, moved by the love which He bears toward us and not being able to give us His life, gives us the life of His Son. To spare us the pains of hell and to procure for us heaven's joys, Christ suffers prison, flagellation, an ignominious and painful death. For the same end God, who could not undergo death in His own nature, sought and found a means of undergoing it in His own person. This burning and flaming will which possessed Christ's human nature to die for men was only a flame which was lit by the fire of love and desire, which burnt in God's will, to become man and die for us.

"This subject is infinite. The more I unfurl the sails, the more space I see to be traversed, and the more I navigate, the more I discover new seas; the more I contemplate this face, the more I discover in its aspects the being and the perfections of God. But it is now right to return to port. I will do it, by saying only that, since God is triune and one, triune in persons and one in essence, in the same way Christ and his faithful, who also represent God, are numerous and different in persons; however, as we have already begun to say, and we will say it more fully, in spirit and in a secret unity which is explained badly with words and which is understood by those who take delight in it, they are one and the same. Although the qualities of grace and justice and the other divine gifts which the just possess are similar in principle but divided and different in number, the spirit which lives in all of them, or even better, He who causes them to live a just life, who inspires them and moves and excites them and activates the same qualities and gifts is, as I said, one and the same spirit in everything; it is the spirit of Christ. He lives in His own, they live through Him, all live in Him, they are one divided by multiple persons, entirely simple by the quality and spiritual substance, as Christ had asked His Father when He said (John 17:21), 'That they all may be one, as thou Father art in me, and I in thee.'

"We also say that Christ is the face of God because we are recognized by our faces and in the same way God wants to be recognized through Christ. Whoever recognizes Him without this means does not recognize Him. It is because of this that Christ says of Himself that He showed men the name of His Father (John 17:6, 10:9). He is called 'port' and 'entry' (John 10:9) for the same reason, because He alone guides us, directs and introduces us to the knowledge of God and to His true love. But we can now satisfy ourselves with what has been said on this name."

This said, Marcelo was quiet, and Sabino continued:

WAY

"Christ is called also 'way' in Holy Scriptures. He Himself is called this in St. John 14:6: I am, He says, the way, the truth, and life. To this we also refer what Isaiah says (3, 5:8): 'And a highway shall be there, and a way, and it shall be called the way of holiness.' To this what is said in Psalm 16:11 is not strange: 'Thou wilt show me the path of life'; and even less strange is what is said in Psalm 67:2: 'That thy way may be known upon earth,' and this explains then which 'way': 'thy saving salvation among all nations.'

"It will not be necessary—said Marcelo as soon as Sabino had read this—to prove that 'way' is a name of Christ since He gives it to Himself. But it is necessary to see and understand the reason for which He gives it to Himself and what He wanted to teach us by calling Himself the way. Doubtlessly, this has already been said in part because of the kinship of this name with the one which we have just spoken of, because to be face and to be way are in certain respects the same thing. But since this name includes in itself many other considerations, it would be advisable that we speak of it in particular.

"To this end, the first thing which it is necessary to note is that in Holy Scripture the word way is taken in different ways. In fact, it is there designated often as the character and the temperament of each person, his inclinations, his manner of proceeding, and what we usually call 'style' and 'disposition.' It is the meaning which David gives to it in Psalm 102 when in speaking of God he says: 'He made known his ways unto Moses.' Because the ways of God which he mentions here are the same which the Psalm speaks of and which is what God revealed of His condition in Exodus when He appeared to Moses on the mountain and as He put His hand on his eyes, passed before him, and said in passing: 'The Lord, the Lord God merciful and gracious, long-suffering and abundant in goodness and truth. Keeping mercy for thousands, forgiving iniquity and transgression and sin—visiting the iniquity of the fathers upon the children, and upon the children's children unto the third and to the fourth generation' (Ex. 34:6–7). Thus, His ways are these good and strange qualities of God.

"In another sense we call way the profession which each one of us chooses for his life, his intentions, that to which he pretends in his existence, in some particular affair, and the goal which he proposes to reach. It is in this sense that Psalm 37:5 says: 'Commit thy way unto the Lord, and he shall give thee the desires of thy heart.' David wishes to tell us that we must place our intentions and our projections under the eyes of God and in His hands, putting our cares in Providence, and to abandon ourselves to the assurance that He will take them in charge and they will come out well. If we put them in His hands, they must be what they must be, that is, of a nature that God may take charge of them, for He is justice and goodness. With the same words, the Psalm warns us of two things: the first, not to undertake things nor to conceive projects which cannot merit God's help; the second, after having purified and justified them, not to place confidence in our own powers and to confide ourselves in Him with assured hope.

"The work that each of us does is called also 'way.' Wisdom says of itself in Proverbs (8:22), 'The Lord possessed me in the beginning of his way, before his works of old,' that is, 'I was set up from everlasting, from the beginning of his way, before his works of old.' Of the elephant it is said in the book of Job (40:19) that he is 'the beginning of the ways of the Lord' because among God's works when He created the animal he is one of the notables. In Deuteronomy (32:4) Moses says that 'his ways are judgment' to express the holiness and justice of His works. In Psalms (119:5) the just desires and demands that 'my ways,' that is, the goals of His steps and actions, are to do what God orders to be done.

" 'Way' means also the precepts and law. Thus David uses the word: 'For all his ways were before me and I did not put away his statutes from me' (Ps. 18:22). And more clearly in another place, 'I will run the way of thy commandments, when thou shalt enlarge my heart' (119:32). In this fashion the name 'way' in addition to its proper meaning, which designates that by which one goes to a place without getting lost, also communicates analogously this signification to four other things: the inclination, the profession, the works of each, the law and the precepts, because each one of these things leads man toward a purpose, and by them is led toward an end as if by a way. It is certain that the law guides, that works lead, that profession directs, and that inclination leads each to his goal.

"Let us now see what are the reasons that Christ is called way or let us see if He is the cause of all of them, which He doubtlessly is. For the propriety of the word, as well as this way—and Marcelo showed it with his finger, because it could be seen from the place where they were—just as this way is that of the Court because it leads to the Court, to the residence of the King, for all those who take and follow it, in the same way Christ is the 'way of heaven' because if one does not put his steps into His and doesn't follow His signs, one doesn't go to heaven. I do only say that we must put our steps in His and that our works, which are our steps, must follow those which He has accomplished, but that our works, as it is suitable for a way, must go along with His, because if they depart, they are lost. It is certain that when we do not support ourselves in Christ, and do not take Him for our foundation, our behavior and works represent no progress and do not bring us closer to heaven. Many of those who have lived without Christ have embraced poverty, loved chastity, practiced justice, modesty, and temperance, and whoever would regard these things closely could judge that they followed Christ's route and that their steps imitated His. But, since they did not support themselves upon Him, they followed no road and did not gain heaven. The lost lamb, that is, man, the shepherd who found it, as it is written in St. Luke (15:3–6), did not return it to the flock by making it go and pushing it before him; he carried it on His shoulders. Because it is only on His shoulders that we can go, I want to say that it would be useless to try to go to heaven by following another's path.

"Have we not seen some mothers, Sabino, who, holding with their two hands the two hands of their children, make them put their feet upon theirs and move them, forward them, embrace them, and are thus their ground and their guide? Oh, what goodness is God's! In the same way You act, Lord, toward our weakness as children. You give us the hand of your support, you make us put our steps into yours, which do not go astray; you make us ascend, you cause us to progress, you stir us always in our behavior to come close to you in a way that is satisfactory to you; you unite us to you by the tightest bond in heaven.

"Since the roads, Juliano, are not all the same, for some are level and open and others narrow and sharp, some are long and others shortcuts, in the same way Christ's true and universal way, to the degree that it depends upon Him, contains in itself all the variations. We find in Him large avenues where there is no risk of stumbling and by which the weak souls travel without fatigue, and steeper, narrower paths for those who have more strength; detours for some, because this is suitable to them, and similarly, what is necessary for those who wish to hurry, shortcuts and abridgments. Let us see what Isaiah says about this way:

> And a highway shall be there and a way, and it shall be called the way of holiness; the unclean shall not pass over it; but it shall be for those. The wayfaring men, though fools, shall not err therein. No lion shall be there, nor any ravenous beast shall go thereon; it shall not be found there. But the redeemed shall walk there. And the ransomed of the Lord shall return and come to Zion with songs and everlasting joy upon their heads: they shall obtain joy and gladness, and sorrow and sighing shall flee away." (Isa. 35:8–10).

"In the original text the word 'path' designates every passage by which one goes from one point to another. But it is not a question of any particular passage, but it is a question of a passage a little higher than the rest in relation to the ground to which it is close, and of a smooth passage, either because it is paved or because it is free of stones and obstacles. Consequently, this word designates at times the steps of stones through which we climb, at other times the paved and raised embankment, at still others, the path neatly laid out, twisting from base to summit. All this applies very well to Christ because He is highway, path, and steps united and firm. This means that this way has two qualities, which are height and facility. They are fitting as well for what we call steps as for what we denote as path and highway. Because it is true that all those who follow Christ's road go to the heights and without obstacles. They go, at first, into the height because they mount, and they mount because their going consists properly in ascending, knowing that Christian virtue is always amelioration and progress of the soul. Thus, those who practice it and exert themselves in it progress greatly, and their going rends them greater and greater. On the other hand, those who follow the path of vice don't cease descending because by giving themselves over to vice they destroy themselves and grow smaller, and the more they go on, the more they are reduced and diminished. Slowly, they become at first a beast, then less a beast, and finally nothing. "The children of Israel, whose voyage from Egypt to Judea was an image of this, never ceased to ascend because of the terrain and disposition of the land. In the ancient temple at Jerusalem, which is also a figure, one could not enter any part without mounting. Thus the Sage, although he uses a comparison with the brightness of light, says the same thing of those who travel with Christ and those who don't wish to follow Him. Of the first he says: 'But the path of the just is as the shining light, that shineth more and more unto the perfect day' (Prov. 4:18). Of the second, in a passage which concerns them particularly: 'For her house inclineth unto death, and her paths unto the dead' (Prov. 2:18). Thus it is for the second. As for the first, they go into the heights because they always go far from the earth which is the lowest, and they go far from it because what it loves, they hate; what it follows, they flee; what it esteems, they despise. Finally, they go because they trample underfoot what the opinion of men has placed at the top: riches, pleasures, honors. Such is the first quality, height.

"We see the same thing in the second, the smooth and obstacle-free road. Because he who directs his steps according to Christ does not come up against anyone; he cedes the advantage to everyone else, he is not opposed to their pretensions, he does not undermine their plans, he suffers their angers, their injustices, their violence, and he does not maltreat or despoil them. He does not show himself to be despoiled, but relieved and made more agile for his journey. On the other hand, for those who follow another way they encounter at each step innumerable obstacles because others seek what they seek; thus all travel toward a sole and similar goal, and they hinder each other. They run into each other at every turn and they jostle each other, they fall, they stop, they fall back in despair of reaching the point they want. But in Christ, as we have seen, there is no obstacle. He is like the grand 'road' where everyone who wishes finds room without hindering anyone else.

"The Christ is not only steps, highway, path, because of the mentioned qualities which are entirely common to three things, but also because each of them has a property which can be applied to His name. In fact, it is steps that are needed to enter into the temple of heaven, a path which leads unerringly to the height of the mountain where virtue resides, and a dry and solid highway upon which one makes no mistakes and where the foot glides along, never stumbles. The other roads are in truth slippery inclines on precipices, and, at the moment the most unforeseen, either they are cut off or they crumble underfoot; the unfortunate person who travels quietly is thrown into the void. Thus Solomon says: 'The road of the wicked is a ravine and a deep crevice' (Prov. 4:19). How many have lost their lives in and through riches by seeking and having found them! How many have found their shame going in pursuit of honor! And of pleasure can we say that it does not end in pain? He who follows our 'path' does not slide and is not hurried because he has his feet on sure ground. This is why David tells us: 'The law of God is in our hearts, his steps lead us not astray' (Ps. 37:31). And Solomon says: 'The way of the slothful man is as a hedge of thorns, but the way of the righteous is made plain' (Prov. 15:19). But Isaiah (35:8) adds: 'And a highway shall be there and a way, and it shall be called the way of holiness.' In the original the word 'way' is repeated three times in this manner: 'He will be way and way and way called holy.' Christ is the way for all mankind. All those who go with Him are of three kinds: the beginners in virtue, as one calls them, those progressing, and those whom we call the perfect. These three degrees form the elite of the Church; similarly, its image, the temple of long ago, was composed of three parts—portico, palace, and sanctuary—and the apartments which were attached to it and surrounded it on two sides and in the rear were divided into three different kinds—ground level, entresol, and floor level. It is thus that Christ is three times way: He is the large and smooth road for the imperfect, way for those who have more force, and holy way for those who are already perfect in Him. He also says: 'No impure person will pass there' (Isa. 35:8). Doubtlessly in Christ's Church and in His mystical body there are many impure people, but those who pass through Him are all pure; I mean that when we go in Him, we are always pure because the steps of those who are impure are not steps made on this way. Those are pure who pass through Him and not those who only begin there, but all those who begin there and attain the milieu and continue to the end, because if one is impure, one stops or retreats or leaves the way. Consequently, he who will not stop but will continue, as we have said, will necessarily be pure. This is revealed more clearly from what follows: 'And it will be a sure road for you' (Is. 35:8). Here the original exactly says: 'And he will walk with them the road' or 'he is for them the road which they follow.' Thus, Christ is 'our way' and also He who follows the road because He goes when we go, or better, we go, we, because He goes and His movement draws us. Thus, He is Himself the way which we follow and He who goes with us and incites us to go. It is certain that Christ does not accompany the impure. He who is deity does not travel here, and he who has sinned does not progress because no one goes there if Christ does not go with him. From this comes the following: 'And the ignorant will not go astray' (Is. 35:8). In fact, who would go astray with such a guide? But how proper to say the ignorant! Because the learned, confident in themselves and having the presumption to open the road for themselves, go astray easily and they go astray necessarily if they trust in themselves. Besides, if Christ is Himself the guide and the way, that convinces us that He is the way clearly and without detours and that no one loses such a way without deliberately wanting to lose it. 'And this is the Father's will which hath sent me, that of all which he hath given me I should lose nothing, but should raise it up again at the last day' (John 6:39).

"And assuredly, Juliano, there is no clearer thing to the eyes of reason nor less exposed to error than the way of God. David

BOOK I

said it well (Ps. 19:8–9): 'The Commandment of the Lord is pure, enlightening the eyes . . . the judgments of the Lord are true and righteous altogether.' But since the way is always sure, must we think that there are perhaps wild beasts which make it perilous by their attacks? He who has removed the difficulties and laid out the road has also assured its peace. Because it is this that the Prophet adds, 'No lion shall be there, nor any ravenous beast shall go up thereon.' He does not say 'will go' but 'will ascend.' In fact, the savagery of passion or the demon, similar to the enemy lion, could not attack those who travel there; never will they dominate them nor have control over them. On the contrary, the devils will depart abased and humiliated. If it is not they who travel along the road, who else will travel there?—'but the redeemed shall walk there' (Isa. 35:9). Yet, one begins by being redeemed before traveling, and Christ, by the grace and justice which He grants them, begins by liberating them from the fault of which they are captives and removing the chains which hinder them. It is thus only that they begin to travel. We are not redeemed having at first traveled, nor for having made the happy steps; it is not by ourselves that we arrive at justice. 'Not by words or righteousness which we have done, but according to his mercy he saved us' (Titus 3:5). Thus our redemption is not the fruit of our travel and of our merit. Once redeemed, we can go on and have merit, due to the virtue of this goodness.

"It is true that only the redeemed and freed travel there and that they are free before they travel, that those who are free and just travel and advance only through the steps which they have accomplished as just and free men, because the redemption and the justice, the spirit which forms them, is enclosed in ours, its impetus and the works which are born in us from this impetus and in conformity to it are the feet which make us go on this 'way.' We must be redeemed, but be redeemd by whom? The original word shows it because it designates he who is redeemed by way of parentage and alliance, and who is freed, as we say, for the desired sum or ransom. Consequently, if only those who are redeemed by a parent or by parentage travel there, it will be clear that only those who are redeemed by Christ travel, for He is our parent, having taken on our nature, and He redeemed us because of who is His. In fact, as man He suffered for men; as their brother and their head, He paid for them the price which they owed by right, and He redeemed us for Himself, as people who belonged to Him through blood and lineage, as we shall explain later.

"He adds, 'But the redeemed shall walk there' (Isa. 35:9). This concerns fittingly the members of the Jewish people, who must rejoin the Church at the end of time. When they rejoin, they will begin to travel by this way which is ours, with great steps and by proclaiming Him the Messiah. Because He said: 'They will return to this way.' It is the one who they at first followed in truth when they served God with faith and hope of His coming. They then pleased Him. But they subsequently went astray and they didn't wish to recognize Him when they saw Him, and now they do not go with Him. He, however, prophesied that they would return. It is said that those whom Christ has redeemed will return again to the way. Each of these words has a particular reason which demonstrates the exactness of what I say. At first, in the original, where we say 'Lord' is found the proper name of God, which expresses particularly a pity and a mercy full of tenderness. In the second place, instead of 'redeemed' the text reads literally price or ransom. It is said that the ransoms or redemptions by the Very Pious One are still to come. He calls ransoms or redemptions what He granted this lineage because He has not ransomed them only once from their enemies but often and in many ways, as the holy letters state. At this place He calls Himself very merciful. Although He may always be so with us, there is something which stirs our admiration: the extreme of generosity and love with which God treats this people although not merited by them. In addition, because after having so rejected and so separated Himself from them, rejected and separated so justly, after the infidelity and murder for which He reproached them, and when it seemed that they no longer remembered Him, since so many centuries had passed without appeasing His anger, after so long a period of rejection and forgetfulness, to want to bring them back to His grace, to bring them back to Him meaningfully, is an evident sign that His love for them is full of tenderness and depth since neither the long vicissitudes of time, nor ardent anger, nor all the flagrant and constant offenses made this love disappear. We see that this love has in God's heart very intimate roots, since, cut and apparently dried up, it comes forth with such great vigor. Thus it is that Isaiah calls the Jews ransom and calls God merciful because it is uniquely His invincible mercy in their regard, after so many ransoms made by God and after all their bad repayments which He received from them, which will end by their liberation one day. Once free and reunited to those who have been freed and who are now within the Church, He will put them on the way which leads to the Church and He will lead them along it.

"But what a privileged fate and what a voyage full of mirth and happiness where the way is Christ, where the guide of the road is Christ Himself, where the protection and security are still Christ and where those who follow Him are His creatures and His redeemed! In this way all are noble and free. Free from the demon, I say, redeemed from sin, protected against his pursuits, protected against his maliciousness, encouraged to the good by the joys and satisfaction which He brings, and promised a recompense so delightful that its expectation suffices to make them in some way happy. And it is thus that God concludes with these words: 'And the ransomed of the Lord shall return and come to Zion with songs and everlasting joy upon their heads; they shall obtain joy and gladness and sorrow and sighing shall flee away' (Isa. 35:10).

"It is in this way that Christ is called the way in conformity to the proper sense of the word, and in the manner that we apply it to things we call it the same by comparison. In fact, if as we said, the way of each, are the inclinations that bring His spirit and taste to it, in all truth the Christ is the way of God because He is, as we have said a moment ago, His living image and the true portrait of all His inclinations and of His character. Or, to say it better, He is the execution and realization of everything which pleases and is most agreeable to God. And if the end and purpose which each man proposes for the direction of his actions is his way, Christ is without doubt the way of God. Indeed, as we said today at the beginning, Christ is the principled end which God regards in everything which He does.

"Finally, how could Christ not be the way if what we call way is law, rule, commandment, which orders and directs life, since it alone is the law? Because He is not content to say everything that must be done, He does what He tells us to do and He gives us the forces to do what He tells us to do. Thus He does not command only the reason, but He imposes on the will the law of what He commands; He establishes Himself there, and, once established in it, He is its good and its law. But let us not only speak of that. The subject has its appropriate place and we will treat it later."

This said, Marcelo was quiet. Sabino opened his paper and said:

SHEPHERD

"Christ is also called 'shepherd.' He Himself says it in St. John (10:11): 'I am the good Shepherd.' In the Epistle to the Hebrews (13:20) St. Paul says of God, 'that brought again from the dead our Lord Jesus, that great shepherd of the sheep.' And St. Peter says the same: 'And when the chief Shepherd shall appear' (1 Pet. 5:4). The prophets call Him in the same way" (Isa. 40, Ezek. 34, and Zach. 11).

And Marcelo then said:

"What I said about the previous name I can also say about this one. It is useless to demonstrate that it is a name of Christ; He gives it to Himself. Although this is easy, it also requires much consideration to comprehend all the reasons for which He gives Himself the name. In fact, in what we call 'shepherd' we can consider many things—those which properly concern this office and those which touch upon the characters of the person and the life of those who exercise it. In the first place, pastoral life is a tranquil one, which flows far from the noises, vices, and pleasures of the city. We find in this tranquil life a great innocence, similarly in its labor and the activity to which it is attached. It has its pleasures, born from things simpler, purer, and more natural: from the view of the open sky, from the purity of the air, from the forms of the countryside, from the green of the grass, from the beauty of the roses and the flowers. The birds with their song and the waters with their freshness charm and serve this pastoral life. For this reason it is a very natural and ancient way of life among men, because there were already shepherds among the first of them and it was practiced by the best men who existed. Jacob and the twelve patriarchs practiced it, and David was a shepherd. This life is highly praised by everyone, as you know, Sabino; there is no poet who does not sing and praise it."

"Even if no one had praised it," Sabino said, "it would shine, for it was indeed praised, with what the Latin poet* said of it, who in everything he wrote surpassed the others and who on this point seems to have surpassed even himself, so elegant and well chosen are the verses where he spoke of the pastoral life. But since we speak, Marcelo, of the life of shepherds, and of the poetry inspired in shepherds, we ask you, with great surprise, for what reason poets every time they want to evoke tales of love attribute them to shepherds, have had recourse to them, and have preferred to display this passion among them. This is what Theocritus and Virgil did, and who did not do it, since the Holy Spirit itself in the book of Canticles chose two shepherds to represent as actors to express the unbelievable love which He had for us? On the other hand, shepherds do not seem to be fitting persons for this representation because they are rustic and crude, and the delicacies of love in its seriousness and proper nature do not seem to agree with peasant grossness nor to find a place in it."

"It is true, Sabino," Marcelo answered, "that poets have recourse to pastoral life when they wish to speak of love. But you are wrong to think that there are persons other than shepherds who can be more representative. It can be that in towns one speaks better, but the purity of feeling belongs to the country and solitude. In truth, the ancient poets, and with even more care as they were more ancient, tried with effort to avoid the lewd and the artificial which fills the love which is born in the towns and cities and which allows much artifice and impurity. Since the shepherds have simple souls which vice has not contaminated, pastoral love is pure and aims at good ends, and—since they live in peace and without worries and they enjoy with complete tranquility and freedom the solitary life which the country offers them and where there is nothing to distract them—their love is lively and deep. They are helped by the free spectacle of the sky, of the earth, and the other elements from which they constantly benefit, so that their life is a clear image or a school of pure and true love. It shows the fullness of friendship and agreement among them, linking one to the other, allying and mixing, and by this mixture and alliance continually revealing and producing fruits which embellish the air and the earth. On this point the shepherds

---

*The poet referred to is Virgil.

surpass other men, and the other thing which comes forth in the shepherd's character is that he is well disposed to honest love.

"The third characteristic concerns the shepherd's occupation, which assuredly consists in ruling and directing but which is very different from other governments. In the first place, his government doesn't consist in issuing laws or in giving orders but in feeding and nourishing those whom He governs. In the second place, he doesn't apply always to everyone the same general rule, but at each moment and on each occasion he adapts his government to the particular case he is directing. In the third place, he governs without dividing among the several ministries the authority which is his. He alone administers his flock in a way that is convenient to it; it is he who feeds it, waters it, bathes it, grazes it, watches over it, punishes it, causes it to rest, recreates it, makes music for it, and protects and defends it. Finally, he is obliged to gather the scattered sheep and to lead back to the same flock many who without him would have gone their own way. This is why the holy writings, when they speak of the one who is gone astray and lost, compare him always to sheep without shepherd, as we can see in Matthew (9:36), in Kings (3:17), and elsewhere. The life of the shepherd is innocent, peaceful, and pleasant; the nature of his condition inclines him to love; and his activity consists in governing by nourishing, by adapting his government to the particular reality of each person. For those whom he governs, he is the only one who is necessary, and his actions never had any other purpose than to keep his one flock.

"Let us see now if we can find this nature in Christ and the superiority which He shows in it. We will see to what degree He merits the name 'shepherd.' Christ lives in the countryside; He enjoys the open skies, He likes solitude and tranquility, and it is in the silence of everything which agitates life that He has his joy. In fact, in the same way that everything that is in the countryside is the purest in the visible world, in essence and like the original of everything which is tied to and mixed with it, in the same way this region of life where our glorious good lives is pure truth. It is the essence of the life of God, the explicit original of everything that is, and the vigorous roots from which are born and from which are supported all creatures. They are the pure elements, the fields eternally filled with flowers, the sources of the living waters, mountains veritably covered with thousands of very noble goods, somber and withdrawn valleys, woods filled with freshness where, sheltered from every injury, gloriously thick with beech trees, olives, and aloe trees, with all other perfumed trees, and where in their glory rest armies of buds whose music never deafens. To compare with this region the miserable exile in which we live is to compare agitation with peace, the disorder, trouble, tumult, and malaise of the most turbulent city with purity, tranquility, and sweetness. Because here one suffers and there one rests; here one imagines, there one sees; here there are the shadows of things which frighten and shock us, there it is truth which soothes and charms us. This is only darkness, tumult, uproar; that is a very pure light at the core of an eternal peace.

"Rightly and with reason his spouse, the shepherdess, implored the shepherd to show her this place where he feeds his flock. 'Tell me, O thou whom my soul loveth, where thou feedest, where thou makest they flock to rest' (Cant. 1:7). In fact, it is the middle of the day, in this place, that she asks where the light is at its height without being contaminated, and where in the profound silence of all things we heard only the sweet voice of Christ surrounded by His glorious flock. It resounds without noise in the ears of His flock, and it acquires from Him incomparable pleasures which penetrate the holy souls, put them beyond themselves, and cause them to live uniquely in their 'shepherd.' Thus Christ is shepherd by the land in which He lives; He is shepherd also by the kind of life He loves, which is tranquility and solitude, which He shows toward His own, whom He invites always to the solitude and the retreat of the country. He says to Abraham, 'Get thee out of thy country, and from thy kindred and thy father's house, and I will make of thee a great nation' (Gen. 12:1). To show it to him He made Elijah enter the desert (1 Kings 19:4). The children of the Prophet lived in the solitude of the Jordan. Of His people He Himself said through the voice of the Prophet, 'I will allure her, and bring her into the wilderness and speak comfortably unto her' (Hos. 2:14). And under the form of the Husband, what other thing than this retreat is to be asked of the Wife? (Cant. 2:10–13). 'Rise up, my love, my fair one, and come away. For, lo, the winter is past, the rain is over and gone; the flowers appear on the earth, the time of the singing of the birds is come, and the voice of the turtle is heard in our land. The fig tree putteth forth her green figs and the vines with the tender grapes give a good smell. Arise my love, my fair one, and come away.' What He wants is that what He loves be pleasant to His flock; and thus since He, being shepherd, loves the countryside, those who are His sheep must similarly also love the countryside because the sheep find in the countryside their nourishment and their subsistence.

"In truth, Juliano, those who must be nourished by God must also renounce the food of the world and shake off the chains of darkness to reach the shining freedom of the truth, in the little-appreciated solitude or virtue and in separation from every agitation which encumbers our life. It is there that is born the nourishment which preserves our soul in an eternal happiness and which is never diminished. In fact, where the shepherd lives and rejoices, there must be the sheep; as one of them said, 'Our conversation is in heaven' (Phil. 3:20). And as the Shepherd Himself said, 'His sheep follow him, for they know his voice' (John 10:14).

"But if Christ is shepherd by the circumstances of His life, how much more would He be by the nature of His character and by His loving tenderness, about which no language and no praise could express the intensity not even remotely? All His actions are love from birth; because He loved us He lived in us loving, He suffered death for our love, and all that He did in His life, all that He suffered in His death, what He now does and conceives in His glory, seated at the right hand of the Father, all that He did through love for our good. Beyond all His actions there is the love, affection, and tenderness of His heart, the disquiet solicitude of His love, the ardor and force of His will which inspires the same acts of love which He accomplishes for us, exceeding everything that we can imagine and say. There is no mother so attentive, no wife so affectionate, there is no amorous heart so tender and so submissive, no friendship more proven and carried to such a point of refinement. Because, before we love Him, He loves us; when we are foolish enough to offend and scorn Him, He seeks for us, and neither the blindness of my eyes nor my callous stubbornness can conquer the warm sweetness of His very benign mercy. He arises with the dawn, while we sleep without concern for the peril which threatens us. He rises with the dawn, I say, and before there is day or, to put it truly, He never sleeps nor rests, but, always attached to the doorknocker of our heart, He does not cease to strike it at every hour, saying, as it is written in the Canticle (5:2), 'Open to me, my sister, my love, my dove, my undefiled, for my head is filled with dew, and my locks with the drops of the night.' 'Behold he that keepeth Israel shall neither slumber nor sleep,' says David (Ps. 121:4).

"In truth, as in divinity, He is love, as St. John says (1 Epistle 4:8), 'God is love,' in the humanity which He borrowed from us He is also love and sweetness. And, as the sun, which by itself is the source of light, its action consists in perpetually causing light by emitting rays of light unendingly, in the same way Christ, the living source of a never-exhausted love, flows continually in love. Upon His face and in His person this fire is always burning. Across His countenance and being the flames of this fire never cease to transpire and to strike our eyes, and all that shows itself is only the rays of love. This is because when He showed Himself to Moses (Ex. 3:2) He manifested Himself in the form of flames which embraced the bushes with fire. He wanted to represent ourselves and Himself in the form of thorn bushes, symbol of our harshness, surrounded with the living fire of His loving tenderness to reveal in a visible way the violent fire which the love of His people inflamed secretly in His breast. We see the same thing in the figure which St. John gives of Him at the beginning of his Apocalypse when he says that he sees the image of a man whose face shines like the sun, whose eyes were like shining flames, whose feet seemed of brass in a burning furnace, whose seven stars cause his right hand to sparkle, whose breast was surrounded by a belt of gold, and who had about him seven lighted torches in their holders (Apoc. 1:13–16). This means that Christ emitted flames of love which appeared from all sides, which reddened His face and came through His eyes, which embraced His feet, which shone through His hands, and which surrounded Him with their glow. It is like the gold, which in Holy Scripture represents love, girded His clothing on His breast; in the same way the love of His vestments, which in holy letters designates the faithful who approach Christ, surround His heart.

"Let this all be and let us pass now to the role of the shepherd and what fittingly belongs to Him. If the function of a shepherd is to rule by nourishing, as I said a short while ago, there is no other truer shepherd than Christ since, among all those who ever governed, He is the only one to have been able to employ and use perfectly the form of governing. This is why in the Psalm where it speaks of this shepherd, David has united in a single act feeding and governing. He said, in effect (Ps. 23:2), 'He maketh me to lie down in green pastures; he leadeth me beside the still waters.' Because the proper governing of Christ, as we will say later, consists in giving us His grace and the efficacious force of His spirit which guide us as well as feed us; or, to say it more truly, their principal task is to furnish us food and substance. In fact, Christ's grace gives life to the soul, health to the body, force to all weaknesses which are in us, atonement to everything which is exhausted by vices; it is the efficacious antidote against their venom and poison, it is the healthy refreshment, and finally a nourishment which produces in us a resplendent and glorious immortality. And thus all the happy people who are governed by this shepherd in all that they do or undergo under His impetus grow, progress, acquire a new vigor, and everything becomes for them an abundant, substantial, and very savory nourishment. It is what He Himself says in St. John (10:9): 'I am the door, by me if any man enter in, he shall be saved, and shall go in and out, and find pasture.' Because the entry and departure, in the true sense of these words in Holy Scripture, comprehend the whole of life and the different actions which we achieve in it.

"It wants to signify by that, that in the entry and the departure (i.e., in life and in death, in prosperous times as in difficult and adverse times, in health and weakness, in war and in peace) His followers, guided by Him, find relish—and not only relish, but the substance of their life and substantial and healthful nourishment. This is in conformity to Isaiah's prophecy about the sheep of this shepherd when he says (49:9–10), 'They shall feed in the ways, and their pastures shall be in high places. They shall not hunger nor thirst; neither shall the heat nor the sun smite them, for he that hath mercy on them shall lead them.' As you see, in saying that they are nourished in their ways, He says that the steps which they take and paths which they travel feed them, but that the woods are precipices and mortal obstacles for evil, for as they say, 'We roamed . . . along the paths of wickedness and ruin" (Wisdom 5:7), but they are for this shepherd's sheep a nourishment and a solace. He says also that in the steep heights as in the flat and cavernous places, that is, as I said, in everything which happens in this life, they have their food and nourishment without fear of hunger and sunstroke. Why? Because, He says, He who had pity upon them is also the one who will guide them, because He is the only one to have had pity for men in His true behavior. This explains what we said before, that is, in His actions He gives them at the same time government and substance, and He always leads them to the springs filled with water, which are in Scripture the grace of the Spirit which refreshes, causes to increase and magnify, and which nourishes.

"The Sage* has noted this also when he said that 'the law of wisdom is the source of life' (Prov. 13:14) by reuniting to what one sees, the law and the source. At first because in giving a law to His flock Christ caused to be born and to grow in them strength and health to practice it with the aid of grace, as I have said. Then because the one that commands us is also the one who feeds our rest and our true life. In fact, all that He commands us is to live in tranquility, to enjoy peace, to be rich and joyful, and to reach true nobility. Because it was not without reason that God put into us the desire for these goods, and God does not condemn what He himself puts in our minds. But the blindness of our misery— moved by desire, ignorant of the good which true desire seeks, and deceived by other things which have the appearance of what one desires—by aspiring to life begins to seek death, and instead of riches and honors runs breathlessly after dishonor and poverty. Christ gives us laws to lead us without error to this veritable good to which our desire aspires.

"Since His laws give life, and what He commands us is nothing other than our sustenance, He makes us feed in health, joy, honor, and repose, thanks to these rules which He gives us for living. As the Prophet says (Ps. 36:9), 'For in thee is the fountain of life; in thy light shall we see light.' For the life and the vision which are true being, and the works which are fitting for such a being, are born and come forth from the grace which He gives us, and from those commandments which He prescribes for us. It is also the cause of this complaint, so just and moving, which is uttered against us in this passage of Jeremiah (2:13): 'They have forsaken me, the fountain of living waters, and hewed out cisterns, broken cisterns, that hold no water.' Although He leads us to fresh pasturage and to the good, we choose with our own hands what

*Solomon.

leads us to death; although He is a spring, we seek wells; although he is gushing water, we prefer broken cisterns which hold no water. Truthfully, in the same way, what Christ commands us is what feeds our life; in the same way, our error makes us choose, and the roads which we follow, led by our caprice, cannot be better designed than by the Prophet's expressions. In the first place, he mentions cisterns dug from the soil with unbelievable difficulty, that is, goods searched for with infinite diligence in the vileness of the soil. If we see the sweat of avarice in its depths, the anxieties which the ambitious feels in his career, the pain which is paid for debauchery in voluptuousness, there is no greater misery nor pain to be compared. In the second place, he speaks of pierced and dried-out cisterns whose great appearance attracts from afar those who see them and promise water to quench their thirst, but which in reality are only deep and obscure holes, not providing what they promise, or better said, filled with what is opposed and repugnant since instead of water they offer mud. Thus the richness of avarice is in fact poverty, the honors which the ambitious seeks make him slave, and the impure pleasure will torture and sicken the one who takes it.

"But if Christ is the shepherd because He governs by feeding and because His commandments are the nourishment of life, it will also be because in His government He does not measure all His sheep by the same standard, but takes account of what is proper to each whom He governs, because He governs by feeding, and the food is measured by the hunger and need of each of those who graze. From this it is clear that among the qualities of the good shepherd enumerated by Christ in the gospel, it is said (John 10:5) that He calls by name each of His sheep, that is, that He knows what is individual in each one, that He governs each and calls it to its good in the particular manner which is best suited to it, that He doesn't treat them all in the same way, but that He treats each individually. Christ nourishes the weak in one way, and in another those who are strong; in one way those who are already perfect, and in another those who have to progress. There is for each a particular style, and it is a marvelous thing His secret commerce with His flock and His different and admirable procedures. In the same way, during the time that He lived among us and in His healings and His kindness He did not observe with everyone the same manner of doing; because He healed some only

BOOK I

with His word, others by His word and presence, others by touching them with His hand, while others were not healed at all for the moment after having been touched but when they had taken again their path and they were already at a distance they recovered their health; others still asked Him for healing, while others regarded Him in silence. In this secret commerce which He had with His flock and in this secret medicine which He continually applied to them, it is a strange miracle to see the variety He employed and how He became different for each and bent to every person and to every character. This is why St. Peter (1 Eph. 4:10) is right in calling His grace 'multiform': He assumes for each a different form.

"It is not something which has a single form or face. On the contrary, like bread (that in the ancient temple was placed before God and was a clear image of Christ), and Holy Scripture calls it 'bread of many faces,' Christ's government and the nourishment which He gives His own have a great number of faces and they are bread. Bread because it feeds, and bread of numerous faces because He adapts Himself to each according to his character. And thus, according to Wisdom (16:20), each found in the manna the taste which was pleasing to him, and thus Christ diversifies His feeding by conforming to the differences which there are among everybody. His government is an extremely perfect one if we think with Plato (Rep. 1:4) that the best government is not one of written laws because they are one and unchanging, while particular cases are numerous and change at each moment according to circumstances. It happens that it may be not just in the particular case what has in general been established with justice. Dealing with only the written law is like dealing with a stubborn man who understands no reason and who at the same time is powerful enough to carry out what he says. Painful and violent situation! The perfect government is inspired by the living law capable of always judging what is the best and always willing to judge in such a way that the law is nothing other than the sane and right judgment of the one who commands, who always adapts himself to the particular case of the one he governs.

"However, since this government does not exist on earth, because no present ruler is wise or virtuous enough not to be deceived or doesn't want to shun injustice, the government of men is thus imperfect. Christ's rule is different. As he possesses perfection, wisdom, and virtue, He discerns infallibly what is just and doesn't desire what is bad; He always sees what is good for each. It is to this that He leads him, and as St. Paul says of Him, 'I am made all things to all men' (1 Cor. 9:22). This makes us refer to the third trait of the shepherd's life. We have said that it consists of forming a trade filled with a multitude of other tasks, and that the shepherd exercises all of them. It is truly so. All the things that concur in the happiness of men are so different and numerous, yet it is Christ principally who executes and realizes them. He calls us, corrects, purifies, heals, sanctifies, gladdens, and dresses us with glory. All the means which God employs to guide a soul, it is Christ who merits them and is author of them.

"But the Prophet speaks well and he speaks fully of this:

> For thus saith the Lord God, Behold, I, even I, will both search my sheep, and seek them out. As a shepherd seeketh out his flock on the day that he is among his sheep that are scattered, so will I seek out my sheep, and will deliver them out of all places where they have been scattered in the cloudy and dark day. And I will bring them out from the people, and gather them from the countries, and will bring them to their own land, and feed them upon the mountains of Israel by the rivers, and in all the inhabited places of the country. I will feed them in good pasture, and upon the high mountains of Israel shall their fold be; there shall they lie in good fold, and in a fat pasture shall they feed upon the mountains of Israel. I will feed my flock, and I will cause them to lie down, saith the Lord God. I will seek that which was lost, and bring again that which was driven away, and will bind up that which was broken, and will strengthen that which was sick, but I will destroy the fat and the strong, I will feed them with judgment (Ezek. 34:11–16).

He says Himself that He seeks His sheep, that He brings them back when they are lost, that He redeems them when they are captives, that He cares for them when they are sick. He Himself delivers them from evil, establishes them in the good, makes them go to the highest pasturage. Near all the rivers and in all the places He feeds them because in all circumstances He finds them pastures, and food in everything which remains or passes away; and as everything relates to Christ, the Prophet immediately adds: 'And even my servant David; he shall feed them, and he shall be their shepherd. And I the Lord will be their God, and my servant David a prince among them' (Ezek. 34:23–24).

"We can see three things. The first is that in order to execute all that God promises to His own, He says to them that He will give them Christ, a shepherd, whom He calls first His servant, and then David, because Christ is descended from David, in the flesh, where He is less than his father and subject to him. The second is that for so many tasks He promises only one shepherd, as much to show that the Christ has power over eveything as to teach that in Him, he who guides is always one single being. In fact, among men, even if there were only one to rule the others, it never occurs that there is only one to govern, since ordinarily many others live in him, which are his passions, affections, interests, and each commands from its perspective. The third thing is that this shepherd that God promises and has given to His Church, He says that He will be raised from amidst His flock, which means that He will reside in the most secretive part of their entrails so as to make Himself master and that He will make them feed in His own being. In fact, it is certain that man's true nourishment is inside man himself and in the lofty principles of which each is the master. Because it is necessary, without doubt, to see the foundation of the good in this division of values by which the philosopher Epictetus begins his book when he says:

> Of things some are in our powers and others are not. In our power are opinions, pursuit, desire, aversion, and, in a word, whatever are our actions. Not in our power are body, property, reputation, command, and, in a word, whatever are not our own actions.
>
> Now, the things in our power are by nature free, unrestrained, unhindered, but those not in our power are weak, slavish, restrained, belonging to others. Remember, then, that if you suppose things by nature slavish to be free, and what belongs to others your own, you will be hindered. You will lament, you will be disturbed, you will find fault with gods and men. But if you suppose that only to be your own which is your own, and what

belongs to others such as it really is, no one will ever compel you; no one restrain you; you will find fault with no one; you will accuse no one; you will do not one thing against your will; no one will hurt you; you will not have an enemy, for you will suffer no harm. (*Manual*, trans. E. Carter [Everyman], p. 255)

"Since the happiness of man consists in the good usage of these acts and of things of which he is entirely the master, that is, of these acts and things which he has in himself and within his control, far from everything external, the result is that ruling and nurturing men means to make man use what is his and what he possesses enclosed within himself. Thus God, with reason, places the Christ who is His shepherd in the entrails of man in order that, by acting upon them, He guides his opinions, judgments, appetites, and desires toward the good which will feed his soul and always give new strengths so that he will realize in this way what the same Prophet says, that is, that he will be nourished in all the best pastures of his own country, that is, by what is purely and properly the happiness and felicity of man. It is not only in these pastures but also on the 'highest mountains' of Israel which are the sovereign goods of the heavens and which surpass in every way natural goods because the lord of them all is the same shepherd who guides them, because He possesses them all united in Himself.

"Since He possesses them in Himself, being in the midst of his flock, He attracts his sheep always to Himself. He does not only put Himself among them, but He climbs and elevates Himself with them, as the Prophet says of Him, because in Himself He is raised through the accumulation of the sovereign goods which He possesses. In them He is raised, for in feeding them He lifts them and separates them as much as possible from the earth; He attracts them always to Himself, He perches them on His summit by elevating them even further and introducing them to His possessions. Remaining with them, He dwells in the breast of each of His sheep, and as making them feed consists in uniting them to Himself and making them enter into Himself, this, as I said a little while ago, is the final quality suitable for the shepherd, to realize the unity of the flock belongs to Him. It is what the Christ does in such a marvelous way, as we will subsequently express it. Suffice to say that clothing is not so united to the body which it covers, that the belt does not grip narrowly enough the waist which it surrounds, that the head and the members are not joined strongly enough, that parents and children are not so strongly tied, that husband is not so close to wife, as Christ, our divine shepherd is with us when He makes in Himself the union with his flock.

"That is what He wishes; it is what He aims at; it is what He does effectively. The other men who, before Him and without Him, introduced into the world laws and sects did not sow peace, but division. They didn't come to reunite the flock, but like Christ said in St. John (10:8 and 12), they were thieves and mercenaries who entered into the fold to divide, to distort and massacre the flock. In fact, although the multitude of evil forces gathers together to fight Christ's sheep, the evil ones are not united for that; they do not form a unified flock, but all their desires, passions, ambitions—which are numerous and different—make them different and divided among themselves. Their flock is not one of unity and peace, but a gathering of war and a gang of enemies who in their multitude detest each other and fight with each other because each has his own will. But Christ, our shepherd, because He is truly a shepherd, gathers His flock in peace. For this reason, in addition to what we have said, God calls Him the sole and unique shepherd, in the passage referred to; because His task causes Him to bring unity. Christ is the shepherd through everything that has been said and because it is incumbent upon the shepherd to take care to protect and increase his flock. Christ constantly takes care of his own and surrounds them in solicitude. As David says (Ps. 34:15), 'The eyes of the Lord are upon the righteous, and his ears are open unto thy cry.' 'Can a woman forget her sucking child? . . . yet will I not forget you' (Isa. 49:15). If it belongs to the shepherd to work for his flock in the cold and ice, who has worked like Christ for the good of His? Jacob was right to say in his name (Gen. 31:40), 'Thus I was; in the day the drought consumed me, and the frost by night; and my sleep departed from mine eyes.' If it is fitting for the shepherd to serve in humiliation, to live with a despised dress, and to be neither adored nor served, then Christ—similar in clothing to His sheep and dressed in their humble fleece—served to gain His flock.

"After having said how everything that belongs to the shepherd belongs to Christ, let us now say how Christ shines above all the other shepherds. He is not only a shepherd, but He is a shepherd as no other has previously existed, which he expresses in relation to Himself (John 10:11–14) by saying, 'I am the good shepherd.' In this phrase the word 'good' marks excellence, as if to say He were 'the best shepherd of all.' His first superiority is that the other shepherds are such accidentally or by chance, while Christ is born to be a shepherd, and before birth He wished to be born for that, so that He descended from heaven and He became man-shepherd, as He Himself says, to seek out man, the lost sheep. And since He was born to lead to pasture, it is to the shepherds that at the time of His birth He made His coming known. In addition to that, the other shepherds guard their flocks which they find, but our Shepherd constitutes Himself the flock which He must protect. What we owe to Christ is not only that He governs us and makes us feed in the manner just spoken of; it is above all that we, who are savage animals, He transforms into sheep, that He goes to find the lost ones, and He infuses into us the spirit of simplicity, of sweetness, and of holy and faithful humility by which we belong to His flock.*

"His third superiority is that He died for the good of His flock, which no other shepherd did, and that He snatched us from the teeth of the wolf; He consented to offer Himself as victim to the wolf. The fourth is that He is at the same time shepherd and pasture and that in feeding His sheep He gives himself to them. To govern His own and to lead them to pasture, Christ did no other thing than to place Himself among them, to permeate Himself with them, incorporate their life in Himself and in the warmth of this faithful love, make His sheep go through His entrails in such a way that once gone through He transforms His sheep into Himself. They feed themselves from Him, removing themselves from themselves and taking upon themselves the qualities of Christ. The flock grows, thanks to his happy pasture, and slowly they become one with its Shepherd. Finally, if other names and offices are fitting for Christ, either from some beginning, or for a certain end, or during some period of time, this name of Shepherd is endless because, before being born in the flesh, He

---

*It should be noted here that Fray Luis uses the past participle *ganado*, "gained," also in the substantive meaning "flock." The interplay of the two meanings is of great significance.

nourished creatures as soon as they appeared; because He governed and conserved things, He Himself fed the angels and 'These wait all upon thee, that thou mayest give them their meat in due season' (Ps. 104:27). In reality, after His birth as man He feeds men from His spirit and flesh. As soon as He ascended to heaven, He made His nourishment rain upon the earth. Then and now and later, in all time and at every hour, He nourishes men in a thousand secretive and marvelous ways. On earth He feeds them, and in heaven He will also be their Shepherd when He will lead them there; then the centuries will be consumed, and insofar as His sheep will live, they will live eternally with Him; He will live in them, communicating His own life to them, having become their shepherd and their pasture."

Marcelo became quiet at this point, indicating to Sabino to continue. The latter unfolded the paper and read:

MOUNTAIN

"Christ is called "mountain" as in chapter 2 of Daniel (34–35), where it is said that the stone which struck the foot of the statue which the king of Babylonia saw, and which crumbled and demolished it, was transformed into a very vast mountain which occupied the whole earth. In chapter 2 of Isaiah (2): 'And it shall come to pass in the last days, that the mountain of the Lord's house shall be established in the top of the mountains, and shall be exalted above the hills.' And in Psalms (68:16): 'The mountain of God, a mountain of cliffs and filled with fat.' "

He stopped with these words. Juliano then said: "Since our paper, Marcelo, resembles Pythagoras and affirms, without giving reason, it would be proper that you give us reason. These passages, especially the last two, certainly could be questioned as to whether or not they speak of Christ."

"Many biblical quotations say many things," replied Marcelo, "but the paper enumerates and reproduces the most certain and the best among them. In the passage of Isaiah, in what precedes and in what follows, there is not a word which does not seem to designate precisely Christ. 'In the last days,' or as you know, the end of days, or the last days, are expressions which in Holy Scripture designate the epoch in which Christ is to come, as the prophecy of Jacob shows in Book of Creation (Gen. 49:1) and in other places. Because the epoch of His first coming, in which the light of the gospel began to be seen together with the Christ, is the period of the revolution of this light—which is that of his preaching, similar to a sun which makes its tour of the world and which passes from one nation to another—since the turning, the appearance, and the duration of this enlightenment is called a day; it is like the rising and setting of the sun in day, and this is called the last day since, once the course of the evangelical sun is ended—what it will have produced when it will have enlightened all the nations is similar to our sun—no other day will come to succeed it. Christ says, 'And this gospel of the kingdom shall be preached in all the world for a witness unto all nations; and then shall the end come' (Matt. 24:14).

He says also that 'It will be established.' The original word designates a foundation and installation free of change, not shaky or subject to the injuries and vicissitudes of time. The same is said in the Psalm (103:19) with the words 'The Lord hath prepared his throne in the heavens.' In fact, is there any other mountain or grandeur not subject to change than Christ's alone, whose reign has no end, as the Angel told the Virgin? (Luke 1:32.) Now, what do we read? 'The mountain of the house of the Lord.' In this expression a word is the explication of the other, and we must understand 'the mountain, that is, the house of the Lord.' This excellent house among all the others is Christ our redeemer, in whom God rests and lives eternally as it is written. 'For in him dwelleth all the fullness of the Godhead bodily.' The text says, 'above the summit of the mountains,' something which can be said only of Christ. In fact, 'the mountain' in Scripture and in the secret manner of speaking which Holy Scripture employs designates all that is eminent, either in earthly power, such as princes, or in virtue and spiritual knowledge, such as the prophets and the prelates. And to say 'mountains' without limitation is to say all mountains (as that is understood from an article which is in the primitive text), that is, 'the most remarkable of all the mountains' as much by their height as by their other qualities and characteristics. To say that He will be established on 'all the mountains' is not to say that the mountain is raised higher than the others but that it is placed on the summit of all, so that its lowest part is above what among the others is the highest.

BOOK I

"Thus, to summarize in clear terms all that I said, the following interpretation comes forth: The root, or as we say, the womb of the mountain of which Isaiah speaks (i.e., the lowest and most humble part) has under it all the most notable and highest summits, temporal as well as spiritual. Well, what summit or what peak will be so great if it is not Christ? What other mountain in God's domain will be suitable for such a greatness?

"Let us see what Holy Scripture says when it speaks of Christ in unadorned and simple terms, and let us compare it with the circuitousness of this passage of Isaiah. If we find that the two texts say the same thing, we will no doubt know that they are speaking of the same thing.

"What does David say (Ps. 110:1)?—'The Lord said unto my Lord, sit thou at my right hand, until I make thy enemies thy footstool.' And the apostle St. Paul (Phil. 2:10): 'That at the name of Jesus every knee should bow, of things in heaven, and things in earth, and things under the earth.' And the same apostle, speaking directly of the mystery of Christ, says (1 Cor. 1:25): 'Because the foolishness of God is wiser than men; and the weakness of God is stronger than men'; because the mountain is placed there on the mountains, and here the height of the world and of hell is placed as a footstool under Christ's feet. Here what is created kneels before Him; there everything that is raised is submitted to Him; here His humiliation, debasement, cross are said to be wiser and more powerful than what men can know and do. We see in Isaiah that the root of this mountain is placed above the summits of all the mountains. We must not doubt that Christ is this mountain of which Isaiah speaks and that He is also the one of whom David sings in the previously cited Psalm. This Psalm is obviously a prophecy, not a single mystery, but of all those which the Christ has brought about for our salvation. Apparently it is an obscure Psalm. However, it is obscure for those who do not discover the core of its true meaning but abandon themselves to their personal imagination. Since the Psalm does not agree and cannot agree with them, they wish to make it agree; they turn around the text, they obscure and trouble the meaning, and at the end they tire themselves in vain. On the contrary, if we grasp once the thread and its design, the same things explain and refer to each other and they link together among themselves with marvelous art. Now, for what refers to our purpose—because it would detour us too much to comment on the whole Psalm—what the verses of this Psalm point to is the comprehension that the mountain is Jesus Christ; it suffices to see what follows: 'mountain where God is pleased to reside and surely he will reside there eternally.' If that is not Jesus Christ, it can be said of no other. We must study each word as well as this verse and the verse which precedes it. But let us avoid confusion and trouble.

"First of all, let us say what it means to call the Christ 'mountain.' Then we will return to these same passages and we will express some characteristic words which the Holy Spirit attributes to this mountain. I will say this: Beyond what these mountains possess over the rest of the land—that is, a superiority as remarkable as that of the Christ, as man has above all other creatures—the principal reason for which Christ is called mountain is the abundance or the plenitude and riches of different goods which He has amassed and which He bears in Himself. Thus we know in Hebrew, a language in which the sacred books are in their original state, the word which designates mountain, in its proper sense, designates in our language 'he who is full' so that what we call 'mountains' is called properly 'full' in Hebrew.

"This name is fitting in a perfect way, and not only because of their elevated form, round and, as it were, inflated on the surface of the earth, which makes of them its belly, and not an empty and flabby belly, but pregnant and full; it is also because they carry in them—in order to beget and to bring forth at the proper time—almost everything which is esteemed on the earth. They produce trees of different species, some which furnish wood for construction, others which by their fruits sustain life. More than any other part of the earth, they beget herbs of different kinds with secret and efficacious virtues. The mountains are the sources of the rivers which are born there and afterward they spread and turn across the plains and make fertile and embellish the earth. There the mercury is produced and the tin and all the lodes of silver, gold, and the other metals, precious stones, and the quarries of hard rocks which are still more useful, with which we strengthen the walled towns and ennoble them with sumptuous palaces. Finally, the mountains are like a store and a reserve of all the greatest treasures which the earth contains.

"As Christ is our Lord, and since He is God—because of this title, Christ being the divine Word, through which God created all things, He possesses them all in Himself with a value and a being which is superior to what they are in themselves. Yet Christ, still as man, is a mountain, an accumulation, a plenitude of all that is good, of everything profitable, delectable, glorious that is in the desire and core of men, and of many other things which are not in this core. In Him are the remedies of the world, the destruction of sin, and the victory over the Devil. The springs and the mother lodes of grace and virtue which flow through our souls and hearts find in Him their abundant principle. In Him are their roots, from Him they grow and, thanks to His virtue, take in beauty 'all trees of frankincense, myrrh and aloes,' as it is stated in Canticle 4:14, and the apostles, the martyrs, the prophets, and virgins grow in grace and beauty. He Himself is at the same time the priest and the sacrifice, the shepherd and the pasture, the doctor and the doctrine, the advocate and the judge, the reward and the distributor, the guide and the road; the physician, the medicine, riches, light, protection, and the consolation, He Himself, and He alone. In Him we have joy in sadness, discernment in doubt; in danger and desperation we find protection and health.

"To obligate us further and in order that, by seeking what is necessary in other places, we do not set ourselves apart from Him, He placed in Himself riches and abundance, or, in some way, the boutique and the market, or, better said, the treasure liberally offered to us of all that is necessary, useful, and sweet, in adversity as in prosperity, in life as in death, in the long years of our exile as in the eternal felicity toward which we travel. As a high mountain covered with clouds at its summit transcends them and seems to touch the heaven, while its sides produce vines and crops and furnish healthy pasture to the flocks, in the same way the summit and head of Christ is God which goes beyond the heavens and which is made from the very profound advice of wisdom to which no mortal spirit can attain. But His humility, His unstudied words, the poor, simple, and very holy life which He led among us, the works which He accomplished as man, the sufferings and pains which He endured for men and because of men are pastures which bring life to His faithful sheep. It is there that we find the wheat which fortifies the heart of men, the wine which gives them the true joy, and the virgin oil of olives, the oil, giver of light which puts aside our darkness. 'The rocks,' says Psalm 104:18, 'are the refuge of the rabbits.' In You, the true support of the poor frightened ones, Jesus Christ; it is in You, O sweet and sure protector, always faithful gatherer, that the afflicted and persecuted come to hide themselves. If the clouds pour out from the water, if the rivers of the heavens are pouring down on us, if the sea goes out of its bed, deluges the lands, and if the waters submerge the mountains as in the time of the flood, on this mountain which is above all the mountains we dwell and we are not afraid. And if the mountains, as David says, 'are torn from their place and fall into the heart of the sea,' on top of this mountain which does not change we have nothing to fear.

"But what do I do now? Where does my enthusiasm carry me? Let us return to our subject and since we have said why the Christ is a mountain, let us explain the qualities which Scripture gives a mountain.

"Daniel (2:34–35) said that 'a stone was cut out without hands, which smote the image upon his feet ... and broke them to pieces ... and the stone that smote the image became a great mountain, and filled the whole earth.' This shows us, in the first place, that this very great mountain was first just a little stone. Although Christ is called 'stone' for different reasons, here stone means strength and smallness. It is a worthy point of consideration to see that the stone does not fall upon the statue nor destroys it as a great mountain, but does so as small stone. To destroy tyrannical power and pride of the demon, usurped adoration, and the idols which exist in the world, Christ did not use the greatness of His forces and did not beat them with the arm and weight of His hidden divinity; He used what was humble in Him, what was low and small, that is, His sacred body and His shed blood, His imprisonment, condemnation, and His very cruel death. This smallness and weakness are strong forces, and all the magnificence of hell and its kingdom are dominated by the death of Christ. The stone becomes the 'mountain.' At first He humiliated Himself and conquered through His humiliation; then glorious conqueror, He revealed His light and filled heaven and earth with the virtue of His name.

"But what the Prophet expressed circuitously, the Apostle expressed simply. Speaking of the Christ, he said (Eph. 4:9–10): 'Now that he ascended, what is it but that he also descended, first into the lower parts of the earth? He that descended is the same also that ascended up far above all heavens, that he might fill all things.' And elsewhere (Phil. 2:8–9): 'He became obedient unto death, even the death on the cross. Wherefore God also hath highly exalted him, and given him a name which is above every name.' And as we say of the tree that the more it causes its roots to penetrate the depths, the more it grows toward the heights and is raised above space, similarly to the humility and smallness of this stone replies the immense grandeur of the mountain. The more it is diminished at first, the more it increases subsequently. Even though small, the stone which one throws strikes a great blow if the arm which sends it forth is strong, and we could think that if this small stone reduced the statue to pieces, it was through the strange and powerful force which threw it. It was not so, and the Holy Spirit did not wish that we imagine things thus. For this reason, it added that it struck the statue without the aid of its hands, that is, it struck with a borrowed force; it struck a surprising blow by virtue of its own power. This is what truly happened.

"In fact, the despised weakness of the Christ, His passion and His death, this poor man, scoffed at and covered with spittle, was a very hard stone; I want to say so firm in His suffering and so strong and constant that He strikes down whatever is held to be strong in this superb world, nothing being able to resist. On the contrary, everything fell, broke, and was destroyed as the thinnest glass. In addition, what is even more wonderful, the stone did not hit the head of this frightful figure, but only the feet, where the wounds are never mortal. In spite of that, this blow to the feet caused the breast, the shoulders, the neck, and the golden head to crumble. What in effect happened is that the beginning of the gospel and the first blows which the Christ struck in order to destroy the power of the corrupt world were to its feet and to what seemed to languish upon the earth, that is, people low and base both in their condition and in their occupation. Once the latter were struck by the truth, conquered and broken by the world, and dead before it, and once placed under the stone, the heads and breasts, that is, the wise and the powerful, all fell; some under the stone, others broken and pulverized by it, some in order to continue to grow in their evil. And thus, some destroyed and others converted, the stone became a mountain and it occupied the whole world.

"The Christ is also a true mountain, and He is as if born from a stone, so that we comprehend that this mountain is not made of crumbling earth and that it cannot be decreased or diminished in any way.

"Let us see what the venerable David said on this subject. 'The mountain of the Lord,' he says, 'a thick mountain, a rich mountain' (Ps. 72:16). This means a fertile and abundant mountain, in the same way we are used to calling the good earth, rich earth. The nature of the good earth consists in being thick, compact, and massive, and not light and sandy; it is an earth which drinks much water and which the latter does not inundate or dissolve, but which on the contrary, after having entirely absorbed it, grows rich and is swollen with juices. Thus, later, the harvests which it produces are in conformity with this abundance; they are thick and high with straight stems and vigorous ears of corn.

"It is indeed true that where we say 'thick' the original text says 'Basan,' which is the proper name of a mountain in the Holy Land and which is located on the other side of the Jordan in the portion which fell to Gad and Reuben and half of the tribe of Menasseh. But this mountain was remarkably fertile, and thus our text, although it passes over the name in silence, has preserved the meaning and has expressed the same idea. Instead of 'Basan' the text put 'thick mountain' as is the case with the 'Basan.' Christ is in no way compatible with light earth and moving sand. He is, on the contrary, a consistent and robust earth which drinks and contains in itself all the gifts of the Holy Spirit which the Scripture usually calls waters; and thus the fruit which comes forth from the mountain and the harvests which are produced there show us very clearly how thick and fruitful is the mountain. Of these harvests, David (Ps. 72:16), with the images of wheat, harvests, and fruits of the earth, speaking of the kingdom of Christ, tells in his song, 'There shall be a handful of corn in the earth upon the top of the mountains; the fruit thereof shall shake like Lebanon; and they of the city shall flourish like grass of the earth.' In saying this, it came to mind, I want to say, as our common friend said it, translating into Castilian verse this psalm:

O centuries of gold
When only an ear of corn
sowed on the hill
produced such a treasure,

BOOK I

harvests which swayed
like the high summit of the Lebanon
when with more riches and abundance
than the grass in the cities
the fields of wheat will swell.

"And in order that we see clearly that this fruit which we call wheat is not wheat and that this abundance is not from the good nature of the earth, nor from the sweetness of a clement sky, but that it is the fruit of justice and of spiritual harvests, never previously seen, which is born by the virtue of this mountain, he than adds:

By which the fame
unfolds through a thousand centuries
the name of this king and lifts it to the heavens.

"But this name, was it born perchance with this fruit or did it already exist? Was it living in the heart of His Father before the wheel of the centuries began to turn? David says, in this version,

The name which was resplendent before the sun gave forth light and in which the last of the mortals will be blessed whom people, celebrating it night and day, bestow praises and benedictions and will say in praising him: Lord, God of Israel, what language can express the glory which is yours?

"I am separated from my path, carried by the flavor of the verses. We must return to it."

After having said that and having taken a short breath, Marcelo was ready to continue when Juliano stopped him and said to him:

"Before speaking, tell me one thing, Marcelo. This friend who is common to all of us, of whom you were speaking and who has written these verses, who is he? Although I am not a great poet, they seem to me excellent. Who gave them this quality? It is in the nature of this material, I believe, that poetry is made to soar."

"It is a great truth, Juliano," replied Marcelo, "what you say, because such is indeed the sole subject worthy of poetry. Those who are distanced from it and do violence to it in order to use it or to lose it in frivolous tales should be punished for having publicly corrupted two very holy things: poetry and morals. They corrupt poetry because, without any doubt, God inspired men's intelligence in order that its movement and spirit transport them to the heaven from which poetry comes. Because poetry is only a communication of the celestial and divine breath, and almost all the prophets, as well as those who were truly moved by God, as those who spoke through the action of other supernatural causes, the same spirit excited them and made them see what other men did not see; this inspired, composed spirit poetized in some manner the words in their mouth, with the necessary meter and rhythm, to aid them to express themselves in a more elevated way than other men, and in order that the style of their discourses accorded with their sentiment and that there was conformity between the words and reality.

"Thus some frivolous poets corrupt this holiness and, what is a greater evil, they corrupt also the sanctity of morals. Because the vices and the hidden honeyed turpitudes, in the harmony and the artifice of verse, are gathered with greatest pleasure by the ear, from where they pass into the spirit, which by itself is not good, and they penetrate it with great power. When they dominate and they chase from it all proper meaning and reflection, they corrupt the spirit, often without awareness. I would say that it is a pleasantry—but it is not a pleasantry, it is a blameworthy frivolity that mothers guarding the virtue of their daughters forbid them to talk with certain women and do not forbid the verses and couplets dealing with indecent subjects which speak to them at any hour. On the contrary, without hindrance, the latter teach and sing to them and thus they attract them, they secretly persuade them, they spread their poison slowly in their hearts and end by poisoning them completely. In the same way that the city, whose citadel has been lost and has fallen into the enemy's hands, is entirely lost; similarly, once conquered, I say once lost, the heart attached to vices and made to slumber by them, there is no defense strong enough or no sentinel vigilant enough and attentive to guard it and save it. But this point belongs at another place, although the necessity and the ravages which usage has created, more widespread today than ever, ever acting among people, make it possible to deal with it wherever and whenever.

"Let us leave this for the moment. I am surprised, Juliano, that you asked me who was the common friend of whom I spoke, because you cannot forget that although each of us has numerous friends, we have only one who is my friend and yours almost equally, because He likes me as Himself, and you He likes as I like you, which is hardly less than the friendship which I feel for myself."

"You are right," replied Juliano, "to criticize my distraction. Now I understand very well what you are talking about. And since you must have in your memory some other psalms which our friend has translated I would like—and Sabino also, if I am not mistaken—at this time that you refer to them and recite them to us."

"I don't know," replied Marcelo, "if Sabino will be happy to hear what he already knows. In fact, he is younger and more in love with poetry, he has at his fingertips the language of the Psalms of which we have spoken. However, I want to give you this pleasure and I rely on Sabino to recall them if my memory fails. He will recall them, or if he prefers, he will recite them personally. It is better that he prefers it because he will recite them with greater charm."

These last words did not fail to make Juliano and Sabino laugh a bit. When Sabino said that he would act thus and would be happy, Marcelo took up again the thread of his considerations and said:

"We said that this mountain, as the Psalm says, was of exceptional fertility and we have shown its fecundity by the number and the height of the crops which are born there. We also recalled what David said about this, that a handful of wheat spread on the summit of this mountain 'would produce plants and stalks so high and thick that they would be equal to the highest cedars of Lebanon' (Ps. 72:16). Thus each stalk and each ear of corn would be like a cedar, all would cover the summit of the mountain, and moved by the wind they would stir at the top of the cedar trees and the other trees which give the Lebanon a sovereign crown.

"Above, David indicated three very remarkable qualities. He says in the first place that there are harvests of wheat, useful and necessary for life, and not like trees, which are more beautiful in their branches and foliage than profitable in their fruits. This was the case of the ancient philosophers and those who through their hard work alone wished to achieve virtue. Then he affirms that these harvests are better not only because it is wheat, but that they are much greater in height than the groves of the Lebanon. It is something which strikes the eye, if we compare the greatness of the renown which the sages and the great leave behind them with the merited honor which the Church always gives to the saints and which grows each day as long as the world endures. In the third place, he says that this fruit originates from very small beginnings, from a handful of wheat sown on the top of a mountain where ordinarily the wheat grows badly. In fact, on the top there is no soil, but rock, or if there is soil, it is a very light soil and the place is too cold because of the altitude. It is one of the greatest marvels that we see in the virtue that is born and is taught in Christ's school: From a beginning that is very small and hardly seen you do not know how and in what manner its members grow, come forth, and attain, in very little time, an incomparable greatness.

"We all know to what degree ancient philosophy attempted to make men virtuous—its precepts, disputes, and foggy problems—and we see at each point the beauty and sweetness of its contrived and artificial words. We also know, despite the appearance, the minor results which it produced and how little it gave in relation to what we expected from its great promises. This was not what occurred in Christ. If we consider the totality of his person, which is said to be 'a single grain of dead wheat' (John 12:24), and not several grains, we see it managed with twelve lowborn and simple men and their teaching, with rough words and brief phrases, to fill the entire world with incomparable virtue. We will expand this in a later and more convenient place. Similarly, if we view the detail of what happens each day to many people, can we contemplate this spectacle without being filled with admiration? He who lived yesterday without law, who abandoned himself without limit to his desires and was already hardened in evil, who was a servant to money and sought only enjoyment, filled with pride toward others, and haughty and cruel toward his inferiors; today, because of a word having touched his ear and then passed into his heart, planting a delicate and small seed which he hardly feels, this man begins to change into another and through the secret force of a small seed which spreads through his soul, he becomes completely different. We see the nobility of his virtues and attitudes grow in such a manner that the dry leaves, destined for the flames, now form a green tree, rich with flowers and fruits; now the lion has become the sheep, he who used to steal now distributes his goods to others, and he who wallowed in stink now spreads around him and afar the good smell of purity.

"And, as I have said, if we return to the beginning and compare the grandeur of this planet and its beauty to the small grain from which it was born and the little time it had to develop, we will see in such a surprising smallness an admirable and unforeseen virtue. Similarly, the Christ is said to be similar to the mustard seed which is small and then expands; elsewhere, he is compared to the oriental pearl which is of small size and yet of great value; and there is finally a passage where it is said that he is like the yeast which looks small and lowly and yet, placed in a large dough, penetrates it quickly, and at the end permeates all of it (Luke 13:19, 21; Matt. 13:14). At this point it is useless to search for further examples; their multitude would submerge us. But the text of St. Paul is the most celebrated from among them all, and it is his feast which we celebrate today. Who was he and what happened? How fast and with only a single word did he transform himself from darkness to light, from poison to the tree of life of the Church!

"Let us go on. David adds, 'curdled' mountain. The word originally means 'cheese.' It designates also what is 'deformed' and in a proper and original way it is applied to everything which possesses parts which come forth and form a swelling above the other parts which it already contains. This is how cheese and hunchbacked are designated by this single word. If we add to it the name 'mountain,' as David did here, and if we put it in the plural as it is done in the first text, it signifies, as St. Augustin read it, 'mountain of cheeses' (Enarrat. in Ps. 67:22–23, P.L. 36:827), or as certain people now translate it, 'mountain of humps.' This fits very well with one or the other expressions. In saying the first thing, we understand and make more precise the fertility of this mountain which is not made solely of thick earth and apt to produce harvests, but forms also a mountain of cheeses or curdled milk, that is, by designating the cause by the effect, when I say a mountain of beautiful pastures for the animal, I mean a good mountain producing bread, no less good to nourish herds.

"As St. Augustin has said, the wheat and the size of the mountain which produces it are the sustenance of the perfect ones. The milk which is curdled into cheese, the pastures which produce it, are the proper food for those who begin in virtue. It is what St. Paul says (1 Cor. 3:2): 'As little children I have given you milk and not solid food.' And according to that, we understand that this mountain is the general sustenance of everyone, as well by its importance for those who have grown in virtue as by its pastures and its milk, for those who are newly born there.

"However, if we say 'mountain of humps or of swellings' we express a pointed truth—that mountains exist which suddenly arise to the summit and which form there a unique and round peak, and others which form a great number of peaks which are of different heights; yet the Christ is not a mountain like the first one, eminent and excellent on only one point, but a mountain made from mountains, and a greatness filled with greatnesses, diverse and incomparable, and in some way a mountain made entirely from other mountains so that, as St. Paul divinely writes (Col. 1:18), it has primacy and superiority in all things.

"Then he says, 'What do you suspect, mountains of heights, this is the mountain which God desireth to dwell in; yea, the Lord will dwell in it forever' (Ps. 68:16). He addresses himself to all those who consider themselves superior and who are opposed to the Christ, assuming to challenge Him; he says to them, 'What do you suspect?' Or as St. Jerome has said elsewhere, 'What is this case or what is this struggle against this mountain?' This actually means: O mountains, what presumption and what thought is yours, however eminent you may be in your opinion, to oppose yourself to this mountain, to pretend either to conquer it or to put in yourself what God has decided to put there, that is, his perpetual dwelling? In other words, it is totally in vain and profitless that you tire yourself. That shows us two things: that this mountain is envied and contradicted by many mountains, and that it is chosen by God from all the others. Concerning the first, that is, jealousy and opposition, it is the destiny of the Christ to be always envied, and yet this is of comfort for those who follow Him, as the old Simeon said to them when he saw the child in the temple and, speaking to his mother, said, 'Behold this child is set for the fall and rising again of many in Israel; and for a sign which shall be spoken against' (Luke: 2:34). And the second Psalm had said the same: 'The kings of the earth set themselves, and the rulers take counsel together against the Lord, and against His anointed.' The event was in conformity to what was foreseen, as we saw in the opposition which pitted the leaders of the people of Israel against the Christ during His whole life and in the plot which they hatched among themselves to bring Him to His death. When we regard it closely, it is assuredly a surprising thing because if the Christ was treated as He should have been, as He should according to the height of His rank, if He had courted temporal authority on all things, if in words or acts He had shown Himself haughty and desirous of domination, and if He had intended not to do the good but to amass goods, to subjugate the nations, to live from their sweat and work, in rest and abundance, if many envied Him and opposed Him for their interests, there would not have been anything marvelous here. On the contrary, it would have been what happens every day. Yet since He was simplicity itself and He didn't want to go before anyone else and didn't want to chase anyone from his office and preeminence, since He lived without pomp and humbly, since He did good in a way never before seen by man, without seeking or demanding or even wishing to receive honor or profit, the fact that the people hated Him, the great detested Him, a poor man, and the potentates and high ecclesiastics hated a humble benefactor, is something which fills us with stupor.

"Well, did the opposition disappear with His death and did His disciples and His doctrine escape the contradiction and opposition of men? What happened in the head also took place among the members. As He Himself says, 'If they have persecuted me, they will also persecute you' (John 15:20). It is what happened to them, to the emperors, king, princes, and wise men of the world. And so our blessed light, which in all justice should be loved, is persecuted, likewise His disciples and His doctrine, although they made all reasons and causes of jealousies or hatreds to disappear, have become the victims of the world's cruel enmity. Because those who taught against the accumulation of fortunes or the pursuing of honors and dignities, the conserving of a humble state, and the elimination of all jealousy, yielding before everyone all their rights, becoming poor themselves in order to help the poverty of the other, returning good for evil, those who lived as they taught, became public benefactors, who would have ever thought that they could be detested or persecuted by anyone?

"And even if we turn our eyes toward the beginning and the first origin of this hatred and jealousy, we will find that this hatred began before He became the Christ of the flesh and in this we come to know the cause. The first to be jealous of Him and to hate Him was in fact Lucifer, as the glorious Bernard affirms (in *Cantica*, sermo 17:5; P.L. 183:857), and in a way conforming to true doctrine. Lucifer began to hate Him as soon as God revealed to him and to some other angels a part of His mysterious design, and when he knew that God was planning to make a man the universal head of all things. This he knew from the beginning of time and before he fell. In fact, he turned his eyes toward himself, he considered with pride the very high perfection of his nature, he saw at the same time the singular abundance of gifts and grace which God had conferred upon him, more than upon any other angel, and happy with his person and seized by a miserable infatuation, he aspired for himself this excellence. This aspiration led him to a refusal to submit to the order and decree of God, to flee His holy obedience, and to change grace into arrogance, in the same way that the Christ is everything that is simple and humble. If someone skips a step in descending a stair, his fall is not limited to the step, but from step to step he tumbles down to the bottom. Similarly, Lucifer, from disobedience toward God, fell into the hate of Jesus Christ. He conceived against Him jealousy, then a bloody hatred, and this hatred caused an absolute determination to be born in him to combat Him forever with all his power. This is what he attempted at first against his parents by killing and condemning in them, insofar as it was within his power, the succession of men, then in the person of the Christ by persecuting Him through his ministers, condemning Him to death, and then exciting against His disciples and believers, unceasingly, until the end of time, his principal ministers, that is, all who are held to be wise and great in this world. This war and struggle has been a tale of power always fighting against weakness, pride and arrogance against humility, ruse and craft against simplicity and goodness, yet finally those who seem at first conquerors are conquered. It is against this enemy that David directs the words which we comment upon. In fact, this angel and the other angels who followed him, so boastful and inflated with qualities which they owe both to nature and to grace, this angel he calls 'elevated and crooked mountains' or mountainous mountains, and he speaks to them thus: Why, O boastful mountains, are you jealous of the greatness of man in the Christ who is revealed to you; why do you war and create difficulties for Him; why do you pretend that it was for you that this glory was intended or that your opposition will help take it away from Him? I assure you that this enterprise will be in vain and that this struggle will lead to His greatness and you will have raised yourself in vain; He will crush you, and Divinity will be in Him with a peaceful sweetness till the end of time."

With these words Marcelo was silent. Then Sabino, believing that he had concluded, again opened the paper, looked at it, and said: What now follows is brief enough in words, but I suspect that concerning the things just spoken of there will be much to say. Here is what he reads:

THE EVERLASTING FATHER

"The sixth name is the Everlasting Father. It is what Isaiah calls Him in chapter 9:6: 'We shall call him the everlasting Father.' "

"I had not yet finished with the mountain," Marcelo then said, "but since Sabino has gone ahead and there will be doubtlessly a better occasion for what I have to say, let us continue as Sabino desires. Besides, there is reason to say that the passage which he has just submitted to us, if it is brief in words, will be long in commentary. At the least, if it is not long, it is extremely profound, because it contains in great part the mystery of our redemption. If, as is the case, the subject could be held in my spirit and come forth through my mouth dressed in the words and phrases which it deserves, that would suffice to fill our souls with celestial light and love. But let us repose on Christ's favor and, aided in this enterprise by your holy desires, let us begin to say what inspires us. Here is how we will begin.

"It is certain and demonstrated in Holy Scripture that to live in God we men must be born a second time after we were born and left our mother's womb. It is certain that all the faithful are born again in this second birth where the principle and origin of holy and faithful life resides. This is what the Christ affirmed to Nicodemus, who, being master of the law, came to Him one night to be His disciple. Then Christ, to establish the doctrine which He wanted to present to him, posed this: 'Verily, verily, I say unto thee, except a man be born again, he cannot see the kingdom of God' (John 3:3). By the force of correlations which mutually respond to each other, we deduce easily that when there is birth, there is a child, and when there is a child, there is a father. If we the faithful, being born again, become children again, we have a new Father whose force brought us forth; this Father is the Christ. It is for this reason that He is called the Everlasting Father, because He is the principle and origin of this new and blessed generation and of the innumerable multitude of descendants who were born from it. To further understand this thing, to the degree that it can be understood by our weakness, let us take all this reasoning from its beginnings and let us say why it becomes necessary for man to be born a second time. Then after that, proceeding gradually and orderly, let us say everything which is fitting to a clear understanding of this subject. We will always keep our eyes fixed on the light of Holy Scripture, which will guide us as a star and we will follow the traces of the doctors and saints of the past.

"According to what I said a moment ago, since the infinite goodness of God, pushed by its sole virtue, decided before time to raise to God man's nature, to make it participate in His greatest goods, and to make it master of all His creatures, Lucifer, from the moment he perceived it, was inflamed with jealousy and was prepared to corrupt and dishonor the human species as much as he could, to destroy man's body and soul in such a way that he would be rendered inadequate for heavenly goods, and could not achieve what God had decided for in his favor. 'It is through the devil's jealousy,' says the Holy Spirit in Wisdom (Wisd. of Sol. 2:24), 'that death entered the world.' What happened is that as soon as he saw the first man created and favored by God's grace, placed in a state of happiness and beatitude and on a level close and near to the eternal and veritable good, he observed that God, at the same time, had denied him the fruit of the tree and if he ate the fruit, the pain of death would be immediately incurred for the life of the soul and later for the body; and on the other hand, the Devil knew that God could not, in any way, retract what He had once decided. He imagined at once that if he could deceive man and cause him to transgress this commandment he would leave him necessarily lost and condemned to death both in body and soul and that he would render him incapable of the good to which God destined him. But he realized that even if this man sinned, those who were born after him God could lead to the good because he had decided in men's favor; he resolved to throw his venom into the first man, as into the first source, as the seeds of his pride, impiety, and ambition, the roots and principles of all the vices, and to stir them up continuously so that this evil would spread and extend itself in those who would be born of this first man, that they would all be born guilty and detestable in God's eyes, inclined to continuous and new faults and incapable of becoming what God had ordered. This is what he thought; he thought it, and right away he put it into action. He succeeded in his plan. Induced and persuaded by the Devil, man committed sin and the Devil believed his work done, that is, he believed man to be definitely lost and believed God's design destroyed and overthrown.

"In fact, everything which touches man remains strangely laborious and confused. Thus, we saw two divine decrees mutually contradict each other and at war with each other, and it didn't seem possible to settle nor to find a mean term which was good. On the one hand, God had decreed the exaltation of man above all other things, and on the other, He affirmed that if he sinned He would take away from him the life of soul and body. Man had sinned. Thus, if God carried out His first decree He would not execute the second, and if He carried out the second He annuled and effaced the first. At the same time, concerning both points, God could not but respect His word because God cannot change what He says and no one can put an obstacle to what He has ordered. In both cases His will seemed impossible to execute. In fact, one could think it would have been good that God create other men not descending from this first man, achieve in them the decree of His grace, and carry out in others the sentence of His justice; God could doubtlessly do it, but then the promise would remain of an incomplete and diminished fidelity because the grace of the promise was not made to anyone but to the men whom God created in Adam, that is, to Adam's descendants. When there didn't seem to be a remedy, God's incommensurable wisdom found it and He imagined a result to a situation which the difficulties made all but impossible. The means and result were not to create a new species of men but to cause these same men, already created and born through generations, to be born again, in order that they, remaining themselves, die to their first birth and live according to their second, and that for the first, God apply the decreed punishment and for the second God accord the promised grace and grandeur. In everything He would remain true and glorious. Pope St. Leo says, briefly, what I have just said:

> The devil took pride that man deceived by his ruse had been deprived of his divine gifts, and that, deprived of the privilege of immortality, was under the cruel sentence of death. It was for him a sort of consolation in his faults and evils to have thus found a companion in the new sinner. God himself, following the demands of a just severity toward the man he had created for such a high degree of honor, had modified his first decision. It was necessary, according to the economy of God's new secret design, that who does not change and whose will cannot be thwarted in his munificence, carried out through a hidden mystery the first decree of his clemency, that man, led into error through the deception and deceit of an infernal evil, might not perish contrary to the will of God (in *Nativitate Domini*, Serm. 2, P.L. 54:194).

"Such is the necessity for man to be born a second time. But we must now know what is this new and second birth, what force it has, and in what it consists. For this, I presuppose in principle that at our birth, with the substance of the soul and body with which we are born, there is also born in us a base corruption and an evil spirit which, spread and diffused in all the parts of man, overwhelm them all, corrupt and destroy them. Because in the understanding darkness is introduced, in the memory forgetfulness, in the will error and revolt against God's law, in the appetites, passion and rage, in the senses deception, in works evil and sin, in the body decay, weakness, and suffering and finally death and corruption. All this St. Paul usually expresses with one word when he says 'sin' and 'body of sin' (Rom. 6:6). St. James declares 'that the wheel of our birth,' that is, its principle or the substance with which we are born, 'is embraced with the fire of hell' (James, Ep. 3:6). Thus, in the substance of our soul and body is born—when it is born, imprinted, and attached—this evil force which many names can hardly define. It dominates in such a manner that not only does it infect and contaminate our soul and make it into something else, but it pushes, inflames, and leads it where it desires, as if our soul were another substance or another spirit, established and grafted upon ours.

"If we want to know the reason which causes us to be born thus, we must, to understand it, note in the first place that the substance of human nature, in itself and in accordance with its first birth, is imperfect and becomes so; but it has complete freedom and will to realize and take fully the good or bad form, whichever pleases it the most, because in it it has neither. It is capable of receiving all of them, and it enjoys a marvelous faculty of adaption to each of them like wax. In the second place, we must remark that that which is lacking in man and which he can acquire—like the achievement and end of work—cannot give him the being, the life, the movement when he already possesses man. They are his as a good or bad being, they are his in a determined way, his good and his proper form, and it is the spirit and form of the soul itself which leads it and decides the nature of its actions, what extends to and shines through them all, so that it may act as it lives and in order that what it does be in conformity with the spirit which characterizes it and causes it to act.

"This is what happened to us. When God formed the first man and formed us all who were born in Him as from His seed, He formed with His own hands, and as from God's hands nothing comes forth unfinished or imperfect, He added to the natural substance of man the gifts of His grace. In particular, He formed him in a supernatural manner in His image and spirit, and He caused him to come forth all at once complete and divinely complete—in fact, he who, because of his natural facility, could receive in character and aptitude the form either of an animal, demon, or angel, is given the form of God and in whom God places an image of Himself that is supernatural and very close to His own, in order that it, like us who are in Him, would always preserve the form if our first father did not lose it.

"But man lost it when he transgressed the law of God and he was immediately deprived of this divine perfection with which he was endowed. Once deprived, his fate did not wish that he remain naked, but, like the exchange between Glaucus and Diomedes, who unequally exchanged their arms, he was both dressed and undressed; undressed of God's supernatural form and spirit, and dressed with the error and the misery, with the Devil's garment of form and spirit whose suggestion he had followed. In fact, since he had lost what he held of God because he was separated from Him, he, because he heard the Devil's voice, received into himself his spirit and his errors; consequently, God allows, in all justice, with this visible nourishment, by secret means and power, the Devil to put into man an image of himself, that is, an evil force very similar to himself. This force we call venom because the Devil is shown at times in the form of a serpent, at times like burning fire because he inflames and embraces us with an incredible ardor, and at other times with sin because this force consists entirely of trouble and disorder and it leads always to disorder. It has thousands of other names and all hardly sufficient to express to what degree it is evil. The best is to call it another devil because it possesses and brings together in itself all the characteristics of the Devil: pride, arrogance, envy, disdain of God, attachment to sensible goods, love of sensual pleasure, lies, anger, and deception, and everything which is vanity. This evil spirit, which followed the good which man previously had, in the form of the damage which it caused, imitated the good and the profit which the first had produced. Since the latter perfected man, not only in the person of Adam, but in all of us who were in him, and it was a general good which we possessed potentially and rightly, which each of us would really possess at birth, this poison did not only infect Adam but all his descendants in the root and seed of their origin and each of us when we are born, evil is born at the same time and is attached to us. Such is the reason why we are born infected and sinners, as I said at the beginning. As this good spirit made men similar to God, so this evil and sin added to our substance and, being born with it, conforms to it and gives birth to it, although in human form, with the Devil's character and veritably serpentine and immediately hostile and culpable toward God, daughter of anger and of the demon, and condemned to hell.

"Besides all that has been said, this evil poison possesses other properties which I am now going to expose; this will help us greatly in what follows. First of all, between the two things which

BOOK I

I spoke of, one being the substance of both body and soul and the other this poison and evil spirit, there is the following difference relating to our purpose. In itself the substance of body and soul is good; it is God's work, and if we refer the thing to its principle, we hold it from God alone. In fact, the soul, He Himself created it and the body; when He made it at the beginning from a bit of mud, He was its sole creator. Similarly, when He produced man from this first body and gradually as time passed the body comes forth in each of us who is born, He is also the principal artisan of the work. On the contrary, this other spirit, poisoning and boastful, is in no manner God's work, and it does not engender itself in us through its own decision and will. It is entirely the Devil's work and that of the first man—the Devil's insofar as it inspired and persuaded the first man; man's who received it freely and is culpable. Thus, this is what Holy Scripture calls in us the 'old man' or the 'old Adam' because it is Adam's own work since it is not what Adam received of God but what he made in himself through his error and the Devil's action. We call it the 'old garment' because Adam, beyond the nature which God had placed in him, took on this form and caused us to be born dressed with it. We call it also 'the image of the terrestrial man' because this man which God made from the earth transformed himself through his own will. Such he did, he engendered himself in us, we resemble him in this, in it we are completely his sons because in it we are only the sons of Adam. In fact, by nature and the other natural properties with which we are born, we are only and primarily the sons of God as it is stated above. Such is the first point.

"The second point is that this evil spirit has another property. Its poison and the damage which it produces affect us in two ways, one potentially and the other in a formal and declared way. It is because they affect us potentially, in one way, that they then affect us formally. They touched us potentially when we did not yet have being in us, but our being was only potential in him who was the common father of us all, and it touched us, in an effective and real way, the day we were born with this conception. At first this evil appeared clearly only in Adam, but we knew that he puts his poison secretly in all those who were hidden in him. Later on, it is born openly and plainly in each of us. If we now take the core of an apricot or some other fruit where the future tree has its origin and root, its trunk, its leaves, flowers, and fruits, and if by means of some infusion we introduce into this core a strange color or flavor, we see and feel immediately this color and flavor. On the other hand, what is potentially enclosed is not yet seen, in the same way that this being is not yet visible; but we know that this color and flavor have already been introduced and they are included in the same way that everything which is included in the core then openly appears in the form of leaves, flowers, fruits. When they leave the core or the grain, in which they were hidden, they are discovered and shown in full light. Such is the manner that things of which we have been speaking occur.

"The third property, which follows from what we have just said, is that this force or spirit is born in us from the beginning, not because we have acquired or merited it voluntarily in our person, but because of what another has done and merited who had us inside Himself, like the ear of corn contains the grain. This is the way His will was held over ours and, loving as He loved, to be Himself infected in the way we described; we thus seemed to have wished the same thing for ourselves. Although at the beginning this evil or this spirit of evil was born in us without our having merited it, later on we wished to give ourselves to its force and let ourselves be led by its violence; it grew, established, and affirmed itself more and more as the consequence of our errors. Thus, after having been born evil and having followed the evil spirit with which we were born, we merited becoming worse, and we are so, in fact.

"Finally, in the fourth and final place, this seed and this poison which I so often said are born with the substance of our nature and spread there, insofar as it is in them they destroy us and lead us to our perdition, and they guide us all so sweetly toward an abyss of misery. The more they grow and fortify themselves, the more they weaken and debilitate, and to use this word, they annihilate. In fact, if it is true, as we have already said, that our nature is made of wax so that we can do with it as we would like, it remains a creature of God and in this sense a good creature; the evil character, temperament, and spirit which we induce there, although it receives them because of its capacity and facility, receives them with pain because it is like the work of a good artist, good in itself and given to what is best. As the termite destroys the piece of wood, similarly our nature has in vain adapted itself to this malice or evil spirit; being absorbed in it, it is almost entirely destroyed. In fact, established in its core and growing continually, it places disorder and trouble in all parts of man. It plunges our whole kingdom into tumult; it divides it against itself; it denounces the ties which attach and unite this whole which is our body and soul. It prevents the body from being submissive to the soul, and the soul from being submissive to God, which is a sure and brief path leading to the death of both body and soul. Since the body draws from the soul all its life, it lives even more as it is more submissive to the soul, and on the contrary, it separates itself from life as it removes itself from subjection and obedience. This detestable fury works to withdraw the body from this obedience and subjection; this occurs from the moment it unites with the body and becomes alive in it, making it liable and subject to evils and infirmities. As it grows with it, it weakens and debilitates it more and more, until that moment that it detaches and separates the body completely from the soul and reduces it to dust, and it remains forever dust and is nothing but dust.

"What it does in the body it does equally in the soul. It is from the soul that the body lives, and similarly the soul lives from God; the more this fury grows, the more it separates itself from God and continues to separate each day. But it cannot lay waste the soul entirely nor reduce it to nothing since it is like a metal which does not corrode; yet it destroys it to the point of letting it have only life necessary for the awareness of its death. This death is what the Scriptures call the 'second death,' the principal death, or what is the sole true death. This is something which we can show with reason, make it clear; but we must not say everything here. However, what is proper to this subject and what is proper to say is what St. James declares, putting into a single word all that I have said: 'Then when lust hath conceived, it bringeth forth sin: and sin, when it is finished, bringeth forth death' (Ep. 1:15). This is worthy of attention, that when God wished to put fear in man so that he would not let sin enter his heart, the pain which He menaced him with was the death which man produced and its fruit. This is a perfect and total death. As it seems that he did not wish to put His hands upon man nor to decree extraordinary punishments for him, but to let the punishment be born of man's will: that he find his own executioner in his choice.

"But I will not go further, but I will return to what I

proposed at the beginning: What is the nature of this last birth? I will say that it does not consist of the birth in us of another substance of body and soul because that would not be born a second time, but born differently, through which, as it has been said, we would not obtain the desired end. It consists in the absence of this evil spirit and of this primal force in our substance at the moment of its birth and in the presence of another spirit and force which is contrary and different from it. This force and spirit in which the second birth consists is called the 'new man' and 'new Adam' in Scriptures, and this previous other man who is opposed to the new is called the 'old man,' as we have said already. As the previous force is spread through both body and soul, so the good is spread throughout. As the former brings disorder, the latter brings order, and finally it sanctifies and leads us to the glorious and eternal life, while the other condemns us to a miserable and endless death. It is the reverse of the first: The latter is the light in the heart, the presence of God in the memory, justice in the will, temperance in the desires, guide for the senses, fruit and profitable merit to the hands and their works, life and peace for all men, the veritable image of God, which makes all men His sons. This spirit, its good effects, all its efficacy and virtue, the sacred writers speak of under diverse names and say much in many places; for instance, St. Paul says, writing to the Galatians, 'But the fruit of the Spirit is love, joy, peace, long-suffering, gentleness, goodness, faith, meekness and temperance': (5:22–23). Similarly to the Colossians, 'Seeing that ye have put off the old man with his deeds and have put on the new man, which is renewed in knowledge of the image of him that created him' (3:9–10). What is the second birth of men but to be clothed in this spirit and to be born not with another being and substance, but to acquire different traits and characteristics and to be born with a breath different from the first? I had only promised to say what this birth meant, but in speaking as I have done I explained not only what this birth is, but even what is born and the nature of the spirit which is born in us the first as well as the second time. We must now continue, say what God has wrought and the means which He used so that we could be born in this second way. With this explanation we will have almost entirely ended what belongs to this subject."

Marcelo was now still and began to prepare himself so as to

BOOK I

begin again to speak. But Juliano, who from the beginning had listened attentively and who had often shown his surprise by his attitudes and gestures, intervened and said to him:

"These things which you are now expressing, Marcelo, you are not drawing from yourself and you are not the first to express them. These are strewn and diffused in the divine books, and in the holy Fathers of the Church in divers places. But among those whom I saw and heard, you are the first to have united them with others that correspond to them, to have assembled them, given them their proper place, a structure, and an order, and to have made of them one body and one fabric. If it is true that each of these things, when we read them in books or wherever they are, enlightens and instructs us, I do not know how to describe the effect of grouping and arranging them as you have just now done, so that they fill the soul with light and admiration and seem to open it, like a new door, to knowledge. I don't know what others think; from my point of view I will affirm that when I see that gathering of ideas and this very close harmony of the divine plan which you have been speaking of, and have not finished exposing, when I see what you have explained up to this point, I believe I see in the holy books many things which, I will not say, I was not knowledgeable of, but rather that I had not noticed before today and had passed over too quickly. It seems to me even—I don't know if I am mistaken—that this single mystery, grouped in this way and well understood, suffices to clarify many errors which in this sad time are upon the Church and to chase away the darkness which they cause. In fact, these single words which you have said, and without going further into them already show me and make clear to me how this new spirit, in which is our second birth, and new birth, is something introduced into our soul which it transforms and renews, similar to its contrary, the first birth, which lives in it and infects it. It is not an imaginary affair, an external appearance, as is said by those who speak foolishly today. Because if it were, there would be no new birth since, in all truth, nothing new would be introduced into our substance which conserved, on the contrary, its first old age. I see also this new spirit and new creature are things which receive growth by the grace of God and by the industry and merits of good actions which are born in them, while its contrary, which makes us live in Him and conform to Him, grows much more every day and acquires ever greater strength as our unworthiness grows. I see that this spirit grows by working, I mean that the actions we take under its impetus provoke its own growth and that they are its proper food and nourishment; similarly, our sins feed and cause growth for this same evil spirit who impels us toward sin."

"Indubitably," replied Marcelo, "because this new generation and God's plan in this regard—if we organize them into a whole, if we explain and comprehend them well—destroy in its principal source the Lutheran error and show clearly its falsity. Once we have understood that, we find clear and comprehensible many sacred texts which appear confused and obscure. If I possessed the talent and necessary knowledge for this and if God gave me the leisure and favor which I asked of Him, perhaps I would undertake to serve the Church in this question and explain this mystery, applying it to our struggle with the heretics, freeing the truth through the light of this light. In my opinion, it would be a very profitable work. With the means that I have I will not abandon the idea, but will give myself to it at the right time."

"When is there not a time for a concern of this kind?" asked Juliano.

"All times are good," replied Marcelo, "but everything does not depend upon me and I do not belong to all times. You see all the concerns I have and the great weakness of my health."

"As if we didn't know," said Sabino, coming to Juliano's help, "that with all your concerns, with your poor health, you find time for other writings which are not less difficult and of less use."

"These things are," replied Marcelo, "quantitatively numerous, but each is separately brief. On the contrary, here we are dealing with a long writing, tightly organized and very serious. Once begun, we couldn't abandon it before its completion. I was hoping for the end of the conflicts and rivalries in and among the Schools in order to have a little tranquility and peace. If it pleases God to use me for this task, His goodness will grant it to me."

"He will grant it," both Juliano and Sabino replied in one voice.

"Nevertheless, our readings of Scripture must happen before anything else. May it happen so," said Marcelo, "but that will be in due time; now let us return to what we have begun."

The two became quiet and attentive. Marcelo began to speak again.

BOOK I

"We have explained how men are born a second time, the reason and necessity for this birth, and what constitutes it. It now remains to be said how God acts, which is to say, what He does so that men are born a second time, which is short and long at the same time. Short because it suffices to say that He has made another man, who is the Christ man, in order to engender us a second time, as the first man engendered us the first time; and we said that everything that exists, exists in this regard. Long because to make this comprehensible and well known we must explain what God has put into the Christ so that He truly is understood to be our new Father and we also understand the manner by which He engenders us. Now these first and second points cannot be briefly explained. Let us begin with the first point. I will say that God wished in His infinite goodness to give men a new birth since the first was lost through their fault. As it is His character to lead things to their end with sweetness and gentleness, by the means which their nature requires and imposes, when He wished again to make new sons, He made Him, in a fitting way, a new Father from which they were born. To do it meant to place in Him all that is necessary and all that is fitting to be a universal Father. In the first place, since He should be Father of men, He decided that He would be of the same lineage and of the same substance; on the other hand, our whole substance was spoiled and infected in the person of our first father. For the same reason, if the second Father took him from the first, it would seem as if He made Him similarly spoiled; if He took Him, in this manner, we would not be able to be reborn in Him pure and stainless as God wished for our second birth. Facing this difficulty, God's infinite wisdom, which when facing the greatest difficulties shines forth even more, found a way so that the second Son was a man of Adam's lineage and nevertheless was not born with the evil and imperfection which afflicted us from our birth in Adam. He formed Him of the same substance and lineage as that of Adam, but not like the other men, formed by Adam's hands and action, which spoil and deteriorate all things. He formed Him with His own hands and with the single virtue of His spirit in the sovereign Virgin's pure entrails, daughter of Adam. From her very holy blood and substance which she gave without vicious passion and with an ardent love of charity, He drew forth the second Adam, universal Father of our substance and completely strange to our fault, but similar

131

to a virgin honeycomb made of pure matter fashioned by heaven's hands or from the flower of virginity and purity. Such is the first point.

"In addition to this, God pursued His work since it is proper that all the qualities which are in the flower and the fruit are, at first, in the seed from where they are born; for what should be the stem of this new and supernatural descent? He established and placed in abundance, in an infinite way, all the good from which are reborn all those called to be born in Him: grace, justice, celestial spirit, charity, and knowledge, with all the other gifts of the Holy Spirit; and He established them as principles endowed with virtue and efficacy so that they may be born from Him in the others; they are transmitted to their descendants and are goods capable of producing from themselves other goods. As in the principle are found not only qualities of those which are born of Him, but also those which are born before they themselves are born, they are in the principle potentially. Consequently, it is clear that those which are born from this first Father were at first placed in Him in principle and in the form of a seed by a secret and divine virtue. This is what God did. We must understand that by a manner of spiritual and ineffable alliance God united all the members with Christ as man and brought them all together in Him. Those even who, each in his time, were existing by themselves were to be reborn and to live in justice, and those who after the resurrection of the body—just, glorious, and deified throughout, distinct in person—will be one spirit as much among themselves as with Christ. We all will be one Christ; we even, not in actual form, but in original virtuality, have been in Him before having been reborn through God's action and will. For it pleases Him to unite us secretly and spiritually to the one who was to be our beginning, our source, to be so in truth and that we proceed from Him by not being born of the substance of human nature, but by being born again according to a new life in the spirit and justice of His grace. In addition, this is something that the condition of father demands, and moreover, this flows necessarily from what we have previously said. In fact, if God has placed in Christ the essential grace and spirit to the highest and most eminent degree to engender in Him the new life and spirit of all beings, in the same way He put all of us in Him. It is comparable to fire: It possesses heat to the highest degree and is at the same time the source of all that is warm; in it resides everything it can be, even before it was, like in the source and in the principle.

"But to make things clear it will be good to prove them by the words and witnesses of the Holy Spirit. St. Paul, moved by the Holy Spirit, writes in the letter to the Ephesians (1:10) what I have already alleged: that 'he might gather together in one all things in Christ.' The word here in the Greek text belongs properly to the language of numbers and designates what is done when several different qualities are reduced to one. It is what we call in Castilian 'to add up to.' In the total are found all the qualities not separated as they previously were, but brought together in the total. St. Paul means that God 'has united all things in Christ' or that the Christ is like the total of everything. Consequently, in Him everything is placed and assembled by God secretly and spiritually according to the manner and being in which everything can be reformed and reengendered again, like the effect is joined to the cause before coming forth from it and the branch is in the root which is its principle. In fact, this is the conclusion we draw from St. Paul when he says 'that if one died for all, then were all dead' (2 Cor. 5:14); it is upon this evident reality that it rests and is supported by this union of which we have spoken. His death makes us die since we are all in Him in the form which I have stated. This is even more clearly concluded in what St. Paul writes to the Romans (6:6): 'Knowing this, that our old man is crucified with him.' If he were crucified with Him he was surely in Him, not by touching His person, since the Christ was always free of sin and age, but because a secret virtue reunited in His person our own persons. This same union and alliance are the reason which makes him write elsewhere that Christ 'bares our sins in his body and that he nailed them on the wood of the cross' (1 Peter 2:24). The phrase of St. Paul to the Ephesians that God 'hath raised us up together and made us sit together in heavenly places in Christ Jesus' (Eph. 2:6) even before the general resurrection and glorification; this is written and spoken of with great truth because of this union. Isaiah says that 'God put in Christ all our sins' (Isa. 53:5–6) and that 'his wounds saved us all.'* Christ

---

*The text reads: "But he was wounded for our transgressions, he was bruised for our iniquities: the chastisement of our peace was upon him; and with his stripes we were healed.

Himself while He suffered on the cross said in a high and plaintive voice, 'My God, my God, why have you forsaken me? Why art thou so far from helping me, and from the words of my roaring?' (Matt 27:46; Ps. 22:1). Before His Passion David had prophesied it. In fact, how true would this be if Christ did not suffer in person for all of us and consequently we were united in Him by a secret force, like children are in the father and parts are in the head? The Prophet, does he not tell us 'that he carries the realm upon his shoulders' (Isa. 9:6)? Jesus explains it when in the parable of the lost sheep He says, to gather them He put them upon His shoulders. Thus His empire is His—those who are submitted to his commandment, those whom He bears upon himself—because to regenerate and save them He has to unite them first to Himself. This is what St. Augustine says clearly concerning Psalm 22, and he says it in this way: 'Why does he say it, if it is not because we are also in him?' (Enarrat. in Ps. 21:5, 2:3; P. L. 36:172). We need no more arguments when truth shines so clearly. Let us listen to what Christ says in the sermon of the Last Supper: 'At that day ye shall know that I am in my Father and ye in me, and I in you' (John 14:20). Thus God made Christ the Father of this new lineage of men and to make Him a father He placed in Him all that belongs to a father, a conformity of nature with those who are born from Him, all the goods which they must possess, those who could be born in this way, and in particular those who should thus be born, enclosed and united to Him like to their source and origin.

"But now that we have said how God has put all the faculties and qualities of a Father in Christ, let us pass to what we still have to say and to what we have promised to say, which is how this Father has engendered us. When the form of this generation will be explained we will see and know better the secret mystery of this union, and by explaining how we are born of Christ we will see clearly how it is that we were at first in Him. But before undertaking this explanation it is fitting to ascend a little higher through the spirit and to recall and place before us the understanding of what we have already said of the evil spirit with which we are born at our first birth and how it is communicated to us, at first, potentially and how we find it embodied in our principle, and then expressed in reality, coming forth from us and made clear, when we begin to exist in ourselves. We must understand that when this second Father comes to destroy the evils which the first had caused He follows the path made by the other to injure us and He advances on the same road to do good for us. Indeed! I say that in this way Christ has reengendered us and raised us to Himself. We find ourselves united to Him, then He engenders us, renews each one in Himself and in reality.

"Let us speak of the first point. Adam put in our nature the spirit of sin and disorder by placing the disorder in himself and opening his heart to the serpent's venom, introducing it into himself and into us. From this moment, everyone who came from him was infected and evil in the form which is ourselves. Christ our joyous Father caused our life to begin in justice, forming at first in Himself what must be born in us. He put into the grain the quality which He wanted to find in the corn; in this same way, we possess everything, united in Him in the form which we have already spoken of, that He made in Himself. In all that depends upon Him, He began to make us and raise us again potentially so that He would engender us later in effective reality. Since our birth and appearance were not a first appearance but a birth after a birth, and after a birth which was lost and spoiled, it was necessary to do not only what was necessary to give us a good spirit and life, but even to suffer to free us from the evil spirit with which we entered our first life. As a master who takes a student who is already badly educated, we say that he has two tasks, those of uprooting evil and implanting the good. In the same way Christ, our good and master, made two things in Himself so that, made in Him, they were made in us who are in Him, the one to destroy our evil spirit, the other to produce our good spirit. To kill sin and destroy the evil and disorder of our first beginning, He died in the person of all of us; in Him we have all received death by the fact that we are in Him, and we find ourselves dead in our Father and dead so as never again to revive in this form of being and life. Because in this form of suffering life, which bears the image and representation of sin, Christ, our Father and head, will never again live as the Apostle St. Paul says, 'For in that he died, he died unto sin once, but in that he liveth, he liveth unto God' (Rom. 6:10). With this first death of sin and of the old man which had taken place in a general and original way for the others is born the force of argument which St. Paul used writing to the Romans: 'What shall we say then? Shall we continue in sin, that grace may abound? God forbid. How shall we, that are dead to sin, live any longer therein?' (6:1–2). He goes on to explain, 'Knowing this, that our old man is crucified with him, that the body of sin might be destroyed, that henceforth we should not serve sin' (6:6). This says again to them that when Christ died unto their suffering life, which has the form of sin, everything died in Him which belongs to this life. Since they died in Him because the Christ was dead and did not again take a similar life, if they are in Him and if what took place in Him similarly took place in them, it is completely impossible that they should want to become again what they had ceased to be forever by the fact that they were in Christ. The same thing can be found in what Paul says in Romans: 'Wherefore my brethren, ye also are become dead to the law by the body of Christ' (7:4). A few lines further, 'For what the law could not do, in that it was weak through the flesh, God sending his own Son in the likeness of sinful flesh, and for sin, condemned sin in the flesh' (8:3). In fact, as we have already said and as we should repeat often, in order to be better understood, Christ underwent death and accepted the sacrifice which He Himself made, not as a particular person, but as a person who represented mankind and its antiquity, in particular, all those who benefited from this second birth and that secret union of the spirit which He placed in Him and upon His shoulders. Thus, what He did in Himself, He achieved in all of us.

"That Christ mounted the cross like a public person in the manner that I have already described is something already proven, but it is even better proven by what Christ did and wanted us to comprehend in the sacrament of His body which, close to death, He consecrated under the species of bread and wine. Taking the bread and giving it to His disciples, He said these words (Matt. 26:29): 'Take, eat; this is my body, which will be given over to you.' He wished to make clearly understood that His body was truly under the two species, that it was there under the form that He had offered Himself upon the cross, that these same species of bread and wine manifested and represented the form under which He was going to offer Himself. In the same way that the bread is a body composed of many bodies, that is, of many grains which have lost their original form under the action of water and fire and which form a bread, in the same way our 'bread of life' is added to our nature by a secret force of love and spirit and becomes like a single body with itself and with us all—with itself in full reality and with others potentially—since it is not as an isolated person but as a principle which contained them all that He mounted the cross. In the same manner He ascended the cross narrowly embracing us; He embodied Himself in this relationship so that this meaning, although veiled to our eyes, illuminated continuously our heart and told us that we were contained in Christ, not in an arbitrary manner, but in the same way He mounted the cross, carrying us in Him and joined with us by a spiritual union, like the bread which contained the grain was a mixture made of several grains. In this way these singular and similar quotations say two things at the same time: the first, that 'this' which appears as bread 'is my body which will be given over to you'; the second, that similar to the bread which seems to be here, 'is my body which is here and which will be handed over to death for you.' It is the same which the young saint Isaac revealed, who did not go to the sacrifice bearing nothing, but whose shoulders were burdened with wood and who was to be burned with it (Gen. 22:6). It is known that in the secret language of Scripture dry wood is the picture of sin. Let us recall the scapegoats which the priests sacrificed in expiation of sins and which were a clear image of Christ's sacrifice. The people all together put their hands upon their heads to show that in this sacrifice our Father and head carried us all in Him. But why speak of goats? If we seek images of this truth, there are none more alive and exact than the high priest of the ancient law, dressed in pontifical vestments in order to perform the sacrifice. In fact, as St. Jerome says (Ep. 64, Ad Fabiolam), or, in truth, as the Holy Spirit explains it in the book of wisdom (18:24), these pontifical vestments—their form, their elements, and all their colors and characteristics—were like a representation of the universality of things. The high priest so dressed was a complete universe, and as he wished to treat with God in the name of all, he carried them all upon his shoulders. In the same manner, Christ, the true high priest, whom every former high priest had preceded as an image, when He mounted the cross, sacrificing Himself for us, was dressed with our bodies and souls in the form we have described. Sacrificing Himself, and us in Him, He brought to an end, in this way, our ancient infirmity.

"We have said what Christ did to uproot in us our first evil spirit. Let us now say what He did to produce in us the new man and good spirit, that is, after we died to the evil life, to give us the good life and cause our second generation. Because of His divinity and because, according to the laws of justice, He was not obligated to die, since His human nature was innocent from birth, Christ could not remain dead, and as St. Peter (Acts 2:24) says, it was not possible that He was held in the pains of the tomb. Thus, He, on the third day, came again to life, but not in suffering flesh which would have the appearance of sin and which was subject to pain, as if He had sinned—because this died in Christ not to be revived ever again—but in an incorruptible and glorious body as only engendered by God's hands. In fact, at the time of His birth in the flesh, born of the Virgin, God His Father, and no man, intervened; He was born free of sin, but since He was born from a suffering and mortal mother, He was born apt to suffer and die, which belonged to the origins of His birth and to each element of it. Indeed, it was the same for His resurrection, which Holy Scripture also calls birth or generation. No human being intervened to be His father or mother, but God alone, by Himself, and without any intermediary. He came forth whole from God's hand, not only free of sin, but of all the consequences of sin; free from suffering and death and, at the same time, endowed with splendor and glory. Since this body was reengendered by God alone, it was alive again with God's traits and qualities to the degree that they are possible for a body. Thus, God took pleasure in this act as an act which belonged only to Him; as the Psalmist says, 'this day have I begotten thee' (2:7).

"We now say that since He laid to rest the old man, He died for us by representing us, because by a secret mystery He held us in Himself as our Father and head; for the same reason, when He came to life again, our life was reborn with Him. What I call life in this moment is conformity to justice and to spirit. It comprehends not only the beginning of justice, when the sinner begins to become just, but the growth of justice itself, with its march toward perfection, until man reaches the immortality of the body and full freedom from sin. In fact, when Christ came to life again, by this very fact all this process began in us which we found in Him, as in our principle. It is one and the same thing which St. Paul expresses in a brief and significant way when he says (Rom. 4:24), 'Who was delivered for our offenses, and was raised for our justification.' He could say by extending it further: He took us into Himself and He died as sinner, so that the sinners died in Him and He came to an eternally just, immortal, and glorious life so that we could come to life in Him in justice, glory, and immortality. But perhaps are we not born again with Christ? Let us listen to the Apostle (Eph. 2:5–6): 'God hath quickened us together with Christ and hath raised us up together and made us sit together in heavenly places in Christ Jesus.' Thus, what Christ did in Himself and in us since we were in Him was what I have said. We need not conclude that this suffices to cause us to be reborn in reality and in ourselves, to render us engendered anew, dead to the old sins and alive to the spirit of heaven and justice. We begin only to be reborn, to be reborn again in reality. This was like the first foundation of another building. To express it more properly, from the noble fruit of justice and immortality which appeared among us, which grew, increased, pierced the heavens, these were the first germs and roots. When Adam sinned we all sinned in him and received a spirit of poison and death. However, in order that the sin infects us and penetrates us, we must be born from Adam by natural generation. Similarly, in order that the spirit of fault dies really in us, and the spirit of grace and justice lives in us, this seed, foundation, and principle do not suffice. On the other hand, what has been made in us through the person of Christ, without being concerned with our person, does not suffice to make us just and saved, as those who stray from the truth claim today. We must be really born in Christ for this birth to be effective, so that it flows in our person and is established there, that same birth which had already begun in our origins. To use again the same comparison, we see that the ear of corn is not necessarily in the grain as it will be later; to become what it is and acquire all its characteristics and aspects it needs water and sun to come forth from the grain and be born. Similarly, we will not begin to be such as we are in Christ until we are really born in Christ.

"We will perhaps ask, how will we be born, or what will be the form of this generation? Should we return to our mother's womb, asks Nicodemus (John 3:4), marveling at this new doctrine, or return to the earth or even consumed by fire be reborn from our ashes like the phoenix? If this new birth is to be born in flesh and bones, it would follow one of these ways. Since it is a question of birth in the spirit, this is done in the spirit and by a secret virtue. 'That which is born of the flesh is flesh; that which is born of the Spirit is spirit' (John 3:6), Christ says. Thus, what is spirit must be born by the means and potentiality of the spirit which effects this generation. By His spirit Christ realizes effectively in us what we begin to be in Him and which He does in Himself for us, that is, 'He destroys our sin' and chases it from the soul; this poisoned fire which the serpent has blown into our flesh and which incites us to sin, He redeems and contains so that He will completely kill it in the last days. He also adds a germ of His life, that is, a grain of His spirit and grace which, enclosed in our soul and cultivated as it must be, increases progressively, takes strength, and increases until, as St. Paul says, it attains the size of a 'perfect man' (Eph. 4:13). When Christ puts this in us we are born of Christ in a true and real way. However, a question and a doubt come forth immediately. Has Christ put this in all men? Has He put it at all ages and in all times? When and in whom does He put it? It is certain that He doesn't put it in everyone, but only in those who are born from Him. Those who are baptized are born from Him, and in this sacrament this generation is operative and effective. When the visible water touches the body, and where the virtue of the invisible Christ acts in secret, the new Adam is born, while the old dies and is buried. In this as in all things God has followed the direct and simple path of His divinity.

"In fact, in the manner that fire inflames wood, and the wood becomes the illuminated fire, we at first must bring fire near to the wood, and in the nearness the wood becomes like the fire through the dryness and heat which it receives; then this similarity grows to the desired point, and the fire penetrates the wood and gives it its form. In a similar manner, Christ puts and introduces in us, among the treasures of life and goods which He joined through His death and resurrection, the images suitable for us; in order that we are born in Christ, that is, as His children, He wished that a representation of His death and new life become effected in us, and that in this way we become similar to Him. We received from Him, being similar to Him, what responds to His death and life. To His death corresponds the suppression and the death of sin, and to His resurrection the life of grace. To enter into the water, to plunge into it, is in some way to find ourselves and to live there entombed as the Christ died and was put in a tomb, as St. Paul says (Rom. 6:4): 'Therefore we are buried with

BOOK I

Him by baptism.' In the same way, coming out of the water is like coming alive out of the sepulcher. To this figure the truth corresponds: Becoming similar to Christ in this way, if we are receptive and a well-disposed subject, we immediately receive the good spirit, the Christ is born in us, and the sin, which by His death He had destroyed in its root and in general, He had destroyed in particular in each of us who died in the sacred water. The life of everyone, which by His life He resurrected, He puts in each of us, in particular when leaving the water they seem to be resurrected. Thus, there is image and truth: What appears outside is an image of life and death; but what happens in secret is the true life of grace and the true death of sin. If you desire to know, since this figure of death could wear many other aspects, why among all God chose water, I like very much what the glorious martyr St. Cyprian said (Sermon on Baptism). The sin which dies in this image of death is a sin whose nature and character are those of a poisoned being, like one born from the bite and breath of a serpent. We know that the serpent's venom is lost in the water, that the snake—if it enters the water—abandons its venom. Thus, we die in the water so that the venom of our fault may die there. Nature causes the venom to die in the water. All this applies to the death of sin. About life we must say that if sin dies completely, the life which is then given us is however not entirely perfect; I mean that the new man does not live immediately in us in his perfection, but as the character of the second birth requires: He lives as a feeble and tender child. In fact, Christ does not put immediately in us all the being of the new life which was resurrected with Him; He only puts, as we have said, a grain of this life and a small germ of His spirit and grace, small but very apt to live, to progress, to chase from the soul the remains of the old man, its enemy, to spread with force and completely dominate us and make us perfectly good and happy. How marvelous are God's wisdom and the grandeur with which He disposes of the things which He makes, uniting them all and harmonizing them in such a surprising way! In philosophy we are used to saying that as a thing is born, so it grows and develops. Thus, God acts in the new man, through this grain of spirit and grace which is the germ of our second and new life. In fact, in the same way that He began in our soul when baptism made us like Christ, similarly, the more we become similar to Him, the more He grows and progresses, even though in a different way. To receive the principle of this life of grace, we resembled Him in spirit, since in reality we could not be like Him before receiving this life. To make it grow, we must imitate Him by our deeds and works.

"On this point as on all the others we have discussed, this new man and spirit is the balanced contrast to the old, perverse spirit. In fact, in the same way, the latter is distinguished from our substance in that our substance is God's creation and the other has nothing of God but is entirely the creation of the demon and of man. Similarly, Adam, the first father, in obeying the demon caused his fall and that of those in him. Likewise, Christ, our second Father, in obeying God suffered to heal those who were in Him. As our first father ended life and caused the death which he merited by his evil conduct, so our second Father by His divine patience gave death to death and rendered life to life. Although the former transgressed, we didn't actually wish it, but, being in him as in our father, we were supposed to have wished it. Similarly, Christ suffered and redeemed us, and this He did without our will but not without what was potentially our will; this we know by what has been said. In the same way, this venom has tainted and infected us in two ways: one, in general and potentially when we were all in Adam; the other, particularly and in effective reality when we begin to live in ourselves after being brought forth by this virtue and grace of Christ, as we also explained above. He ennobled us at first generally and in common, since we were supposed to find ourselves in Him because He was our Father; and in fact in each one individually, since each begins to live in Christ after being born through baptism. When we were born we fell into corruption, this great evil, without having earned it ourselves but in the patriarch that contained us. We came out guilty from our mother's womb though we had committed no fault before leaving it. Even so, when we were reborn in Christ, the spirit which came from Him and begins to live in us is not the work nor the compensation of our merits. In the same way, this venom, by being born at first in us, without our wishing it personally, when we want to use it, obey it, and abandon ourselves to its evil tendencies and inclinations, augment and aggravate it through the malice of our own actions and deeds, it having penetrated into the core of our soul without any of us having opened the door for it willingly, guided by us, it invaded, tyrannized, and in a certain way transformed in itself, our soul. This life and spirit which we have from Christ and which, without our merit, was given to us from Him, we do not resist, and if we give ourselves to its power, we increase and fortify ourselves. By what grows from us and from the power, we merit by seeing it grow in us. Since the acts born from the evil spirit were evil in themselves and grew, increased, and fortified this same spirit from where they were born, in a similar way we are guided and encouraged by the fact that this life which we hold from Christ is good in itself, pleasant and beautiful in God's eyes, and merits that the spirit from where it draws its source attain a higher degree of good and power.

"Thus, the venom introduced in man remains there; it spreads little by little in him and contaminates and corrupts him to the point that it leads him to a perpetual death. But if it lasts in us, health becomes stronger and greater each day and makes us completely healthy. So that if we follow the impulse of the spirit with which we are born and which, put in our souls, excites and brings them to act in conformity with what it is at the origin of their birth, which is Christ, the more we act so, the more we are similar to Him. Thus, as we approach Him, He approaches us and we have the advantage that He penetrates more and more in us because to the first spirit there is added another quantity of spirit, a great degree is added to the first; the germ of life which He planted grows in our souls, becomes greater and stronger, and reveals more of its virtue. Because if we act according to God's impulse and if we go this route with well-directed steps, we will merit being sons of God, for in reality we are. And we who were born in baptism were made similar to Christ by His grace, before being so by our acts, we who, being now just, have acted justly, making us similar to Him through our acts, we progress with justice in the resemblance to His being. The same spirit which impels and pushes us to do good works, grows, thanks to their merit, becomes strong, progresses and dominates us, gives us more health and life, and doesn't rest until in the final days it gives us perfection and glory, having raised us from dust."

Having said this Marcelo was quiet for a moment and then said:

"I explained how we are born from Christ, the necessity of being born from Him, the profit and mystery of this birth, and the abyss of secrets contained in the Holy Scriptures on the subject of this generation and of this divine parenthood. I explained the little which my inadequacy could achieve, considering the time, and the occasion, as well as the nature of things which are delicate and obscure. Now, leaving these thorns and brambles for a more open terrain, I say that here we see the reason Isaiah named Christ the Father and said of Him that He is 'the Everlasting Father': He wanted to designate the new generation of man and the men engendered in this manner, and the long, indefinite duration which will benefit this generation. In fact, the present age, which in comparison to the one Isaiah calls the age to come, is called the first age, that is the life of those who are born of Adam, began with Adam, must end and finish with the life of Adam's last descendants and, certainly, this life will not endure in any of them more than Adam endures in the present life. But the second age begins with Abel and extends through time, and when time reaches its end it will grow stronger and will last forever. And it is called 'future age' although it is already present among many as it was also when the Prophet so named it, because the other mortal age had already begun. It is called 'age' because it is a world apart, yet similar to this other old visible world and different from it. Similarly, God, before making man, made the heavens, the earth, and the other elements; at the time of the creation of the second and new man, in order that everything be new for him, He made in the Church His heavens and earth and filled the earth with fruits and the heavens with stars and lights. What He did in the visible world, the same He did again in the new invisible world, following the same path in both cases, as the divine singer David noted in a psalm which is of very great beauty and elegance (Ps. 104). He uses the same words and the same voice to tell, by praising God, the creation and the government of these two worlds, and by saying what is seen he makes understandable what is hidden, as St. Augustine has shown (Enarrat. in Ps. 103; P.L. 37: 1336) with all his talent and his spiritual sense.

"St. Augustine says 'that God unfolded the heavens like one unfolds a tent, that He covered the roof with waters, that He ordered the clouds and that He roamed among them flying on wings of air accompanied by thunder, lightning and storm.' Here we see the heavens, the clouds which are condensed water, placed in the air which we call sky. We hear the thunder at times; we feel the wind which flies and billows and the flash of lightning which wounds our eyes. Below in the new world and in the Church, in the same way that the heavens are the apostles, the sacred doctors, and the other saints, elevated in virtue and who infuse virtue; the doctrine which they teach is the clouds which they direct toward us and transform into rain. Upon the latter God moves, flying, and with it comes the breath of His spirit, the flash of His light, and the crash of His thunder which deafens our senses. Speaking of God, the Psalmist says, 'Who laid the foundation of the earth that it should not be removed forever' (Ps. 104:5). And as it had, at first, been plunged into the sea, 'Thou coveredst it with the deep as with a garment; the waters stood above the mountains. At thy rebuke they fled, at the voice of thy thunder they hastened away.' As soon as they parted 'the earth revealed its image, damp in the valleys and sovereign in the heights.'* Below, the firm and massive body of the Church, which occupied the whole circumference of the earth, had been established by the hand of God on the unchanging foundation of Christ, where it will rest with an eternal solidity. At the beginning it had been covered and submerged by the Gentile nations, and this great tempestuous sea of tyrants and idols had almost engulfed it. But God caused it to arise toward the light by the power of His word, and He separated from it the bitterness and violence of waves, and He crushed them all into the thinness of fine sand which made the form and harmony of the Church appear, elevated in the bishops and spiritual masters and humble in the humbler faithful laity. As David said, 'They went up upon the heights and they appeared in the depths of the valleys.'

" 'There as here,' as the same psalm says, 'God brings forth Cymes from the pools of water,'† great spirits which between two mountain chains, without going to the extremes, follow directly the simple path toward truth; 'in them the (spiritual) birds bathe' and, placed close to them, they sing sweetly in the orchards of virtue which grow there. But not only the birds bathe here. The other faithful who are more earthly and less spiritual do not go

---

*They go up by the mountains; they go down by the valleys unto the place, the place thou hast founded for them."

†These and the following texts are interpretations of Psalm 104, which is a vital text for an understanding of the aesthetic dimension of the creation.

just to bathe there, but 'they drink and quench their thirst there.'
Upon the Church as upon the world He 'sends the rains' of
spiritual goods from the sky. They fall at first 'upon the heights,'
then they form the streams which descend from them and which
'water the fields.' They make the hay grow for the ignorant as
well as for the beasts; and for those who live with more reason
'they give nourishment. The wheat which gives strength, the oil
which gives light, and the wine which gives joy' and all the gifts of
the spirit flower because of this rain. Because of it the sterile
deserts are covered with religious 'beech and cedar trees.' These
same cedars are covered with green and with fruit, and they offer
the rest of a sweet and protecting nest 'to those who have fled' to
them, fleeing from the world. God is not content to furnish a nest
to those who flee; to each kind of faithful He has arranged 'his
proper retreat,' and as upon earth the rocks are made for the goats
and 'the rabbits have their burrows in the rocks,' it is the same in
the Church. In it the 'moon' shines and the sun of justice 'shines,'
and 'it rises and sets in turn,' as much the one as the other. It also
has its 'nights,' with hard and cruel times, where the bloody
'violence' 'from savage enemies show themselves, bellowing and
applying their savagery.' But after the nights it knows also the
dawn which 'then shines,' 'the malice is hidden' before the light,
reason and virtue become resplendent.

" 'How great are your grandeurs, O Lord!' If 'you fill us with
admiration by this order,' corporal and 'visible,' you inspire us by
it even more by the spiritual and invisible order. There another
'ocean' is no longer lacking and its magnitude no longer short, its
depth no longer narrow as those which surround the earth, and
whose waters, although faithful, remain carnal and bitter, and
their violent desires agitate storms. 'It engenders innumerable
fish,' and the infernal 'leviathan' goes there. In it and across it
'travel a thousand boats,' a thousand people are hastened from the
world and enclosed in the boat of their secret and holy plan. But
happy are those who reach port safe and sound. 'All,' Lord, 'live
by the liberality of your largesse.' However, as in the world, in the
Church, also, you hide and you shorten your hand when it seems
good to you, and, as soon as your love and spirit fail him, the soul
'again becomes earth.' But, if you let us fall so that we know
ourselves, so that we praise and celebrate you, then 'you restore
us.' Thus you cause growth, you govern and perfect your Church

to lead it to its final goal where after the entire consumption of the old metal you will show it in its pure unity, resplendent and with a truly perfect newness. When will this happy and loving time come which will no longer be time but changeless eternity! When will it come, that the 'arrogant pride of the mountains will tremble and be crushed and will disappear in smoke,' and under the act of your majesty, all the power, all the carnal appetites, and all mortal wisdom? At the same time, you will enchain tyranny in the abyss, and the kingdom of the new earth will belong to yours. They 'then will not cease to sing your praises and you will find it agreeable to be praised in this manner.' They will live with you and you with them, giving them a very rich and sweet life. They will be kings, you will be king of kings. You will be in them, in all things, and you will reign forever."

This said, Marcelo was quiet. Sabino then said:

"The psalm with which you have ended, Marcelo, your friend has also put into verse and so as not to break your thread I do not want to recall it to you. But since you gave me this responsibility and you have forgotten it, I will say it myself, if you agree."

Marcelo and Juliano replied that it would be good and that he should immediately recite the psalm. Sabino, young, charming of soul and body, raised his eyes to the heavens and, inspired, recited in a harmonious voice:

"Praise, O my soul, God, what language would be capable of praising your greatness? Covered as you are with glory, beauty, and resplendent light.

"Unfolded above the heavens you set forth the waters; the clouds are your chariots, your winged horses are the winds.

"Your messages are a burning fire; they are thunder and storm, and the lands are held by your hand on everlasting foundations.

"At the beginning the seas covered the heights, but at the powerful sound of your voice they fled in terror.

"At once the heights of mountains and the depths of the valleys increased, and if the waters swell savagely, they do not overflow their limits.

They do not overflow the limits and boundaries which you have fixed for them and they do not inundate the earth. You reveal springs among the hills and the waters flow from the mountains.

"Here the deer and the wild animals come to quench their thirst; here the birds bathe and sing in the branches.

"With the rain you water the mountains and you satiate the plains. Thus you feed the animals with grain and innumerable foods for men.

"Thus the wheat is formed and the vine grows for our joy, the green olive shines in our eyes, and the bread gives courage.

"From this the woods, the trees, and the mighty cedars draw their sustenance, the birds make their nest; there the kite builds its dwelling.

"The rocks give shelter to the young deer and crevices to the rabbits. We owe you the light of the sun which is upon us and the sister lights of the moon which guide us.

"And time. You give darkness when the deer comes forth and the tiger whose cruel hunger asks food with his roaring.

"You awaken the dawn and together they return to their homes, while men free of all fear go to their occupations without concern.

"How noble and wise are your acts! Who will describe the immense sea, its vast abysses, and all the fish which it feeds, the ships which traverse it, and the frightful whale which stirs it? All await from you the substance of life because you do good immeasurably.

"We take if you give, your open hand leaves us satisfied. If you flee from us, our being dissolves and we are nothing but dust.

"But your breath will return, and with it anew you will restore the world. Your glory is limitless and you are praised ceaselessly.

"You who inflame the mountains if you touch them and make the earth tremble, I need thousands of lines and mouths to sing your praise.

"My voice will please you and I will have great joy in this work. Upon the earth no evil or bloody tyrant will be seen.

"Evil men will be forgotten; you, my soul, sing the glory of God."

Sabino stopped. Marcelo then said: "It doesn't seem just or possible to add anything to this. Since Sabino ended so well our conversation which has already lasted so long and the sun seems to have risen above our heads in order to listen to us, but it begins to blind us, let us now think of resting. This afternoon, after the siesta, at our leisure and without allowing the night to hinder us, let us say what remains to be said."

"Fine," said Juliano.

And Sabino added:

"I would propose finishing our conversation in that little wooded island which is formed by the river and which can be seen from here. The sun, which I see is like a furnace, today hardly allows for any other place."

"You are right," replied Marcelo and Juliano. We will do as you propose.

Marcelo arose, the others did the same, and their conversation came to an end for the moment.

Book II

DEDICATION

THIS SECOND BOOK OF THE NAMES OF CHRIST
IS DEDICATED TO DON PEDRO PORTOCARRERO,
MEMBER OF HIS MAJESTY'S COUNCIL AND OF THE
COUNCIL OF THE HOLY INQUISITION.

Nothing reveals more clearly the weakness of our human condition than the ease with which we commit sins and the large number of sinners. This despite of the fact that by nature we should crave goodness and in spite of the fact that the evils of sinning are so obvious. If the ancient philosophers who tried to delve into the hidden causes of our physical world and our behavior had taken into account these facts, they would probably have come to the conclusion that there was in man's nature some mysterious illness, some hidden flaw. They would then have understood that our nature was no longer just as pure as when it came from the hands of our Maker, and that it had been damaged and corrupted either through a disaster or through our own will. For upon reflecting on this subject, how could anyone believe that nature, as a mother and a diligent provider to her sons and daughters, could create man so full of evil thoughts and inclinations and at the same time so weak and powerless to resist and overcome his perverse inclinations? How could we believe that nature, which has guided toward their goals, as we can see, animals and plants and even the smallest objects helping every being to reach its full and healthy development, how could this very nature create the best and most illustrious of her creatures so inclined toward sin, so often incapable of reaching our goals, so prone to anguish and ruin?

In the same fashion that it would be most unwise to entrust the reins of two crazy galloping horses to a small inexperienced boy, having him ride down on a stony or rough road, or to entrust to this same boy a ship tossed by the winds in the middle of the storm, these examples should show us that it is not reasonable to assume that God in His wisdom should place in charge of our restless bodies, tossed by the winds of vice, our mind as it finds itself when we are born, with weak reason and unadorned by wisdom and good doctrine. We cannot assume that God put our soul in charge and placed it in the middle of enemies, all alone in the middle of many, unarmed against their fury, simply hoping that the spread of good religious tidings and the passing of time would finally strengthen our reason. For it is well known that before our reason has time to wake up, there arise in us the lowly desires inspired by our senses. These desires take over our soul and give it bad advice before the soul has time to know itself. How true it is that as soon as reason opens its eyes it finds nearby, waiting at the door so to speak, the ignorant crowds and the bad companions with a style of life full of perverse errors, together with the pleasures of the body, ambition, gold, and shiny riches. Each one of them has the power to darken and surround with the gloom of night the humble spark of our just born reason. These enemies attack it all at once as in a plot and after deceiving our reason and taking away the reins with which she might direct our body, they subject her to the wishes of the body and induce her to love and desire that which would destroy her.

Therefore, it is sufficient to reflect upon our inner turmoil and our inclination toward evil in order to realize that our nature has been basically corrupt for a long time. As I have mentioned in the first book of this work, although God made man wholly master of himself and wholly perfect, as a punishment for man's disobedience his bodily appetites and his senses no longer obeyed reason and after rebelling against the principles of reason, they darkened its light and limited its empire. Man's soul became prey to whatever could harm it, falling into confusion and ultimately becoming slave to sin. And yet, it's strangely marvelous to note in the same fashion how experience allows us often to avoid things and situations that we hold to be bad or dangerous, just as a traveler who slumbers and falls down in the difficult part of the road avoids the spot if he has to follow the road once more. Yet there is one mishap: the falling into sin which seems to have the opposite effect on us. Once we have tried sin, we seem to open a door through which we penetrate more deeply into darkness. Our first sin is like the first step up the ladder, which allows us to reach a second step. The more our soul destroys itself, the more it seems to find pleasure in its own self-destruction. This strange satisfaction is one of the worst consequences of sinning, perhaps the worst consequence of all. Because of it, a small sin becomes like a link in a long chain leading to even larger transgressions. Our human heart becomes hardened to the point that one would say the surface becomes callous. The soul's wounds become incurable as we proceed from a small sin to a mortal one. The very habit of sinning makes us accept as normal and sweet what is in itself—and also to the eyes of a sane judge—ugly and abominable. If the sinner could go back to the very beginning and reflect upon the enormity of his behavior, he could avoid the very thought of sinning and fear sin more than death; this can be seen in the lives of saints of which history gives us numerous examples.

A clear example is offered by the Hebrew nation, both in the past and in the present. As soon as they started to wander away from the path that led to God, they seemed to have hardened their hearts and although they occasionally came back to the right path, they proceeded then to offend God once more, one sin following another, until the gravest offense—that is, the death of Jesus, took place. And since the wages of sin are always a severe punishment, it was this offense that was the cause of a great calamity. I do not want to underline here the fact that they lost their kingdom and their temple was razed to the ground and their city was destroyed while the glory of the true cult of God was passed on to other nations. I do not want to point out in detail the loss of many material goods and great number of inhabitants that died in the war, as well as the eternal captivity in which they live now, surrounded by enemies, degraded by their neighbors and turned into patent examples of God's wrath.

There is something else: Can one imagine anything worse than having been promised them that the Messiah would be born of their blood and their lineage and after waiting so long to reach the splendor and glory through such a birth, taking hope and faith by this thought in the middle of moments of anguish and oppression; yet when the Messiah arrived among them they did not want to acknowledge him. Blind, they turned homicidal and destroyed their glory, their hope and their great good. When I reflect upon it my heart fills with grief.

If we understand properly the magnitude of such crime we will find out that it was born of other excesses. When the doors were opened to sin and their souls entered the darkened threshold further and further away from God, they became blind in the middle of the light, since light and clarity are precisely what surrounded Christ. The light shone from His marvelous miracles as well as in the Holy Scriptures that described Christ's life. All of which seems to show that none can be as blind as Christ's contemporaries were, unless it was because they had become great sinners. The events are equally frightful and awesome, for there is the blindness and cruelty of Christ's contemporaries in one hand, and on the other the severity and rigor of God's justice against those who sinned at the time. Every time I reflect upon this subject my heart fills with wonder. At this moment I have been brought back to this subject by some words uttered by Marcelo that I have still not written down. It is the time now to go back to Marcelo's speech.

INTRODUCTION

It so happened that the three of them, having eaten and rested for some time after the intensity of the sun's heat had diminished, came out of the barn and walked toward the river running by. They climbed aboard a small boat and following Sabino's advice they rowed toward a small island in the middle of the river near a dam and a mill. This island was covered by a luxuriant grove, small but dense. The air was calm and serene and the trees had abundant foliage. Some had grown there naturally, others had been planted by the hand of man. The island was divided into two parts by a noisy brook nourished by the water that escaped from the river through the stones of a dam.

Having entered the grove, Marcelo and his companions proceeded to reach the thickest and most central part of it, a place where the rays of the sun could scarcely penetrate, and gather around a tall poplar which grew almost in the center of the island. They leaned their backs against the poplar and faced the other side of the grove, the shadows and the green grass. Their feet almost reached the running water. Having sat down and after commenting on the contrast between the strong heat of the sun and the coolness of the place they had found, they thanked Sabino for his good advice to which Sabino replied: "I am happy to have found this spot and especially because of you, Marcelo, since I know that in order to give me pleasure you never hesitate to follow me even when, like today, you are in poor health. I would not want you to talk too much today, unless the coolness and quiet of this spot turns out to be a sort of medicine for your ills. And yet, when one has been accustomed to the discipline of school life which compels us to read numberless books even during the hottest days of summer, he can also discuss philosophical and religious matters in the coolness of the grove during a whole day. Let us pretend simply that we are playing hooky from school."

"Sabino is right," Marcelo answered looking at Juliano, "for it is almost a sin to work ourselves to death reading so many books one after another and it is a cruel life that compels us to work so hard. You may proceed with your speech, Sabino, without fear, for this place is ten times better than a schoolroom and besides the subjects that we are discussing are much sweeter than our school-work."

Then Sabino unfolded a paper he was carrying and proceeded with his speech, which follows:

ARM OF GOD

"Another name for Jesus is 'arm of God.' In chapter 53, Isaiah writes:

Who has believed our report?
And to whom is the arm of the Lord revealed?

and in chapter 52 he writes:

The Lord has made bare his holy arm
in the eyes of all nations
and all the nations of the world shall see
the salvation of our God.

and in the Virgin's Canticle (in the gospel according to Luke) we read:

He hath shewed strength with his arm,
He hath scattered the proud in the imagination of their
hearts.

and also quite clearly in Psalm 70 where David, speaking in the name of the Church, states:

> Now also when I am old and grayheaded, O God, forsake me
>   not;
> Until I have shewed thy strength unto this generation,
> and the power to every one that is to come. (Ps. 71:18).

We find this idea in many other biblical passages."

Here Sabino finished his short speech. Marcelo was getting ready to speak when Juliano took him by the hand and stated:

"I am not sure, Marcelo, that the Hebrews would accept that Isaiah, whom you have just quoted, was referring to Christ."

Marcelo answered, "They will not acknowledge it. They are blind on these matters and yet it is true. They are like a poor and rebellious patient who refuses a medicine that can restore his health. Such an acknowledgement would dissipate all their shadows and errors, yet they refuse to take this step. It is easier for the sun that shines above to lose its brightness than for them to accept our truth. For if Isaiah is not alluding to Christ, may I ask, who is he talking about?"

"You know what the answer to this question would be," retorted Juliano.

"I know," Marcelo said, "they claim the quotation refers to themselves and to their present condition and yet, do you think we need to reason at length in order to destroy such an obvious error?"

"No doubt it is obvious," Juliano answered, "and in any case, a strong proof on our side that the person alluded to by Isaiah is said to be entirely innocent and devoid of all sin. The Hebrew people in their present state, no matter how blind and arrogant, would not dare attribute to themselves such innocence and purity. Even if they were to think so, they stand condemned by God's word in Hosea, when He states that at the very end after the long captivity in which they find themselves, they will finally acknowledge the Lord, because logically, if they are to be converted at the very end, this means that at the present moment they are far from the Lord, that they are not His servants."

BOOK II

"Even if we set aside this matter, we may quarrel with them with respect to the meaning of the word. They may admit it refers to Christ and accept, as is true, that to be an 'arm' means to be God's strength and God's victory over his enemies—but they claim that the enemies that God destroys and will overcome through His Messiah, through His arm, and His strength, are the enemies of His chosen people, the visible enemies of the Hebrews, those who attacked and enslaved them such as the Chaldeans, the Greeks, the Romans, and all the other nations that made war upon the Jews. They hope to be avenged through the strength of their Messiah, the Messiah that in their error they are still waiting for, and they call him 'arm of God' because of the victory and revenge they have been talking about."

"That is but a dream," Marcelo added, "and since you have alluded to it, we must clear up the matter once and for all. When a field is about to be sown, the first thing that a farmer needs to do is to pull out the weeds, after which he plants his seeds. In the same fashion, we must pull out such a mistaken dream so that truth will have a clean and fertile land from which to grow.

"Pray, tell me, Juliano, did ever God promise His chosen people that He would send them His arm and His strength in order to assure their victory over their enemies, in order to give them not only freedom but also supremacy and lordship over other nations? Did He state anywhere that the Messiah would be a strong and valiant warrior who would overcome through His courage and His weapons, spreading to all lands in victorious battles, subjugating to His empire every nation?"

"Yes, He did state and promise such victories," Juliano answered.

Marcelo continued: "And did God make the promise only once, in a single text, perhaps while dealing with another matter?"

"No, indeed, this thought appears in many places," Juliano answered. "It is clearly underlined, expressed in beautiful and lofty language."

"How did God express this thought, where did He state it? Quote me some texts if you know them by heart," Marcelo added.

"That is a long story," Juliano stated, "and although you are asking me to tell you something you know very well, and I still do not know what the purpose of your question is, I will offer you a few quotations: In Psalm 45, David, speaking directly to Christ, tells Him:

> Gird thy sword upon thy thigh, O most mighty,
> With thy glory and thy majesty.
> And in thy majesty ride prosperously
> Because of truth and meekness and righteousness;
> And thy right hand shall teach thee terrible things.
> Thine arrows are sharp
> In the heart of the king's enemies;
> Whereby the people fall under thee.
> Thy throne, O God, is forever and ever:
> The sceptre of thy kingdom is a right sceptre.

"And in Psalm 97:

> The Lord reigneth; let the earth rejoice;
> Let the multitude of isles be glad thereof.
> Clouds and darkness are round about him:
> Righteousness and judgment are the habitation of his throne.
> A fire goeth before him,
> And burneth up his enemies round about.

"Isaiah in chapter 11 writes,

> And it shall come to pass in that day,
> That the Lord shall set his hand again the second time
> To recover the remnant of his people,
> Which shall be left, from Assyria,
> And from Egypt, and from Pathros,
> And from Cush, and from Elam, and from Shinar,
> And from Hamath, and from the islands of the sea.
> And he shall set up an ensign for the nations,
> And shall assemble the outcasts of Israel,
> And gather together the dispersed of Judah
> From the four corners of the earth.
> The envy also of Ephraim shall depart,
> And the adversaries of Judah shall be cut off:
> Ephraim shall not envy Judah,
> And Judah shall not vex Ephraim.

BOOK II

But they shall fly upon the shoulders of the Philistines
toward the west;
They shall spoil them of the east together:
They shall lay their hand upon Edom and Moab;
And the children of Ammon shall obey them.

"And in chapter 41:

Who raised up the righteous man from the east,
Called him to his foot,
Gave the nations before him, and made him rule over kings?
He gave them as the dust to his sword,
And as driven stubble to his bow.
He pursued them, and passed safely;
Even by the way that he had not gone with his feet.

"And the same Isaiah a little further on:

Behold, I will make thee a new sharp threshing instrument
    having teeth:
Thou shalt thresh the mountains, and beat them small,
And shalt make the hills as chaff.
Thou shalt fan them, and the wind shall carry them away,
And the whirlwind shall scatter them.

"And when this same prophet talks about the Messiah and his
enemies he declares:

The Lord shall go forth as a mighty man,
He shall stir up jealousy like a man of war:
He shall cry, yea, roar;
He shall prevail against his enemies.
I have long time holden my peace;
I have been still, and refrained myself:
Now will I cry like a travailing woman;
I will destroy and devour at once.
I will make waste mountains and hills,
And dry up all their herbs;
And I will make the rivers islands,
And I will dry up the pools.   (42:13–15)

"It is, as you see, a long story. The same prophet, using different words, makes the same statements in chapters 63 and 66. Joel affirms the same things in his last chapter, so does the prophet Amos in his last chapter, and Micah repeats it in his fourth, fifth, and last chapters. Is there any prophet that does not sing about God as almighty captain and about God's mighty victories?"

"It is so," Marcelo stated, "and yet, tell me, is it not true that the Assyrians and the Babylonians were famous for their warlike nature, and they fought under aggressive and victorious kings, bringing under their rule the whole world or the greatest part of it?"

"This is true," Juliano answered.

"And the Medes and the Persians who came after them," Marcelo added, "did they not use their weapons with courage? Did they not lord it over the world when among them flourished the famous king Cyrus and powerful Xerxes?"

Juliano conceded that it was so.

"It is equally true," Marcelo continued, "that the victories of the Greeks were even more glorious, and that they always were victorious. Alexander the Great, sword in hand and swift as lightning, in a very short time galloped from one end of the world to the other, astounding and subjecting all nations. After his death we know that his successors ruled long years in all of Asia and in a great part of Africa and Europe. And in the same fashion the Romans, who succeeded Alexander in the empire and in military glory, conquered all enemies and grew until the whole earth and their empire were one and the same thing. And this empire, albeit diminished and made up of different parts, some weak and others quite strong, as Daniel could read upon the feet of a certain statue, has been preserved century after century until our time. Without mentioning the names of princes who fought and conquered during modern times we still must remember the names of Scipio, Marcellus, Marius, Pompey, Caesar, in the past centuries, for whose valor and glory the whole earth was but a small place."

"I still do not know what you're driving at," Juliano complained.

"You shall soon see it clearly," Marcelo proceeded, "only tell me, these great victories, these vast empires that we have mentioned, were they granted by God to the kings we have mentioned or did they by themselves, without any help from God, achieve all these victories?"

"There is no doubt about it," Juliano answered, "that those who acknowledge God's divine designs are favored. And it is said in Proverbs (8:16): 'By me Princes rule.' "

"You speak the truth," Marcelo continued, "and yet I would ask you whether all these rulers knew and worshiped God."

"They did not acknowledge nor worship God," Juliano stated.

"One more thing," Marcelo continued, "before God granted them His favors, did He promise them anything, did He address to them long speeches, did He send them messengers to announce his promises in detail?"

"None of these things took place," Juliano answered, "and if anything of the sort is mentioned in the Holy Scriptures, as it may happen in some cases, it is mentioned in passing and the main message of the text is a different one."

"Then I ask," Marcelo added right away, "how is it possible to think that God granted and is still granting, to people who do not acknowledge Him, people who live without laws, barbarians, infidels, sinners, that is to say, earthly power, victory in war, the glory and nobility of ruling over all or almost all men; I repeat, who could believe that God grants all of this to men who are no better than slaves, granting it to them without promises, without explanations as if He were granting something insignificant? Indeed these victories are in and by themselves insignificant, and yet let us consider what He did with His own chosen people. The only ones that while others worshiped idols would acknowledge and serve Him. In order to grant them victories—if we follow the interpretation of the blind descendants of the chosen people—God would have to make numerous promises and take a long time to fulfill them. Almost every century new promises were made by the prophets, and still they had to wait and wait until today, more than 3,000 years after the first promise, it has not been fulfilled, and it never will, because it is not what God had promised them. It is almost a joke, or rather a pitiful error, to think that God's love and friendship had to be translated into weapons, banners, the beating of drums, castles besieged, fortresses torn down, knives, blood, attacks, the captivity of thousands of innocent people. It is a mistake to believe that the arm of God, spread out, surrounded by invincible strength, that God promises in His Holy Scriptures and of which He is so proud, is a descendant of David, a valiant captain clad in iron, sword in hand followed by a mass of soldiers, smiting the vanquished with his sword and unfolding all over the world his victorious banners. Cyrus would have been a messiah of this sort, and the same could be said about Nebuchadnezzar, and Artaxerxes. That kind of messiah, if we follow this definition, would make a messiah out of Julius Caesar the dictator, out of the great Pompey, and in this manner Alexander the Great would be a better messiah than all of the others. Is there such courage in killing mortal men, in bringing down the stones with which fortresses are made, stones which will eventually fall down by themselves? We do not need God's strong arm to achieve all this. How true what Isaiah expressed, speaking in the name of God:

For as the heavens are higher than the earth,
So are my ways higher than your ways,
And my thoughts than your thoughts. (55:9)

"These lines always come to my mind when I think about their error. For there are other victories, I would like to explain to these blind and confused people, there are other empires and lordships much bigger and better that have been promised to you by God, and his arm and strength are different, and better, from the ones you imagine. You have been thinking about victories in a world that is perishable and must crumble, while God's Holy Scripture is a promise about heaven. You are asking about freedom from your bodies and a prosperous life, which still will not free your soul from sin and vice. Yet God has promised you freedom from these mortal diseases. You had hoped to be masters of other men, while God only promised to make you masters of yourselves. You feel satisfied if you can find a successor to David who can bring you back to your land of origin, ensure justice, and defend and protect you against your enemies; yet God, who is incomparably more generous, had promised you not merely a son of David but rather His own son—and also David's son—who, enriched with all the goodness that God possesses, would liberate you from the powers of the Devil and from the embrace of eternal death and would allow you to trample upon everything that is really harmful to you, carrying you in glory, immortal and holy, to a land of eternal life and peace. These are gifts truly worthy of God, these are the gifts hinted at in God's repeated promises.

"And truly I tell you, Juliano, that their mistake implies, among several drawbacks, the sad error of judging God's mercy in a debased and limited fashion. God's heart is not as ungenerous as the human heart often is. The earthly goods and earthly glory that we appreciate so much, and which, by the way, God is the only one capable of distributing among us, He knows to be impermanent gifts, basically alien to man, gifts that not only do not make us better human beings but often make us worse and more corrupt. This is why God does not boast about such gifts or about being able to distribute them, and most of the time gives them to those who are not deserving, with aims only He knows. Those He despises, who are to Him as vile slaves, receive from Him such a brief consolation. On the other hand the people chosen by God, the ones He loves as a father loves his children, receive only meager earthly gifts, because He knows our weaknesses and is aware of the ease with which our heart pours out in the love of earthly goods and is also aware that almost always they destroy or weaken the sinews of true virtue.

"Yet some may claim, 'We are awaiting what the holy texts have told us, we are satisfied with what God has promised and do not despise. We read the word *captain*, we hear about *wars, horses, arrows, swords,* and we read about *victories* and *triumphs,* we hear promises of *freedom* and *revenge,* we are told that *our city and our temple will be restored,* that *other people will serve us* and that *we shall be masters of everything and everybody.* We are waiting for all of these things we have heard about, and with this hope we live happily.'

"Yet it is always a weak defense to cling to the letter when reason and common sense uncover the true meaning of a text. Such a defense is even weaker in this case since the very same Holy Scriptures uncover the true meaning of these passages in many other places. One should wonder why Isaiah, when speaking about Christ in a clear and direct manner, describes Him in Godlike fashion thus: 'Behold my servant, whom I uphold; mine elect, in whom my soul delighteth; I have put my spirit upon him: He shall bring forth judgment to the Gentiles. He shall not cry, nor lift up, nor cause his voice to be heard in the street. A bruised reed shall he not break, and the smoking flax shall he not quench: He shall bring forth judgment unto truth' (42:1–3). It is obvious that Jesus Christ, the arm and strength of God, does not show military strength or soldierly courage and that the deeds of such a humble land as Isaiah described in this passage are not deeds of physical and bodily war, a war from which spring pride and cruelty, a war in which noise, wrath and fury agitate our hands. '*A bruised reed shall he not break,*' the Prophet writes, and yet there are still some people who in their sad mistake think the Messiah will come to upset the world as a warrior.

"Another clear message can be found in another chapter written by the same prophet: 'And he shall smite the earth with the rod of his mouth. And with the breath of his lips shall he slay the wicked' (11:4). For if the weapons with which he smites the earth and with which he slays the wicked are living and burning words, it is obvious that the deeds of such an arm are not physical fighting and victory over human bodies but rather a fight against vice with the weapons of the spirit. This is why, in agreement with this conception, in another paragraph Isaiah depicts the Messiah fully armed with all his weapons: 'For he put on righteousness as a breastplate, and a helmet of salvation upon his head. And he put on the garments of vengeance for clothing, and was clad with zeal as a cloak' (59:17). All of this goes to show that the arrows sent by the strength of His arm to pierce our body are actually sharp words clearly aimed at us and capable of piercing through our hearts. And His famous sword was not tempered with steel in Vulcan's forge with the aim of cutting flesh and pouring blood, because it is not made out of visible iron but is rather a ray of invisible virtue which cuts off everything that in our souls is an enemy of God. His helmet, breastplate, and other garments are consequently heroic and heavenly virtues against which all the blows of evil shall prove impotent. Yet there are those who ask God for a song and a word but are incapable of uplifting their eyes in order to understand the words which God has already sent them.

"I wonder how it is possible to ask God for favors related to our mortal life, the flimsy quality of which we see daily simply by looking around, when God says through His prophet Isaiah that the goodness of God's promise is so high, so surpassing, that since the beginning of the world men have not heard, nor perceived by the ear, neither hath eye seen, what God has prepared for him that waited for God (64:4). We know quite well what happens when a people defeats another people. We witness daily the deeds of armies, and we know quite well that our weak flesh prizes before all other things wealth and power. This is not what God had promised us: What His promise announced goes beyond our wishes and passes our understanding. The fact that God could become man is something of which our flesh is incapable; the fact that God could die in the human state that He had acquired in order to give new life to His fellow men is something that goes beyond our understanding. Who has ever heard that a man could through his own death turn the tables on the Devil, who terrorized mankind, and make the Devil subject and slave to mankind? How could we ever wish or imagine in our wildest dreams that those who served hell would become citizens of heaven and sons of God, making the souls shine in beauty and justice, turning them into sources of light, destroying a thousand sinister evils, clothing the souls and the bodies with glory and immortality?

"Why should I stop here? Does not the same prophet Isaiah describe clearly Christ's nature, the kind of war Christ was to wage, in chapter 61 of his prophecies, in which he puts these words in the mouth of Christ: 'The spirit of the Lord God is upon me; because the Lord hath anointed me to preach good tidings unto the meek'? Do you not understand the meaning? What is indeed the meaning? Good tidings to the meek, not the assault of arms climbing up the walls of a fortress. There is more: 'He hath sent me to bind up the brokenhearted.' And yet the mistaken interpreters keep thinking about uplifted swords and bloody corpses. 'To proclaim liberty to the captives.' To proclaim liberty, not to make war or to enslave. Not to give vent to rage, but to spread indulgence and generosity and 'to proclaim the acceptable year of the Lord' and the day in which as if vengeance had taken place, God's wrath will vanish. 'To comfort all that mourn,' to give strength to those that cry out. To give garments of praise instead of the spirit of heaviness, to replace mourning by oils of joy; and so that no doubt can remain he concludes, 'The Lord God will cause righteousness and praise to spring forth before all nations' (61:11). How do those who deceive themselves hoping for strength in weapons and armies while God has promised strength in virtue and justice explain all this?"

And then Juliano, looking at Marcelo merrily in the eyes, stated:

"It seems to me, dear Marcelo, that our conversation is heating up, as if the heat of this weather were not enough, but I am not sorry to have enticed you to go on speaking because I have fully enjoyed what you had to say. And in order to exhaust this matter I would like to ask you now for what reason God, while promising His people such great things, wished to disguise His spiritual gifts in the shape of physical treasures and victories, being aware that His audience would be too weak and too much in love with earthly goods to find out the true message."

"There was no deceit," answered Marcelo right away, "since almost at the same time God's word pointed out the right interpretation and God's hand lifted the veil that hid the true meaning. Yet God's audience had made up their mind they wanted to be blind to the truth."

Then Juliano intervened, "I had spoken before, and yet my question was practically the same. Since God knew His chosen people would be blind to His true message, why did He not speak in a perfectly clear fashion? Since He wanted to make His will known, and wanted to be understood, why make it possible for errors and mistakes to lurk in some corner of the text? We cannot suspect that God wished to be misunderstood. He could have instead kept silent. We cannot believe that He was incapable of expressing His thought."

"God's secrets," Marcelo answered, while he seemed to recoil, "are like deep abysses which we can hardly penetrate or fathom. Our faith, our Christian attitude, should make us understand that God's wisdom and knowledge would be meager indeed if human intelligence could penetrate them completely. We must not presume to be able to find all the answers. This is true with respect to all of God's words and actions, and especially with respect to the blindness of His chosen people. With respect to that fact, even St. Paul seems to shrink away from any conclusions, and although inspired by the very breath of the Holy Spirit he avoids any personal opinion on this matter and writes:

Oh, the depth of the riches both of the wisdom and knowledge of God! How unsearchable are his judgments, and his ways past finding out! For who hath known the mind of the Lord? or who hath been his counsellor? (Rom. 11:33–34).

"And yet, though truth be hidden, since it is made of the essence of light, there are always a few rays that come out of it and illuminate the path for our humble souls. It seems to me that the errors and sins of some men should not force God's wisdom to change the language with which He speaks to us, the actions with which He rules us, or the order of created beings. Since all this matters, He has found ways that are fitting and proper to the nature of the world. As you know, there are malefactors who like to work during daylight, while others prefer night and its gloom for their sins. A pirate needs the rising sun's rays in order to detect and follow his prey, while the adulterer waits for the sun to set before staining his neighbor's bed. God gave us intelligence, reason, sharpness of understanding, all of which are occasionally misused by many human beings. Yet if we had not received such gifts, we could not call ourselves real human beings. Does not St. Paul say about the doctrines contained in the gospels that they bring the zest for life to some and the gloom of death to others? What would happen to the world if in order to heal the sins of some we were to spread the guilt among everybody else? Therefore, dear Juliano, the style of expression that God has made use of, a style in which through similes and metaphors related to things that we may know, see, and love, God gives us a description of His true gifts and offers them to us in a fashion that could be understood by our limited intelligence, is both useful and proper. It is useful because when we realize the parallel between the gifts we know and those that are promised, our intelligence, which is always inclined to comparisons, is made sharper. When we notice something in common between things that are in principle very different, we seem to rejoice and keep forever in mind the similarity which we have discovered. We must remember that through the message that reaches our senses and through our experience, we know how pleasant and sweet some earthly goods could be, but we still do not know what the taste and sweetness could be in the gifts that belong to heaven.

"That is the reason God offers to us the gifts that are unknown to mankind disguised as gifts that we love and enjoy, so that since we understand that the unknown gifts are even better than the familiar ones, we should become more and more interested in these unknown gifts just by remembering the known pleasures. In the same way God became a sweet loving man, so that the side of His nature that is all sweetness and love could be understood by us and fill our souls with love. In the same fashion through the Holy Scriptures God talks to us as a man would talk to other men: He describes His spiritual and lofty gifts through words and images of earthly goods. This way, spiritual gifts are honeyed and made more desirable. This is a general phenomenon but seems to affect more strongly the people that we have previously mentioned because of their innate weakness, and as St. Paul said aptly, their infinite childishness. It is because of this childishness, just as a tutor will offer candy to a young child so that the child will learn his lessons, that God tried to uplift their eyes and their wishes toward heaven while offering them what seemed to be earthly goods. They could clearly see the infinite power of God and also His infinite love for them in acts such as the calamities that afflicted Egypt and the parting of the Red Sea.

"They had almost in front of their eyes the burning bush and the cloud over Sinai; they could almost hear God's voice dictating the precepts of the law; they had tasted the manna that God had rained upon them. They could gaze at the cloud that guided them during the day and shone during the night and yet, when they reached the border of the land of Canaan, when God was guiding them, when they heard that its inhabitants were courageous, their hearts were filled with fear and mistrust: They withdrew among tears of weakness, not believing that He who could part the sea would be able to destroy the walls of earth. Neither the wealth of the land they could see far away, nor their experience of God's strength could make them advance. Now, pray tell me, if God had promised them in clear and direct language the incarnation of His son, and an abundance of spiritual gifts, yet not gifts for the present but rather for a new life in heaven, would God have been believed and understood? His words would have been completely barren. And thus, all the lofty promises made by God become more understandable and desirable; they become a source of immediate satisfaction and pleasure. Specifically, the mystery and the promises that reside in Jesus Christ are offered to us in the holy texts almost always transformed in one of the two following images: in talking about the grace that flows from Christ into our souls and the fruits of these graces, all this is symbolized with parallels and images inspired by the cultivation of fields by agriculture. As we said earlier this morning, the texts talk about the sky, earth, clouds, rains, mountains, valleys, and mention in a beautiful and accurate way the fields of wheat, vineyards, olive groves. Yet there is another aspect of Christ's life: His victory over the devil upon the cross, His triumph over hell and death, and the ascension of His body to heaven. All of this is depicted through the mentioning of wars and visible victories. Flags and banners are displayed. We hear the blasting of trumpets and see shiny swords: The descriptions are so lively that we seem to hear the noises of clashing weapons and the scream of fleeing soldiers displayed in front of our eyes. We almost see a triumphant army. And, dear Juliano, if I must tell everything I feel, we are dealing with people whose hearts have been hardened. Their trust in God was always incomplete. They sinned grievously against God from the very beginning: Their ugly and enormous sins, their ungratefulness, were other reasons God's message to them was indirect and not wholly clear. The same thing happens with prophets; God gives them greater or smaller clarity and impact according to their greater or smaller heart, mind, and personal qualities. The same truth can be communicated to some people in their sleep, to others while awake, but through material and obscure images that arise in their brain. This truth will reach others through pure and simple words. The same way that our face looks different when we look at it through several different mirrors, some clear, some dark, some accurate, and some full of distortions, God revealed in an obscure and hidden fashion the truth about His son, about Christ's life and deeds. He chose to do so because He knew that His message would be clear enough for those who among them were good and faithful, and the ungrateful and wicked ones did not deserve to be enlightened.

"And it thus happened that God thought some men would find a healthy mental exercise and a holy pleasure in seeking and finding God's hidden message. Other men might not easily find it, since their many sins would make them go astray. They were walking without guide, without control, and little by little sank into an evil and dejected situation. They could have chosen life but embraced death. They despised salvation when it was made available; neither their eyes nor their ears were of any help. They were surrounded by light yet they went groping into darkness. Blind, they seized Christ and amidst blasphemy they denied Him and killed Him, reaching the extremity of sin. Is this something that has occurred to me or did not God speak to them through Isaiah a long time ago?

> And he said, 'Go, and tell this people,
> "Hear ye indeed, but understand not;
> And see ye indeed, but perceive not."
> Make the heart of this people fat,
> And make their ears heavy, and shut their eyes;
> Lest they see with their eyes, and hear with their ears,
> And understand with their heart, and convert, and be healed.'
>
> (6:9–10)

and Christ himself points out how God's message couched in parables and images was bound to confuse some men: 'Only to you it is given to know the mysteries of the kingdom of God: but to others in parables; that seeing they might not see, and hearing they might not understand' (Luke 8:10).

"Since there are people that are blind and deaf and stubbornly cling to their blindness, let us pass on and try to define the strength of God's invincible arm."

After saying this, Marcelo looked at Sabino and added: "Unless Sabino thinks that we should add something to our previous discussion."

Marcelo spoke thus because he had noticed that Sabino twice had indicated, leaning forward and with a movement of his eyes, that he was ready to ask a question. But Sabino answered: "I was not going to deal with anything important. I was ready to keep quiet, but since you invite me to speak I will do so. My question is this: "If God spoke to the Jews in figured language as a punishment for their sins and they were unable to understand God's message because they were sinners, after which they rejected Jesus and put Him to death, could you point out what were the earlier sins that brought about the last enormous sin which they committed later?"

BOOK II

Marcelo answered: "It is hard to point to one single sin when there were so many and grievous sins, and yet, your question is not meaningless, dear Sabino, for if we pay attention to Moses' message, we may come to the conclusion that the sin of worshiping that golden calf must have motivated God to allow them to reject Christ. From that early source flowed the poisoned waters which, mixed with other currents, have become an abyss of evil. For if we analyze all the shades of evil which can be found in that old sin, we will realize that its punishment, blindness in front of Jesus, and all the anguish that followed, were richly deserved. I do not want to mention now that God allowed them to escape their slavery in Egypt, and that in a wondrous gesture had opened for them a path through the sea. The memory of such generosity was fresh in their minds. In order to appreciate the gravity of their sins we must remember that they turned their backs to God at a time in which God was in front of their eyes, present on top of the mountain when they were camping on the slopes of Mount Sinai, and could see the cloud and fire of God's presence. They knew that Moses was speaking to God, and had just received the law, the Commandments, which they started to hear from God's very lips and seized by deep awe, did not think themselves worthy to hear the whole message and asked Moses to do it for them. Thus they forgot God when they were looking at Him. They denied Him while they were beside Him, they erased Him from their memory while they were still gazing at Him. And why did they erase Him from their minds? We cannot say it more concisely than is said in the Holy Scriptures, because they fell in love with a 'similitude of an ox that eateth grass' (Ps. 106:20).

"It was not even a real ox or calf that ate grass, but rather a carved image of a calf that seemed to eat, carved by their own hands at that time. The crazied worshipers exclaimed, addressing the whole of Israel, that was their God. The one that freed them from bondage in Egypt. And I ask what weakness or lack of love they could have found in God until that time, and what strength they thought they could find in a badly carved lump of gold? What words could depict such blindness, such wickedness? Those who through malice and lack of wisdom erred their path at that moment did so because God allowed them to go astray.

"We are not the ones that point to this situation. Moses,

173

speaking through God and in an allusion to the worshipers of that same golden calf, has these words:

> Whosoever hath sinned against me, him will I blot out of my book. Therefore now go, lead the people unto the place of which I have spoken unto thee: behold, mine Angel shall go before thee: nevertheless in the day when I visit I will visit their sins upon them. And the Lord plagued the people because they made the calf, which Aaron made. (Ex. 33:10)

And also in Deuteronomy (32:20):

> They have moved me to jealousy with that which is not God;
> They have provoked me to anger with their vanities:
> and I will move them to jealousy with those which are not a
>   people;
> I will provoke them to anger with a foolish nation.

"Let us now remember what happened then, what Moses carried out by order of the Lord, for those events will make my meaning clear.

"Does not the Holy Scripture state, in Exodus 31:19, that Moses turned around and went down from the mountain carrying two Tables of Testimony in his hand, but seeing the disordered behavior of his people, he cast the tables out of his hands and broke them on the ground? And also that the Tabernacle to which God descended to talk to Moses was taken by Moses out of the camp, far from the tents of the Hebrews, and pitched in a far-away place? How could we interpret all this as a prophecy through an image, a metaphor, about what was going to happen to the Jewish people as a punishment of their excesses? The meaning is that the Tabernacle where God dwells forever, which is the human body and nature of Jesus Christ, born among them, residing among them, was bound to go far away from them because of their diffidence. And the law that had been given to them, the law that they so zealously try to follow at present, would be for them fruitless and meaningless. Then, as now, they were bound to see only Moses' back, that is to say, the shadow and outer surface of the Holy Scriptures. The real meaning of the Holy Scriptures, although given to them, can no longer be understood by them and has fled to other quarters. Because of their sins and especially because of their worship of the golden calf they were punished thus, for God did not speak clearly to them and they did not have wisdom enough to understand God's hidden message. We have now, I think, said everything that had to be stated about this point. We should discuss now all the qualities related to God's arm and try to define its strength."

Marcelo here made a short pause, after which he spoke again: "It has been said about Firmianus Lactantius, as you probably know, that he was far more eloquent when he wrote against heathen mistakes than when he tried to explain Christian truths. He was better in his description of errors than in convincing anybody about true values. I hope to do otherwise. If I can express in simple words the great deeds that God accomplished through Jesus Christ—and hence recall Jesus, God's arm—I will be able to convince you of the truth of my interpretation and at the same time confound those who oppose it.

"And in order to enhance my reasoning I would like to assume that since God is infinitely strong and powerful there would be no great merit for Him to carry out a deed simply by making use of His absolute power. What should impress and awe us with the infinity of God's power and knowledge is that He carries out great enterprises without seeming to do anything. When the work is finished no law of nature has been broken, no violence has taken place, great things seem to appear or happen by themselves, as if untouched by God's hand. God's strength walks hand in hand with God's prudence and knows how to accomplish difficult goals through easy efforts and without changing the order that regulates the world. And in this kind of action God always rejoices since this is the way in which His infinite wisdom shines best. And as for our human rulers, good and wise rulers have always imitated this attitude, although those who rule us today are often unaware of it. So many other inspirations from God have diminished and become like shadows that our rulers very often are obsessed by small goals and in their pursuit of these goals tend to forget the larger ones: They may be successful on one small point but fail elsewhere. So blind are they that they feel proud of their new laws even when such laws clash with other better laws. They do violence to nature in their acts and seem proud of it. If this were the occasion I could give you numerous examples of such an attitude.

"In order to realize the great deeds carried out by God through the power of His arm, we must remember how many difficult things had to be reconciled and were powerful. And yet with great ease and with great dexterity, God through Christ took care of all the problems as if in one blow. This underlines the greatness of God's power and the reasons to call Christ God's arm and God's courage.

"We know that Lucifer, in love with himself, wanted to appropriate what God had prepared through Christ for the honor and help of mankind, and then, astray from the path of obedience and God's grace, fell to the lower depths of grief: started hating God and envying mankind. Spurred by his passion he applied all his tricks and his ingenuity to the task of making mankind break God's law and stray from God's path. If that was accomplished mankind would not find the happiness that divine Grace was offering it, and God could not accomplish His goals. Men were persuaded to break God's Commandments and they did so. After this the Devil thought he had won since he knew that God could not go back on His word and had given a pledge that man would die as soon as he would break God's law. We can now see that after mankind's fall, after God's advice had been disregarded, the Devil started to congratulate himself, and yet God's honor and greatness compelled Him to come to the rescue and find a solution. Many different problems, some requiring almost opposite solutions, had to be attended to at the same time.

"First of all man had to be punished; he had to die since otherwise God would not keep His word or mete out justice. And yet, so that God's advice could be finally heeded, man had to go on living and his anguish had to be alleviated. Finally Lucifer's daring act had to be punished. The Devil had acted out of pride in front of God and out of envy of mankind, wishing not only to have man stray from God but also trying to turn him into the Devil's vassal and the servant of sin. Moreover, he used all his tricks and in a certain way wanted to compete with God in wisdom, trying to fight God through God's own words and with God's own weapons. Such pride had to be punished and the punishment had to fit the crime. Lucifer wanted to be God's equal, and God made him servant and slave to man. And also, since envy leads often to sorrow, the Devil, who was envious of man, was punished by man being made blessed and glorious. And the effrontery of trying to compete with God in wisdom and advice would be punished when God decreed that the Devil's advice and cleverness would ensnare the Devil himself and that his weapons would turn against him.

"As a consequence of all this it was God's wish that sin and death, which were rooted in man by the Devil, should become the occasion and the cause of man's greatest happiness. Life would spring out of death, joy out of pain and grief. And the life-saving death and grief would be a product of the Devil himself, ironically turning against himself. It was important that while carrying out this plan, God should not make use of His absolute power and that natural law should not be broken. The surface of the world would appear the same as before. Thus were coordinated the Devil's wickedness, man's misery and fall, and God's wisdom and honor. God's plan would fail if any link in the chain were to be broken or if absolute power were made use of while carrying out God's grand design.

"And I ask myself, what did God decide to do? Did He give up such a confused and confusing problem? Not at all. Did He try to solve one of the matters leaving the other matters unsolved? No, rather He tried to solve both. Did He make use of His absolute power? He used rather His equanimity and justice. Did He gather large armies of angels? Did He start an open war, a field battle against the Devil and take away the Devil's prey? No, since victory was achieved through only one man. And just by allowing the Devil to put a man on a cross and kill Him in this manner, all the problems that I have mentioned were fully solved in a satisfactory way. This is because of Christ's death on the cross, to which he was nailed by God's permission and at the hand of the Devil and his followers, since the man who died was also divine and since the human nature that He had taken was innocent, free from all sin, holy and perfect, and also connected with our image as mortal beings; Christ's death did in true justice stand for the death to which all the human race had been condemned. It was almost a symbolic death, and by redeeming all our sins it freed us from the Devil and placed us on the road toward immortality, glory, and God's abundant grace. And because the Devil lay his hands upon an innocent being, one who being without sin was not his subject, he overstepped his bounds and justly lost the obedience that man had given him. A thousand precious spoils were taken away from his claws, and he became a slave of the innocent man he had killed. His victim, who had been born without having had to pay tribute to death either in His person or that of His followers, could treat the devil as a rebellious and fugitive servant. Thus the proudest and bloodiest enemy was abased and vanquished by God's law. And the one who had tricked a weak and innocent mankind, enslaving it through false promises, is now trodden by man, who has become his master by the grace of God's death. The Devil suffers with envy when he sees mankind, after having lost the earthly paradise because of his machinations, now identified with Christ and God in the heavens. The Devil boasted about his great knowledge but God decided that he was to wound himself with his own hand: By killing Jesus Christ he destroyed himself and gave life to the world. The devil then ranted and raved turning everywhere in anguish, but can complain only to himself, since through Christ's death he plunged himself into an abyss of misery while man, whom he hated, was rising toward glory and God's wisdom and power shone brighter than ever, which is what hurts the devil the most. For God's greatness is limitless and the proof of His infinite strength and immeasurable wisdom is everywhere.

"What can today's Jews criticize in God's actions, with what weapons can they defend their error: Can they deny that the first man sinned? Were not all men subject to death and misery, enslaved by their sins? Could it be claimed perchance that it wasn't God's role to remedy this situation by destroying the Devil's power and redeeming mankind, making us free from our old chains? Would it be a lesser deed, one less worthy of God, to vanquish this diabolical beast, than to turn to flight the armies of mortal men? Could we, no matter how we try, find a more efficient, faster, wiser, more honorable, more conducive way of revealing God's wisdom than the one that He made use of through the sacrifice, the blood, the obedience of Jesus Christ? Even more, if among men the names of great warriors that achieved victory are famous and shining, could we deny Jesus Christ the glory, a glory both infinite and shining above all, of having undertaken all alone such a great enterprise and having carried it out to complete success?

"All of these wonders were achieved through Christ's death.

BOOK II

And even after such death, Christ descended into hell, destroyed Lucifer's pride, chained him, and came back to life on the third day, never to die again, made a triumphant ascent into heaven, and placed our blood and our flesh to the right hand of God where the Devil had wanted to be. He had become the Lord, as man of all creatures, their judge and salvation, and in order to carry out the grand design and thwart the Devil's work on the earth, Christ sent back from the heavens His spirit. Inspired by it His humble disciples became more powerful and could wage war against tyrants and idolaters, against vain and pompous pseudo-philosophers who were carrying out the Devil's work. A great architect and builder always chooses for himself the hardest part of the work leaving for the other workers and masons the light tasks: In this fashion, Christ, after defeating through His actions the spirit of evil, sent His followers after the followers of the Devil. And it was so: Victory was achieved and the prince of Darkness lost his earthly dominion, his throne and scepter fell forever into the dust. The new deed, the new wonder, which is Christianity, is a source of amazement when we talk about it. Let us imagine again what we know happened in reality. On one hand, we see twelve men devoid of what most people hold in esteem. They are from humble origin, are not famous, speak simply, have not read any books, have no friends in high places. They are confronting a world empire and the religious establishment that has become entrenched through the passing of centuries, with its priests, its temples, its devils. The laws decreed by the rulers, the decisions by institutions and communities, the very rulers and the very communities are all united against those twelve men. There they are, the twelve men, alone, facing everybody else, every other man and every devil with their knowledge and power.

"It is indeed something that moves us to wonder, something that we could not believe unless our eyes attested to it, to have a handful of men wage war against everybody else. And another wonder, that once the war started and after seeing how the enemies' hearts were consumed by fire, by rage, the small group still went on fighting. Another wonder is the journey to Rome of a poor, strange man, one who later on will be called St. Peter. Rome held the scepter of dominion over the whole world, was the seat and throne of a huge empire. This did not deter the poor man: He screamed his truth from streets and squares, he claimed that their idols were devils and that the religion and the way of life that the Romans had inherited from their ancestors were empty and wicked. It is amazing that such daring could succeed and yet this happened. It would have been easier if the old religions had contained many harsh and painful precepts and regulations, and if the apostles had started to preach an easier, more pleasurable, more sensuous religion. Even in that case, it is hard to break customs, habits, values, which are based on respect for our ancestors and on the authority of many writers and historians. Much can be accomplished when a new religion tries to flatter man's basic instincts. But it happened otherwise: The Romans had followed a religion that was based on the tolerance of every human wish and vice, while the apostles were demanding continence, fasting, poverty, rejection of earthly goods. As far as the new beliefs, the apostles had come to announce news that seemed incredible to reason and common sense. The gods given to them by their parents had to be rejected, to be replaced by a man whom the Jews had crucified. Only the man who had died upon the cross was to witness forth and give strength to this strange news.

"And that is why we state that the facts we are remembering are actually marvels and miracles. It was marvelous to see how little effort was invested in the beginning of the process and then how fast things happened, and how the process became speedier, and developed and achieved its goal. It could have happened otherwise. The apostles could have persuaded a small group and this group in turn persuaded others; then, all together, weapons in hand, they could have taken over the city. Fighting on, they could have conquered a region and gathering strength slowly taken over a whole kingdom. This is what happened with Rome: First, it took Italy and then started to conquer the world. If the new movement had taken over the world by force of arms and then changed the laws and beliefs of the whole world, this would have been much less surprising. What Rome did was also possible in part for the city of Carthage. Many powerful kingdoms have humble beginnings. Thus, the followers of the false sect of Mohammed have increased their power; the strength of the Turks, of which everybody is fearful, was only meager at first.

"Every man, every group of men tries to grow and lord it over others. But the deed we are talking about unfolded in a different fashion since it was through the work of God. The apostles never came together. Their followers gathered together not in order to wage war but in order to suffer and become martyrs. Their weapons were not made of iron and steel; they were made out of unheard-of patience and humility. They died and won their victories by doing so. When they fell down beheaded, new disciples arose to follow their ideas. The earth, fertilized by their blood, sent forth new fruits of faith. Fear and death instead of making their followers escape attracted more and more people to the new Church. In the same fashion that Christ won his battle in his death, thus in order to show God's real courage, He allowed the Devil to display His enemies armed with cruelty, with iron and with fire. He did not take away their weapons as He could have done, neither did He make His followers invulnerable to weapons, as they say Achilles was, but rather, He delivered them to their enemies and their cruelty. This is the paradox: The infidels screamed 'let's kill them,' and the believers whispered, 'let us die,' and then it was infidelity that perished while faith grew until it covered the whole earth.

"And victory was thus assured: Our enemies were utterly crushed, as the prophet Zechariah writes eloquently:

And this shall be the plague wherewith the Lord
will smite all the people
That have fought against Jerusalem;

Their flesh shall consume away
while they stand upon their feet,

And their eyes shall consume away in their holes,
And their tongue shall consume away in their mouth. (14:12)

"And as you can see, it is not said that anybody would attack them physically, weapon in hand, in order to slay them, for they themselves were to wither away as happens to those afflicted with tuberculosis, and finally they would no longer be able to stand on their feet and would totter and fall down. Because although it is true that the Church's enemies always attack it cruelly putting to death the faithful, treading on Christian blood, it is also true that after our martyrs fell down it was the turn of the idols and of the executioners, for the death of martyrs always increased and spread faith in others until faith ruled all of us.

"I would now like to ask a question of those who trust only their senses and who, by following only the literal sense of the text, are hopeful of earthly battles, victories, political power. They do not want to put their faith in a secret spiritual victory, in the redemption of souls which were chained to evil and which were liberated by Christ on His cross because all this cannot be seen by their physical eyes and because they do not possess the eyes of faith that would give them the right vision. Yet, I ask, could they claim that the falling of the idols and the spreading of Christianity is an insignificant fact, something daily and normal, something easily imagined before it happened? Isn't this spiritual victory more in agreement with God's promises, isn't it worthier of God than the victorious armies of their mistaken dreams? How could they compare any earthly victory with a spiritual one? What victory parade will not pale by comparison? What foundation can they find for their persevering error?

"I am convinced that the conversion to Christianity of the diverse nations of the world proves the truth of our religion without any possible doubt and destroys completely the reasoning of infidels, no matter how clever, because, my dear Juliano and Sabino, I would like you to tell me—and if my wits are not strong enough you must help me with your sharp vision—when we discuss Jesus Christ and the great deeds that are known to all, the deeds carried out during His life and by His disciples after His death, is it not obvious that such deeds were carried out, either by the grace of God or through the Devil's strength, since no man unless helped from outside could have the strength to accomplish what Christ and His followers did accomplish? I have no doubt this is so because of the many marvelous happenings that can be read even in the books of infidels and especially the conversion to Christianity of all pagan nations, perhaps the greatest wonder of all. Such miracles, we must conclude, were either false miracles or true ones. If false, they were the work of the Devil, but if true, the work of God.

"If this is so, if not the work of the Devil, we must conclude this was the work of God. Obviously, the Devil was not going to favor an enterprise through which his power would be destroyed, men would pull down the temples where he was worshiped and would reject him with curses. What took place in the past throughout the Roman Empire is also taking place today in the New World recently discovered, where the holy gospels are displayed in flags of victory and idol worship is being stamped out. The spread of Christianity is due to either the power of God, or to the forces of evil, and we must now conclude that the Devil is bound to fight such an enterprise, since it weakens him. We see in it, therefore, inescapably the strength of God's arm.

"Truth is indeed like a shining light, like a beacon; it fights darkness with its rays; it seems to float in the air out of reach, out of contradictions. It attains its goal with simple and short words. That is why I come back for the third time to this simple idea: If Christ's presence among us was not the result of a mistake committed by the Devil, the inescapable conclusion is that Christ came to bring us God's light and truth. And if Christ destroyed the Devil's knowledge and power, which he did, it should be obvious that he was not the Devil's minister or servant.

"Let the infidels bow down their heads in front of truth, let them confess that our beloved Jesus Christ is not an invention of the Devil but rather God's truth, strength, justice, courage, God's famous and powerful arm. We admire the courage of the deeds accomplished and the deeds to come in the future: As St. Paul writes in *1 Corinthians* (15:24), God will empty, that is to say, deprive of their being and existence, all the earthly powers and kingdoms, subjecting everything to His power so that only God will reign. It is then that sin and death will disappear and the head and body of evil will be plunged in hell forever and ever.

"Much more could be said on this matter. But other holy texts await us, and the sun has begun to set."

At that moment Juliano raised his eyes toward the sun which was coming close to the horizon and said:

"Dear Marcelo, time flies but we are hardly aware of its flight because we were absorbed in what you were saying. Yet a cool night will not be less favorable than a hot day to the unfolding of your speech."

And Sabino added, "The night is even better for our purpose. The moon will come out and the shining choir of stars will follow giving Marcelo a large audience, listening to him across the silent night spaces. Try not to disappoint such a crowd."

THE NAMES OF CHRIST

After which he unfolded a paper and read what follows:

KING OF GOD

"In the second Psalm of the *Books of Psalms,* it is said: 'Yet have I set my kingdom upon my Holy Hill of Zion' and in chapter 14 of Zechariah it is said: 'and all the peoples will come and they shall admire the King of God our Lord.' "

After having read these texts, Sabino continued: "Not much more is said about this matter in my text. Therefore, in order not to have to unfold my pages time and time again, I will read on to the end."

And then he said, "Another name for Jesus is Prince of Peace and also husband. The first name appears in the gospel according to St. John: 'He who has the bride is the bridegroom. The friend of the bridegroom, who stands and hears him, rejoices greatly at the bridegroom's voice' (3:29). And elsewhere in the Holy Scripture: 'The day will come when the bridegroom is taken away from them, and then they will fast' (Matt. 9:15)."

And then he ended his speech, while Marcelo started to reason:

"I think, dear Sabino, that what you have just told us is apt to create some confusion. Every night I try to establish a dialogue with the stars in the sky. They may be deaf to our problems and yet they are not speechless, for it is said in Psalm XIX:

The heavens declare the Glory of God;
And the firmament sheweth his handiwork.

"And the Glory of God and His handiwork are the deeds of Jesus which we have previously mentioned. Let the heavens hear a message that came to us from them, and which now we try to broadcast. My only regret is that my voice is feeble and the noise of the river going over the dam may blot out many of my words.

"Let us proceed nevertheless. When God calls Jesus His king, and since whoever is king is so by the grace of God, we should understand that Christ is not a king just like the others but rather an unusual, extraordinary kind of king. As I see it a king should have three great qualities. He should be personally fit to rule, he should be able to rule over good subjects, and finally he should be able to carry out his task and improve their life. No one has ever had these conditions fulfilled as perfectly as Jesus. That is why He was such an extraordinary king.

"Let us count these blessings God endowed Christ's human nature with, humility and a kind heart, as Christ himself states:

Take my yoke upon you, and learn of me;
For I am meek and lowly in heart: and ye shall
find rest unto your souls. (Matt.11:29).

"And as we pointed out not too long ago, Isaiah said of him:

He will not cry or lift up his voice, or make it
heard in the street;
A bruised reed he will not break. (42:2–3).

And also the prophet Zechariah,

Lo, your king comes to you;
Triumphant and victorious is He,
Humble and riding on an ass. (9:9).

"Perhaps many people will conclude that humility is not a fitting quality for a king, yet God, who chose Christ above every-body else and called Him His own king, a king that would translate God's ideas and make them intelligible to all men, came to the conclusion that the most essential quality of a good ruler was to be humble and kind. The magnificent building that God envisaged could have no other cornerstone. In music not every voice can be a soprano or bass voice. When singing a madrigal you hear several voices which all mingle and combine harmoniously. So too God found that the humility and meekness that were so much a part of Christ's soul would harmonize in a most beautiful fashion with the highness and universality of wisdom and power in which Christ's life and mind excelled over every other created being. For if such intelligence and such power were to be given to a proud and haughty individual, no good and proper result could come of it. And moreover, even if humility had not been a requi-site from the viewpoint of Christ's own preferences, He, as well as his subjects, were bound to find it useful. For the efficacy of His rule and the many gifts that come from it are coming to us through our faith and through the love that unites us to Him. It is well known that the leader whose majesty and greatness are beyond compare does not create in our hearts love and affection, but rather admiration and awe. It would be impossible for our mortal and weak hearts, face to face with the boundless excellence of Christ, to feel the tenderness and brotherly love with which He wants to be loved by us. Only His humility makes this possible, making us more daring, more hopeful, bringing us closer to Him.

"In truth, if one wishes to be a fair and honest judge, one will state that humility and meekness are most necessary qualities for a king. Sometimes we err in our judgment and since we see that princes have been acting all the time in a haughty and proud fashion, we have concluded that humility and plainness are virtues reserved for the poor. We lose sight of the fact that the very nature of God, which should be an example of majesty and inspiration to kings, is both elevated and humble. God came down to create with care, with His hands, even a lowly worm, taking care to keep the worm alive. God painted with a thousand glowing colors birds' feathers, covering the trees with green leaves. What we seem to despise by treading upon fields and meadows, God did not disdain but carefully painted with grasses and flowers. Therefore, with praise and admiration David sang:

> Who is like unto the Lord our God,
> Who dwelleth on high,
> Who humbleth himself to behold
> The things that are in heaven, and in the earth!
> He raiseth up the poor out of the dust
> And lifteth the needy out of the dunghill;
> That he may set him with princes,
> Even with the princes of his people. (Ps. 113:5–9)

"And, it is sad to say, we no longer expect our rulers to be humble. We have become perverted by past history—and the behavior of princes has been very influential in this perversion. God made His son a prince among princes, the only true king, and made Him humble. How did this happen? How can we define Christ's sweet humility?

BOOK II

"Let us do it obliquely, by defining another one of Christ's virtues. For Christ was not only humble. He, among all other human beings, became an expert in suffering and anguish. All of His sad experiences were sent by the Father to His Son because Christ had to become a true king, a perfect one. As St. Paul has written:

> For it became him, for whom are all things, and by whom are all things, in bringing many sons unto glory, to make the captain of their salvation perfect through sufferings. For both he that sanctifieth and they who are sanctified are all of one. (Heb. 2:10–11)

And a few lines below,

> Wherefore in all things it behooved him to be made like unto his brethren, that he might be a merciful and faithful high priest in things pertaining to God, to make reconciliation for the sins of the people. (Heb. 2:17–18)

"Let us remember that since Jesus suffered by being tempted and having to resist temptation, He can also help us in our temptations. I do not know which to admire most, God's love, a love that inspired Him to give us a king that would last forever, a king from our lineage, so human, so humble, so full of compassion, so familiar with pain and grief, or the infinite humility and patience that Jesus wanted to assume and accept fully in order to give us a good example and also because thus He could better understand us when we became afflicted by troubles and anguish.

"And since some men are afflicted by certain troubles, other men by other troubles and problems, Christ, whose empire had to last through the centuries, and whose charity and compassion were infinite, wanted to try in Himself almost all the different kinds of grief and trouble. What did He not suffer? Some men suffer from poverty. Christ knew poverty better than anyone else. Some men are born from lowly parents and are therefore despised by society: Christ's father, according to the human opinion of that time, was a humble carpenter. Exile is always bitter: Jesus as a child lived in exile and had to flee to Egypt. He was hardly born when His troubles began. It is always sad to be the cause of grief to one's own family: Jesus in His flight was compelling His poor and beautiful mother, as well as holy and poor Joseph, to travel through strange alien lands. He lived through the anguish that children fear the most, that is, being alone, separated from their parents: Christ wanted to be, was to become for a while, a lost child.

"And then let us think about His mature years. How could we describe His grief and suffering during those years, His fortitude in accepting them? He seemed to invent new troubles daily and to rejoice in them. He suffered from hunger and from cold, lived in abject poverty, tired His body in long marches along roads and pathways, just to carry to men His unsurpassable gifts of wisdom and grace. And crowning all these sufferings, from these days of anguish, were to spring forth the torment and anguish of His final days. And His efforts were to be rewarded with grief and persecution. His love was rewarded with hatred. His efforts to give us a new life with a bitter death. Poverty, nakedness, anguish, are all horrible, but become even worse when crowned by ungratefulness, disdain, and persecution. David says in one of his psalms:

> All that hate me whisper together against me:
> Against me do they devise my hurt.
> 'An evil disease,' say they, 'cleaveth fast unto him:
> And now that he lieth he shall rise up no more.'
> Yea, mine own familiar friend, in whom I trusted,
> Which did eat of my bread,
> Hath lifted up his heel against me. (Ps. 41:7–9)

Which seems to indicate that ungratefulness brings the sharpest sufferings.

"Christ's experience was even more bitter, because He was not only persecuted by His own people, but also by those who had received from Him innumerable favors, by those who turned love into hatred, gratefulness into ingratitude, which reminds us of what Isaiah says about himself:

> But I said, 'I have labored in vain,
>   I have spent my strength for nothing
>   and vanity;

BOOK II

yet surely my right is with the Lord,
  and my recompense with my
    God. (49:4)

"We would never end if we tried to list Christ's sufferings. Let us mention the crowning torture, His death, and we shall realize how cheerfully He accepted such a bitter draught. Our words are insufficient to describe such sufferings. Let us try to indicate at least the bitterest moments of His final days.

"Misery is always more painful when it comes after prosperity and happiness. A few days before His arrest and crucifixion, Jesus was acclaimed and entered Jerusalem in triumph. He already knew that He was soon to be tortured and killed. In order to increase His sufferings later on, He wanted to retain the memory of the applause that those who were to despise Him had granted Him barely eight days before. He heard the enthusiastic shouts, 'Hosannah, Son of David' and also 'Blessed be He who comes in the name of the Lord,' and such shouts almost mingled in His ear with the contrasting 'Crucify him, crucify him' and also 'You who would destroy the temple and build it in three days, save yourself, and come down from the cross!' (Mk. 15:29–30) and also 'He saved others; he cannot save himself' (Mk. 15:31). The clash and contrast between the words of glory and the words of death were bound to darken His heart.

"It is often a consolation to those who leave this world, not to see the tears, the sobs, the afflicted sadness of those they love. Yet Christ, during the night before the last day of his mortal life, gathered together all His friends and disciples and had supper with them, and then He told them He was going to depart, witnessing their anguish, which made His own anguish sharper and deeper. Such words He had for them that very night, such expressions of love, which move our hearts today when we read them after so many years; they were bound to be even more powerful when they were heard by His friends as He walked away toward the Garden of Gethsemani. Each one of His steps along that road was like a nail that wounded His flesh, bringing to His mind and His imagination the prison and the death which were coming nearer and nearer. Everything He did in the garden was bound to increase His grief: He chose three disciples that were to keep Him company and comfort Him and yet allowed them to fall asleep, so that His care and anguish would increase through their carelessness.

"Later on, kneeling in prayer and addressing His Father, He was to ask that such a bitter draught should be taken away from Him—and yet He did not want His request to be granted. He let part of His will wish something that He did not want to attain, and in this fashion He felt the grief that comes from wishing in vain and seeing that which we wish refused. As if the torment of His approaching death were not enough, he wanted, in a manner of speaking, to rehearse His death, to die twice, once in fact and once through His imagination. For He deprived His human side of the consolation and power of the heavens, and He imagined, as a mortal man, the very sufferings of death, doing so in such a realistic way that neither the crown of thorns nor the wounding nails were as cruel and powerful as His own imagination. He seemed to crave sufferings and to experiment beforehand all the pain that His body was to suffer later on. For a sudden death gives us but little suffering, but He wanted to anticipate all His torments within His soul, feeling in detail and slowly each one of His coming wounds, the grievous blows and lacerations, combining the fear of death and agony itself.

"I mentioned the fear of death, and yet if I have to express what I have always thought about Christ's agony, I will tell you, dear Juliano, that it was not fear that opened His veins and made Him sweat drops of blood. Indeed He wanted to experiment and fear bodily consequences, but fear does not act this way in the human body, it does not make blood come to the surface of the skin, but rather brings it deeper into the body and around the heart; the very pores seem to constrict. It was not, therefore, fear that brought to the surface Christ's blood but rather courage and the effort of His soul which was fighting fear and in an inner struggle seemed to tear off parts of His body. We know that Christ, as I have mentioned, wanted to experience all our pains in order to achieve victory over them and show us the way so that we would in turn overcome. In this fashion, He hurled against Himself all the forces of anger and fear, like a cavalry charge hurled against His very soul. Both His body and His soul were tortured by infinite pain, and at the same time His soul was examining and weighing the reasons He was submitting to this: These reasons were mankind's past and future sins, their heavy ugliness, God's wrath and indignation. At the same time He may have thought about the coldness and indifference of man to His own suffering.

"So many thoughts, so vivid an imagination, all present in His mind at the same time, almost drowning Him. But He did not try to flee or surrender or in any way diminish His anguish. On the contrary, He brought it to its peak, trying not to think about His own divine nature and the heavenly glory to which He was getting near in His agony.

"It was without any weapon except His courage and His desire to obey His Father that He faced His tormentors and won His last battles. The effort was so great that He was bound to sweat blood. He became thus acquainted with our human suffering, our fears and anguish, and knew what it is to fight against oneself, against one's wishes and imagination, until He became the master of His own fears and trembling. He was also afflicted by a sad experience: to be betrayed and sold out by one of His friends, as He was by Judas, a certain night; to be abandoned by other friends in His moments of trouble, to be rejected by those who loved Him so much and delivered Him into the hands of those who hated Him bitterly. The sadness of being falsely accused by false witnesses, the wounds of injustice, the hardness of a bloodthirsty judge, are evils that can be understood only by those who have lived the same experience. The same thing can be said of His being interrogated by cruel tyrants, shielded hypocritically by religion in spite of their blasphemies, for their hatred of God was carefully hidden by a false mask of pretended piety. All this bitterness was found by Christ and to this experience were added insults, the blows, the mockery, the smile in the face of His enemies, the accusations of madness, the crown of thorns, the cruel lashes, and what may be even more painful, the mixture of hope and hopelessness that He experienced during His last hours.

"He also suffered the blow of treason: He was betrayed by His own friends such as Judas. Those who owed Him love and affection abandoned Him in His hour of affliction. Not only did they reject Him, they delivered Him to His mortal enemies. He suffered the lies of His accusers, of false witnesses; He suffered injustice and fell in the hands of judges anxious to shed innocent blood. Such grief is fully understandable only to those who have suffered a similar destiny. Under the disguise of legality He found only tyranny, under the cloak of religion and piety only unbelief and blasphemy, under the pretense of worship of God He found hatred of God. Such was the bitterness that He had to endure, and to it was added insulting words, blows, mockery. He saw the smiling faces of His enemies as He was dragged from court to court, crowned with thorns, cruelly whipped: He knew hope briefly, but it was soon replaced by despair.

"Thus when Pilate found out about the envy and lies of the Pharisees there was a glimmer of hope: Pilate spoke with Christ and decided to submit the matter to Herod, whose opinion of Christ was high. At that moment it was possible to think that a happy solution was at hand. And when Pilate submitted the trial to the will of the people hope was renewed. The people had to choose between a murderer and a man who had resuscitated the dead and whose good deeds were known by all. And the judge's wife let him know about her vision and asked him to free the innocent. At that moment we reached the threshold of victory. And yet the light vanished soon and was replaced by darkness. As in a tempest a ship is tossed upward by a wave and soon afterward seems to fall into an abyss, the waves of hope and despair battered our Lamb. He had decided to explore every corner of the realm of unhappiness.

"The subject is endless but our tongue grows tired of enumerating Christ's sufferings. I forgot to mention the unjust sentence at the trial, the town crier's voice, Christ's weak shoulders under the heavy cross (our king's true scepter), the screams of the crowd, some inspired by joy and others by grief, all equally moving.

"Let us not forget Mount Calvary. Being undressed in public is something a mature man finds shameful: It happened there to Christ. Having one's hands and feet pierced with iron nails is a cruel torment: It happened there to Christ. He, who showed pity and charity to all, seems to have been without pity with respect to His own body. He rejected even the gesture of mercy His executioners had offered Him: In fact it was the usage of that time that those who were condemned to die on the cross would be offered a strong drink made with wine, myrrh, and incense, that had the power to dull pain, and Christ rejected it when it was offered to Him.

"And thus, defying pain and rejecting any weapons against suffering, His body naked but His heart armed with strength and patience, our king rose nailed to His cross. He was carrying upon

BOOK II

His shoulders our salvation, suffering all the punishment that the world deserved because of our sins: His pain was indescribable. For every part of His body and senses became a part of His grief. His eyes showed Him His mother before Him, His mother alive and dead at the same time. His ears made Him aware of the blasphemous screams of His enemies. When He was thirsty He had to taste gall and vinegar. His sense of touch, with His skin in tears and with open wounds all over His body, did not show Him anything that was not bitter and cruel. He finally started to bleed copiously: His blood seemed anxious to wash our sins and poured out incessantly. Then came the cold of approaching death; finally He experienced agony and death.

"Why should I dwell upon these details? Even now Christ, as Lord of the whole world, is still suffering: He was never afraid of pain. How many men, or rather how many nations even today reject His principles and curse His name? He is and should be in principle exempt from misery and suffering, but accepts these insults in His mystical body because He does not want to reject grief and pain."

"This is a new and better way to be a good king," Sabino said turning toward Juliano, "as Marcelo has just described it. I do not know whether the writers who have dealt with the education of princes have described it thus but I know too well that the princes and kings who are alive today have not followed Christ's example, for their main goal is to avoid all suffering."

"It is true that some ancient writers," Juliano stated at that point, "wanted a young prince to have a hardy and tough education, but it is also true that they were thinking about toughening the prince's body to make him strong and courageous. As far as I know none of them prescribed exercises and experiences that would improve the prince's soul and teach him to be compassionate. But of course we are dealing with human writers and human projects, while the king about whom Marcelo was talking inspired His life in divine principles and the straight path that leads to truth and avoids the lies and deceptions of our world. It is therefore no wonder, dear Sabino, that today's kings do not follow Christ's example, since their aims and goals are different. For Christ organized His kingdom for our advantage and betterment, acquiring all the qualities that are necessary to improve the lot of His subjects, while the kings of today rule in order to gain advantage for themselves and care little for us, selfishly taking advantage of us and even harming us when they feel they can gain by it. And whenever they neglect to follow God's teachings our daily experience shows us that this very fact prevents them from reaching true greatness. Why do you think, Sabino, that they burden their subjects with such heavy yokes, establishing cruel laws and executing them without pity, if not because they have never experienced in themselves the pains of affliction and poverty?"

"That is so," Sabino answered, "but what tutor would dare educate a prince in misery and need? And if he did dare, what would the reaction of the court be?"

"This is our blindness," continued Juliano, "to approve what harms us and to be afraid to have our prince experience everything in life, although it would be beneficial for us to have a prince that had lived through good and bad times. Those who educate our princes do not want them to lower their eyes and look kindly at their subjects. They would rather spoil them, regale their body, serve them four meals a day, dress them in silk. But we are wandering from our main subject."

"Dear Juliano," Marcelo continued, "this was not a digression but an inspiration to me. And you, dear Sabino, you must know that it is impossible to dream that our princes and kings can ever follow the perfect example of our Lord. If they were not so different God would not have designated Christ his king. Besides, Christ's kingdom is eternal while our princes' rule ends with their life. So each would follow its own path: Our kings will be haughty and reject every unpleasant experience, while God following his path, in order to create in Jesus a true king, made Him humble and subjected Him to grief and pain so that He could be compassionate with His suffering subjects. God also made Jesus aware of the personality, devices, and virtues of His subjects. For a king also must be a judge, giving his just desserts to each one of His subjects, distributing rewards and punishments, and if the king does not know the truth there will be no real justice in his kingdom, for the indirect knowledge that the king receives from those who surround him is the source of error, not of truth. Those who surround the king not only make many mistakes but often try to deceive their king in order to further their own private purposes; that is why it is almost impossible to find out the truth.

But our king has a mind that, like a perfect mirror, shows Him everything we think and do and therefore He does not pass judgment, as Isaiah points out, nor does He punish or reward by following whispered insinuations or by concluding from appearances, because both senses can be deceived. He does not follow the opinion that His courtiers want Him to follow: He follows the truth, which He can recognize without any problem.

"The same way that God allowed Jesus to be able to know what is in our souls, God also gave Him all the power needed to grant us favors. He Himself in His own person holds all the goods and riches that can make prosperous and happy the inhabitants of His kingdom. We are always depending on Him because in a way we are all members of His family. This establishes the spiritual climate of Christ's kingdom: Let us describe further this heavenly kingdom.

"Its main feature is that all its inhabitants are generous, noble, and belong to the same lineage, race, or family. For although Christ's kingdom in the whole universe embraces all mankind, all creatures, good or bad, yet the kingdom that we are talking about and in which Christ shows His noble condition of king, the kingdom that will last forever in glory (for the wicked will be set aside, plunged in darkness, forgotten) comprises only the just, the good human beings, and they are all generous, noble, all belonging to the same family. They may differ in their birth, but as we mentioned before such a difference is insignificant and does not matter at all with respect to this new kingdom, which is composed by what St. Paul calls 'the new man' or 'the new creatures' in his Epistle to the Galatians, 'For in Christ Jesus neither circumcision availeth any thing, nor uncircumcision but a new creature,' and therefore all these inhabitants descend from the heavens, they are all brothers and all sons of Christ.

"David understood how excellent the new kingdom under his divine nephew would be, and he describes it in a short and elegant fashion in his Psalm 110:

The Lord shall send the rod of thy strength out of Zion:
Rule thou in the midst of thine enemies.
Thy people shall be willing in the day of thy power, in the
  beauties of holiness

THE NAMES OF CHRIST

From the womb of the morning: thou hast the dew of thy
    youth

and thus we see that when Christ finally rules and the rays of His
light dissipate the mist and darkness that still oppose Him, his
vassals will become true princes: Each human being will be a king
and Christ, as truthfully He is called in the Holy Scripture, will
be King of Kings and Lord of Lords."

At that moment Sabino said, turning toward Juliano: "That is
indeed a noble kingdom in which no vassal can be called low
because of his lineage or despised because of his family and social
class, and all are equally well born. It seems to me that a king who
wants to be truly and honestly a king should not have any vassals
who can be despised and called vile."

"Yet in our present time, dear Sabino," Juliano answered,
"our kings seem to be forced to despise some of those they rule in
the same fashion that when we want our body to be healthy
sometimes we have to make a limb or part of it suffer so that the
other limbs and parts of the body are not lost, and therefore, we
should not be too critical of our princes."

"It is not so much that I criticize them," Sabino said, "but
rather I feel sorry for them, because compelled by the need which
you have mentioned they have become lords of despised and lowly
vassals, but what can we say about kings and princes who not only
lower and despise some of their subjects but think that this is the
only way they themselves can feel important, and try their best so
that the groups they have lowered and despised will be held down
and despised generation after generation?"

To which Juliano answered, "They are in that case everything except true kings because a true king must always try to
make his subjects happy, which is the opposite of making them
feel harassed and worthless. And besides, the king who debases his
subjects debases himself. If the king is the head, what honor is
there in being the head of a deformed and vile body? If the king is
like a shepherd, why should a shepherd want to have a sickly
herd? Seneca was right when he wrote, 'it is beautiful to lead
illustrious people.'

"Not only do kings damage their own honor when they try to
stain the honor of their subjects but they also damage their interests and endanger the peace and the very existence of their king-

dom. In the same way that oil and water will not mix, it is impossible to establish peace in a country in which there are groups that are held apart from one another, one group with honor and glory, the other group rejected and without honor. In the same way that a human body with damaged limbs and whose humors are in disharmony is close to sickness and even death, we can see that a country in which many groups and many families are mistreated and wounded and because of customs and law cannot mix and harmonize with other groups and other families is a country about to sicken and on the edge of civil war. For each individual feels in his own self the wounds and insults with which society is rejecting him and will always be ready to rise, strike, and take vengeance.

"Let us now set aside these sad situations which have been produced either by necessity or by ill advice and error and let us now hear again Marcelo, who was explaining why the vassals of our only and true king are noble and generous."

"They are noble and generous," Marcelo answered right away, "because they were brought up by someone who had such qualities and also because they were noble and generous at first. They are the effect, the fruit, of a generous soul, because it was the generous decision of God and Christ to inspire justice and friendship in those who by themselves may not have deserved such qualities. It is true that just and upright men deserve God's favor, but to inspire justice and righteousness in human beings who were God's enemies can be the result only of God's generosity and thus James writes, 'Of his own will he brought us forth by the word of truth that we should be a kind of first fruits of his creatures.' The Greek text uses the word *bouletheis*, which means 'of his own will' and has the same meaning in Hebrew, his mother tongue (if per chance he wrote in Hebrew), where it is said *nadib*, a word close to, and with its roots in, *nedaboth*, a word which, as we pointed out earlier, means magnanimous and princelike. Thus the text means that God created us magnanimous and princely, that is, not only because He wanted to create us and was inclined to do so by Himself, but also because He wanted to show His grace and justice with an abundance of generosity and kindness.

"For truly, everything created by God is born out of His will and is created by His pleasure, for no one compels God to create—and yet when He places so much energy and a divine spark in men, this comes not only because of God's will but rather out of God's extraordinary generosity. For God gives His favors, among the greatest of His favors, to beings that do not really deserve such favors and rather would deserve to be punished than rewarded. I shall give only one example and try to be brief. Let us remember what happened with mankind's common ancestor: Adam, and remember what God did to Adam: in spite of the sin committed by Adam, yet God did not destroy him. This should remind us of God's generosity in His creation of mankind.

"Adam sinned and in this sin condemned himself and all of us, yet God later on forgave him and made it possible for his descendants to be saved. Who can count the infinite resources of kindness that God poured out when forgiving mankind? First of all God forgave the man who trusted the serpent, a serpent who had not given man any tokens of love, and yet Adam followed the serpent's advice and forsook the Lord's. Then we must remember that God forgave a sinner who appreciated more the vain promise of a small advantage and forsook a true experience and the possession of true great riches. Thirdly, God forgave someone like Adam who did not sin out of need or passion but rather out of ungratefulness. Moreover, God forgave Adam who did not ask for forgiveness but rather fled and hid. God forgave him shortly after his sin, almost right away.

"And there is more: In order to forgive Adam, God became indebted to Himself. And when man's grievous wickedness arose in God's heart a just wrath, yet God's mercifulness gained the upper hand: In order to save mankind God decided to diminish His own powers and take flesh as a man. As St. Paul puts it, God paid Himself for man's sins, and in order to give man eternal life God decided to die in His incarnation as a man. It was generous to forgive the early sin, an unmotivated sin, and more so since the sin was so swiftly forgiven, and even more so to look for Adam in order to forgive him, when Adam had fled into hiding. Yet all of this pales beside the fact that at the same time that God realized that man was sinning He pledged His own life to the redemption of mankind. Man had forsaken God in order to follow the Devil, but God drew near man and became a man in order to save him from the Devil's dominion. What happened in the past to all of us (because in Adam's sin we all sinned) is happening daily to each of us, in a way that is uninterrupted and secret at the same time.

BOOK II

"For it is impossible to enumerate the many ways in which God in His kindness and pity helps us not to fall into sin and perdition, even though we try hard to sin and condemn ourselves. He inspires us in a thousand ways, never growing tired or giving up, no matter how ungrateful we prove to be. We remain aloof, as if in a castle besieged by God. He tries to enter, knocks time and time again at the door, beseeches us to open the gates, just as in the Bible the voice of the beloved is heard, saying

> Open to me, sister, my love, my dove, my undefiled:
> For my head is filled with dew,
> My locks with the drops of the night. (The Song of Songs 5:2)

"Let us not forget: The just, the men who are just, are generous and open-hearted because they are the living proof of the kindness and generosity of God's heart. They are called just because of the wonderful qualities that God has introduced in their hearts. Nothing is truer, more generous, and nobler than a perfectly Christian heart. The heroic virtue dreamed by the ancient Stoic philosophers pales beside the virtue that Christ has brought to our souls. When we consider the ancestry and lineage of the just man, of the Christian, we realize that his roots are to be found in God, and that the grace that inspires him is like a living portrait of Jesus Christ. Think of the just man's attitude, behavior, life-style: Everything is ruled by the image of God engraved in his soul. Gold and sensuous pleasures may interest others, not him. He is his own master, and despises the vain honors created by society. He does not know anger. He has infinite riches inside his soul: His main goal is to help other people.

"His generosity spreads out beyond his neighbors, his province, his country. He tries to help all the inhabitants of our earth. He can even be friendly and generous toward his enemies, who attack him with bloodstained hands. He can risk his life, and in fact will do so in order to save the lives of his sworn enemies. He rejects everything low and subject to time's ravages, wanting only to draw near to God and the values that can be found only in heaven. Whatever is enduring and eternal, noble, and solid, such as God's friendship, God's embrace, is what he desires. A good example of all these traits can be found in St. Paul, who about himself says in his Letter to the Corinthians: 'But we have this treasure in earthen vessels, that the excellency of the power may be of God, and not of us. We are troubled on every side, yet not distressed; we are perplexed, but not in despair; persecuted, but not forsaken; cast down, but not destroyed' (2, 4:7–10). And writing to the Romans, full of generous courage, he states in chapter 8: 'Who shall separate us from the love of Christ? shall tribulation, or distress, or persecution, or famine, or nakedness, or peril, or sword?' (8:35).

"I have stated briefly what God's efforts were in order to make Christ a king, and us Christ's subjects. It remains to be described how and in which manner Christ as a king rules over His subjects. It is a unique way, much different from today's usage, unlike the way our earthly kings deal with us.

"For it is obvious that the basic tool of rulers is the law. And through it the king can become rich, if he is actually a tyrant and his laws are tyrannical, or, on the other hand, if he is a true and genuine king, he can make his subjects, in that case, happy and prosperous. It often happens that because of man's weakness, because of man's evil mind, laws are misinterpreted and misapplied. They should protect us against evil and foster good behavior, and yet quite often it happens otherwise: By forbidding something the law makes it more desirable. Often laws make us aware of ways to break the law, and as St. Paul points out, they induce us into sin in spite of the best of intentions. That is why Christ, our redeemer, has found a better way: Not only does He teach us to be better human beings, but He makes us better, what no one else could do in the past. In this respect He differs from other teachers.

"A system of laws should carry us toward goodness and away from evil. It can achieve it through the mind or through a training of the will. This is why we can talk about two types of laws. The first ones talk to the mind and through reasoning tell us what should be done and what should be avoided. The second ones talk not to our minds but to our will, creating a craving for the good things and the noble behavior, teaching us to avoid crooked and evil actions. The first kind is full of commandments and rules. The second kind restores our health by reconciling us with wisdom and reason.

"We know in truth that Adam's sin has affected and wounded us all, diminishing our minds and wills. Two kinds of laws were needed if we were to be helped, one directed toward the mind and the second intended to restore our lost will power. Yet the law that gives guidance and light to our mind is often unable to influence our will, and by forbidding some activity makes us more aware of it and of its possible pleasures. Often the intention is thus frustrated: The basic idea was to make mankind better, the result is just the opposite. We wanted to underline the darkness of evil and succeeded only in making evil more desirable. Yet and most fortunately the second kind of laws uproots the evil altogether, since it makes our will desirous of all that is straight and good and honest, and makes sweet all that can be healthy to our soul, and at the same time pulls us away from whatever harms us, is evil and bitter to the life of our soul.

"The first set of laws is the Commandments, all of it full of negative injunctions. The second set of laws is the law of grace, mercy, and love. It does not tell us what to do or not to do but it helps us to love what we should accomplish. The first law is hard and harsh: it condemns and attacks what our corrupted will accepts as good, and by doing so confronts it in a mortal contradiction. The second is sweet and beneficial, allowing us to love its commands, or in other words implanting in us the desire of goodness, making us fall in love with goodness and virtue. The first law is imperfect because of the contradictions it creates. The second law is perfect because it brings us closer to perfection. The first law makes us afraid, the second law turns us into lovers. The first law may make us worse in the secret recess of our souls, the second law will help us become just and saintly. As St. Augustine points out in *De littera et spiritu* (chapters 28–31) following as usual the trail blazed by St. Paul, the first law is perishable, the second law is eternal. The first law turns us into slaves, while the second law makes us sons of God. The first law is like a stern tutor while the second law gives us mercy and comfort, no longer servitude but rather honor and true freedom.

"This being so, without a doubt, I claim that Moses and those who before or after him gave us laws and commandments and helped us to organize our countries were only acquainted with the first kind of laws, more apt to order than to induce understanding and love in their subjects. This explains their failure. Christ, our redeemer, did much better: His law was always inspired by love.

"His mind and spirit have changed our souls, made us acquainted with virtue. Christ inspires us with chords and melodies of love, not through thunder and lightning, as Moses used to do. The law came to us through Moses, the grace came down to us through Jesus, as St. John has written. Moses gave us commandments, laws, not justice. He spoke to our rational minds yet could not heal our souls. As in the Burning Bush in the book of Exodus: It burned and yet did not set our souls on fire. The old law would light up the rational mind but could not set our hearts and wills on fire.

"Yet Christ could give us a law full of grace. Through it our will would turn toward good deeds. As St. John said in a succinct statement, the law was given unto us by Moses, grace by Christ. Moses gave us precepts, not justice; he talked to our rational minds not to our souls. This was wholly in agreement with the main characteristics of the old law, always close to our rational vision yet far from our wills. Only Jesus Christ gave us a law full of grace: It influenced our souls, our will power; we forsake evil and seek goodness, in the same manner that Jeremiah stated, as a prophet, that a day would come, as the Lord had said, in which a new testament would be brought to the house of Israel and also to the house of Judah. Not like the testament that was delivered to their parents on the occasion when God took them by the hand in order to help them flee from Egypt, for they did not abide by it: 'Forasmuch as they broke My covenant, although I was a lord over them, saith the Lord. But this is the covenant that I will make with the house of Israel after those days, saith the Lord, I will put My law in their inward parts, and in their heart will I write it; and I will be their God, and they shall be My people; and they shall teach no more every man his neighbor, and every man his brother, saying: "Know the Lord"; for they shall all know Me, from the least of them unto the greatest of them, saith the Lord; for I will forgive their iniquity, and their sin will I remember no more' (Jer. 31:28).

"And we now have the new laws given to us by Jesus, and also His new rule. I need not dwell upon the beauty, virtue, and advantage of this new system. We love what we do, we love goodness and understanding and see they are one and the same thing. Will does not need the help of our rational understanding in order to embrace what is fair and just. We now see that our new king will be eternal. God calls Him king. Other sovereigns are bound to perish. Christ's reign is free from errors, faults, blemishes, and is bound to last forever. A kingdom perishes because of the tyranny of the king (for nothing based upon violence endures too long) or because of the vices of the subjects, who cannot agree with each other, or else because of the harshness of laws and the cruel way the laws are applied. All of which, as we know, cannot and does not apply to Christ's kingdom and reign. Jesus, who experienced every pain and travail, could not possibly become a tyrant. He also possessed every treasure in the world, and therefore could not be interested in oppressing His subjects in order to become wealthier. His subjects, moreover, are all tied together in a knot of friendship and peace. They are all noble, all come out of the same father, the same family, all endowed with the same spirit of peace and generosity. The laws are based upon love, they induce us to love what is to be done. This is why the angel who carried our king's message to the virgin said, 'He shall be king over the house of Jacob forever; and of his kingdom there shall be no end" (Luke 1:33). And David, much earlier, had said much the same thing, as Sabino well knows."

Sabino said right away, "I suspect the text you have in mind is as follows:

They shall fear Thee while the sun endureth,
And so long as the moon, throughout all generations. (72:5)

And with respect to the kindness of his rule and the happiness of his subjects the text goes on to say,

May he come down like rain upon the mown grass,
As showers that water the earth.
In his days let the righteous flourish,
And abundance of peace, till the moon be no more"
(Ps. 72:5–7).

And then Marcelo went on speaking, adding: "It is obvious that a work that endures forever and cannot be destroyed by time and age is a work that is worthy of God, since He is eternal and whatever comes from Him lasts forever. Our earthly kings and kingdoms are bound to perish and disappear, and this is unavoidable. May all kings relate to God, but only Christ be king of kings, lasting forever and ever."

Here Juliano added, thinking Marcelo was about to end his speech, "Yes, indeed, Marcelo, and you might as well point out now how the Holy Scriptures underline the difference we know exists between our earthly kingdoms and the kingdom of Christ, since it is fitting to all that has been said before."

"I was about to do just that," Marcelo added, "and finish my speech with it. The Holy Scriptures are clear and to the point. One of these kingdoms is solid and eternal, the others change and perish. The prophets call these earthly kingdoms by the name of winds, or of wild beasts, but the everlasting kingdom of Jesus Christ they call it 'mountains' (Ps. 72:3). And Daniel, speaking about the four royal dynasties which history records, the Chaldeans, the Persians, the Romans, the Greeks, tells us he saw the four winds fighting each other, and then he talks about four great beasts, diverse one from another. And Zechariah, in chapter 6, after mentioning four chariots drawn by horses differing in hair and color, states, these chariots go forth to the four winds of heaven. For in truth all the earthly power which our history describes is much ado about nothing, noise without substance, it vanishes like a wind or a cloud, is born of small causes. Just as wild beasts lack reason, are ruled by cruelty and violence, so do these empires come out of the bestial element in mankind, out of fierce ambition, greed for power, bloody revenge, naked wrath. They are bound to perish through these same blind forces.

"On the other hand Daniel designates Christ and his kingdom by the word 'mountain,' as in his chapter 2, and elsewhere by the word 'man' as in chapter 7, where it is said that someone resembling the son of man came in front of the ancient of days, who gave him dominion over all peoples. In this way the word *mountain* expresses the firmness and everlasting quality of such a reign, and the word *man* indicates that such a holy monarchy is not ruled by bestial instincts or disordered passions: Every action is grounded upon good judgment and reason; it is a kingdom ruled not by fierce cruelty, but by human kindness."

Then Marcelo paused. Sabino then spoke: "If you allow me, Marcelo, I have two questions for you. The first one is as follows: both Zechariah and Daniel, in the passages you have quoted, mention only four earthly empires or kingdoms, and in truth there seems to be five, for the empire of the Moors and the Turks, which flourishes in our time, is different from the four ones quoted before and yet is not less powerful than most of them. And if Christ by His coming and by establishing His kingdom had to get our earth rid of any other monarchy, as Daniel seems to have announced, when he talks about a stone that smites an image upon its feet of iron and clay and breaks them in pieces, how can we accept the fact that after Christ came to the world, after Christ's doctrine spread over most of the earth, there should arise an empire alien to him, as powerful and vast as the one I have mentioned? My second doubt has to do with the kind and loving fashion with which Christ, as you stated, will rule His kingdom. For in the second Psalm we read that the Lord says to His son:

Thou shalt break them with a rod of iron;
Thou shalt dash them in pieces like a potter's vessel."

And Marcelo, then, "These are not questions easily answered, my friend. The first one is so hard that I would rather listen to someone else's opinion than give my own. It may take more time than is available now to us to give a complete answer to it. I will do the best I can. There are scholars well known to you, dear Sabino, and well liked because of their wisdom, who claim that this new empire of the Moors and the Turks is not basically different from the Roman Empire but rather an offshoot of it and still part of it. Zechariah says about the fourth chariot that its horses were grizzled and bay: He may be defining this offshoot of the Roman Empire, which in the part occupied by the Moors and the Turks can be described as grizzled or strong, and in the western section which is Germany, where the emperors do not succeed one another by lineage but are elected from different families, could be described as variegated or bay.

"And as far as I can tell Daniel seems to favor such an interpretation when, in his second chapter, he describes the statue that symbolizes the earthly empires; he explains that the legs were made of iron, and the feet part of iron and part of clay. These legs and feet do not symbolize two different empires but rather allude only to the Roman Empire, which in its first period was all iron, because of its strength and greatness, but now at the end its western part is weak like clay, and the eastern section, with its capital in Constantinople, is strong and hard, Daniel seems to point out that the hard iron in the feet, which we have said may symbolize the Turks, when in Daniel's Latin text it is said that the iron in the feet had its source, or if you prefer its roots, in the legs of iron. And in his seventh chapter when he describes the terrible beast—no doubt the Romans—he seems to say the same thing: He describes the beast as having ten horns, and says that later a new horn, a small one, grew and it had the effect of destroying or plucking up by the roots three of the first horns. We could interpret this to mean the expansion of the Turkish Empire, which arose out of humble and low beginnings yet with its growth has broken and brought into submission two powerful seats of the Roman Empire, the section around Constantinople and the sultans of Egypt, and is attempting to do the same with other sections. And if this horn symbolizes the Turkish Empire, this means that such an empire is part of the Roman Empire, since it is a horn, as Daniel has it, which is born in the fourth beast, and we know such a beast is a symbol or allegory for the Roman Empire. This is, dear Sabino, a possible answer.

"And yet it is one which I have never accepted with enthusiasm. For what can we find in the Turks that will allow us to call them Roman, how can we pretend their empire is part of the Roman Empire? History tells us there is no linkage by lineage. Their laws are quite different. Their systems of government have nothing in common. Language, customs, life-styles, religion: all different. If we claim that the Turks are Roman because they replaced the Roman dominion over Constantinople and the eastern Roman Empire, then we are saying that the four empires are actually one and the same. For the Persians overthrew the Chaldeans and took over their capital, Babylon, where the Persians ruled a long time, until the Greeks under Alexander the Great took over from them, and then it was the turn of the Romans to rule. If taking over means identity of empire, then only one empire has existed. And yet we cannot accept such a statement.

"I sometimes think that the prophets of the Old Testament mentioned only four kingdoms, as you Sabino have pointed out, and did not mention, or know, the Turkish Empire. Their goal was to forecast the order and succession of empires on earth until the beginning of Christ's empire, the main object of their prophecies. Whether another empire was to come to power after Christ's birth and the establishment of his Church, until the end of time, was probably not something the prophets wanted to discuss: They left such matters to God's Providence and to the writers of the New Testament.

"And thus we see that St. John in his Apocalypse, if I am not mistaken, mentions clearly—as clearly as this is possible to the writer—the Turkish Empire. Not as one of the four empires, but as a fifth and new empire. In chapter 13 he describes a beast coming up out of the sea, having seven heads and ten horns, and upon these horns ten diadems, much like a leopard, and its feet like the feet of a bear, and its mouth like the mouth of a lion. We cannot ignore the possible allegory and allusion to a great empire, because of the name *beast,* and the diadems, heads, and horns, and because John writes that the beast was allowed to wage war with the saints and to overcome them, and received authority over every tribe, people, tongue, and nation. It is also obvious that this beast is not one of the four that Daniel describes, rather it is quite different, according to its description by St. John. If we accept that it symbolizes an empire and is unlike the other four beasts, it follows that a fifth empire would be established on earth after the birth of Christ: It is the one we have mentioned above, the Turkish Empire.

"To what you object—that is, that if Christ and his gospel were to crush the earthly kingdoms, as announced by Daniel with his symbol of the stone that destroyed the statue, how can it be that after Christ was born the Roman Empire endured and after its fall a new and powerful empire arose, it can be answered as follows: The crushing of the statue, and the overturning of the earthly empires, is not something that happened in one second. It is rather a long process which was started with the birth of Christ and the preaching of the gospels and that will continue until all the enemy forces are destroyed. The kingdom of heaven is coming little by little, smiting the statue, and will go on hammering it until all the spiritual forces reach glorious perfection.

"These blows weaken and destroy step by step the power which Satan had usurped in the world. Satan's idols are falling one by one. As Satan's head is wounded the Devil's limbs weaken. This does not mean the total destruction of earthly empires, which are still necessary in this world, but rather destroying and changing the principles and the people rebellious against Christ, until a more ethical and happier situation is established on earth. From the ruins of the old customs and attitudes emerges the body of Christ's Church. When the task is done and the virtuous are separated from the sinners the latter, as useless straw, can be sent to the eternal fires of hell and Christ and his Church, alone and openly, will reign gloriously forever. This, dear Sabino, is my answer to your objection.

"Because we must understand that Christ's Kingdom is being established in two steps (this applies to individuals as well as to all of mankind) and the first step is full of contradictions and tensions, the second will be full of victory and peace. During the first period Christ finds vassals but also rebels. During the second we will all obey and serve Christ most willingly. In the first period Christ smites with an iron bar the rebels and rules his subjects with love. In the second love will reign alone.

"It can be said that in a certain way Christ already reigns in the hearts of those men who are just and virtuous. His rule later on will be even more thorough. For nowadays it is the highest part of our soul which is subject to Christ's divine grace, which acts as an image of Christ, as a lieutenant sent to rule our souls. Yet the flesh, our dark passions, are often in rebellion against it. The struggle is constant: If man allows himself to be helped by grace, little by little his bad instincts are overcome. Like idols they are toppled and destroyed. Finally grace is firmly established in our souls and shines in the throne of our spirit. The rebellious forces are trampled and banished from the soul. This is bound to happen in the day of the Last Judgment, when the first period of God's reign will come to an end, struggle and war will cease, and victory and peace will be established.

"About this period St. Macharios has this to say:

For then will come out what our souls now contain. Just as trees after winter is past, under a warm sun and caressed by soft breezes, bring forth leaves, flowers and fruits, and just as grass in the same season is covered with flowers, so will the soul of every good Christian flower in such a day. For every soul devoted to God, that is to say, every true Christian, will know such a month of April, the day in which they shall be reborn to a new life. The warmth of the sun of Justice will bring forth the glory of the Holy Spirit. Their bodies shall be clad by the glory that now inhabits only in their souls. The first month of Spring is a month of joy, trees wear a new dress, animals and even things seem happy. And the day of resurrection is the April of the just, clothing their bodies in glory and light, in spiritual strength, the best garment with its joy, peace and eternal life. (*Homil.* 5)

"This is what St. Macharios says, and it is relevant, since from that day on our souls and bodies will be infused with grace, and our souls will take charge of our bodies. Our souls, full of reason and virtue, will become almost like God, and our bodies, influenced by our souls, will become almost pure spirit. Our souls, clad with God, will see Him and converse with Him. Our bodies will be immortal, full of light and without weight, and the grace sent to us by Christ will inspire our every thought and movement.

"The same will happen in society and history. At present Christ rules amidst some resistance: Some obey him, others reject him. Sweetness and light, yet also war. By a slow and secret action Christ is fighting and destroying His enemies. He first attacks the heads, the leaders, in other words the devils, who had taken over and were lording over many men. This was so in the past and is now taking place in the New World. For it is only by preaching the gospel, that is to say the virtue and the words of Christ, that idols will be toppled over and destroyed.

"After the idols Christ confronts those men who followed them blindly and who in their behavior were much like devils. Truth has to be accepted by them, and if they refuse they must be destroyed. Our gospel is much like the sun, sending its rays all over the world, and when it rises somewhere it sets somewhere else. Our gospel advances, moves on, lights first here and later there, making converts and also leaving in darkness those who are unable to accept its principles.

"And if divine grace allows some infidel kingdoms to grow in power it does so in order to test and make harder the human stones with which its Church is being built. The victories of infidel nations are but temporary, the victory of the Holy Spirit will be everlasting. At last God will be the only ruler, forever and ever. As St. Paul accurately and briefly states (in Corinthians 1, 15:25–28)

> For he must reign, until he has put all his enemies under his feet. And the last enemy to be destroyed will be death, for he has put all things under his feet. But when he says all things are subject to him, undoubtedly he is excepted who has subjected all things to him. And when all things are made subject to him, then the Son himself will also be made subject to him who subjected all things to him, that God may be all in all.

"It is, he states, convenient and needed for Christ to rule until his enemies are destroyed: The state of tension and war will have to go on until the complete victory is achieved. The last enemy is death: At the end of time there will be no more corruption, death or change, the just will come back to life, eternal life of glory: The first period completed, Christ will offer His kingdom to His Father, who will henceforward rule it together with His Son in eternal bliss. In this second period God will be master of everything and everybody. Firstly because all men, in their minds and wills and senses, will be His obedient subjects: His will shall be established securely both in earth and in heaven. Secondly because God will be fully in charge, He will be the ruler, the prime minister, the advisor, the source of life and pleasure to all of us.

"Plato states that rulers should be like good shepherds. Homer also had called or defined kings as shepherds of men. They have to behave toward their subjects in the same way as the shepherd who cares for his flock, finds pastures for it, guides it, takes care of the sick ones, washes them, shears them, looks after them. God will be our shepherd, He will be the soul in the body of His beloved Church, He will inspire and guide our senses, He will make our bodies shine with His glory. White hot iron shows us the rays and heat of fire: In the same way our bodies and souls will show the rays of God's light and glory. And we will only sing praises about His kingdom. Then the Daughter of Zion shall praise the Lord, Israel shall rejoice, for the Lord hath ended all punishment, the enemies have departed, and with the Lord at hand all fear must disappear.

BOOK II

"Or, in the words of Isaiah,

Violence shall no more be heard in thy land,
Desolation nor destruction within thy borders;
But thou shalt call thy walls Salvation,
And thy gates Praise.
The sun shall be no more thy light by day,
Neither for brightness shall the moon give light unto them,
But the Lord shall be unto thee an everlasting light,
And thy God thy glory.
Thy sun shall no more go down,
Neither shall thy moon withdraw itself;
For the Lord shall be thine everlasting light,
And the days of thy mourning shall be ended.
Thy people also shall be all righteous,
They shall inherit the land forever;
The branch of My planting, the work of My hands,
Wherein I glory.
The smallest shall become a thousand,
And the least a mighty nation;
I the Lord will hasten it in its time. (60:18–22)

And elsewhere:

And he that sweareth in the earth
Shall swear by the God of truth;
Because the former troubles are forgotten,
And because they are hid from Mine eyes.
For, behold, I create new heavens
And a new earth;
And the former things shall not be remembered,
Nor come into mind.
But be ye glad and rejoice forever
In that which I create;
For, behold, I create Jerusalem a rejoicing,
And her people a joy.
And I will rejoice in Jerusalem,
And joy in My people;
And the voice of weeping shall be no more heard in her,
Nor the voice of crying.

There shall be no more thence an infant of days, nor an old
    man,
That hath not filled his days;
For the youngest shall die a hundred years old,
And the sinner being a hundred years old shall be accursed.
And they shall build houses, and inhabit them;
And they shall plant vineyards, and eat the fruit of them.
They shall not build, and another inhabit,
They shall not plant, and another eat;
For as the days of a tree shall be the days of My people,
And mine elect shall long enjoy the work of their hands.
They shall not labor in vain,
Nor bring forth for terror;
For they are the seed blessed of the Lord,
And their offspring with them.
And it shall come to pass that, before they call, I will answer,
And while they are yet speaking, I will hear.
The wolf and the lamb shall feed together,
And the lion shall eat straw like the ox;
And dust shall be the serpent's food.
They shall not hurt nor destroy
In all My holy mountain,
Saith the Lord."   (Isa. 65:16–25)

After these words Marcelo remained silent for a while. And
then he continued: "It seems to me that we have said enough
about the name *king*. More could be said, and yet we have to direct
our attention so as to deal with other biblical names defining
Christ."

And then he remained silent. He lifted his eyes to the starry
sky and after a while he spoke:

PRINCE OF PEACE

"Even if our reason could not prove it, even if we did not
know in many ways how wonderful a thing peace is, it would
suffice to look up to the starry night heavens to understand
everything at a glance. Every star shining above us bears witness

212

BOOK II

to the harmony and peace of a world created by God. What is peace, in any case the perfect image of peace, if not what we now see in the sky and can give us such pleasure just by our looking at it?

"St. Augustine states that, in few words, one can define peace as a peaceful order, in other words a tranquil and firm approach to the world's balance and order, and that is precisely what a starry night sky is teaching us. We can see now a whole army of stars, an army as if on drill, on parade, each star shining in its great beauty, each star clinging to its place, not attempting to take over the place of the neighboring stars, not bothering other stars, never breaking the laws that bind each to the whole universe. On the contrary, they seem to act like loving sisters, they seem to speak to each other with their rays, one would say that they respect and love each other. Sometimes they seem to mix and combine their light, their attraction, to mingle their power in one single peaceful whole: The universe is one whole and strong unified presence.

"We can therefore say that the stars are a symbol of peace and order, and also a prayer and a hymn of praise to the Glory of God. Each star seems to sing out, each one has her own voice, and all together in a heavenly choir tell us about the wonderful advantages and the shining beauty of peace as it spreads all around us. It is a song without words, a noiseless song. It reaches our souls, it pierces them, it convinces us of the need for peace and harmony. For our souls soon realize how useful and beautiful peace is and begin to look for harmony and peace in themselves. If we look inside ourselves we realize that the harmony and order of the stars in the skies seems to soothe and calm our souls by just looking at them. We may not be fully aware of what happens to us and yet our dark desires, our stormy feelings, little by little calm down and disappear: Everything seems to fall into place. And in the same manner that stars keep silent, in their humility, the main force in our souls, the noblest element, that is to say, reason, rises in us, recovers its strength, its right, as if inspired at the celestial panorama. Our thoughts rise ever higher, as if reminded of their early divine origin. Everything low and vile is cast aside and rejected. Reason rules then, sitting in its throne as an empress, the other elements in our soul fall into place, we are invaded by a wave of peace and order.

THE NAMES OF CHRIST

"The shining stars have an even greater power, not only over reasoning mankind but also over less refined beings in our world, the elements of nature, earth and air, and even wild animals: Everything and everybody seems to calm down at nightfall. Do you not sense the silence that envelops everything at that moment, do you not agree that each being then seems to look into a huge shiny mirror made of a thousand stars, seems to like what it sees and, at peace with itself, become serene and peaceful?

"There is no doubt that our world has as its highest goal a complete and eternal peace. Wherever peace is to be seen we fall in love with it. Not only do we fall in love with peace, we also fall in love with the image of peace, we feel then that we should look like it, because everything seems to bend us toward the kingdom of peace. Even when we admit, as one should acknowledge, that peace is beloved by all, we shall see that the goal of reaching it is and should be our only goal. Everything we do in this earthly life, every human effort and project, has as its goal to reach the golden treasure of peace. There is no doubt that peace is our constant goal. Merchants send their ships to stormy seas, always with the aim of calming down their nagging wish for riches. Peasants work hard, their faces bathed in sweat, tilling their fields, because they want to keep at bay their harsh enemy, poverty and hunger. In the same fashion those who run after pleasure, those who crave after honor, those who look for revenge, in a word, everybody and everything, we are all running after peace, for either we try to reach something that we need in order to feel happy and rest, or we try to escape some evil force that troubles us.

"Whatever we are seeking, whatever we try to avoid, are sources of trouble, of anguish, to our souls. We feel surrounded by enemies at war with us. Every gesture, every step of ours is inspired by our wish to escape from war and struggle, to look for peace and calm. If peace is such a great goal, such a supreme value, who can rightfully be called Prince of Peace, that is, the source and origin of peace, if not the one that was at the source and at the root of all our values and our most precious things, Jesus Christ, our Lord and God? For if peace can be defined as the absence of evil, the avoidance of tormenting desires, and the presence of balance and serenity, only Jesus delivers our souls from fear, making them so serene and happy that they wish for no greater glory.

BOOK II

"It remains now for us to define peace, and also in which way is Christ the creator of peace, its main standard-bearer."

"It seems to me that your first question," Sabino declared, "or rather the first definition you want to spell out, is already fully defined in your previous statements and backed up by the authoritative quotation from St. Augustine."

"It is true," Marcelo answered, "that peace, as St. Augustine has stated, is a peaceful, serene ordering of things, a well-ordered serenity. We should reflect upon St. Augustine's definition, for in it we can find two elements: serenity and order. Peace is an idea that takes for granted the presence of order, or rather we have peace only when each thing, idea, object, being, keeps its proper place in the world. Whatever is and should be high and lofty should be in a high and lofty place, low things should be also in their place. Servants are supposed to obey, lords are supposed to command. Each one is supposed to do his or her duty, and moreover each one should pay his or her neighbor the respect and courtesy that is due to them.

"Moreover, peace demands rest, quiet, serenity. Even if everybody keeps his place, if each individual is nervously trying to elbow his way into a more privileged place, their anxious struggle destroys peace, brings us closer to chaos and war, which means that order, by and in itself, is simply not enough. It is unable to bring us peace. And on the other hand rest, quiet, serenity, again if only they are present, they are not enough if order is absent, they cannot create peace by themselves alone. Let us think about a peculiar situation, one which we might define as a situation full of 'quiet chaos,' if this is at all possible, if we can logically envisage it. It seems to me that successful wicked people are apt to create such a climate of chaos that is accepted as part of daily life. We are still dealing with a situation of tension, or anguish, of war and suffering. We must reject such a possibility.

"Coming back to peace: Let us define it as a serene harmony. And moreover this serene harmony is projected upon a large group of human beings: the third element of the definition is that both serenity and harmony are going to be spread upon a vast crowd, are going to influence it, to pervade and uplift it. Let us think about man in general. Man is related to God and can be defined, up to a point, by this relationship. We can also relate to others with courtesy and respect. And we should not forget that disorder can still be masked and made to look like peace, yet it is war that lurks underneath. Peace can be established in three ways: by respecting God; by respecting ourselves; by respecting other human beings.

"In the first case we see that our souls are in tune with God, subject to God's will, God's laws, and God, in turn, looks with favor and with love upon such a soul. The second case can be defined thus: Let us analyze man himself into his parts, comparing them among themselves. Thirdly, let us compare one man to the other human beings with whom he lives and talks. All of which tells us that we can define three kinds of peace: In the first one, peace is a relationship of harmony between man and God; in the second, peace exists when man lives in harmony with himself; in the third kind, man is not clashing with his fellow men.

"This first kind of peace will take place when man is subject to God and has accepted God's will, obeying divine laws in their entirety, and God, accepting man's submission, treats him with sweetness and love and sends him the gift of grace. The second kind of peace depends upon the rule of reason over human senses and passions. The latter must obey with alacrity, with pleasure, so that no rebellion is ever contemplated, but rather a harmonious collaboration of each part with the others. The third kind of peace is based upon the respect of the rights of each individual, and the granting of justice to each without struggle or delay. Each type of peace gives mankind a great deal of prosperity and when they are all present at the same time man reaches happiness and serenity.

"We experience daily the need for the third kind of peace, which brings us close to one another like brothers, and we also feel painfully its absence: It means quarrels, struggles, bloody wars.

"We are not as familiar with the benefits that the second kind of peace can bring us. Yet it allows us to live in harmony and peace with ourselves without being tormented by fear or fired by passion, without being perturbed by groundless joy or sadness, without being debased and paralyzed by grief. Our lack of familiarity with this type of peace is due to the fact that not too many men allow themselves to be ruled by reason. And yet the need to do so should be obvious. For what can we say about the life of those who allow free rein to their appetites and passions, changing their mind at whim, wishing to have and to hold what cannot be had at the same time, changing in a second from joy to sadness, from confidence to mistrust, from cowardice to arrogance? What life is this, when we are captivated by anything that comes in front of our eyes, when we wish to possess anything we see, we fret if we cannot own the whole world and explode in a rage if we do not succeed in this endeavor? And if we obtain something today, tomorrow we may come to despise it: Our only rule is to have no rules. How can we claim anything to be good among such sudden changes. How can such erratic taste have pleasure in anything? Rather, how can such an attitude fail to pervert and render tasteless anything that approaches our eyes, our ears, our palate? Let us hear what one of your favorite poets, Horace, has to say about this subject:

> No house and farm, no heap of tin or gold,
> Can drive a fever from its owner's weakened flesh
> Or his worries from his soul.
> He must be well if he must have good use
> from everything he has gathered through hard work.
> If one drinks from a dirty glass or vessel
> the best wine, the sweetest honey, will taste sour.
>
> *(Epistles,* Lib.I, 2)

"Even better and shorter is the Prophet Isaiah when he writes:

> But the wicked are like the troubled sea;
> For it cannot rest,
> And its waters cast up mire and dirt. (57:20)

For no stormy sea tormented by furious winds can compare with the huge waves unleashed by passions in our human hearts. These inner storms darken our days, make us afraid about the coming of the night, prevent us from sleeping. Our beds seem to be made of stone, we can no longer eat, in short there is not one minute of peace and joy left in our lives. Thus Isaiah continues,

> There is no peace,
> Saith the Lord concerning the wicked. (57:21)

And if such a chaos is obviously harmful, the absence of it, in other words peace, must indeed be good and useful to man. This should teach us how important it is to be at peace with God, who is the source of every type and kind of peace.

"For the sad results of God's war upon man, when man has displeased Him, show us how important it is to be at peace with Him. Jeremiah, through the voice of the city of Jerusalem, cries out about the ruins and suffering brought about by God's wrath:

> Is Israel a servant?
> Is he a home-born slave?
> Why is he become a prey?
> The young lions have roared upon him,
> And let their voice resound;
> And they have made his land desolate,
> His cities are laid waste,
> Without inhabitant. (2:14–15)

"And the Book of Job shows us clearly, as if etched in the victim's heart, the power of God's wrath:

> A sound of terrors is in his ears:
> In prosperity the destroyer shall come upon him.
> He believeth not that he shall return out of darkness,
> And he is waited for of the sword.
> He knoweth that the day of darkness is ready at his hand,
> Distress and anguish overcome him. (15:21–24)

Job is outstanding in his description of the havoc God created with His wrath:

> He hath fenced up my way that I cannot pass,
> And hath set darkness in my paths.
> He hath stripped me of my glory,
> And taken the crown from my head.
> He hath broken me down on every side, and I am gone;
> And my hope hath He plucked up like a tree.
> He hath also kindled His wrath against me,
> And He counteth me unto Him as one of His adversaries.
>   (19:8–11)

218

BOOK II

Such is the harm that comes to those who antagonize Him and it ensues that those who avoid His wrath will lead happy lives, lives of happiness and prosperity. God can be our worst enemy, and also our best, sweetest friend. Isaiah so states:

Rejoice ye with Jerusalem,
And be glad with her, all ye that love her;
Rejoice for joy with her,
All ye that mourn for her;
That ye may suck, and be satisfied
With the breast of her consolations;
That ye may drink deeply with delight
Of the abundance of her glory.
For thus saith the Lord:
Behold, I will extend peace to her like a river,
And the wealth of the nations like an overflowing stream
And ye shall suck thereof;
Ye shall be borne upon the side,
And shall be dandled upon the knees.
As one whom his mother comforteth,
So will I comfort you;
And ye shall be comforted in Jerusalem. (66:10–13)

"All of which helps us to understand that each one of three kinds of peace is of great importance. They are all related one to the others. For if we are at peace with ourselves we are also at peace with God and can equally establish peaceful relationships with other human beings.

"When God tells us He is our friend He does not change: He is simply as faithful to the past and also wants to improve us by lavishing upon us His grace, thus giving light to our souls. We are the ones that change and improve. He asks us, through his prophets' voices, to change, to improve our souls and our habits. As Zechariah puts it, 'Return unto me, Saith the Lord of Hosts, and I will return unto you' (Zech. 1:3), which seems to say, if you turn your eyes and your hearts to me you will find me looking at you with eyes of love, with a heart full of love. As David sings in Psalm 34, (verse 16), The eyes of the Lord are toward the righteous, and His ears are open unto their cry.'

"Thus He looks upon what is good with eyes that express love

219

and approval. God, as you know, is always looking at His beloved, and they exchange glances. Divine Providence is always present. As David puts it, and as we have quoted above, the eyes of the Lord are always looking at the righteous, and we know He listens to our prayers. And also,

> Behold, as the eyes of the servants unto the hand of the master,
> As the hands of a maiden unto the hands of her mistress,
> So our eyes look unto the Lord our God,
> Until He be gracious to us. (Ps. 123:2)

And in the Song of Songs, the Beloved asks the Shulamite that she should return, so that he may look at her face. Time and again God asks the just not to hide, to come forward, so that he may look at their faces.

"Two beings face each other, one of them is immutable, and then if they stop facing each other it must be because the one that could move and change had displaced his body and face. Now, God is unchangeable, His will and His behavior are one, but we turn our face away from Him—and then try to look at Him again—a thousand times. If I change, then I think God changes, yet it is not so. A soon as darkness disappears and my soul becomes clear and pure once more, God is again in front of my eyes, all love and forgiveness. And the second kind of peace is thus born.

"There is no doubt that being at peace with ourselves is of great help if we want to be at peace with others. For it is mainly our uncontrolled desires that pit us against other beings, and the spring of our evil thoughts and desires is to be found in our uncontrolled appetite, because men fight usually in order to control a limited number of goods or riches, or rather things that we think are good and will make us rich; they are not enough for all, so we try to take them away from others. We quarrel, we argue, we fight, and we finally go to war over such quarrels. St. James puts it accurately: 'Whence do wars and quarrels come among you? Is it not from this, from your passions, which wage war in your members?' (4:1).

"And the other side of the coin is that a man who is at peace with himself has suppressed and eliminated practically all the occasions to quarrel with other men. Possibly they are running after these earthly treasures; our wise man will not hinder them: Wealthy in his own inner self, in his own rich soul, he might even applaud the efforts of those men who are striving for riches and power.

"A cornerstone is a sound contribution to a building, and a string properly tuned helps an instrument played by a clever musician and the whole sound is sweet and harmonious. In the same manner our soul at peace with herself harmonizes with God and helps create a climate of peace and goodwill among all of us. And as we have pointed out previously these three kinds of peace are linked one to another, interdependent, and basically are built upon the first kind, that is, our being at peace with ourselves. St. Augustine is well aware of this, when he writes on this subject:

> Men of peace are those men who first of all manage to harmonize all the forces within themselves, and making these strains subject to their reason, which is the main seat of power in their soul, then manage to curb down their passions and desires. They become part of God's Kingdom, in which everything is well ordered. Let reason shine, let reason excel and rule us: reason in turn depends upon the great truths of Religion and to the presence of the Son of God, Who is truth made flesh. For reason cannot hold in check what is less prominent, less noble, unless it accepts the rule from above, from God's Son, who is the very image and the very presence of Truth. Reason cannot rule its lower subjects unless it accepts to be ruled by these higher principles. This acceptance creates peace, the very kind of peace every wise man and woman craves. (*De Sermone* I.2)

"And now let us find out how Christ established peace in our souls, and why we call Christ Prince of Peace. Only Christ could carry out this endeavor, although others may have tried to do the same thing. Let us state that a religious doctrine that does not strive to create in our souls a feeling of peace and harmony, a feeling of respect toward other human beings, is not truly Christian: This is a touchstone of true Christianity. Only Christ could accomplish such a wonderful transformation of our souls.

"Since Christ is the only one capable of such a wonder it is fitting that we should call him Prince of Peace. There have been people who thought that we were so ignorant that the only solution was to give mankind laws, commandments, regulations, and mete out punishments to those who would transgress. Such is the message of the old law, the Old Testament, and many weighty treatises were written by ancient philosophers dealing with this endeavor.

"Yet other writers took into account our weaknesses. Our flesh is weak, they reasoned, and perhaps this weakness is rooted in our bodies, and in the food we eat. They made rules about certain foods, since the wrong type of nourishment might increase our wrong appetites, our lust. Fasting, exercise, bathing, could clean our bodies and our minds. Hindu philosophers, as well as wise men from other cultures and the followers of Moses, tried to lead us along this path, and yet in vain: These rules and codes of behavior may be partially useful and yet even when we follow all of them at the same time they are not capable of giving us a perfect feeling of peace and getting us rid of our troubling passions.

"We must realize that man possesses both a soul and a body, and man's soul is endowed with will power and reason, yet because of the basic weakness that resulted from man's original sin all our resources were severely damaged. Reason was tainted by ignorance, our flesh and body by uncontrolled passions, and our will, so decisive in everything we do, more prone to evil than to good deeds, as if infected with the poison of the primeval serpent that seduced our ancestors.

"Of all our weaknesses the main one, the most severe and damaging one, is the weakness of our will. This is what failed in Adam, and from him corruption came down to us all. Adam did not sin because his senses betrayed him, or because his flesh overcame his reasoning powers, or his mind was blinded by some serious error. St. Paul points out that man did not sin because he was deceived, but because he decided to sin, opening his heart to the Devil and departing from God's advice, from which came disorder and chaos in his mind and body. We all suffer through hatred and through wars from this primeval transgression.

"The first givers of laws endeavored to better our rational faculty. Others who came afterward tried above all, through regulations about food and diets, to improve our poisoned bodies. And yet the very source and root of our troubles could not be found either in our reason or in our bodies: It could be located only in our will, our damaged and perverse will power. This is why all these attempts at bettering mankind were bound to fail. Only Jesus guessed accurately the source of our affliction and was able to heal our disease.

"For the remedy against our diseased souls can be found only in a heavenly soul, a spirit, that is to say, divine grace, which contains in itself health and truth. This spirit, this grace, only Christ could deserve and obtain, and only Christ can give it to us, for we should not forget what St. John said: 'For the Law was given through Moses; grace and truth came through Jesus Christ' (1:17). Which means simply that Moses gave light to our minds with his laws and commandments; many other lawgivers tried to do the same and succeeded in part, and Jesus could and did give us much better laws. And yet what can save us, and what can come only from Christ, is not laws and commandments and regulations. We can have a clear mind and a perverted will, a reasoning brain full of cynicism, and therefore this is not the way: The path can be found in grace, in kindness, in love. Neither Moses nor any other wise man could give us all of that, only Christ, and that is precisely what He did.

"This truth is so obvious because often the rays of light that carried information to our brain, the laws that were supposed to light our way into a better life, could not be of any help, on the contrary, led us astray. The light of wise advice was in itself good, yet it became useless or perverted because of the way we human beings, poisoned and perverted, were bound to interpret it. St. Paul says it in a few words, 'Once upon a time I was living without law, but when the commandment came, sin revived, and I died, and the commandment that was unto life was discovered in my case to be unto death' (Rom. 7:10). And also 'Now the Law intervened that the offense might abound. But where the offense abounded, grace has abounded yet more; so that as sin has reigned unto death, so also grace may reign by justice unto life everlasting through Jesus Christ our Lord' (Rom. 5:20–21). And also, 'Sin, that it might be manifest as sin, worked death for me through that which is good, in order that sin by reason of the commandment might become immeasurably sinful' (Rom. 7:13). Which means that when we sin in such a fashion, thinking that we obey a law, we sin in a worse way, and evil triumphs in our sinning.

"For indeed, as Plato shows in his *Second Alcibiades*, those whose will is sick or damaged, and do not know much about mankind's true goals and high moral principles, find that ignorance is actually quite useful to them, and knowledge, on the other hand, dangerous. Knowledge does not seem to act as a brake to their runaway desires. They make use of knowledge not for finding the right path but rather they use it for the purpose of refining and perfecting their perverse desires, turning a servant of good and virtue into an accomplice of evil deeds. The smarter and sharper they become, the worse and most corrupt they sink down to be. Without grace there is no peace, no salvation, and grace comes to us from Christ: This must be our final conclusion.

"Let us define this peace, this grace, and its effect upon us," Marcelo said, and while he was speaking he was gazing at the flowing current of the river, pure and shining, a mirror to all the heavenly stars, and then, pointing out toward the river with his hand, said, "This flowing river, this dark water reflecting the stars and that reminds us of a starry sky, can help us understand the meaning of God's grace. The same way that the sky is reflected in the water, which acts as a mirror, and turns the river into something very similar to the sky, in the same fashion divine grace coming down to our souls and taking over our minds turns us into an image of God, not because we look like God but because we reflect God's truth and intelligence, inasmuch as it is possible to do so without changing our nature and being in a radical fashion. Grace is not to be compared to an element of nature, to a metal, it is not air, it is not fire, but something deeper, stronger, loftier in its origin. Elements are born out of nature, grace is born above it. It is like a portrait of God, it carries God's imprint, and nothing in the world can be just like it.

"And thus grace can be compared to a deity, to a living image of Christ, which, having penetrated our souls, uplifts them from the inside, and, if I may use this expression, becomes the soul of our souls. The same way that my soul, spreading its influence over all of my body, can lift it up in spite of its clumsy weight, can give it strength and project it forward, filled with vigor and fire, grace can move and energize our soul. Our soul is imperfect and damaged, part of a body damaged by sin, and yet when moved by grace our will helps us lift up the whole to the heavens, grace spreads out and penetrates every pore, giving us the style and the nobility of heavenly creatures, brings us closer to God, and finally we feel no longer like God's creatures but God's sons and daughters, so close to Him that we feel part of Him and God ourselves.

"And, as we said before, grace acts at first upon our will, and because God's will is the essence of justice, in other words, goodness, what God wishes, and only what God wishes is good, truly good, this is why the first consequence of grace acting upon our will is to make it work toward good goals, not by imposing such goals but by making us fall in love with sweet goodness. We have said that the law can work in two different ways. The first, the way of prescriptions and orders, tells us what we should do and what we should not do, establishing in a public statement what our behavior should be. The second way is this: not by pressure, not by commandment, but by giving us the pleasure, the inclination, to love all that is healthy and sound and good. Because then our love for goodness will rule us and by ruling us become a sort of law to us, telling us what should be done. Philosophers call a law whatever rules our behavior and organizes our strength. It is a law that makes bodies fall down toward the earth's center, that tells fire to send up its flames, up into the air. Each being follows a set of laws that are given and prescribed to it, by acts of nature, and rule its life.

"The first way the law can work is in itself good and yet not very effective with us because of our greed for pleasure and our damaged roots. The second way is much more effective, and this is the way in which and through which Christ acts upon our souls. It writes upon our will what the old lawgivers wrote upon paper with ink, or upon stone with a chisel. The old laws inspired fear in our souls, but grace spreads such honey in our souls that it turns our minds toward goodness and justice and makes us wish for the victory of the good and the fair, as Jeremiah had prophesied.

"We should conclude that grace is an image of God that penetrates into our souls and influences our wills toward everything that is just, fair, and good. When this happens our inner kingdom, the kingdom of our souls, begins to enjoy a marvelous peace. Harmony replaces turmoil, serenity and peace bring joy to our inner life.

"For the first thing that the presence of grace in our soul accomplishes is this: The keen fear of God's wrath that tormented us disappears right away. This is what St. Paul says, 'Having been justified therefore by faith, let us have peace with God through our Lord Jesus Christ, through whom we also have access by faith unto that grace in which we stand, and exult in the hope of the glory of the sons of God' (Rom. 5:1–2). We no longer see God as an angry judge, we see in Him a loving Father, our sweet friend, not our powerful enemy. Through grace we have come closer to Him, and we have learned to love what is so much like us and we trust He loves us because we resemble Him.

"And the second result is that reason and will are going to find a peaceful accommodation and will no longer be at war with each other, for their goals and desires will become identical, and thus we shall see an end to our internal tragic and bitter struggle thus described by St. Paul, when he writes:

> For I do not do the good that I wish, but the evil that I do not wish, that I perform. Now if I do what I do not wish, it is no longer I who do it, but the sin that dwells in me. For I am delighted with the law of God according to the inner man, but I see another law in my members, warring against the law of my mind and making me prisoner to the law of sin that is in my members. Unhappy man that I am! Who will deliver me from the body of this death? (Rom. 7:19–24)

Reason and will become partners and friends from that moment on, the light created by love's fire helps both, and they become like brother and sister.

"One more thing: The senses and passions recognize the fact that a new master is in charge, they retreat, they stop their mischief, and our newly reinforced will can deal with any attempt at insurrection; nothing escapes the vigilance of the new team. Even the senses seem to accept the situation and change their pulling and pushing so as to help the projects being expounded by grace and our will power. Feelings and passions come closer to reason and seem to pull in the same direction. Just as in the changes that take place between day and night, as they are described by David in Psalm 104:

> Thou makest darkness, and it is night,
> Wherein all the beasts of the forest do creep forth.
> The young lions roar after their prey,
> And seek their food from God.
> The sun ariseth, they slink away,
> And couch in their dens.

In this same way our passions roam in the night of our anguish and slink away when the rays of light of love and grace begin to shine. Then what is truly human in us comes to the surface and we can work in peace day after day at the business of being true human beings.

"For indeed, is there any power in our body that can countermand the powers of a human being ruled by such a will helped by reason and grace? Mad wishes and desires, wild fears, count for nothing. Ambition, the blows of adverse fortune, the fear of losing his fortune, all of this is powerless to trouble the heart of the man who is at peace with himself. What does it matter if his fortune is lost? His burden, as a matter of fact, is lighter because of it. Do his friends disappear? God is still his best friend. He can be the target of hatred and envy, but knows no one can take away his inner riches. Everything may change and crumble around him, yet he will keep firm and serene. As Cicero has written, he will shine in darkness and although anybody may try to push him around, yet he will keep his place.

"One more good thing seems to spring out of our peace of soul: We have gained God's confidence and friendship, He is now on our side, and we no longer have anything to fear. How could anyone intimidate us? As Sophocles' Antigone speaking to the tyrant, the power of our free mind backed by God is invincible in us.

"In this way our peaceful soul brings forth the safety provided by God's protection, and such safety makes our inner peace sweeter and stronger. David in Psalm 4 (verse 8) seems to have defined best what we then feel:

> In peace will I both lay me down and sleep;
> For Thou, Lord, makest me dwell alone in safety.

"As he sees it, peace brings sleep, and we sleep best when we feel safe and protected. St. Chrysostom states that one more favor from God is to grant us peace, and quotes Psalm 119 (verse 165):

> Great peace have they that love Thy law;
> And there is no stumbling for them.

"For nothing helps us so much if we want to create and establish peace as our knowledge of God and our acceptance of a life of virtue, which banishes inner troubles. A man who does not know how much happiness this peace brings will be unhappy no matter whatever happens to him. No barbarian, no Scythian army, can wage a crueler war than the war waged against us by our secret thoughts and desires, making us lust for power, money, social standing, or any other wish dear to us.

"And yet this situation is in many ways logical and normal. We are dealing with a war taking place outside our mind, and another war taking place inside. And we can see that the inner turmoil is more severe and harsher than what takes place outside. Let us think about the fact that the disease that grows from inside us is usually more severe than the infection that comes to us from outside. Think about a big wood beam: The worms and termites that attack the beam from inside are more dangerous than any forces that attack from the outside. The same is true about the human body. And the same can be true about a city and about a state: The enemy attacking from outside is often less dangerous than the inner rivals and home-grown critics and destroyers of the peace. And we must state that the very same thing applies to our soul: Passions and inner diseases are its worse enemies.

"This is why we must state that if we could in any way prevent our souls from becoming enamored of evil wishes and projects, if we could in any way get rid of such evil desires, we would get closer and closer to happiness. St. Paul expresses our thoughts when in his Letter to the Ephesians (1:2) he writes, 'Grace be to you and peace from God our Father and the Lord Jesus Christ.' And whoever is in charge of protecting this peace is no longer afraid of any barbarian enemy, he is not afraid of the very Devil, and mocks the Devil and the whole Devil's army. He lives alone in peace and happiness, and neither poverty nor disease bothers him in the least, for his courageous soul takes care of every problem. He is not envied by anybody else: Why should he be? He does criticize himself, he does attack himself in his own mind, if he is envious: The envious man sees enemies everywhere and is easily offended; but this is not the case with those who enjoy God's grace. Those that do not possess such a blessing are always at war, especially inside their own souls and minds, and so external peace is of no use, no benefit, to them. They feel rage in their hearts when they see someone else happy and prosperous. The same is true of those who love riches: Their greed prevents them from living normally, even breathing seems to be a strain to such people. Quite different is the fate of the human being free from such passions: He has reached a safe haven and avoided all the storms that afflict those less fortunate than he (*Expositio in Psalm.* 4:2).

"This is, in brief, what St. Chrysostom has to say about the problem that concerns us. And he also points out how much joy they feel those who are at peace with themselves. For in the same way that when our humors are out of balance we find pleasure in no food, in no kind of drink, those at war with themselves cannot enjoy the wonderful and refreshing taste of truth and of life itself. Just as you can see through pure clear still water, you can see through a soul at peace. We see, we enjoy, we love. For being at peace with God we can then be in harmony with ourselves and enjoy being alive. Micah the prophet shows us how much better we may become through this process when he writes,

> Nation shall not lift up sword against nation,
> Neither shall they learn war any more.
> But they shall sit every man under his vine and under his fig-
> tree;
> And none shall make them afraid. (4:3–4)

Peace, Christian peace, is our safe passport to safety and joy.

"David sums it up quite accurately in one of his Psalms, when he writes, 'Glorify the Lord, O Jerusalem' (147:12) since Jerusalem means City of Peace and all of its inhabitants should praise the Lord for the peace they are enjoying. It is a statement and also a prophecy, for as soon as our will receives divine grace it is bound to make peace with God, whence more love and praise for the Lord.

"And David adds,

> For He hath made strong the bars of thy gates;
> He hath blessed thy children within thee. (147:13)

By which he defines the second wave of peace, the wave of feelings that follow the first peacemaking with God: after which all the powers of the soul feel in harmony. David is right when he writes that the gates have been made strong: Since reason is in charge and desire has been checked, no one can enter the soul and upset our inner peace, we are satisfied with our relationship with God, and as Ausonius puts it, for a man of wisdom no enemy force can find a hold, wisdom is like a smooth and round surface which cannot be penetrated (*Idyls* 14). How can the world hurt a wise man that has no wordly goods to care for?

"David makes his message clearer by adding, 'He maketh thy borders peace' (147:14). For if our peace has spread all about our souls it is obvious that such peace will also spread outside us, and will make us safe and sound. We no longer compete with our neighbors nor pine away after gold and riches: This means our soul is at peace, like a huge field without rich mines or fertile vineyards, without farmhouses or gardens. All that we treasure is locked inside our soul, we are the only ones to enjoy it, we eat the best and whitest bread. And those who do not live at peace with themselves may seem prosperous and yet they eat a dark and bitter bread, they look for crumbs under the table, no food will ever appease their hunger. Meanwhile the man of peace eats all he wants, enjoys the taste of the whitest bread, basks in the golden sunlight, finds pleasure everywhere, in life and in death, in prosperity and in hard times. He eats of the food angels eat, fears no enemy, enjoys sweet peace: This is the meaning of Christ's grace.

"And this is why we must celebrate Christ all the time: He has fought for us, given us peace and harmony, made us free from greed and fear. He is the source of our peace and happiness: it is only right that we call him our Prince."

After these words Marcelo remained silent, and Juliano then spoke:

"I have no doubt after hearing what you had to say that Jesus in truth is really our Prince of Peace. I would like to add that only through Him can we attain such a feeling of peace."

At that moment Juliano and Sabino faced each other, and Sabino spoke,

"I do not fully understand, dear Juliano, what you have said. It is, I suspect, a wise statement: I would like to hear more about it."

"I am glad to speak further on this subject," Juliano went on, "and I would like to ask you, do you think that all those who are born into our world are truly happy, or is it perhaps that some are happy and others are unhappy?"

"I am convinced that not all of them are happy."

"Are some of them happy?" Juliano added.

"Yes, no doubt about it," Sabino answered.

And then Juliano, "Then please tell me, are they happy because this is the way they were born, or else they managed during their life to get close to happiness?"

And Sabino replied, "It is not a matter of being born happy or of being lucky, rather the will power of each individual, the personal decision to lead a happy life."

"I agree," Juliano said, "and you also imply that some people cannot be happy even when lucky."

"Yes, this is what I claim."

"All right, then," Juliano said, "those who are not happy, is it that they do not want to be happy? Are they not trying to be happy?"

"No" Sabino said, "they certainly want to be happy."

"All right, then, is good luck hiding from them? Are not the rules that allow us to reach luck and happiness the same for us all?"

"That is true, I agree," Sabino answered, "and luck may come into our home but since we do not know her we may try to lock her out of our house."

"In other words," Juliano said, "lucky people do not know anything about luck and most of the time they reject luck."

"That is the truth," Sabino answered.

"And then pray tell me," Juliano continued, "how can something be longed for when the person who is supposed to wish for it actually has no idea about the existence of such a desirable object?"

"I agree," Sabino answered, "that is simply not possible."

"Then you claim, my friend, that those who reach the highest and most blessed state of happiness are still too ignorant and dumb to acknowledge their good fortune."

"This is true," Sabino conceded.

"And, once more, those who do not reach this lofty happiness have no experience of it?" Juliano stated.

And then Sabino answered that this was indeed the case.

"Well, moreover, you have stated previously that even those human beings who are not blessed and holy in some ways wish and desire to become blessed and holy. Is this true?"

And then Sabino conceded he had said so.

"Well, then," Juliano continued, "they desire something they know nothing about. Which means one of two things: Either something which is not known can be desired, or else that those people who suffer from bad luck are not interested in becoming lucky. Both of these possibilities contradict, my dear Sabino, what you said earlier. Would you like to change your mind now?"

Sabino reflected for a while and then said, "I cannot help but think I will have to change my statements."

Then Juliano, taking Sabino by the hand, said, "Let us reason together a little longer. Perhaps we will reach truth this way. Tell me, do you think good luck is something alive, something that is endowed with existence, or else how do you define it?"

"I do not grasp your meaning," Sabino answered.

"Well, now, for instance, does the miser love something?"

"Yes, indeed," Sabino answered.

"And what does he love?"

"Gold, no doubt, and riches."

"And those who spend gold and riches in parties and banquets, what do they seek?"

"Their pleasure, their satisfaction."

"That is so, dear Sabino," Juliano went on, "but then, the pleasure that arises from spending money, does it have a true existence, a true reality? Gold and silver do exist, they have substance, they weigh, we can feel them with our hands, we can see them. But pleasure and satisfaction are different. Their presence is part of our inner perception, or perhaps we imagine we feel that way. They are not a piece of metal you find in a mine or a vegetable you grow in a garden, not something you can keep in a box, but the result of possessing something important and valuable."

"I agree," Sabino nodded.

"Then now my question shall be clear: Is good luck like gold and riches, or rather like pleasure and satisfaction?"

"Like pleasure and satisfaction," Sabino conceded, "and I even think good luck is nothing but a whole and perfect satisfaction, when we feel safe from danger and rich with love."

"You are right. But if good luck is like satisfaction, if it is a form of satisfaction, and since we said that satisfaction or contentment comes from our having something of great value, or imagining we have it, there must be something valuable that is at the root and origin of good luck."

"I will not deny it," Sabino said.

"Well, is there one root to this feeling or several?"

"In my opinion there is only one."

"And you are right again," Juliano added, "because man's satisfaction can come only in one way and has only one origin. But this origin or root, and which as you said is one and only, do all men love it and look for it?"

"No, they do not love it," Sabino answered.

"And why?"

"Because they do not know it," Sabino continued.

"And yet," Juliano said, "no one stops loving, as we said previously, good luck?"

"That is so."

And Juliano: "We do not love what we do not know. Which means, dear Sabino, that those who love being happy but do not succeed in reaching happiness know in a general way what is bliss and satisfaction, yet they do not know the precise and true spring from which they flow, nor the way to create them. They are propelled by desire but since they do not know the right way they are unable to stop and unable to reach their goal, just the opposite of what happens to those who are blessed by good luck. And then, Sabino, pray tell me, those who look for happiness and cannot reach it, do not they love something too, do not they look for something that could become the source of the happiness they seek?"

"I do not doubt it," Sabino answered.

"And yet their love does not make them happy?"

"We have said so," Sabino answered, "because the source they seek is not the real source, the real origin, of happiness."

"Then, if their love does not bring happiness, can it have some other effect upon them?"

"Isn't it enough to state what it does not do, in other words, it does not bring them happiness?"

"I do not want to paint their situation in somber colors, and certainly I am not responsible for it," Juliano continued, "but we must examine it more closely."

"It seems to me," Sabino said, "that their situation should remind us of a Greek tradition. Paris stole Helen from her husband, and thought he had found in her joy and happiness. Yet he found nothing but the destruction of his homeland, his own death, and all the disasters sung by Homer. In the same way many who seek happiness find only tears and misery, because they seek it where it cannot be found, and no matter how hard they try they are unable to find it. They are tormented by frustration and anguish, and therefore they are not only deprived of happiness, they are actively sad and unhappy."

"Let us sum up," Juliano said, "all that we pointed out previously. First, that everybody wishes to be happy and tries to reach happiness. Second, that most do not succeed. Third, that the reason for this failure can be found in our love for the so-called sources or roots of happiness: The true source is only one, the others are fakes. Finally, the same way that our love for the true source of happiness will bring us good luck, our love and affection for the false sources of happiness is bound to bring us sadness and sorrow."

"I agree. But what can your conclusions be?"

"I have two conclusions. The first one, everybody loves and wants something. Good people, wicked people, happy people, unhappy people, we are all in love with something or somebody: One cannot live without love. The second conclusion is, love can be the source of happiness in some people, of misery in others."

"I agree."

"Shall we look for the reason explaining this uneven effect?"

"And where shall we look?"

"The reason, the cause, is always the same, love," Juliano replied.

"Yes," Sabino added, "and yet although you call it love, it may not be the same in every instance. In some cases it is love of what is noble, good, high, and happiness flows from it. In other instances it is love of what is evil and base: Only sadness and pain will grow from such an attachment."

And then Juliano, "Can anyone love something that is evil?"

"I do not think so," Sabino answered, "and by the same token a man cannot and should not hate himself. The evil kind of love I have mentioned, I call it by this name not because the object of such a love is in itself evil but because it is not the source, the origin, of the supreme good."

"And this is why," Juliano went on, "my doubt and my questioning seem more urgent than ever. For if men could love sorrow and misery, we could accept that love would make miserable those who chose such a negative kind of love. But if we always love what is good, even if it is not the good that gives birth to the supreme good, then even if their love did not make them entirely happy, at least some happiness should come to them out of their love. What we said before, about love creating sorrow, just does not ring true to me."

"Well, perhaps you are right," Sabino acquiesced.

"Please do not give up so easily. Let us try to ascertain more about love. Perhaps only thus will we find the answers we are seeking."

"And how can we find out what is the essence of love?"

"You must have heard before, dear Sabino, that love is a way of discovering an identity, a union."

"Yes, I have heard and read that love is union and unity, it is a tight bond that brings together those who love each other, and through this bond the one who loves is transformed into the object of his love, becomes one and the same thing."

"Do you think all kinds of love are like this?"

"Yes, I do think so."

"Do you think, for instance, Apollo was in love when, as Ovid writes, he was following Daphne and she was fleeing him? Or in a play by Terence, when one of the characters asks where he can find someone he liked but could not find anywhere, was this character also in love?"

"It would seem so."

"And yet these characters were so far from being one and the same with their loved ones that the first, Apollo, was hated and despised by Daphne, and Terence's character simply could not find the person he was looking for."

"This is true to fact, and yet in their mind they were together with the ones they loved, because such unity and togetherness was precisely what they wanted, if they were in love."

"Then," Juliano parried, "love is no longer union, but rather our wish and desire for union?"

"It seems you are right."

"And then pray tell me," Juliano added, "the characters and persons you mentioned and I talked about, or anyone else in love, when they achieve their wish and reach union with their beloved ones, do they stop loving after achieving union or are they still in love after it?"

"If one can stop loving oneself," Sabino commented, "in the same way one can stop loving someone who is now very much part of oneself."

"That is plausible," Juliano went on, "but tell me now, is it possible to desire something you already have?"

"No, it is not possible."

"And you stated before that these people in love earlier mentioned had reached union with their beloved ones."

"That is so."

"We must then conclude," Juliano stated. "that they no longer wish or desire such unity."

"It seems so."

"And they still love each other. Therefore it is not true that love is a desire of unity."

Sabino reflected for a while. Then he said, "I do not know why you are trying to trap me into such contradictions and paradoxes. Yet I must tell you that there are two ways, two manners or styles, of loving. One is founded upon desire, the other one upon joy and happiness. And both kinds have something in common, the idea of union or unity. The first kind wants it, desires it, and achieves it if possible. The second kind has it, enjoys it, embraces it, gets pleasure out of it. The first kind is a drive, a striving toward something. The second is a pause, contemplation, enjoyment. The first one is a beginning, the second a peak, a perfection. Both turn around the idea of unity, the first kind of love by trying to reach it, the second kind by enjoying it."

"In any case my trap has caught a good-sized prey, my dear Sabino, for what you have just said is very intelligent indeed, and is helping me a great deal toward my conclusion. Since each kind of love either tends toward union or has already achieved it we can therefore conclude that anything that harms or destroys union and unity is an enemy of love and will torment those who love. The same thing happens with our body: If we cut off a part of it, a finger, a limb, we produce a sharp unbearable pain. When we sever the link of love we create in our soul a deep grief, a pain that words cannot describe."

"I cannot doubt what you have just said."

"If this is true, can you tell me what is capable of severing the bonds that unite two lovers?"

"Anything capable of destroying the very existence, the very being, of any one of the two lovers. Or else anything capable of changing, in whole or in part, their will. These possibilities come to my mind: disease, old age, poverty, disasters, finally death, for the first group, and then for the second absence, anger, a clash of opinions, the need to compete, a new love, and our trend toward change. In the first group we can see that death destroys our very being and therefore separates the destroyed man or woman from his or her lover. Disease, old age, poverty, disasters, push us toward death and help to pull us apart from the loved one. As for the second group of forces against love, it is true that absence begets forgetfulness, and anger tends to pull us apart, and a clash of opinions makes conversation difficult, and by making it hard to communicate it creates a void and makes it easier for each one to go his or her own way. It is obvious that a new love destroys the old love, the old bonds. It is also true that our wish for novelties is like a file that slowly cuts what was in the past a solid relationship."

"It is obvious to me that love is a delicate plant that does not grow easily in any soil," Juliano added.

"How is this?"

"There is a legend that some fruit trees give poisonous fruit if planted in Persia and yet if planted in Spain their fruit is succulent and most edible. The same thing may happen with love and friendship. If planted when subject to the accidents we have mentioned earlier it is bound to produce poisoned fruit. And if, as we said earlier, in order to reach happiness we must love something or someone that will become a source of luck and joy, and if Nature ruled that love should be the means, the source and the way of our joy and happiness, it is obvious that the sort of love that is subject to swift change and can suddenly vanish is also a source of sadness and grief. Pain will be our hourly companion, fear will dodge our steps. Even if we enjoy our pleasure for one hour we will have to fear the torment of losing it at any time.

"If love is so full of danger when it does not last, and if most of the time it does not endure, this is why I said that only Christ is a real source of peace, friendship, and happiness. Because only Christ is essentially good and does not change. His love for us does not change. Our relationship flowers and endures when we relate to Christ. Neither old age, nor disease, nor even death, can diminish such love, bad luck has no impact upon it. As the Bible puts it,

> Of old Thou didst lay the foundation of the earth;
> And the heavens are the work of Thy hands.
> They shall perish, but Thou shalt endure;
> Yea, all of them shall wax old like a garment;
> As a vesture shalt Thou change them, and they shall pass away;
> But Thou art the selfsame,
> And Thy years shall have no end. (Ps. 102:25–27)

And also,

> Thy throne given of God is for ever and ever;
> A sceptre of equity is the sceptre of thy kingdom. (Ps. 45:7)

"And if we do not flee from God there is no doubt that God will never stop loving us. We may become poor and dejected, and God will still love us. The whole world may hate us, and God will go on loving us. Disasters, afflictions, hard times, may torment us: God will call us to Him with renewed affection. Absence cannot weaken such love: It is anchored in our souls. The passing of time will rob us of our handsome face and figure, our hair will become white, our limbs will grow cold—not God's love. As an eagle, growing stronger with old age, so the Lord's love toward us, ever closer to us, ever sweeter and more intense."

And then Juliano, "Now, Marcelo, this is your turn, since you are planning to talk about the word *husband*. I spoke at length on other subjects to let you prepare yourself and deal with this subject with all your enthusiasm."

"Well, Juliano, my dear friend, you are helpful more than I can thank you for. Perhaps you should go on talking about this new name, for I really do not know what I can add that is new and original, especially since I have had no experience as a husband."

"We do not agree with you on this matter," Juliano and Sabino said both at the same time; "we believe you quite capable of discussing this subject and now we really want to hear you out."

"In that case I shall go on, and please do not expect too much from me. But then, as some poets ask their muses to help them in composing a long poem, so shall I ask Christ's help so that I can talk about such an important and difficult matter."

And then Marcelo bowed his head in humility. He remained silent for a while. And then, his head high, his right arm extended, he said:

HUSBAND

"There are three things, my dear Juliano and Sabino, that are implicit in this name of husband. The first is the union or marriage between Christ and the Church. Then there is the sweetness and pleasure that this union brings. And finally the preparations and circumstances of such a wedding. For if Christ is truly the husband of all the Church and of each one of the good and holy souls, and such is the case, we have to take into account these three relationships. A wedding is a tight knot making one of two people or it is nothing. And it is a sweet knot, and it requires certain social preparations and ceremonies.

"It is true that other links, other titles, other relationships, can be found among human beings. One can be a relative, a father, a king, a citizen, a friend, and each definition implies links and relationships. Yet the name of husband implies a closer, more intimate link than others, and besides it is normally the source of sweetness and pleasure beyond what the other links can provide.

"It is a source of wonder to think about Christ's sweet love toward human beings. He was and is our father, our leader or king, our shepherd, our healing doctor, and our friend. Yet all this was not enough: He wanted to be our husband, the link that is most closely connected with love, intimacy, unity, sweetness.

"Not only in words but in deeds is he thus our husband. The closest and most loving union between a wedded couple is cold when compared with the union between Christ and our souls. The first union does not fully and completely fuse the two spirits, the two souls, but the union in Christ puts us in touch and makes us one with Christ's spirit. St. Paul says it: 'But he who cleaves to the Lord is one spirit with him' (1 Cor. 6:17). In human marriage two bodies get together and yet retain all their traits and characteristics. But if we draw closer to God, the Word draws closer to our flesh, and as St. John puts it, the Word becomes flesh. Human mating does not mean that one of the bodies will receive new life from the other. Union with God means that our flesh lives and will go on living because of its union with Christ's body. In the first case we are dealing with two bodies quite different in their humors and tastes. In the second we become almost identical to the body of Christ, in such a strange and mysterious manner that we can hardly explain how it happens. This is what St. Paul writes about it: 'For no one ever hated his own flesh; on the contrary he nourishes and cherishes it, as Christ also does the Church (because we are members of his body, made from his flesh and from his bones). For this reason a man shall leave his father and mother, and shall cleave to his wife; and the two shall become one flesh' (Eph. 5:29–32). And also: 'This is a great mystery—I mean in reference to Christ and to the Church' (Eph. 5:32).

"Let us enumerate one by one each aspect of the wonderful union by which a man can become closely linked to Christ, and Christ to him. The soul of a just man wants to become one with the divinity and the soul of Christ because it is impelled by love, because the just man loves Christ as deeply as possible, and is loved by Christ in the same fashion, and yet there are other reasons that draw them together. Christ imprints in man's soul a portrait of himself so lifelike and well drawn that Christ's twofold nature, human and divine, becomes a part of our soul, it clothes our inner being, makes us similar to Christ, just as not long ago we pointed out that divine grace can achieve something similar. Together with Christ's image we receive part of his vigor: It warms our veins, our blood, our whole body, moves us to act, to raise our eyes to heaven, like a flame striving to the clouds. As a craftsman fashioning a tool and then taking it in his hand, moving it, swinging it, applying it to the task, so are we in the hand of God, a living tool, changed by the strength and wisdom of the craftsman. Thus Christ through His grace can handle us, and we then do the work that is expected from us, and then Christ's strength and power is displayed through us and between the two of us we can accomplish the divine tasks that are Christ's projects.

"And yet there is more. Christ is not satisfied with giving us his strength and his virtue: He introduces the Holy Spirit in the very soul of just men and women. He unites His grace to our souls and makes His very Holy Spirit present in us, embracing us in the sweetest and most blessed manner. In the holy Trinity the Spirit seems to spring forth from the persons of the Father and the Son and is the spirit of highest love, as if we were in the presence of a sweet knot that unites both Father and Son. Among us, the Holy Spirit, inspired by our Church, linking all of the Church's parts and inhabiting them, gives them new life, makes them aware of what they have in common among themselves and in common with God. As St. John puts it, 'If anyone love me,' Jesus says, 'he will keep my word, and my Father will love him, and we will come to him and make our abode with him' (14:23). And St. Paul, 'And hope does not disappoint, because the charity of God is poured forth in our hearts by the Holy Spirit who has been given to us' (Rom. 5:5). Elsewhere he states that our bodies are His temple, and He is alive in them and in our souls. And also it is stated in another paragraph of the Holy Scriptures that we were given the soul and spirit of His Son, and this spirit calls out 'Father,' striving to bring him, as Father, closer and closer to all of us.

"Let us remember what happened to Elisha with the son of his guest: The child was dead, and Gehazi laid the staff upon the face of the child, and then Elisha put his mouth upon his mouth, and his eyes upon his eyes (Kings 2, 4:31–35); thus God's embrace means that first God places His grace and His gifts before our soul, then He touches us with His hands, finally He gives us His breath and spirit: Then we become fully alive, we live much the same way as God lives in heaven, as St. Paul puts it: 'It is now no longer I that live, but Christ lives in me' (Gal. 2:20).

"This is, then, the wondrous effect God's presence achieves in our soul, and the divine influence upon our body is no less remarkable. For God became flesh, made Himself human in such a way that the union has become an indissoluble marriage, one in which our flesh and the Word have become one, and the nuptial bed where this union took place was, as St. Augustine states, the immaculate womb of Mary. Having entered human flesh, endowed with a human body, He then joined His body to the body of His Church, to all those who in His Church make use of the sacrament of holy communion. St. Paul writes, 'And the two shall become one flesh. This is a great mystery—I mean in reference to Christ and to the Church' (Eph. 5:31–33).

"St. Paul does not deny that it could be said accurately about Adam and Eve, 'And the two shall become one flesh' (Eph. 5:31) but rather he compares both unions and sees in the first a forerunner of the second, and the first was open while the second union is secret and mysterious.

"This union of Christ's body and our body is also alluded to in St. John (6:54–55): 'Amen, amen, I say unto you, unless you eat the flesh of the Son of Man, and drink his blood, you shall not have life in you.' And the text goes on, 'He who eats my flesh and drinks my blood has life everlasting.' Let us also remember St. Paul: 'Because the bread is one, we though many, are one body, all of us who partake of the one bread' (1 Cor. 10:17). The conclusion is that if we can say that Adam and Eve became one, in the same manner Christ, faithful husband of the Church, and the Church, beloved wife of Christ, through the union that takes place when the faithful receive communion with Christ's flesh, become one and the same.

"Theodoretus comments thus with respect to the Song of Songs, as follows, 'There is no ground to take offense about the fact that the Spouse, the Husband, kisses the Bride in the Song of Songs. We also reach out to our Spouse and Husband, kiss and embrace him' (*Quaest. in Scrip. Sacram. In Cant.*, Lib. I). And Saint Chrysostom writes, 'We are one and the same body, we are members and limbs of Christ, made out of his flesh and bones' (*Ef.*

BOOK II

5:30). 'And not only love makes us one and the same with him, but also the nourishment that he has offered us brings us closer together and makes us feel part of his flesh. He intermingled his body with ours, united both with one single head as a sign of love. He wants to be seen and touched by those who love him, as if saying: I want to be your brother, your relative, this is my message.' "

At this point Juliano took Marcelo by the hand and said, "The same message comes to us from St. Ireneus, St. Hillary, St. Cyprian, St. Augustine, Tertullian, Ignatius, Gregorius Nissene, Cyril, Leo, Phocius, and Theophylactus. It is an accepted fact, for all faithful, that Christ's body, as the Holy Wafer, received in communion, becomes part of our flesh and body, and this means that we become one and the same with Christ, flesh of his flesh, and not only in spirit but also in body we are one and the same. Let no one doubt these conclusions.

"What you should now make clear is this: How is it possible that just because one body touches another body can we say in truth that they have become united, one and the same body, as the Holy Scriptures and the learned holy scholars state? Let me touch you now: My hand touches your hand, and yet this does not mean that my hand and yours have become one body and one flesh."

"You are right," Marcelo said, "and the mere contact is not enough to change anything. A worthless sinner can go through this experience and he will gain nothing by it. One has to be worthy of this experience and receive God's grace through it."

"Could you elaborate further?" Juliano said.

Marcelo kept quiet for a while, and then: "Two points are to be underlined here. First, in order to be able to state that two things are one and the same thing, it is enough to show that they are extremely similar one to the other. Second, that Christ's flesh, when it touches the flesh of a person who receives it reverently in the holy sacrament of communion, makes in a way our flesh similar to it."

"If you can prove these points, Marcelo, all our doubts will vanish. Perhaps your first point is not hard to prove and we might accept it without further discussion," Juliano said.

"I think common sense," Marcelo went on, "can help us here. When two people are deeply in love, do we not say they are one and the same person, since they agree in their love and their way of looking at the world? If our flesh gets rid of its limitations and accepts the qualities of Christ's flesh, it will become one and the same with it. When a piece of iron is red hot we say it is like fire. It is not fire but it is very similar to fire in its high temperature, its color, its effects. In the same way our body, our flesh, can be said to be quite like Christ's flesh and body if it resembles it in so many ways.

"Let us not forget St. Paul's words, 'But he who cleaves to the Lord is one spirit with him' (1 Cor. 6:17). Is it not true that cleaving unto God is receiving in our soul the grace that, as a heavenly quality, puts in us many of the divine essences and helps shape us in God's image? St. Paul has stated that our spirit and God's spirit can become one, and so our flesh and Christ's flesh can also become one, if we acquire some of the qualities that belong to Christ's body.

"Think about a thousand different men, belonging to different families and social strata, with different professions and trades, with differing values and projects, and yet they are all together in a nation, a state, a republic, a city-state: They are surrounded by a protective wall and ruled by the same laws, they are united. Why should two bodies joined by divine grace not be like one? If we wear a perfumed glove our hand smells of perfume even after we take off the glove. Christ's flesh has all the power of true virtue and grace: It cannot fail to give us its virtue and power. Bodies do give each other their warmth, their vibrations. This cool breeze makes us feel cool; a few hours ago it was hot and it made us feel hot. I do not mean that we are talking about a law of nature, a fact of everyday life, because then any body could benefit from such a contact, and yet this is not so: Communion does nothing for those who receive Christ's body in a state of sin and are therefore unworthy of communion. By receiving communion in such a state they endanger their souls as well as their bodies, and, according to St. Paul, accidents, diseases, even death, may result from their rash behavior.

"Let us say now that whatever happens in such a situation is part of the works of nature. And also let us consider that a sinner trying to obtain grace through holy communion will be frustrated and even endangered by such action, and in a parallel and antithetical situation, whosoever is ready to receive Christ's grace in communion will benefit in his body and in his soul. It takes only one positive act: The benefits will follow in abundance.

"Nature and our needs seem to be in agreement with God in such a situation. Let us think back to Genesis, the serpent, our sin, and the way in which this whole situation affected our body and our soul by debasing and poisoning both of them. A new situation, a new food, were needed in order to save us, in order to bring to us justice, purity, wisdom. St. Paul puts it in these words: 'For as in Adam all die, so in Christ all will be made to live' (1 Cor. 15:22). In Adam's sin our spirit and our flesh were damaged, the Devil tempted the soul and corrupted the body of our ancestors. Life fights death, remedy fights disease, Christ gives us life, health, remedy, salvation. The fatal apple upset our body, the holy flesh will heal our tortured flesh. Poison can be held in check, we can still hope for a new life, new health, new grace.

"And St. Gregory Nyssa is right when he writes,

> Let us assume that someone has been poisoned. He tries to counteract the poison. It is useful to have the remedy penetrate his entrails in the same way the poison did. So with us: We did eat poison, we endeavor to be healed. What can cure us? Nothing but the holy body that vanquished death and gave us everlasting life. A pinch of leavening will make a whole of dough rise and be changed. Similarly a body to which God granted immortal life can change our body completely. Poison hurts us, the touch of an immortal body heals us and gives us eternal life. (*Orat. Catech., quae dicitur Magna*, ch. 37).

"St. Cyril is also eloquent:

> Our corruptible bodies, our vile bodies, could not reach eternal life except that they could get to touch a body that is the essence of life. If you do not believe me you should believe Christ, who said, 'Amen, amen, I say to you, unless you eat the flesh of the Son of Man, and drink his blood, you shall not have life in you. He who eats my flesh and drinks my blood has life everlasting and I will raise him up on the last day.' (John 6:54–55). You hear the

holy words that tell you there is no life unless you eat His flesh and drink His blood. You shall not have life in you, that is, there will be no life in your bodies. No life. No spark of life that can make us live again at the moment of the Final Judgment. It is easy to see that Christ's flesh is part of the Word and has the gift of life: Death has no dominion over it, and if it is joined to our flesh it protects us from death: God is always around us and the water that he will give us shall become in us a fountain of water, springing up into life everlasting. (*Cyr. Alex. in Johan. Evang.*, IV, chapters 14–15)

"Another passage from the same source is worthy of note: 'Water is in itself cold, and yet if we apply fire to it it seems to forget its coldness and jumps with energy while boiling. It is the same with us. We are mortal, and yet if we come in touch with a supernatural life, a spiritual body, we gain a new lease on life: Our soul gets new wings when guided by the Holy Spirit, and our rough body becomes immortal when touched by the holy wind of the Word. The Savior's flesh gives life because it is bound to the Word, which gives life naturally, and hence when we eat it we have more life since we are then united with a life-giving substance.' This is why when Christ resuscitated the dead He not only used His words and divine commands but sometimes touched them with His hands, thus showing that His flesh, because it was His, had the power and the virtue of giving life to the dead, according to the same author.

"The forbidden fruit eaten by Adam and Eve corrupted us. The virtuous and clean food provided by Christ gives us new purity and new life. This new life is what Christ's love intended to give us. Love is union and unity, it always strives toward unity, the greater and more intense the unity the greater and more intense the love. We are both flesh and spirit, and our spirit helped by Christ will create a permanent bond and give us life everlasting.

"No one can doubt Christ's love. God can and does carry out this union between Him and us, and when it takes place we feel much better and more powerful. God adds carats of diamonds of light and wisdom to our lives: All perfection flows from Him to us. We cannot doubt His goal and His purpose, and Christ Himself made it clear when He said, 'Yet not for these only do I pray, but for those also who through their word are to believe in me, that all may be one, even as thou, Father, in me and I in thee; that they also may be one in us' (John 17:20–22). Father and Son are one not only because they love each other, or because their will and their judgment are identical, but also because they are a same substance, so the Father lives in the Son and the Son lives in the Father: both live as one and the same person.

"So that our bonds be as perfect as can be it is important that we the faithful can embrace and hold tight together, as tight as possible. We are many and yet since one spirit dwells in our souls and because we are faithful to Christ and the communion with Christ's body, we must all be like one in mind and in body, a divine body, and in touch with God's mind and body we shall endure. As a cloud is surrounded by the long rays of the sun's light, a cloud drenched in light, if you look at it from down below it shines like a sun, in the same way Christ by giving His virtue, His light, His spirit, and His body, to the faithful and just, by mingling all of his graces with our existence, creates light and unity where there was none. Out of our mouths and eyes comes the divine light of Christ: His presence is a part of our intimate being, so much so that at the end of our life no other being will be detected but Christ, and without ceasing to be ourselves we shall be one and the same with Christ.

"A knot, dear Sabino, unites the parts in such a tight way that it is impossible afterward to see which is which, so perfect is their union. It is a marriage, a wedding, a union of two spirits, two souls, cleaner and better than the union of two bodies, and closer, tighter, warmer, much more intimate. It does not imply bodily contact but the elevation and spiritual penetration of the body by the soul. No quarrels, only one will and one goal. No sharing of bodies but rather Christ, the husband, turns his wife into himself—nothing but safety, serenity, unity, contemplation, and noble feelings unmixed by anguish or pain.

"Such a pleasure is so subtle that it is not easy to describe, at least it has never been described in a satisfactory way. Perhaps this in itself is the best proof of the rare and exalted quality of such an experience. The ones that know it the best are the ones that refuse altogether to talk about it. When we experience it we become speechless: Our whole soul is busy and occupied by such intense feelings that we have time for nothing else. This is why the Holy Scripture calls it 'hidden manna' and also 'new name,' which can be read only by the chosen person who receives it (Acts 2:17) and also, in the Song of Songs (2:4–6) it describes lovemaking, sweet embraces, and depicts a bride swooning with pleasure. When we faint we seem to withdraw inside ourselves and our limbs and tongue become useless. The same takes place in the mystic rapture. There is no time for talking.

"The Holy Scriptures say it best. According to David, 'Oh, how abundant is Thy goodness, which Thou has laid up for them that fear Thee' (Ps. 31:19). And elsewhere:

> They are abundantly satisifed with the fatness of Thy house;
> And Thou makest them drink of the river of Thy pleasures.
>
> (Ps. 36:8)

And also: 'Oh, consider and see that the Lord is good' (Ps. 34:8) and still: 'There is a river, the streams whereof make glad the city of God' (Ps. 46:4). And: 'The voice of rejoicing and salvation is in the tents of the righteous' (Ps. 118:15) and: 'Happy is the people that know the joyful shout' (Ps. 89:15). And finally Isaiah,

> And whereof from of old men have not heard,
>   nor perceived by the ear,
> Neither hath the eye seen a God beside Thee,
> Who worketh for him that waiteth for Him. (63:3)

"Everything becomes clear if we define what delight is. In my mind delight is a sensation and a feeling of happiness and sweetness that arises during every activity in which we exert our natural talent and our natural powers without any hindrance. Every time this takes place we achieve something that either by nature or by custom or by our choice is good and worthy of esteem. In the same way that when we lack something we desire intensely its lack or absence brings our heart to agony and frustration, conversely when we attain and possess it its presence gives pleasure to our senses and our desire. Delight is, therefore, the sweet satisfaction of our desires.

"Delight is produced, above all, by the presence and, in a figured sense, the embrace of whatever it is we desire. We reach such a close embrace through some positive activity that we carry out. Finally there seems to be a third party in this harmony, this concert: our consciousness of pleasure, satisfaction, plenitude. For indeed if we are not aware that our correct and sound actions bring us pleasure, then acting in a correct and righteous way simply does not bring any reward. Let us now examine the sources of delight: Much can be discovered and analyzed if we can identify them.

"The first element needed for such a sensation of delight is the presence of our awareness of it. The second, the activity that brings us closer to the desired goal. The third, this very goal. The last element is the presence of this attained goal and its fusion with our soul.

"Our awareness, of course, increases our pleasure. A stone having no feelings experiences no pleasure. In animals the intensity of pleasure is always increased by the intensity of the senses, of their awareness of pleasure.

"Let us go back to human beings. Some people are more sensitive than others and therefore enjoy more intensely the delights that their life provides. Conversely if disease has atrophied our hand we will not enjoy heat in a cold day when we bring it close to a fire. Yet if it heals it will communicate to us little by little a sensation of pleasure. We know, we should know, that the pleasures created by virtue and goodness in our minds are by far more intense than any bodily pleasures. Reason rules the first, flesh the second. The first one is deep, the second one is superficial. Pleasure that comes from our senses is light, it is like a shadow of delight, like a rough and primitive pleasure, while the pleasure that comes to us from our understanding and our reason is intense, refined, true pleasure.

"The pleasures that flow from God to our souls are noble and come from lofty actions on our part: They come from our thinking about Him, from meditation and contemplation, from loving Him and thinking about Him, and from every action and thought that is holy and virtuous. These are actions that define us as human beings and that in themselves make our soul purer and better. On the other hand the pleasures of the body and the senses are sometimes unworthy of a human being, and often low and vile, the result almost always of our need or our vices. Thus a good thought or a kind and holy gesture are pleasurable in themselves even before being rewarded by God. The pleasures of the senses satiate and bring pain and sorrow.

"It is, in any case, difficult if not impossible to compare these two sorts of pleasure. A beautiful painting may please our eyes, a sweet harmony may delight our ears, food can taste sweet or delicious, and yet all these pleasures are necessarily in a different category from the delights that flow from God's embrace. One of the Psalms puts it briefly thus:

> Whom have I in heaven but Thee?
> And beside Thee I desire none upon earth. (Ps. 73:25)

Because if we reflect upon what the Lord is we conclude that He is an infinite ocean of kindness and goodness, and the greatest things on earth are like a drop of water compared with God's greatness, like the shadow of a great blinding light. O Lord, you are what our souls desire, the only goal of our lives, the true aim for which we were born and which we seek even without knowing it in everything we do. For the pleasures of the senses and almost every other value that men strive to attain are but means to some end. Like remedies and medicines to cure some lack or sickness: We seek food because we are tormented by hunger; we gather riches so as to escape poverty; we are captivated by sweet music and handsome proportions because without them our hearing and our eyes languish.

"Therefore the delights afforded by these bodily pleasures are tainted and impure. They are based upon shortcomings and needs, and they last only a short time. Without hunger there is no pleasure in eating, and after hunger disappears pleasure vanishes too. It is also important to respect certain limits: Excesses in sensuous pleasure bring pain. But you, O Lord, you are our goal, our star. You take care of our needs, you fill our void, loving you never diminishes us, rather it makes us stronger and richer. Moreover, those who love you are rewarded in such a manner that the more they are rewarded the more they love you. Since you know no boundaries the delight that you create in our souls is a pleasure without end, one that gets progressively sweeter and more intense, a desire never sated, for, as it has been said, whoever drinks from your sweetness, the more he drinks, the thirstier he becomes.

BOOK II

"And because of all that has been said previously, the Holy Scriptures define the delights offered to us by God with the names of 'overflow' and of 'river,' and in the Psalms it is written that God offers as a drink to His followers a huge river of delights. This expression means that God will reward His followers with a great abundance of joy, and moreover that such a joy is limitless and keeps its impact day after day. It is not to be compared to the water in a glass or a jar, which can easily run out when we are thirsty. It is like the waters of a river, always running, always fresh, always available. God's essence and grace are infinite and beyond compare, and the soul that enjoys such presence and such gifts has reached the ultimate in pleasure and bliss.

"God's essence is the source of such intense pleasures, and yet we should not forget that his love for us can increase even further our bliss. The closer we are to the person we love, the more intense is our rapture. Who can describe what happens to us when God comes closer and closer to our souls? Our sensuous pleasures cannot be compared with the spiritual bliss God offers us. Our senses are limited: They afford us a glimpse, a sliver of reality. We see a beautiful shade of red, we hear a bell's sound, we taste something sweet or bitter, we touch objects that are either soft or harsh. Something totally different happens when God embraces our soul, penetrates it totally, fills every secret chamber, becomes one with it in a most intimate contact. This is why the Holy Scriptures mention more than once that God dwells in the center of our heart. David compares God to a holy ritual oil that is placed upon the head of a priest, running down to his beard, neck, and garments. God has also been compared to mist, which penetrates everywhere.

"God's union with our soul takes place all of a sudden, without the foreplay that is so typical of our bodily union between man and woman. It is more intense and more lasting than our human sexual union, more stable and all-embracing, and this is why the Psalms state that 'there is a river, the streams thereof make glad the city of God' (Ps. 46:4), a river flowing with God's grace, not drop by drop, but as a strong current.

"In conclusion, the marriage of God and our soul is a source of pleasure, delight, and bliss, that nothing can surpass. It is never mixed with doubt or anguish or sadness, it is never tarnished, there is nothing rough or superficial about it: It is an abundant source of joy, it bathes our soul in joy, it makes us drunk with bliss.

"Therefore the Holy Scripture makes use of several images and metaphors when it tries to describe such a unique experience. It calls it sometimes 'hidden manna,' a special and sweet food— hidden, because no one knows what takes place in our soul when God embraces us. It can also be described as a wine, or as a liquor better than wine, or as a cellar full of wine casks and bottles. It can be compared to breasts full of milk to be enjoyed by a baby, for God's presence is even sweeter and more comforting than the mother's breast offering milk to her baby. It is also said that God finds a dwelling place in the middle or the center of our heart. And David compares God to a table covered with food, to a banquet, as does Solomon, and both mean by this image that God can give us nourishment, make us stronger and satisfy our hunger. God's presence is compared to sleep because it restores the spirit of those who are tired and suffer. It can also be compared to a small stone or pebble (Apoc. 2:17) in which a name was written, a name only the person who holds the pebble can read, because according to an ancient custom when the judge threw a white pebble into a vessel or urn this meant a life was going to be spared. The ancients also used white pebbles in order to keep track of happy days and joyous occasions, and in the same manner the bliss given by God to His faithful followers is a token of His friendship and a verdict of innocence which frees us from His wrath, and it also marks a day of happiness and rejoicing. Finally the Bible speaks about feelings of drunkenness:

> I am come into my garden, my sister, my bride;
> I have gathered my myrrh with my spice;
> I have eaten my honeycomb with my honey;
> I have drunk my wine with my milk.
> Eat, O friends;
> Drink, yea, drink abundantly, my beloved. (Song of Songs 5:1)

This is because God's presence in us so overwhelms us that we feel, say and do things that are not reasonable and are similar to what a drunken person might feel, say, and do.

"Truly, Juliano, those who look for such delights but are

perhaps unworthy of them are always marveling at the impact they have upon those who have experienced them. If God's presence in us were not the source of extreme sweetness and bliss, how would it have been possible for the martyrs to suffer the tortures inflicted on them, or for the hermits to live in the desert in solitude for so many long years? It is the intensity of bliss given to them by God that made many men escape to solitude, give up every other comfort, go without food under the broiling sun, the rain, the cold of winter. Stronger than nature's harsh laws, than men's cruel imagination, the soul made stronger by God's presence overcomes every weakness of the human body.

"If we wished to give further examples of God's influence upon our behavior we would need innumerable volumes and many more years than a normal life can stretch. Let us simply go back to the Bible, read once more the Song of Songs, and we shall find depicted there all the pleasures God offers those who choose to follow Him. There is nothing the Shulamite leaves unsaid in order to express the delights offered to her by her Beloved. No sweet endearing word or expression is forgotten, no image or metaphor defining and exalting love is unsaid. The soul is like a vessel with huge sails filled by the winds of love, sailing a sea of honey, burning in secret fire.

"The soul resembles a wooden log not quite dry when fire is placed near it. As heat penetrates each opening and the wood slowly dries the log is now ready to receive a greater heat and it finally catches fire. It smokes, sparks come out of it, fire flares out, seems to stop, then starts again, until every corner shoots out flames and the log is ablaze.

"In the same fashion, when God comes closer and closer to our soul and transmits to it His sweetness, the soul seems to hesitate at first, yet later on as the sweet flavor lingers on and on, bliss increases and the soul grows to appreciate it more and more. There are soft words spoken, sighs of love, tears of emotion, more sighs, more sweet words, until our soul is wholly uplifted by a great wave of love and softly says, 'O my light, my love, my life, my comfort, O infinite beauty, O boundless source of sweetness and power, let me be undone utterly and melt into Thee, O My Lord.' And I would rather say no more, since there are things that words are not able to express."

There was a long silence, after which Marcelo went on, "I

have described the blissful union of the human soul and God. More remains to be described. I shall not mention what moved Christ to become our husband, I shall not underline His pity and kindness. Yet His wedding has given us untold gifts, riches, rejoicings, songs, public partying and dancing.

"Sometimes an old man marries a young girl: he waits until she reaches the right age in order to go through the wedding ceremony. We should understand that the same thing may have happened with respect to the wedding that took place between Christ and His Church. The Church was too young and childish at the very beginning, the wedding could not take place, it had to be postponed. The mature man who is betrothed to a young girl proceeds cautiously and first gives her gifts and caresses her in the way that is suitable to a very young girl. As she grows and matures so does the love for her change and the relationship develops into a more mature one. In the same manner Christ and His church became betrothed, the Church was born and raised in order to marry Christ and the time will come when the marriage is consummated. Christ has treated the Church as becomes the Church's age, first as a child, then as a growing child, an adolescent, and now treats her as a grown girl almost ready for marriage. The whole history of the Church from its birth and origin until the day of the Church's wedding with God, and that is tantamount to speaking about all the time that will elapse between the beginning of the world until its end, can be divided into three periods. The first is the period ruled by nature. The second is ruled by law. The third and last one is ruled by grace. The first period was, and is, to be compared to the childhood of God's future bride. During the second the child grew. During the third and present period she is maturing fast and can envisage getting married. Her fiancé has dealt with her according to her age, although always lovingly, as described in the Song of Songs, which is a good description of the relationship present and future between the two of them, husband and wife, as betrothed, and waiting until the day of the wedding, when history will cease and come to its end.

"The Song of Songs is a picture painted by God's hand which shows the sweet moments, the pleasures and delights that come to pass between two spouses and how they change with time. In the first part, until almost half the second chapter, God describes the beloved future wife in a state of simplicity, which is the natural and primitive state of girlhood. Then in the second chapter we read,

> My beloved spoke, and said unto me:
> 'Rise up, my love, my fair one, and come away' (2:10)

and from that passage on until we read in chapter 5, 'I sleep, but my heart waketh' (5:2) all of this section has to do with what we have called the period or age of law. And from that point to the end of the book we are dealing with the sweet endearments that belong to the period or age of grace.

"For at the beginning of time the Church was an inexperienced child, and we know how tender, impetuous, and impatient children can be: The child seems to demand affection:

> Let him kiss me with the kisses of his mouth—
> For thy love is better than wine. (1:2)

Here 'kisses' mean also His word of pledge, a pledge of marriage that has hardly taken place. For since the moment God decided to take human form and flesh, men's hearts began to behave with greater confidence and familiarity with respect to God, and became suffused with soft and sweet feelings. Childhood is mentioned again in the line 'Therefore the maidens love thee' (1:3) because the maidens are very young girls and they are one and the same with the spouse, the one waiting for her betrothed husband. She comments upon the perfume of her betrothed, compares him to a bunch of flowers, asks him to give her his hand: 'Draw me, we will run after thee' (1:4). They are going to run like children, aimlessly, all of which shows the childish and imperfect aspects of that first period.

"At that moment the Church was conscious of a Paradise lost and of a happy promise of salvation, and then, as if looking at itself on a mirror, the Church states,

> I am black, but comely,
> O ye daughters of Jerusalem,
> As the tents of Kedar,
> As the curtains of Solomon. (1:5)

255

Black because of the disaster of my original sin, which has caused me serious injury, yet comely because of the beautiful hope that has been offered to me after the fall. Air, sun, water, may damage my skin: Yet I have received the right word from God, the word that leads to salvation. And if my mother's sons were incensed against me, because of the slanderous words of an evil angel, and if they turned me into keeper of the vineyards, a harsh work, amidst dust and sweat, and if my own vineyard, that is to say, my primitive bliss and happiness, before the fall, I was unable to keep, yet if I now can find out where thou, O husband, rest at noon, and I know where you and your flock are resting, I hope for a better future.

"And then, for the reasons given above, the husband does not discuss all about their relationship: He suggests that she should follow the footsteps of the flock. The Church was primitive and ignorant at that time, no positive effort came to help her: The Church should follow the trail of the kids. The light that guided the Church was at that moment very faint. The people who believed in that Church were few and scattered, and that is why the Church (the Beloved) is compared to a lily among thorns (2:2).

"All of which describes her growth, her new awareness. Israel in Egypt before being liberated from bondage was truly a rose or a lily among thorns. It was surrounded by unbelievers, Egyptians, it had made damaging mistakes, it was debased by slavery. It is remarkable that in this section of the Holy Book the husband compares Israel, the Church, with products that come out of Egyptian soil:

> I have compared thee, O my love,
> To a steed in Pharaoh's chariots. (1:9)

"A rose among thorns: This image well describes the situation of Israel in Egypt, Israel in slavery, Israel pulling the chariot of the oppressor, the cruel ruler, the Pharaoh,

> To a steed in Pharaoh's chariots
> I have compared thee, O my love (1:9)

which means that Israel was pulling a heavy burden, a chariot as a symbol of servitude.

BOOK II

"This ends the first part of the Song of Songs. There is a change when God says,

Rise up, my love, my fair one, and come away.
For, lo, the winter is past,
The rain is over and gone (2:10–11)

which seems to describe—in a roundabout, poetic way—the flight of the bride from Egypt. Her betrothed husband asks her to come away and get rid of bondage. Winter, the harsh season of servitude, is past, and a spring full of hope is beginning. His Beloved shall be no more a lily among thorns, she shall be like a dove in the clefts of the rock (2:14) which points to the deserted and free spaces where she was led by her betrothed.

"At that moment she, older and more daring, answers merrily to the divine call, and leaving her home she goes out looking for her lover. She then says, 'By night on my bed,' that is to say, in the night of my bondage, 'I sought him, but I found him not' (3:1) and then she asks the watchmen who go about the city, which is a veiled allusion to all the problems that arose since she tried to flee from Egypt, until the moment finally came to carry out the escape. Then, while fleeing, she met her betrothed disguised as a cloud, and also in the shape of fire, and so she tells us that scarcely had she passed from the guards

When I found him whom my soul loveth:
I held him, and would not let him go,
Until I had brought him into my mother's house,
And into the chamber of her that conceived me. (3:4)

For when she reached the Promised Land after walking through the desert she did find her betrothed. A further allusion to the trip through the desert is found below:

Who is this that cometh up out of the wilderness
Like pillars of smoke,
Perfumed with myrrh and frankincense? (3:6)

Afterward (3:9) Solomon's palanquin is mentioned, and the guards are mentioned. Solomon made himself a litter, a palanquin, and in

257

some way this litter is an image of the Ark and the Sanctuary prepared for his bride. Both the description of the litter and the description of Solomon's riches are allusions to the Ark and the Sanctuary which Solomon had built for his bride.

"Then all along chapter 4 she praises her betrothed, describing in great detail all the qualities that enhance and define a great presence, and moreover a being that can also be defined as a huge army organized around a group of rulers under a royal tent. As we can see in Numbers (2:1–34), the royal tent and the other tents in the camp were divided into four sections. The tribe of Judah were placed to the right, together with the tribes of Issachar and Zebulun, at both sides. At the right hand the Reuben tribe, with the Simeon and Gad tribes. On the left side, Dan, Asser, Nephtalim, and at the rear the tribes of Ephraim, Benjamin, Manasseh, and in the middle of the square was the Tabernacle, around which the Levites had erected their tents. When they traveled they followed as a guide and leader the cloud that hovered upon the camp, as a flag, which was followed by the tribe of Judah, and the tribe of Reuben, after which came the Tabernacle, carried by the Levites, followed by Ephraim and Dan at the rearguard.

"The husband does not forget this procession, and actually praises it as if it were one single beautiful person: It praises the eyes, assuming they were like the cloud and fire that were their guiding light, the eyes of a dove, the hair as abundant and beautiful as a flock of sheep, the beautiful white teeth, the crimson lips. Every tribe is praised, and the tribes of Moses and Aaron are commended as the two main sources of nourishment, as well as the tribes of Ephraim and Dan.

"The main goal was to reach the Promised Land, and to occupy and settle it in peace. At the end of the long road they reach their goal. This is why the betrothed says to his wife,

> Come with me from Lebanon, my bride,
> With me from Lebanon;
> Look from the top of Amana,
> From the top of Senir and Hermon,
> From the lions' dens,
> From the mountains of the leopards. (Song of Songs 4:8)

BOOK II

This is an accurate description of the lands of Judea, in which lands the Church grew and prospered for years and years. The husband having given possession of this land to his wife, looking at the many fruits of holiness and religion that the land had produced, calls it 'orchard' and 'fountain,' and goes on,

A garden shut up is my sister, my bride;
A spring shut up, a fountain sealed.
Thy shoots are a park of pomegranates,
With precious fruits;
Henna with spikenard plants,
Spikenard and saffron, calamus and cinnamon,
With all trees of frankincense. (4:12–14)

"This description leads to the conclusion of the section dealing with the second period, that is to say, the adolescence of the bride, after which the third period begins thus:

I sleep, but my heart waketh;
Hark! my beloved knocketh:
'Open to me, my sister, my love, my dove, my undefiled;
For my head is filled with dew,
My locks with the drops of the night.' (5:2)

"Christ at the beginning of this section is born as a man and comes toward His betrothed, and He suffers like a man from hard times, times dark as the night is dark, and therefore He states that He comes drenched with the dew of the night. As a spouse he had never yet made a similar statement. He realizes how difficult it is going to be for His betrothed to open the door of her house and let Him enter, and she says:

I have put off my coat;
How shall I put it on?
I have washed my feet;
How shall I defile them? (5:3)

"After which Christ walks on and looks for other people. Only later the betrothed goes out looking for Him. Those who opened their houses to Christ are those who were persecuted and suffered because of their new faith. This is why symbolically the poem states that she went everywhere looking for him, and she was attacked by the watchmen that went about the city, she was struck and wounded by them, and the guards took away her mantle. The loud cries with which she calls her beloved are symbols of the preaching of the Christian doctrine carried out by the apostles throughout the pagan world. They also were motivated by love. Those who succor the wife and offer their help are all Gentiles moved by the gospels and anxious to follow Jesus. In the meantime the Church develops and grows, reaching maturity: The husband appears, as a man, and describes himself, gives an account of his features, something he had not done previously, for the past was as a dark cloud when compared with such a promising present.

"Love increases, mutual knowledge grows in the third part of the poem. We are no longer dealing with one nation, rather with all the peoples, nations, and races of the whole wide world. This is why the husband compares his beloved betrothed wife to cities (Tirzah, Jerusalem) and declares that she is 'Terrible as an army with banners' (6:10). He praises her, many other voices are also heard in praise of the Beloved. Praise had dealt previously with the beauty of the face, the whole head. It will now deal with the rest of her body and concentrate on her feet, because feet are humble and the Church is and should be humble. Her sister was never mentioned in the first part of the poem. Now she is mentioned: Again, symbolically, we are dealing with a complex situation, many people, many nations, having come to the rescue. She loves and is loved, with less restraint, with more passion than before: she is not content to embrace her beloved in a secluded spot, she will do the same in a public place, seen by all. An adolescent girl cradling a baby brother in her arms: This is how the Church would like to carry Christ for all to see. This is the meaning of the text,

> Oh that thou wert as my brother,
> That sucked the breasts of my mother!
> When I should find thee without, I would kiss thee;
> Yea, and none would despise me.
> I would lead thee, and bring thee into my mother's house,

BOOK II

That thou mightest instruct me;
I would cause thee to drink of spiced wine,
Of the juice of my pomegranate. (8:1–2)

"At that point the only thing that can be anticipated and desired is the coming of the betrothed husband and the celebration of the wedding ceremony. This is the message hidden under the lines

Make haste, my beloved,
And be thou like to a gazelle or to a young hart
Upon the mountains of spices. (8:14)

"She wishes him to come as fast as possible, jumping over mountains over which the sun appears and announces the arrival of the fateful day. A day of light not to be darkened by night, with rejoicing without end, with brilliant ceremonies and handsome clothes to be worn by the newlyweds: About all this wonderful things are said by St. John in his Apocalypse; he says it much better than I could say it now. David, in Psalm 44, also seems to describe such a fateful wedding, one in which the Holy Spirit addresses the bride and groom with words that are both elegant and divine. Perhaps now Sabino will try his mind and his eloquence at describing such an event: As for myself, I do not think I can add anything else."

Marcelo then ceased to speak. Sabino then improvised the following poem:

A deep and guiding thought
    Is stirring in my breast.
To thee, my King, my mind I pledge,
    My heart, each deed of mine.

Of thee I sing, and celebrate
    Thine greatness without peer.
My pen, my tongue, my lips,
    Must sing your glory and praise.

Thy grace and beauty far surpass
    What we see elsewhere;

THE NAMES OF CHRIST

Light and strength are everywhere
Where thou showest thy face.

Come, and win, and dominate,
Give meaning to our lives.
My song will help to show the path:
Let faith and hope arise.

After which, since it was already dark, the three friends
retired for the night.

———————————————

Book III

DEDICATION

DEDICATED TO D. PEDRO PORTOCARRERO, MEMBER
OF THE CROWN COUNCIL, MEMBER OF THE HOLY
INQUISITION

My dear Sir, I have heard that the two previous books that are part of *The Names of Christ* and that have been previously published have been the subject of diverse, even clashing, judgments and opinions. Some readers expected from its author, a theologian, a learned treatise in Latin, and found it disappointing that my book was written in Spanish. According to other readers Spanish is not the right language to write about rather deep philosophical matters, since many readers may be incapable of following the chain of reasoning included in the text. Some claim they would have read the text if written in Latin, but will refuse to read it simply because I wrote it in Spanish. Some readers complain about my style, others complain about the fact that dialogue is the essence of my book, others would like a clear division into smaller chapters, still another objection is that if the language and vocabulary were more current, easier, more common, they would be more understandable. The first edition also added the text of another book of mine, my comments to the Book of Proverbs, a book that bears the title *The Perfect Wife*. This also has been criticized: Some readers think I am not qualified, because of my calling and because of the fact that I am not married, to tell married women how they should act and behave.

I want to respond to these critical remarks. If the critics are my friends I would like to disabuse them, if they are not I would like to see them less happy in their critical attitude. I want my friends to feel happy with my work, my enemies to feel less happy about their reproaches to my work. Perhaps some of my readers and critics expected a book more exalted and sublime would come out of my pen. This is always flattering, and yet I must state that if they think of me as a theologian, then theology, I must tell them, cannot deal with more exalted and sublime matters than the ones I am discussing in this book. I shall add that it is a common mistake to despise a text simply because it is written in a modern language such as Spanish, not in Latin, Greek, and so forth. Spanish can express the loftiest thoughts. We often misuse it out of ignorance, yet this is our fault, not the fault of the Spanish language nor the fault of those writers who strive to bend and shape the Spanish language so that it can convey lofty and exquisite ideas.

Let us now reverse the situation: Our readers should not despise a text because it is written in Castilian, thinking the contents and ideas dealt with in it must be of little importance. Rather, seeing that the matters dealt with in such a Spanish text are indeed lofty and sublime, they should then hold in higher esteem the language that expresses them. Some readers claim that although the ideas in our texts are interesting, they would like to see them translated into Latin. I would like to ask them why should they prefer to read my ideas in Latin? I do not think they can claim to understand them more clearly if they have been turned into a Latin text, and I suspect it would be pedantic for a Spaniard to claim that he or she can understand a text better if it is in Latin than when the same text was read by him in Spanish. Or is it perhaps that they do not want other readers to understand me, thinking that only a few understand Latin, and so the other readers will have to remain ignorant of what I have to say? This would be sad: It is sheer envy not to want to have others share something we appreciate.

Some will then claim that lofty ideas should always be expressed in a lofty language, not a modern one. We should answer them that style and language are two different things. With respect to style it is true that words and sentences should be adapted to the thoughts they try to convey: Humble subjects should be expressed plainly, lofty subjects demand a lofty speech and style, but with respect to languages there is no basic difference among them, there are no languages that should be held in reserve and used only for certain subjects. Each and every language is capable of expressing the whole range of human knowledge. The subject of my book can be expressed in Latin and yet the text could be a total failure if expressed in a lowly and clumsy style. A sentence is not necessarily noble and lofty because it is expressed in Latin. It can be lofty expressed in Spanish or French if it is conceived and expressed as lofty. We call Spanish our common language and yet it is not necessarily, intrinsically, common and low. Plato wrote uncommon, exquisite thoughts in what was then the common language of Greece. Cicero did the same in what was then, when he was alive, the common language of the Romans. Closer to my project, saints Basile, Chrysostom, Gregory Nazianzen, and Cyril have expressed in their mother tongue, Greek language, a language they realized not everybody could understand, many elevated and holy mysteries. They wrote in Greek and realized that many people who could understand Greek could not understand their books. Similarly if I had written my book in Latin I am sure that many readers who can understand Latin could not understand my book. The same can be said about my book in Spanish: Not every reader will understand most of it. Many Spanish texts require from the reader a specialized knowledge of the field, without which the text simply does not make sense.

Some readers are snobbish enough to state that they do not read my books because they were written in the Spanish language and claim they would read them if they had been written in Latin. They are lazy enough with respect to their mother tongue: They have made no contribution to it and always talk about other languages. I claim that they should come to terms with their mother tongue, which certainly they know better than they know the Latin language, even if they are weak in their knowledge of the Spanish language, which is true in most cases. In spite of their ignorance some of these potential readers claim I do not write "proper Spanish," because I do not babble and speak at random; rather I try to order and organize my words and my sentences, I choose my vocabulary with great care. Talking in Spanish, writing in Spanish, does not mean necessarily talking and writing like the crowd, the mob, the ignorant majority. We must think before we speak or write, for speaking correctly is not a commonplace activity but rather the result of good judgment, both in what we say and in how we say it: One must choose, among the words in use, only those most adequate to the task, we must think about their sound, sometimes we must even count the letters, weigh and measure the words so that they may express clearly what we are trying to say, and also so that they do it in harmony and sweetness. If someone were to claim that such a style is beyond the comprehension of humble and simple readers we would then retort that serious and learned readers also have tastes that should be respected, especially when the author is writing a book, such as the present one, that is addressed specifically to such serious readers.

Perhaps my attitude will strike some as a new departure from usage, and I must confess I think so myself, since it is unusual to try to introduce in the Castilian language the ideas of style based upon the length and sound of words, treating words like musical notes, which uplifts our language and gives it dignity. This is just what I have attempted to do, not because I think I can succeed in such an endeavor, since I realize that my talent may not be up to such a task, but so that others with greater talent may, from now on, treat our language as the wise and eloquent writers of the past treated their languages, making our tongue the equal of the great tongues of the past, to which it can and should be compared without forgetting its great and surpassing virtues. With the same goals in mind I tried to give my text the form of a dialogue, following thus the example of the sacred and profane ancient writers who wrote with greatest eloquence.

Something more should be added here: To those who objected my discussing the role of the perfect married woman, claiming that this subject should be off limits to a monk, my answer is simple. The Holy Spirit has dealt with such a subject in the Bible, and my role when writing my book was simply to point out what the Bible has to say about such matters. This role, as a theologian, is proper and normal to me and my training does prepare me for it. A monk should not, probably, tell married people how to behave, but a monk who teaches Holy Scripture, as I do, can interpret God's words and draw the necessary consequences from them. I have followed the path of many other theologians and scholars in this field, and their example weighs more in my mind than the idle criticism of a few readers. I value your opinion much more than theirs, and it encourages me to go on with my task: Let us therefore go back to Marcelo and his friends.

INTRODUCTION

The day that followed the Festivity of St. Peter (and it was during St. Peter's Commemoration that the first two dialogues had taken place) the Church commemorated the anniversary of St. Paul. Sabino rose earlier than usual, at the break of dawn, and went out into the orchard. From there he proceeded into the fields outside, taking the path that leads to the city. He was walking along the path and saying his morning prayers when he saw Juliano coming down on the same path, along the slope that, as we mentioned before, rises near the house. In some amazement he greeted his friend,

"I am not the only one to get up early today. It seems you got up even earlier than I did, and I still do not know why."

"Overeating at dinner," Sabino answered, "keeps people from sleeping soundly, and that is what happened to me last time, not with food, rather with ideas, the ideas we heard from Marcelo, so many and so lofty that my mind cannot digest them yet. That is why I got up before you did: Even before dawn I was walking along these hills."

"Why climb the hills? Would it not be better to walk along the river in such a hot night?"

Then Juliano, "It seems to me our bodies like to imitate the sun's motion: At this time, toward dawn, the sun rises; at the evening it falls down toward the sea. Thus it is natural to want to climb hills in the morning, in the afternoon we shall go down toward the plain and the river."

"If you are right," Sabino argued, "I have no connection with the sun, for I was planning to go down to the river before I saw you."

"Perhaps you have a connection with fishes."

"And yet yesterday I thought I belonged in the birds' family."

"Birds and fishes," Juliano answered, "are actually related, and so you were not far wrong."

"Related? How so?"

"Remember what Moses said," Juliano answered, "God created on the fifth day, out of the waters, both birds and fishes."

"This may be true, yet they try to hide their family connection, because they do not look alike at all."

"I disagree. Swimming is much like flying. In both cases you cut through something, going fast: You cut through air or through water. Both birds and fish are born from eggs, and if you consider the matter closely you will see that the fish's scales bear a certain resemblance to the bird's feathers. Fish also have a sort of wings, their fins, and with them and with their tails they propel themselves in the ocean as birds do in the air."

"On the other hand," Sabino laughed, "birds are mostly fond of singing and chirping, fishes are all dumb."

"God may have decreed such a difference in spite of the family resemblance between fish and birds, so that we men should understand that if we can talk, we should also be able to remain silent, we should be like bird or fish, eloquent or silent as the occasion demands."

"Yesterday was such a hot day," Sabino added, "that I am not sure it called for so much talking as we did. And yet I wish we could go on with our conversation."

"Did Marcelo leave anything unsaid?"

"He was very eloquent, more than anyone else I know. I know him well and think he is brilliant, and yet when I asked him to speak I did not expect him to be so lofty and noble in his thought and his expression. And yet I miss something in all that he said. He was analyzing the names of Christ and overlooked the name of Jesus, which should have been the first priority in such a task."

"You are correct," Juliano answered, "and we must fill such a gap. I am sure this sweet-sounding name can inspire in Marcelo many noble thoughts."

"If this is what you think, it is up to you to make him speak."

"How so?"

"You should take his place and talk about this subject. I am sure you got up early because you were thinking about it."

"I have already told you why I got up early. I am slowly digesting and organizing in my mind and my memory everything we heard yesterday. I have been thinking also about other matters, not about the name of Jesus: I have just realized that it was overlooked yesterday. Let us approach Marcelo and ask his opinion: Our daring will be rewarded."

"Let us do so," Sabino agreed.

They both walked back to the orchard and the house, where they found out Marcelo was still resting. After a while, they went back to the orchard, since they did not want to disturb him. Some time later, with the sun high in the sky, they went into his bedroom, fearful for his health. They found him resting and simply claiming he was somewhat tired. Sabino then said, "I am happy to know that you are in good health, first and foremost

BOOK III

because we all love you, and then because we still have so much to learn from you."

Marcelo smiled, then said, "What is it all about? Have you by chance found another paper?"

"No, and yet," Sabino said, "yesterday's paper is still food for our thought. For instance, among the names it mentions is not to be found the name 'Jesus,' the essential name. We urge you now to discuss it today, the day in which we celebrate St. Paul, who was, as you know, fond of such a name, and so often used it as a glorious centerpiece in his letters and essays."

"It is true that such a name is like the melody in a song, and we have mentioned so far the counterpoint to this melody. So much has been said about 'Jesus' by others that this perhaps is the reason we did not mention it yesterday. Yet, if you want to discuss it, I am willing to hear what Juliano, for instance, has to say about it."

Juliano demurred, in spite of the urging of the other two listeners. Finally Sabino said, "I would like to arbitrate this matter, if you accept my judgment. I find both of you guilty and subject to penalties. Marcelo will have to speak about the name 'Jesus' and Juliano will discuss another name chosen by him or by me."

Both Juliano and Marcelo found most amusing the Solomonic judgment of their friend and both accepted it. They agreed that after the siesta, in the grove, just like the previous day, first Juliano and then Marcelo would speak. As for Juliano, he would choose and decide which name he wanted to discuss. After which Juliano and Marcelo left the bedroom and Marcelo got up. After his morning prayers he rejoined his friends and the three of them passed away the rest of the morning talking at random about several subjects, mentioning repeatedly Sabino's wise sentence, which Marcelo found worthy of merriment and laughter. After a frugal repast Marcelo withdrew to his chamber to rest a while, Juliano withdrew to the cool and pleasant grove of poplar trees in the orchard, and Sabino, younger and more active than his friends, decided he would not sleep the siesta. Later on he would say that he had seen Juliano walk back and forth under the trees, deep in thought, not sleeping even one minute. Finally he took it upon himself to wake Marcelo from his slumber and Juliano from

271

his deep thoughts and told them that they had wasted enough time: The moment had arrived to start thinking and expressing their thoughts. The boat took them to the island and the grove that they had visited the day before. Finally they all sat down and Juliano started to speak.

SON OF GOD

"Since I am to speak first and it is in my power to choose my subject, I have chosen a name given to Christ in the Bible that has not been previously mentioned by any of you. It is the name 'Son.' I could preface my speech with a few remarks about how unworthy I am of the subject and begging your forgiveness for my faults and mistakes, but you know me too well for me to make use of such rhetorical tricks: I will therefore commence with my subject right away.

"The name Son is given to Christ in many passages of the Holy Scriptures: It appears so often that we tend to overlook it when we read it, without realizing that it seems to encompass a mystery, a puzzle that we should try to solve.

"Among other passages we find Psalm 72 where David, while seeming to speak about Solomon, actually describes many of the main traits of Christ and in a hidden yet elegant way makes use of the name I am talking about. David writes,

> May his name endure for ever;
> May his name be continued as long as the sun;
> May men also bless themselves by him (72:17)

where 'to endure' means actually 'to acquire life by being born, to become alive by being someone's son.' With it David declares that Christ is and should be Son, that this name is proper and necessary to name Christ: Christ is to be born bearing such a name. Moreover, this name will last, attached to Christ, longer than the sun.

"St. Paul, in his Epistle to the Hebrews, emphasizes the importance of this name and its relevance to our understanding of Christ, when he writes that Jesus has become 'so much superior to the angels as he has inherited a more excellent name than they. For to which of the angels has He ever said, Thou art my son, I this day have begotten thee'? (Heb. 1:4–5). We see therefore that according to St. Paul Christ is the only one entitled to the name Son of God. This in spite of other passages in the Scriptures where God calls some men sons, as in Isaiah when talking about the Jews God says,

> Children I have reared, and brought up,
> And they have rebelled against Me. (Isa. 1:2)

And we read in Hosea:

> When Israel was a child, then I loved him,
> And out of Egypt I called My son. (Hos. 11:2)

Also in Job (1:6) God calls the angels sons, and the same happens in Genesis (4:2) and several other places. Yet St. Paul affirms with great assurance that only Christ was called Son by God.

"Let us now examine this mystery and let us try to find out why the name Son is so fitting to Christ and what it is that God wants to tell us by such a name."

Then Sabino said, "As far as the divine nature of Christ is concerned I do not see that the name Son should become a puzzle to us. In truth Christ is the only one worthy of such a name."

"I find the puzzle in this name most dark and mysterious," Juliano objected, "because for me the problem is this: How is it that only Christ is called Son and not the Holy Spirit, since both clearly come from the Father. Many theologians have dealt with this matter, and yet I am not sure this is a problem that can be solved by human reason. Yet it may be best to proceed step by step: Let us find out first what being a son entails, and then why such a name fits Christ. A son is someone who is made of the same substance as the father, the same flesh and blood, the same nature. A son is, we could say, a portrait of his father. An artist painting a portrait looks carefully at his subject and then makes use of his talent, his technique, and his art and in order to carry the image to the canvas, translating it into lines and colors. To give life to a child is very much the same thing: It is to create someone who will be very much like ourselves. Of course in nature there are beings that last, that seem to go on and on, through their descendants and other beings that do not fulfill this goal and merely manage to create fleeting portraits of themselves. A good example of this latter category is the sun. It sends us a fleeting image of its light and power: It is lightning. Now lightning does not have as a mission to perpetuate the sun after the sun dies, rather it shows us what the sun is made of, in all its glory and splendor. A son is a living, lasting portrait of his father. He must be created out of the same substance, in every aspect equal or similar to his father, capable of replacing his father if need be, capable of reminding us at every moment of his father's qualities. Father and son should share the same will, the same outlook, the same principles. A son should try to please his father, to take him as a model, a guide, an example to follow, in order to get his inspiration from his father and to turn into love all the messages he received with pleasure, creating thus a pure bond of love between son and father.

"This being so, we see clearly why Christ is called Son of God in the Scriptures. He is the only one that fulfills all the necessary conditions to be called by such a name. He alone is born out of God's essence, similar in all aspects to the one that gave Him birth, since in His birth He becomes closer to God and becomes God's perfect mirror image. As Christ states, 'I and the Father are one' (John 10:30). More about this later.

"Christ is also like us, like mankind. And yet what seems to dominate in His nature is the divine element: This is why Christ said, 'Philip, he who sees me sees also the Father' (John 14:9).

"Eternal life must shine on: Only Christ can make it obvious to all of us. He is the only one that has put us in touch with His Father, by relaying His message and by conveying His style and His virtue. As someone who shares in divine nature, and at the same time in our nature, Christ is the natural bridge between God and man.

"St. Paul writes about God, or rather as Christ as God, that He is 'the brightness of his glory and the image of his substance' (Heb. 1:3). And as man, Christ says about Himself, 'This is why I was born, and why I have come into the world, to bear witness to the truth' (John 18:37). And also, elsewhere, 'I have manifested thy name to the men whom thou hast given me out of the world' (John 17:6). Again, in St. John, we read,

> No one has at any time seen God.
> The only-begotten Son,
> > who is in the bosom of the Father,
> > he has revealed him. (1:18)

"As we have pointed out before, Christ as a Son of God stands alone, is unique: He is also unique in His qualities and attitudes. He alone, belonging to both natures, human and divine, can fuse His will and purpose with those of God Himself. Does not He say of Himself, 'My food is to do the will of him who sent me, to accomplish his work' (John 4:34). And David in a Psalm,

> For Thou art my rock and my fortress;
> Therefore for Thy name's sake lead me and guide me. (Ps. 31:4)

And in the garden at Gethsemane, 'Father, if it is possible, let this cup pass away from me; yet not as I will, but as thou willest' (Matt. 26:39). Always following His Father's footsteps: 'Amen, amen, I say to you, the Son can do nothing of himself, but only what he sees the Father doing' (John 5:19). And elsewhere, 'My teaching is not my own, but his who sent me' (John 7:16). His Father trusts and loves Him, and this love is returned. The Father says, 'This is my beloved son, in whom I am well pleased' (Matt. 3:17) and the Son, 'I have glorified thee on earth; I have accomplished the work that thou hast given me to do' (John 17:5).

"To love is also to obey, and obedience is a proof of love. No one was as obedient as Christ, who obeyed His Father unto death, unto His own crucifixion. Out of obedience He who is the source of life accepted to die, being God He became a mortal man, being a man without blame or sin He accepted and assumed all of mankind's sins and suffered the penalty of death because of them. He chose to forego His power so that His enemies could cast Him in prison and by disarming Himself, so to speak, made His own death possible. He had to work hard in order to set aside His power and His glory, in order to be able to die, and all this He did in order to obey His Father, and this means that it is only fair that

THE NAMES OF CHRIST

Christ and only Christ should be called Son of God: No one else is entitled to such a name. And yet there is more.

"Only Christ was born of God, and He did so in five ways that are unique and worthy of reflection. As God, Christ was born out of God the Father eternally and for all time. As a man, He was born out of a virgin mother, Mary, and His life as a man had to be temporary and finite. Christ's resuscitation and ascent into glory after His death was in effect like a new birth. In a certain way Christ is reborn daily in the Holy Host every time the priests consecrate the wafer. Finally, Christ is reborn and grows in us every time that He blesses us and inspires what is best in us. Let us now deal with each one of these births."

"A noble subject," Sabino said, "is, Juliano, the one that you have chosen. If I am not mistaken we are going to hear many interesting things."

"There are indeed many wonders in my subject," Juliano replied, "but who could describe them all accurately? I have the feeling that I am unworthy of such a subject. Marcelo would feel more at home with it."

"Let us allow Marcelo to rest today, since he spoke at such length yesterday. You yourself are not so lacking in talent as to be in need of his help."

Then Marcelo, smiling, "Today Sabino commands and we obey, dear Juliano: I will be most happy to listen to you."

After a few moments of silence Juliano began:

"Christ our Lord was born out of God, and is truly His son. Both the way in which Christ was born and the consequences of His birth are worthy of analysis. Many non-Christians think, for instance, that since God is eternal, perfect, infinite, there was no point, no need, for Him to have a son. Yet we all associate sterility with weakness and impotence. We also associate riches, abundance, perfection, and power, with fecundity. God should be fecund, since He is the fountain of all abundance, riches and power, He is the essence of kindness, power, and infinite riches. If we know all this we realize that it is in His nature to be fecund and be the source of some offspring. Loneliness is always sad. Since God is the epitome of perfection He had to create a son in a special manner, better by far than any other way of engendering or giving birth to a child.

"He needed no other person in order to create a new being,

differing thus from our human couples: His son was created by Himself primarily, out of His own power: He was basically both father and mother. The Holy Scripture describes this process in a way that makes it intelligible to us in physical terms when it seems to assume that God may have a womb: according to Psalm 110 (verse 3), where we read

> In adornments of holiness, from the womb of the dawn,
> Thine is the dew of thy youth.

"Which means that God's womb, at the dawn of time, is the source of new life, of Christ's life. No other being is needed.

"Another important point: God could not and did not allow the son created by Him to grow apart from Himself. When this happens the resemblance between father and son is blurred. Whence when God decided to have a Son because loneliness is not a good thing He also decided that His son would not grow away from Him, for distance creates lack of knowledge and because God's son could not grow into perfection except near God, in a manner of speaking in God's entrails, in His bosom. The Godhead is one, and cannot be separated or divided. Christ says about Himself that He is in the Father and the Father is in Him (John 10:38). And again in John (1:18) we hear about the only-begotten Son 'Who is in the bosom of the Father.' As a son, Christ is in some ways different from the Father that gave Him life, and yet at the same time, since He is in the bosom of the Father we can also see that His nature, His essence, is actually the same nature, and the same essence, of the Father. Father and son are separate and different so that they can keep each other company, yet they are one in essence of divinity so that the whole universe is a place of harmony and agreement.

"Christ's birth did not take place little by little. It did not occur, on the other hand, once and for all. Whatever has a beginning and an end is limited—yet God is limitless. Therefore from all eternity the Son was born from the Father and is eternally being born from Him, and is always borning whole and perfect, as great as His Father is great. It is in a way a plural birth. Micah writes,

> Out of thee (Bethlehem) shall one come forth
> unto Me that is to be ruler in Israel;

THE NAMES OF CHRIST

Whose goings forth are from of old,
from ancient days. (Mic. 5:2)

"Here 'goings forth' means water springs of light and life that
are eternal. The flowing goes on and on without end.

"By giving birth to Christ we can also assume that it was an
act of pure creation without sensuous passion, troubling sexuality.
It was an act of purity, light, simplicity, like the first flow from a
deep spring, like a light that starts softly to glow from its source,
like the exquisite perfume coming out of a rose. Again the Holy
Scripture: 'He is an emanation of God's virtue and a clear, sincere
presence of the light from the Almighty' (Sab. 7:25). And again, 'I
am like a brook of everlasting water, like a watering canal out of a
river, like a rivulet out of paradise' (Eclo. 24:41).

"It is above all God's infinite and shining mind that cele-
brates the birth of His child. God understands the world and also
understands His own being, since He is the all-encompassing
mind and intelligence. He also sees and foresees in which ways He
can communicate His intelligence to the rest of the world created
by Him. He has planned that by drawing and projecting an image
of His own being the whole world will be drawn closer to His
essence. Such an image was projected into the world: It was that
of His son, Christ.

"When a great artist, a master painter, wants to leave us a
portrait of himself, he looks inside himself first of all, he tries to
understand himself, tries to draw and paint himself in his own
mind. There an image is created, as lively and faithful as possible,
according to the rules and techniques of art. Thus God, who
without a doubt understands Himself, and who wishes to create
an image of Himself, from all eternity has had an image of
Himself clearly drawn in His mind, and then, when He wished to
do so, projected this image outside Himself. Such an image is
God's Son; the portrait that becomes objective outside God is
God's creatures, both each one of them and all together. Which
creatures, compared with the image that God painted inside His
mind and with the norms of art, are like dark shadows, like small
dead parts in front of a living whole.

"Again following the image given above, if we compare the
portrait that a painter paints of himself on a canvas with the
portrait he first drew in his mind, we see that the first is mainly

cloth, spots of color, lines and shadows that lack real life in themselves, while the mental image, when established with care, is almost like a twin of the real person, the real painter; in a similar fashion, each earthly creature is only a glimpse of reality, more appearance than being, more illusion than reality, when compared with the lively and perfect image of God. Everything in this lowly world of ours is born and dies, and in the heavens stars change and go around without rest, but we have our equivalent (a being without change or becoming, a life without death) in God's perfect image. For the being of every thing as reflected in God is a true being, solid, enduring, since it is part of God Himself, while the existence of these same things in our world is weak and precarious, a shadow of true reality. The source of life and truth is also the source of hope. A source has always an advantage: It has the power, the real matter—everything else is a weak reflection of it. God dwells in the heights, upon the pillars of clouds. As the cedars of Lebanon and the roses of Jericho He shines over us. And St. John in his first chapter states,

> All things were made through him,
>   and without him was made
>   nothing that has been made.
> In him was life,
>   and the life was the light of men.
> And the light shines in the darkness;
>   and the darkness grasped it not. (1:3–5)

"Which means that in this image of God everything created was already alive, and that such a holy light was life itself.

"We conclude that such an image of God is the essence of wisdom, since it represents everything that God knows about Himself, and God is the epitome of knowledge and wisdom, our model of order, proportion, harmony. St. John at the very beginning of his gospel calls God 'the Word,' with the Greek word 'Logos,' which means all that was said before. Such an image of God had to touch and change everything created by God: It was the messenger, the model, the shaper of God's thoughts in action. Going back once more to our basic metaphor, if the image that the painter had drawn of himself in his own mind became alive and could think and reason, when the painter wanted to paint his self-portrait on a canvas, it is obvious that it is the image that would take over, move the brush and paint itself. St. Paul in his Epistle to the Hebrews states that God has spoken to us by His Son, whom he appointed heir of all things, by whom also He made the world (1:1, 2). Christ's image was created before any other creature, it is the light that will never fade and will spread all over the earth.

"We now understand fully why such an image is called Son of God. It comes down to us from the Father's wisdom, it is identical to the Father in essence and substance, it lives with the life of God. Christ is Son not only because He is the first and best of all the beings created by God but also because He alone projects completely the image of His Father, He is the forerunner of all the other creatures of God, the first and most successful of God's endeavors. If we think of God as our Father it is because we realize that God did manage to communicate His image and His power to Christ, and can do so, in a degree, with respect to us. As St. Paul puts it in his Epistle to the Ephesians, when speaking about the Father of our Lord Jesus Christ he writes, 'from whom all fatherhood in heaven and on earth receives its name' (3:15), it is an essential attribute of God the Father to have this relationship of paternity with every being in the world, in the same way that the Son of God is the essence and symbol of the relationship son-father, since He was the first to be born from the Father.

"What does St. Paul have to say about this matter? He says about Christ: 'He is the image of the invisible God, the firstborn of every creature. For in him were created all things in the heavens and on the earth, things visible and things invisible' (Col. 1:15). He says Christ is the image of God so that we can understand that Christ is equal to God and God is like Christ. St. Paul in his wisdom writes that Christ is the image of the invisible God, indicating thereby that God remains hidden except in this image, whose role is to give us a chance to see what without it would remain hidden. He adds that Christ is the firstborn, which means that as a son He has to be like His Father and as a firstborn son He comes before every other being both in time and in essence, He is our pattern, our norm, the source of our life and being. Later on Paul underlines, as we have already quoted, 'for in him were created all things in the heavens and on the earth, things visible and things invisible.' 'In him' means 'in him and through him,' in

Him first, as the original pattern, and through Him, later, as our master and guide.

"If we compare Christ to all the other creatures, Christ is the only one entitled to the name Son. If we compare Him with the third person of the Trinity, the Holy Spirit, again only Christ can be called Son. Although the Holy Spirit is God, just like the Father, and is endowed with the same essence of divinity, and is in no way different from God, yet the similarity or rather identity is not translated into an image of the Father but as the Father's embrace and as our reverence toward the Father. Although the equal of the Father, it is not its role to explain and project the Father's image, and therefore it is not in its function and essence to be the Father's Son. In other words: Let us assume I have finally understood myself, my life, my personality, and after doing so I accept and love myself. From this understanding an image of myself is born in me. Thus God from all times understands and loves Himself and has created in Him a live image of every aspect of His being. This love then goes forth and embraces every aspect of reality that is a part of God. Of course what happens with a human being is not the same: In me, in my mind, such an image and such a feeling of affection are accidents without life or substance. Yet in God, to whom nothing can happen casually, at random, and in whom everything that is, is divine and essential, such an image is alive and is God, such a feeling of affection is alive and becomes self-sustaining. The image is God's son because it is God's image. The feeling of affection, on the other hand, is not God's son because it is not an image, it is rather a spiritual feeling, an inclination, a movement of emotional recognition. The three persons, Father, Son, Holy Spirit, are God, one and the same God, because in all three there exists a divine essence, in the Father for and by Himself, in the Son as received from the Father, in the Holy Spirit as received both from the Father and from the Son. In this way the single divine essence is to be found in the Father as fountainhead and primordial beginning, in the Son as self-portrait, in the Holy Spirit as self-understanding. In one body, so to speak, and in one burst of light, reverberating upon itself, in a strange and ineffable way we can see three circles shine. O Sun dazzling and immense!

"I have mentioned the sun: No visible object can be a better illustration of God's essence and God's projection toward us. In the same way that the sun is a body of light that pours its rays everywhere, so God's nature, in its vast immensity, spreads over every created object. And in the same fashion as the sun, with its rays, makes it possible for us to see things that the gloom of night hides and seems to erase, thus God's virtue, shining toward us, brings out from nonexistence to the clear light of being every thing created. The same way that the sun seems to seek our eyes and never tries to hide since it is made of light thus God also seeks us, our minds and hearts, and comes toward us unless we close our hearts to Him: His light penetrates every chink, hole, and crevice. Another parallel: We see the sun's rays shining everywhere, over all things, yet we cannot look straight into the sun, since its direct light would blind us. And about God we can say that He at the same time is clear and dark, manifest and obscure. We do not see God directly, and if we try to do so we will be blinded. Yet we see God in every being created by Him, since His light shines over every creature.

"Let me carry this parallel to the end. In the same way that the sun reminds us of a flowing spring gushing light every second, always in a hurry, we see that God, in His infinite kindness, seems always to bubble over in order to make us better, sending us good tidings and wisdom without limit. And in order to return to our main line of thought, in the same way that the sun creates a ray of light—and indeed the whole shimmering mass of light that bathes the sky and the earth comes from a single ray of sunlight—thus God generates one single Son, who rules and spreads His presence everywhere. The ray from the sun I have just mentioned holds in itself all the rays of light that the sun sends us, and sends us the sun's image, and equally true would be to say that the Son born out of God's essence brings to us this very essence of God and the perfect image of our Creator. The Sun is basically light and sends off rays of its light, of itself: Each ray is a portrait of the sun traveling toward us. In the same manner the Father produced out of His being a ray, a portrait, and sent it to us: It is His son. The sun creates its rays of light continually, not in a haphazard or interrupted manner. It did it in the past and will go on doing so, wholly and perfectly. Thus God from the very beginning and for all eternity did create, creates, and will create forever and ever His son. The sun stays in one place and through a ray of its light appears before our eyes, and spreads over every thing, every being around us. In the same manner, God, of whom St. John says that 'no one has at any time seen God' (1:18), yet manages to shine and spread His light all around us and by doing so makes His Father's presence and being visible to us. Finally, in the same way that the sun through the rays of light it sends us manages to influence the whole world, God manages to create and rule the universe through His son, in whom, so to speak, can be found the seeds, the foundations, the origins, of everything created.

"Let us hear what the Book of Proverbs has to say about this relationship between the son and the Father: It is the son who speaks here:

> The Lord made me as the beginning of His way,
> The first of His works of old.
> I was set up from everlasting, from the beginning,
> Or ever the earth was.
> When there were no depths, I was brought forth;
> When there were no fountains abounding with water.
> Before the mountains were settled,
> Before the hills was I brought forth;
> While as yet He had not made the earth, nor the fields,
> Nor the beginning of the dust of the world.
> When He established the heavens, I was there;
> When He set a circle upon the face of the deep,
> When He made firm the skies above,
> When the fountains of the deep showed their might,
> When He gave to the sea His decree
> That the waters should not transgress His commandment,
> When He appointed the foundations of the earth;
> Then I was by Him, as a nursling;
> And I was daily all delight,
> Playing always before Him,
> Playing in His habitable earth,
> And my delights are with the sons of men. (Prov. 8:22–31)

"The first line, where it says that the Lord made Him at the beginning of His way, means that the Lord would not have followed a way or path outside Himself, that is to say, that He would not have created the creatures He did create, and communicated His wisdom and kindness to them, unless previously and for all eternity He had not created His Son, who, as we have pointed out previously, is the reason and the cause of all that has been created. The Lord made Christ, Christ was set up from everlasting, Christ was brought forth: All of which means that God was preparing a vast creation, in His wisdom and art: His Son would help in many ways, not apart from God, not living in His own house, but—born out of God—from inside God Himself.

"This creation was deliberate, not the product of chance and confusion: God knew what His power was capable of. God acquired a son as one acquires a treasure: Creating Christ was like discovering a mine of gold. And when we read that the Lord made Christ as the beginning of His way, the original text allows the interpretation, as was made by those who translated it into Greek, that God made Him as the origin and head of His way, in other words, that the divine Child is the prince and king of everything God would create afterward, since He is at the origin and beginning of creation. In the same manner, when we read 'the first of His works,' 'of everlasting,' it means Christ has always existed, even before time. Anything coming from God that comes to us in the frame of time can be called modern: What is ancient is the beginning, the everlasting, what existed before time, outside time, in eternity. What we see as modern creation was already existing in the Son of God from all antiquity, outside time.

"When we read 'I was set up' we are reminded of the way an army is set up before a battle, with the squadrons of warriors all in line and by groups, with the captain at the head. Here 'set up' means 'placed in the first rank,' made ruler or commander of the rest, because the word, in the original text, means literally 'made a prince.' It also has another meaning: 'cast,' as used by silversmiths, in other words, pour in the cast the molten gold or silver in order to create a work of art: The metal pours down the mold and takes its shape. Divine wisdom, according to the text, was cast by the Father since before time, forever, because it was made to His image and He shaped it in His mold and became one with it.

"What follows in the same text amplifies and specifies further the main thought by saying that God created divine wisdom (the Son) before the earth was, when there were no abysses, no fountains or springs, before the mountains became firm and settled into their natural shape, before the hills existed, before the fields spread out, before the world was organized. The message is, not only had this wisdom been born from God before God created all other things, but also that, when God created everything, the sky, the stars, the clouds, the sea, the earth, this wisdom was already in the Father's bosom, creating everything together with Him, helping Him in this creation. To create means here to foster, to protect, to bring up, to educate, to carry the creation in your arms much like the nurse carries in her arms a baby she is taking care of. For things were born tender and childlike, and divine wisdom accepted the task of raising them and became their wet nurse. Carrying further the image I shall say that there was no end of sweet talk and tender loving care. Just as a nurse caresses and praises a baby, showing off to all, saying 'see how pretty the baby is,' thus divine wisdom did with the newly created beings in the world, showing off their beauty, or as we read in Genesis (1:31), 'And God saw every thing that He had made, and, behold, it was very good.' Vergil knows about this era at the very beginning of our world and he describes it thus,

> Springtime that was; the great world was receiving spring weather, and the East winds moderated their wintry blasts. Then it was that the first cattle drank in the light and man's iron race reared its head from the harsh fields, and wild beasts were let loose into the forests and the stars into heaven. And tender things could not have endured this world's stress without such long pause between the seasons' cold and heat, and without heaven's gracious welcome to the new-born earth. (Georgics II:338–345)

Divine Wisdom was playing before the Father, as before a mortal father a nurse may play with a baby and exhibit the baby's beauty, and concludes, 'My delights are with the sons of men,' which seems to indicate that she was delighted in meeting men and getting to know them because she had already made up her mind to be born as a man when the time to do so would come.

"About this second birth in which the Divine Son became man, it is not less wondrous than the first. It is something new, never seen before or afterward. The three persons of the Trinity are all equally holy and deeply united, and yet they were not born as a man the three of them, only the person of the Son was. When this happened the Son did not cease being God nor did He mix to man's nature His divine nature, but He remained one single person with two different natures, one from God the Father and one received from mankind, not created anew or from the dust of the ground, but from the virgin blood of a virgin without stain, in her womb, without harming her purity, and the child was of Adam's lineage yet without the stain of Adam's original sin. Out of virginal blood came human flesh, a child's body with all members and organs, and in this body a man's soul endowed with intelligence and reason, together with a thousand qualities and perfections, with spontaneity and freedom, all this together with a knowledge and enjoyment of God, together with a great sensitivity: a blessing and a great capacity for suffering.

"All of this took place in an instant. A man-God was born, a very old child, a great holiness in the tender body of a baby, a perfect wisdom in a tender body without speech, a paradox and a miracle: a child who was a giant, a weak body endowed with great power, wisdom, and invincible courage surrounded by nakedness and tears. And what was conceived in a holy womb was born out of it, after a few months, without any pain and leaving the womb holy and virgin. The newborn babe was a ray of divine light, a shining splendor bringing to us the light from the Father, and such was His birth: The child came out of the mother's womb as a ray of light shines through a window pane, without harming the glass in any way. Flesh and divinity, God and man together, a child without mother in the heavens, without father in this earth: the union of the creator and creation.

"Do listen to Saint John:

And the Word was made flesh,
    and dwelt among us.
And we saw the glory—
    glory as of the only-begotten of the Father—
full of grace and of truth. (1:14)

And do listen to Isaiah:

For a child is born unto us;
A son is given unto us,

BOOK III

And the government is upon his shoulder;
And his name is called
Wonderful in counsel is God the Mighty,
The Everlasting Father, the Ruler of Peace. (9:5)

A child is born unto us: that is, a child generated by God for all eternity is now born unto us, among us, and the Son, who helped in the creation of the whole world, is now among us as a son. He is a child, a son, a baby, yet a king, and is called Wonderful in counsel because He is Himself a wonder and a source of wonder. He helps in carrying out divine counsel, to the betterment of mankind. He is God, He is the Mighty, He is the Everlasting Father, He is the Prince of Peace.

"Marcelo explained yesterday how He did not come from a human father in His second birth. Solomon may have realized that He did not harm His mother's virginity when he stated,

There are three things that are too wonderful for me,
Yea, four which I know not;
The way of an eagle in the air;
The way of a serpent upon a rock;
The way of a ship in the midst of the sea;
And the way of a man with a young woman. (Prov. 30:18–19)

(Here a young woman means a virgin.) Three things are compared in this text, three things that leave no traces of their passage. All of which may mean that when our child-God was born out of His virginal mother's womb He did so without breaking it, without leaving any traces of His passage, just as the eagle leaves no trace in the air while flying, nor does the snake upon a rock, nor a ship upon the sea. This is, therefore, a good description of this holy birth.

"As for how it happened, here we find an ineffable mystery. How can we understand the secret ways of God? St. Augustine says wisely that in matters such as these the main point to be considered by us is the infinite power of the one who carries out the project. How did God become a man? Because His power is boundless. How can the same person partake of man's nature and of God's nature? Because His power is infinite. How can a baby grow in body and be a perfect man in His soul, still keep the senses of a child, yet see and conceive God in His mind, be conceived in a woman without the help of a man, be born of a woman and still leave His mother a virgin? Because God's power is infinite. God would not do much for us if He did only what our common sense can understand. It is, of course, not an easy task to do a favor to someone whose weak understanding and lack of imagination cannot understand what is being done for him and keeps doubting about the favor simply because he himself would be incapable of doing such a favor. How did God become a man? My answer is this: through His love of mankind. It is something so new and strange that love can change the lover, draw him near the beloved, more and more like the beloved. Whoever loves and thinks constantly about the object of his or her love will be deeply changed by all of this and come to resemble the object of his love. Divine wisdom declared that her delights were with the sons of men. More than that, imitating them was part of the picture, before taking human flesh and shape. Divine wisdom talked to Adam in the Garden of Eden as one man to another, as reported by Pope Leo and other theologians. It talked with Abraham when Sodom was about to be destroyed, with Jacob when Jacob fought with the angel, with Moses in front of the burning bush, with Joshua, the warrior of Israel. Such contact with men was bound to leave traces upon it: After wearing for a while the mask of man it finally became a man.

"How can God dwell in human flesh? Let us hear from the great Basil:

> In the same way that fire dwells inside a piece of iron. It does not displace it but rather pours its energy into it. Fire does not move towards iron but once inside it its properties spread out everywhere and influence it. The same is true about God's Word: it inhabits among us without changing its original abode and without leaving its proper space. Do not imagine God coming down from the heavens, for God does not travel from one place to another in the same way our earthly bodies travel. Deity did not change while becoming human flesh, for God is not subject to change. Again, how is it that our flesh's weakness and corruption did not affect God? Think about this: fire does not accept or receive the qualities

and properties of iron. Iron is cold and black, yet after going into a furnace it becomes like fire, with the color and heat of fire, nor does it make fire cold or black. The same with human flesh: It received divine qualities but did not contaminate God with its weakness. Or are we unwilling to accept that God can do as much as fire? (Pseudo Basil, *Hom. in sanctam Christi generationem,* XXXI, col. 1459, Migne, *Patr. Graeca*)

"Another enlightening comparison is this following one: The Ark of the Covenant was built out of wood and gold. Out of wood that would not rot and out of the finest gold. It was both a wooden ark and a gold ark and yet it was one single ark, not two. Thus in this second birth the ark of innocent mankind came to us combined with the gold of God. Gold covered it in all its surfaces yet did not change its being: Two arks had become one, forever.

"In the highest peak of Mount Sinai, when God was giving Moses the tablets of the law, He was surrounded by fire and clad in His full glory, and yet lower down there was smoke and the tremors of an earthquake. Thus Christ, born as a man—and symbolically a man is also a mountain—at the top of His soul was burning in the flames of love and enjoyed a glorious vision of God and the heavens, yet in the lower parts of His body He shook and smoked, weak as a man. Let us also remember Jacob who on the road to Mesopotamia, when night fell, fell asleep in the fields placing his head upon a stone. Outwardly he seemed to be a poor laborer dead tired and asleep. Inwardly he was contemplating the road open to him and to us from earth to heaven, God above us all, angels all around. Thus in this birth the appearances are deceptive: A small baby born in a manger, a baby that did not speak nor cry, and yet in the depth of His soul was absorbed in contemplation of God's greatness. And just as in the Jordan river, when the Ark of the old Covenant rested in the waters of the river, so that the Israelites could ford the river and go on with their journey, the waters above the Ark rose up high, while below it the waters went on flowing as usual (Josh. 3:13ff.), thus when God entered a human body the upper part of this body always gazed at the heavens, yet the lower part of it continued to be subjected to mortal pain and suffering.

THE NAMES OF CHRIST

"This is why St. John in his Apocalypse describes the Word made flesh as a lamb, as a slain lamb, symbol of meekness and humility, and having seven horns and seven eyes, and he alone could reach God, taking from God's hand the sealed scroll, opening it (5:6), discovering the greatness and strength that dwelled in him, and prepared to open the seven seals of the scroll, a symbol of the *why* of this birth of God made man, the third wonder and the meaning of God's advice, hidden until then and sealed with seven seals. When the book has been opened the first thing that appears, after the lamb opens the first seal, is a white horse, a rider, and the rider receives a crown and goes forward as a conqueror (6:1). Then, after the second seal is opened, a red horse, with a rider that carries a sword and takes peace from the earth (6:4). Then a black horse whose rider weighs and measures the fruits of the earth (6:5–6). Then a pale horse, the rider is Death and leads us into hell (6:7–8). Then the martyrs appear, they are consoled and receive white robes (6:9–11). With the opening of the sixth seal there is an earthquake, earth trembles, the sun becomes black. At the opening of the seventh seal the skies become calm and silence is made in heaven. For the sealed secret of God is a complex device ordered with the purpose of making us whole. Grace, in its pure and white wholeness, shines first. It is succeeded by the red flag of fire, the symbol of a clash between reason and passion, passion ruled by mad desire. All this situation is followed by the travail of melancholy and mortification, a sad and pale emblem. It is followed by hell and its cohorts, ever ready to attack and mistreat virtue.

"Yet we should not forget that God protects His followers in many ways, gives them succor and inspiration, allows them to endure until the moment of victory arrives. God's arm reaches far and His mercy is all-encompassing. After the struggle a heavenly silence prevails.

"In principle, as St. John writes, no creature could break the seven seals of the scroll and reveal God's plan. This is why it was decided that the one to do so would be a meek lamb. One, moreover, with seven eyes and seven horns, symbols of wisdom and knowledge and power. God's power would be joined to man's weakness. As a weak man such a being could die; as a being suffused by holiness, his death would be an acceptable sacrifice. As a man-God, his death would be our everlasting life, our rescue from original sin. In such a manner God was born again, as St. Basil writes,

> so that He would deal a death blow to the death hidden in the flesh. Some remedies against poisons manage to destroy the black nefarious effect of the poisonous substance: as the gloom of darkness is dissipated by the rays of light of a lamp, thus death, about to take hold of men, is defeated by God's presence in our body and soul. Ice can rule the cold waters of a lake or river while night lasts, yet when the sun rises and heats the air it will melt away. Thus death had dominion over us until Christ arrived. After our Sun of Justice started to shine death was defeated, no longer able to prey upon life. O kind and loving God! We have been freed. Should we ask how and what for, when we should thank God for such a great favor? What next, man? You searched for God and thought Him hiding in heaven. Now that God has come down to earth and talks to you, instead of thanking Him are you going to ask Him how and why He wanted to be like you? Know and learn: God became like you because it was essential to make pure and holy your flesh, so long accursed. Your flesh, so weak, had to become bold. It was alienated from God, and it had to draw near Him. It was expelled from Paradise, and it had to reach towards Heaven. (*Homil. in St. Chrt. gener.*, XXXI, col. 1462, Migne)

This is so because God wanted to salvage what had previously been lost, and since the holy Word was the tool or bridge through which God created all things, the Word came to the rescue in order to save them. Since among all the creatures it was man that had been most endangered, it was logical to turn God into man in order to protect and save this most endangered being. Moreover, since the medicine had to be clean and health-giving, the being chosen to bring it to man had to be clean and spotless. Moreover, since this being was part of God it was essential that He could enjoy God's presence, therefore since the very beginning of His life He could contemplate and be aware of God's presence inside his soul. And since in order to bring remedy to our grief He wanted to experience grief, contemplation of God did not exclude sad and bitter feelings. And since He had come to heal an old wound He did not wish to wound his virginal mother's womb while being born. And since he was the Word, born without effort or pain from His Father, He chose to be born without inflicting His mother any pain. Finally, since He, as God, is one single being together with the Father and the Holy Spirit, and yet He is also a different and separate person, He was able to join to the divine nature of God the mortal nature of His body and soul— body and soul that, through a last miracle, He was able to join once more, after being dead for three days, causing to be born again what death had plunged into darkness.

"This birth was the third of the five we have previously mentioned. It was indeed a true birth, as the Holy Scripture points out. In Psalms (2:7), speaking about the resurrection of God's Son, it says, 'Thou art My son, This day have I begotten thee.' For God's virtue and grace did shape the body of Christ inside Virgin Mary's womb, and years later, when Christ's body had been placed in the tomb, a cold and bloodless body full of wounds and devoid of life, the very same grace and power of God took Christ's body into His warm embrace, poured new blood into His veins, lit once more the furnace of His heart, and from it life spirits were poured into the arteries, the heart gave its warmth to the whole chest, and lungs started to breathe, and the soul penetrated once more into His body, more powerful and active than ever, in perfect control of the body and the senses, free from suffering, mistress of a perfect, incorruptible, eternally living body.

"This body is sustained without earthly nourishment, its internal heat radiates without effort, humors and spirits ever flowing in balance: Such a body is a victory over death, eternally at bay and incapable of harming it, a body forever shining, a body turned into light, life, grace, and glory, coming out of the tomb as a baby out of his mother's womb, an eternally living body, a living miracle.

"For indeed Christ's second birth, when he was born out of Mary, although unusual in some ways, was quite normal in other ways. The baby took shape inside Mary very much like other

BOOK III

babies, out of the mother's blood, warmth, nourishment, humors, life spirits. Thus when born Christ was similar in many ways to our human condition: He had to eat in order to replenish His strength, He felt the pangs of hunger and the tired feelings brought about by exertion and hard work, He could be wounded, hurt, bruised, He could bleed, and since the knots that tied together the various parts of His body had been tied by His mother, they could be untied by death, as in fact they were.

"But the third birth was quite extraordinary and divine, for there was no natural force that could give heat and life to a cold body enclosed in a grave, nor was there any normal way to bring blood back to His veins, humors to His body. It was only the wonderful powers of God that could bring heat where ice was, fullness where emptiness reigned, tie together what had been set apart and broken. Christ's soul was full of God's essence, which helped God's movement toward Christ: Christ's soul became full to the brim with God's presence, and so was His body, and finally God's presence, warmth, and glory, penetrated every pore of Christ's body and made both body and soul shine with His glory to the point that they outshone the sun's rays, the sun's golden light. Long before this moment David had written,

Thy people offer themselves willingly in the day of thy
    warfare;
In adornments of holiness, from the womb of the dawn,
Thine is the dew of thy youth. (Ps. 110:3)

Yesterday, dear Marcelo, you spoke about the birth of Christ as He became human; the same statement can apply to this other birth. For the Holy Spirit, who sees the whole picture at the same time, may combine in one sentence several truths. It declares that Christ was born when He resuscitated from the womb of the earth, in the dawn of time, through His own will, because He had with Himself the dew of His birth, which helped His bones to green and flourish. All of which took place among rays and splendors of holiness, in beauty and grace, for three sources of radiant light mingled their presences: divinity, a presence made into light; Christ's soul, holy and surrounded by light; His body, also beautiful and seemingly created again anew, radiating beauty.

For God's infinite light reverberated in Christ's soul, and the soul shed its light into the body, and the body then became a beacon of God's ever-expanding light.

"And we read that Christ was born then 'in adornment of holiness,' because when He was thus born out of His tomb He was not the only one born, as had happened when He was born out of Mary, but rather with Him and in Him many other people resplendent in life, glory, and holiness were also born. He brought into a wider horizon of light and freedom many people who were imprisoned in the old law of Abraham, and moreover, as we learned from Marcelo's lips yesterday, in the mystery of the last supper and when He was walking with His cross Christ managed to gather together all His friends and disciples in a spiritual embrace, and He gathered all of them into Himself in such a way that in the death that His mortal flesh was to suffer all the evil and sinful part of their flesh would also die. Condemned to die, it was to be reborn into glory and justice when Christ was resuscitated. This is why in a beautiful metaphor and paradox Christ says about Himself and His new birth, 'Amen, amen, I say to you, unless the grain of wheat fall into the ground and die, it remains alone. But if it die, it brings forth much fruit' (John 12:24–25). Because when a grain has been sowed, if it becomes full of the soil's humidity and the juices of the earth, it becomes pregnant, rots, and out of its womb come a thousand other seeds, a whole ear of corn or of wheat. In the same manner Christ, buried as a dead body and becoming as a buried body part of the earth, managed then to gather into Himself the virtues and properties of the earth, and after a while He came back to the light of the sun as an ear of corn, no longer as a grain.

"We see then that when Christ rose like the sun from His sepulcher this meant that it was not only a ray of sunlight that was arising and shining at that moment, but rather many rays, many shining splendors, life itself, and the very future of the world, being embraced and enhanced by Christ. Joy, birth, a new birth for all of us: a wonderful birth in which we were all reborn, and moreover one that overcame death, anguish, despair. By contrast with darkness light shines brighter. The anguishing hours before such a birth, hours of despair and death, enhance such a birth, since out of suffering, misery, grief, came out victory and life. A paradox: By falling down Christ rose up, out of death life arose and conquered the heavens. In such a manner, we conclude that the deeper the roots, the higher the plant that grows out of such roots, and in a parallel way out of an experience, so deep and poignant, of agony and despair, Christ came to know an existence of bliss.

"We realize now how hard it is for us to understand God's mysterious ways. Christ, born in light, reborn in glory, found a way to be born again every day in the modest, almost secretive yet holy host that priests consecrate. The Son does not boast about His presence among us. Yet His birth is important and helpful. Christ is indeed present in His sacrament, what was bread becomes Christ's body, He does not leave the heavens yet resides among us. Christ is indeed reborn every time the priest consecrates the holy host. The host is much like a womb in which a magical birth takes place after a magical word has transformed into spirit all the material shape and substance of bread.

"The Holy Scripture indicates in other passages the relationship between Christ and bread. We read in Psalm 72, 'May he be as a rich cornfield in the land upon the top of the mountains' where corn, wheat, is a symbol of sustenance, strength, for our hearts. David speaks of the 'bread that stayeth man's heart' (104:15). Even before Christ came bread had acquired the value of a symbol. And you know that the original Hebrew words that we translate as 'firmness, strength' are *pisath bar*, which mean 'fistful of select wheat,' *bar* meaning 'polished select wheat' and meaning also 'son.' The meaning of these prophetic words is that in the kingdom of the Messiah, and when the Messiah's new law will flourish, among many new excellent things we will see a fistful or small heap of wheat shaped like a child, a son, that is to say, God's Son will look like clean polished wheat, it will appear to our eyes like a small loaf of bread.

"The consecration of the holy host is, as we have said, a form of birth, and at the same time a recapitulation and repetition of Christ's other births. For in the same way that Christ was born to divinity through God's word, through the word of God's divine mind, here Christ begins to be born in the host by virtue of the words of the priest that consecrates it. And in the same fashion that Christ was reborn and came up out of His tomb in His flesh and human body, yet such a body had suffered a deep change that adapted it to His eternal life and glory, thus, in the consecrated host we find the true reality of His body, but it is there as a spirit, all of it in all of the host, all of it in each part or piece of the host. When Jesus was born from the Virgin He was born blessed and divine in the highest part of His soul, yet with a mortal body subject to pain and death. His riches were hidden inside; outside He looked poor and humble. The same happens now with the host. If we look at the outside it is but a poor piece of bread, yet it hides all the treasures of heaven. According to appearances it can be broken and eaten. The reality is different: Neither evil nor pain can reach it.

"When Jesus was born out of God the other creatures were molded, as we said before, in Him and in His ideas; when He was born as a man He accepted human flesh in order to cleanse and purify man's flesh; when He was born out of the tomb He brought all of us, together, to eternal life. Each one of His births affected our well-being, increased it, and the consecration of the host is no exception, for it allows us to reach not only His true body but also the mystical body of His members. Each birth tends to draw us closer to Him. In this last one He aims at holding us close to His essence, enclosing us in His spirit, bringing His flesh to the inside of our bodies, so that we will communicate with each other and become, by uniting our spirits, one single body with one single soul.

"This is why the warm bread that could always be found in the Temple at Jerusalem before the Ark of the Covenant, an Ark shaped like a loaf of bread, is called by the Scripture 'bread of faces' to point out that such a bread has innumerable faces, that is to say, it contains the other limbs and features of a body, and in the same fashion that God embraces and holds in Himself all the creatures, thus among us this Holy Sacrament embraces and holds all of mankind. We see therefore that this last birth of Christ has as its aim to bring us closer to our happiness, which is to be close to Christ: In a way this last birth is the crowning of the others, the fulfilling of all the previous promises.

"For indeed Jesus becomes our sustenance, becomes part of us, our flesh and His become one, if we are prepared for such a union. The human flesh becomes purer, our soul is enriched, the forces of vice are routed, death is banished from our presence. We are given His being, His life, we eat Him and in turn are eaten by

Him, by acquiring His qualities we become almost like Him. Thus are the previous births brought to fruition. As David put it in a psalm,

> The Lord is gracious and full of compassion.
> He hath given food unto them that fear Him. (111:4–5)

For in such food, which is nourishing only for those who fear the Lord, all the divine greatness is encapsulated. His infinite power is clearly exemplified, as well as His infinite wisdom, His compassion and love for mankind. Jesus was not satisfied with what He had done previously: He had been born a man out of His love for men, He had died in order to give us life, He had been reborn so as to make us follow Him toward eternal glory, He occupied his place to the right of His Father in order to defend and protect us, always present and loving, offering Himself to us as food, so that, once inside us, He can be reborn inside us for the fifth and last time. I will speak about it now if Sabino agrees and grants me permission to do so."

And then Sabino, smiling, "I am pleased that you ask my permission, or rather my opinion. You have been very eloquent, and I am sure you still have a great deal to tell us. But first perhaps you can solve a doubt I have about this fifth birth."

"Could you not accept that Christ is reborn inside us every time that God sanctifies our souls?"

"I remember," Sabino answered, "that St. Paul writes in his Epistle to the Galatians, 'My dear children, with whom I am in labor again, until Christ is formed in you!' (4:19). Which means that as a soul previously steeped in sin converts to goodness and gets rid of malice, Christ begins to take shape in it, begins to be born. And about those who love Him and follow His path Christ says that they are like His Father and His mother. But the same way that we can say that Jesus is born in the soul that abandons wickedness and becomes holy, we can also say that it is the soul which is born in Christ. He being born in us and us being born in Him are one and the same thing, they have the same root, the same cause, and of our being born in Christ Marcelo said yesterday everything that can be said. Therefore, dear Juliano, it seems to me there is nothing else you can add now: hence my doubt."

Then Juliano: "By your doubt you have given me a point of departure for my chain of thought, for it is indeed true that all the births that we have mentioned are part of one single event, and that each time that we are born in God, Christ is born in us: holiness, love of justice, and the renewal of our souls are what makes these births possible. Yet, although they seem to be one and the same birth, our intelligence and our wisdom can analyze them and see some subtle differences between them. For our being born in Christ is in truth, after setting aside the stain of the original sin that the Devil had introduced in our souls, to receive the grace and the justice that God had created in us: It is like an image of Christ inside us that by growing inside our soul shapes it according to Jesus' shape. But when Christ is born in us we not only receive the gift of grace in our souls, but we also receive the spirit of Christ Himself, coming together with our soul, and like a soul of our soul it pours out from the deep center, it permeates our memory, our will, our intelligence, not for a short while as happens when we meditate and have holy visions, but in a permanent way, in the same way that our soul finds a lodging in our body. In Christ's words, 'If anyone love me, he will keep my word, and my Father will love him, and we will come to him and make our abode with him' (John 14:23).

"Therefore when we are born in Christ we receive His grace and are shaped by it, but when Christ is born in us He comes in spirit to inhabit our souls and bodies. He comes, as I say, to live with us, not merely to give us pleasure and grace for a while. This is why, although yesterday Marcelo explained how we can be born in God, we still can deal today with the birth of Christ inside our souls. In order to understand more completely such an event let us describe the difference between Christ's presence beside us while we are praying, and Christ's first presence in our souls.

"In the first case Christ is still in some way outside us, talking to us. But when He is about to be born in us, His spirit unites with the essence of our soul and begins to exert His strength and His virtue in it, in a tight embrace that is so mysterious that we do not even realize what is going on, penetrating to our very core. In the words of Isaiah,

Cry aloud and shout, thou inhabitant of Zion;
For great is the Holy One of Israel in the midst of thee. (12:6)

BOOK III

"There it lies, resting, at peace, in the center of our soul, and from there the rays of His grace pour out and move our soul in a secret way. Little by little the holy influence gains space and strength. While, on the other hand, when we come close to Christ while praying the contact that takes place is between Christ and the powers of our soul, reason, will, and memory, passing on sometimes to our senses and communicating His message through them as far as this is possible. The soul in turn radiates sweetness and light. Yet it all happens in a flash: The moment of joy comes and is gone almost at the same time. For our powers and our senses are always distracted by the normal cares of our daily life: They have many details to attend to, many distractions and emergencies draw them away from contemplation, prayer, and meditation.

"There is yet another difference. In the union of Christ with our soul, in what we call the birth of Christ in us, Christ's spirit acts as a soul with respect to our soul and becomes the source of activity pushing our soul in the right direction, and both become partners for each new activity. This, as we have said, is different from Christ's presence during our prayers. His presence gives us pleasure and light, yet our soul and its powers are then at rest, it is Christ that is active and gives them ineffable rest and peace. Thus the first union tends to give us greater vitality, the second one greater pleasure and delight. The first union increases our being and our becoming, the second one increases the pleasures that make it so sweet to be alive. The first union turns our soul into God's dwelling, the second makes us taste some of God's blessings. The first union must be lasting and solid, since its lack would diminish our life, the second one is brief because it is more pleasant than necessary, for our life has been given to us so that we may work, act, accomplish something; and when we are enjoying ourselves deeply we no longer act or work, joy is our only aim.

"As for my second argument, it is as follows: Christ is born in us every time that our soul turns its attention inward, in self-examination, finds mistakes and ugliness, and hates what it has found. It thinks then about God's wrath, is anxious to placate it, and turns—with faith, with love, with grief—toward God's mercy, and toward Christ as our Savior. Christ is then born in us. He penetrates then in our soul, His spirit enters it, and while doing so it pours its grace into it, a grace which is like a splendor and like a lightning that take their place in our soul and beautify it. Thus Christ begins to live and to act in us, by inspiring in us virtuous thoughts and acts. Action, as we said, is the essence of life, of being alive. Thus Christ, who lived in the bosom of the Father from before time existed, and who was born perfect out of God, begins to live in us as a babe. Not because He is a babe or because His spirit is in any way diminished: He comes to us whole, complete, but He has to adjust to our weaknesses, and although He has penetrated our soul He cannot act upon it all of a sudden: He has to conquer it little by little. Thus we say that He is born like a babe. But as our soul, guided by Him, surrenders itself to Him, He grows daily in strength and efficacy, until the moment when He reaches, as St. Paul puts it, a point in which we attain 'to perfect manhood, to the mature measure of the fullness of Christ' (Eph. 4:13). Which means, until Christ becomes, in what He achieves in us, perfect, as He is in Himself.

"As perfect, but perhaps not in the same manner. I mean by this that the life and influence that Christ acquires when He reaches perfect manhood in our souls is not equal in greatness to the life and influence that He has in His own being, His own life, yet it shows the same mettle, the same lineage. Thus, His presence in us is slow in developing, resembling first that of a child, then as an adolescent, finally as a perfect adult. The same happens to our soul: As we are born, our soul is born, whole, in our body, yet it does not exert from the very first its full power; it takes time for it to develop. Heat dries up and develops the organs through which the soul acts in us, and the soul becomes more powerful in us. The same with Christ: All His spirit is inside us when He is born in us, but much of its power is unused at first. As we are moved by His spirit and as we manage to get rid of our moral impurities, His influence increases daily. From growth, after birth, He develops into perfection. There are, therefore, three steps in this relationship: childhood and adolescence, at first; then comes a second level of understanding and action, and finally we reach a perfect presence of Christ in us. We can call the first step, 'the period of the law,' for reasons that I shall explain later. The second stage can be called 'the period of grace' and the last one 'the period of glory.'

"Let us describe further each one of these three steps, without forgetting, of course that our soul, as you know, is made up of two parts. The first part is divine, and because of its origin and its nature it aspires to heaven and to everything connected with what is saintly and heavenly, unless prevented from doing so by powerful forces, and by the disappearance of reason and justice. It desires to be near what is by nature immortal and does not change easily, it desires contemplation and love of eternity. Yet there is another part to our soul: It looks toward the earth, it is always in touch with our body, closer to the body's passions and sudden changes, troubled and upset by waves of intense feelings, by fear, anguish, covetousness, tears, pride. In a word, being close to the flesh it cannot act independently from it. These two parts are like twin sisters born from the same womb, yet they are always quarreling and pulling in opposite directions. Although by law the second part should be subject to the first, it happens sometimes that it rebels and, full of fury, takes over the reins of rule, overpowering her better half. This is a sad and sickly situation, since the normal relationship is one of obedience and joy at the rule of her better half. These two parts are like heaven and earth, or like Jacob and Esau, conceived in the same womb and yet quarreling one against the other, as we shall discuss in detail later on.

"It happens that when the soul abhors its wickedness and Christ begins to be born in it, Christ's spirit penetrates to the very core of it, as we said before, and Christ's virtue affects first of all the better part of the soul, the highest part of it. Christ lives and develops there, lighting up this part from the inside, straightening up our instincts, renewing and fixing our feelings and ideas, giving our soul courage so that it can rule us without fear. Yet at this moment Christ's spirit does not destroy the power and energy of the lower part of the soul: The spirit has not penetrated it yet. But even if the spirit does not inhabit it as a lord and master, it can give it a tutor and teacher capable of correcting its childish behavior: This role will be played by the soul's better half, which, from up above, gives it rules for its behavior, urges it to know itself better, corrects and reprimands it when necessary, whence comes sometimes agony, contradiction, tension.

"And Christ, who lives in us, deals with the lesser part of the soul just like Moses dealt with his people: He gives it the law, the Commandments, He admonishes and criticizes it, yet at first cannot get rid of its weakness and evil thoughts. This is why this period or stage is called 'the period of the law.' In it, just as Moses in the past was able to listen to the voice of God, and on top of Mount Sinai conversed with Him, received His grace, saw His light, finally coming down to his people, who were interested in material things, were restless and lustful, and from the slopes of the mountain could see nothing but the shaking earth and the clouds above it; just as Moses, then, gave them God's law and admonished them to control their mad desires, such is the role of the loftier part of our soul. As soon as Christ is born in its bosom it feels itself made holy by such a presence: It feels as if on top of a tall mountain and talking to God. Then it addresses the people on the slope of the mountain, that is to say, the lower half of the soul which because of the many desires and passions that move it all the time can be compared to a noisy crowd. The noble half gives the crowd the divine laws, tells it what should be done, takes charge and rules, sometimes with a soft hand, sometimes harshly and through threats.

"And just as Moses' people rebelled against him time and time again, always reluctant to place their stiff necks under the yoke of the law, all of which was the source of riots followed by punishment, thus the lower half of the soul refuses many times to pay attention to the admonishments of her elder sister, in whom Christ already dwells: The sisters sometimes fight each other bitterly. Moses in order to bring his people to the promised land persuaded them first to flee from Egypt and brought them to the solitude of the desert, guiding them through a winding trail across the waste. He separated them from other men and placed them under the protection and the inspiration of God—in the cloud, in the pillar of fire, in the manna that rained from above, and in the water springing up from a stone, they were uplifted and thought about God's help—until under Joshua, their leader, they crossed the river Jordan, swept away their enemies from the land, and colonized the area until Christ came and was born as a man. In the same manner Christ's spirit, born in the highest part of our soul, wants to be obeyed by the other half, the half that is weak and inclined toward sensuality. From the dwelling place the spirit has chosen, from the seat of reason, as a new Moses, it invites it to leave the pleasures of Egypt. It washes the weak soul in the water of tribulations. It weans it from its rough pleasures and teaches it to love the poverty and nakedness of the desert. It sends it manna. It kills most of its perverse passions. After a holy period of rest, the spirit grows inside the soul, teaches it wisdom and strength, penetrates each nook and cranny and becomes its lord and master; it does not take away its natural traits, such as a well-balanced sensitivity and the experience of suffering and dying. But the worst bad habits at least have been finally eradicated.

"This is, then, the second step, in which Jesus' spirit penetrates and changes both parts of the soul. The first part, the celestial soul, is made holy, is made to resemble God. The second part, in close contact with the flesh, is purified and cleansed from its carnal and low desires. These desires used to besiege and destroy the spiritual soul, and are now in turn besieged and destroyed by Christ's presence. The same thing happened when Christ walked on earth with His disciples. Through word and deed He influenced them, and little by little their sensuous passions became controlled. After His resurrection they were obedient, humble, and gathered in Jerusalem. He sent to them, in abundance, His spirit, and thus made them perfect and saintly. The same thing happens with His presence among us. He influences first our reason, He strengthens it so that it cannot be overcome by our senses. Then, step by step, as Joel puts it,

And it shall come to pass afterward,
That I shall pour out My spirit upon all flesh (2:28)

and the spirit is victorious. And what takes place then is what we ask in our prayer: 'Thy will be done, on earth as it is in heaven.' For God is then all-powerful in the heaven of the soul, and on the earth of the same soul He is obeyed practically in the same way. Christ bathes our hearts with His light and anoints our soul from one end to the other and gives it grace. He may not appear visually before us but makes us aware of our everlasting life: His spirit sustains and protects us much as it will do later forever and ever. This is the sustenance and the bread that we ask daily from God, after Christ's advice, 'give us our daily bread,' that is, our bread, ours because it was promised to us, ours because without it we cannot live, ours because only it can satisfy our yearnings. O Lord, hasten to us with your bread and with the everlasting life you have promised us, and may your son live among us and bring us total, complete life, because He is the bread that nourishes our life.

THE NAMES OF CHRIST

"In this fashion, when Christ's presence in us reaches such a peak we can truly say that He has become the Messiah promised by God. We are now in a stage or period of grace, not of law, nor of servitude or fear. Grace bathes our souls, every command is obeyed with pleasure, Christ has entered the part of our soul that used to be rebellious and needed intimidation and control, and rebelliousness is almost at an end. It is the kingdom of the gospel, because Christ's rule over both halves of the soul, and the blessing of the soul together with our victory over old age are all effects of the good news brought by the gospel and the kingdom of heaven which the gospel announces. This is the task that the Son of God, the Messiah that the Scripture promised, had reserved for Himself. As we read in Saint Luke,

> Be mindful of his holy covenant,
> Of the oath that he swore to Abraham our father,
>   that he would grant us,
> That, delivered from the hand of our enemies,
>   we should serve him without fear;
> In holiness and justice before him all our days. (1:72–75)

And it is the kingdom of joy, for in the whole of our soul the spirit rules and brings to us its fruit, which, as St. Paul writes, is 'charity, joy, peace, patience, kindness, goodness.' Isaiah says about such a stage:

> I will greatly rejoice in the Lord,
> My soul shall be joyful in my God;
> For He hath clothed me with the garments of salvation,
> He hath covered me with the robe of victory,
> As a bridegroom putteth on a priestly diadem,
> And as a bride adorneth herself with her jewels. (61:10)

"Freedom and power are what St. Paul wished for when he wrote to the Colossians: 'And may the peace of Christ reign in your hearts: unto that peace, indeed, you were called in one body' (3:15). In the first level we enjoyed God's peace and grace, yet we were close to our enemies. Now we feel a greater freedom. Christ, through His life, His thoughts, His actions, gives life to our high goals, our lofty ideals, destroys our evil thoughts and passions. St.

BOOK III

Paul explains, 'But if Christ is in you, the body, it is true, is dead by reason of sin, but the spirit is life by reason of justification' (Rom. 8:10). And finally we are dealing with a period of love and peace, for in it the two parts or sides of the soul become united once again, our senses accept with joy to be the servants of reason, Jacob and Esau become friends, and their shining example is a beacon to us all.

"As you well know, dear Sabino, Rebecca, Isaac's wife, was the mother of twins, and they fought and quarreled in their mother's womb even before they were born. She became anguished and managed to discuss her predicament with God. He let her know that she had given birth in her womb to two different lineages and that they would quarrel one against the other, moreover, that the child who would be born last would overcome the firstborn. When the time arrived to give birth to these twins, the firstborn was a child with abundant red hair, and afterward, grasping his foot, another baby, different in looks, was also born. The last-born child was named Jacob. The firstborn was named Esau. They were dissimilar from the very beginning. Esau liked living out, in the fields, in the woods. He liked hunting. Jacob liked living indoors. Jacob, one day, bought from his brother the rights related to being firstborn: It had to do with food. Afterward, through a trick, he secured his father's blessing: His father thought he was blessing his firstborn son. This made the two brothers into bitter enemies. Jacob turned away from a fight, and, following his mother's advice, went away, traveled to the East, was a servant in the household of his father-in-law, and, after marrying, had many sons and untold wealth. Returning home, he struggled with the angel, was blessed by the angel, and, weak in one leg, he changed both his name and his way of walking. He met his brother Esau and both were reconciled.

"All of which gives us a parallel image with respect to our spiritual life. Both sides of our soul are born out of the same womb. Both quarrel while inside the womb, for they are striving in opposite directions, and after they are born from them originate two lineages that keep fighting each other. One of them stands for the senses, passion, violence; the other one, for reason and justice. The senses are born first and manage to exert their influence at the beginning. Reason is born afterward. The senses are clothed in blood, delight in stealing, robbing, killing, violent

305

passions, but reason likes to dwell at home, delights in contemplation and truth. Blessings from the father and the rights that relate
to the firstborn are hers by law. Yet the senses are aroused and try
to attack and destroy their brother. The brother, guided by reason, flees, and while escaping, God appears to him and tells him
he can trust His help, after which his thigh dies symbolically,
since blessing depends upon the death of the wrong impulses. He
will afterward walk in a lame way, and this is a symbol for Israel,
for divine life shines in the life of the race, yet lame, because in
worldly ways there is still the gap of need. Reason and passion
come together, make a pact, rejoice, and rest. Jacob and Esau live
like brothers and the holy spirit of Jesus binds their life into a life
of love. As it is written,

> Behold, how good and how pleasant it is
> For brethren to dwell together in unity!
> It is like the precious oil upon the head,
> Coming down upon the beard;
> Even Aaron's beard,
> That cometh down upon the collar of his garments;
> Like the dew of Hermon,
> That cometh down upon the mountains of Zion;
> For there the Lord commanded the blessing,
> Even life for ever. (Ps. 133:1–3)

For indeed our life becomes sweet and serene when our two
sisters, the two twin parts of our soul, are reconciled and live in
peace.

"Such a sweet and profitable peace is to be compared to
perfumed ointments, to cool dew coming down from the dawn
skies upon the hills of Hermon and Zion, a symbol for the grace of
the Son of God coming down to give us truth and light. The
image that we see is that of a head, also a harsh beard, and they are
symbols for Zion, a mirror of God, and Hermon, the desert that in
its desolation puts an end to our wild desires. Christ comes to us,
lives in us, and finally the words of St. Paul come true: 'It is now
no longer I that live, but Christ lives in me' (Gal. 2:20). He lives
and does not live: He does not live for and by himself, but rather
he lives because Christ lives in him, Christ, embracing him, inside

him, gives him strength and inspiration, has become the life of his life. Isaiah describes such a happy feeling:

> They joy before Thee according to the joy in harvest,
> As men rejoice when they divide the spoil. (9:3)

Harvest always brings us joy because it offers us the fruit of our labors, we realize our hope was not unfounded, God grants us a deserved reward. In the same manner those who reach a high level in their spiritual life gather the fruit of their faith and ascetic penances: They feel rewarded by God's bounty.

"They divide the spoil, the sacred text tells us, because they— the winners—are rejoiced by three thoughts: They are out of danger, they are honored, they are surrounded by riches. All of which applies to those who harvest wisdom and holiness. The negative forces in their senses have been defeated and have almost vanished. Christ's spirit is pouring inside them, penetrating everywhere. They are out of danger: They are both happy and rich. They rejoice before Him because God's presence in their souls, Christ's presence and growth, has brought them rich rewards. Isaiah enumerates some of them:

> For the yoke of his burden,
> And the staff of his shoulder,
> The rod of his oppressor,
> Thou hast broken as in the day of Midian. (9:4)

Indeed the harsh law of sin was a yoke and weighed heavily upon our shoulders, just as the old executioners used to whip their victims upon their shoulders. Christ has managed to break the instruments of torture and paralyze the arm of the torturer. And He has achieved it as in the day of Midian: You may remember how Gideon achieved his victory over the Midianites, without weapons, by blowing horns and breaking in pieces the pitchers, holding a torch in his hand. In a similar fashion, Christ's birth in us is not something that is due to our merit, but rather the result of Christ's overflowing grace. This grace, as a shining light, as a blinding torch, penetrates our soul, breaks the bond of our senses and passions. The light shines, Christ's voice sounds, and the enemies flee and die. An enemy in his dreams saw a bread made out of oat flour, and this loaf of bread would bring down every tent of the enemy encampment. The same is true about Christ, likened to a low bread, and yet when coming in contact with our senses capable of bringing down the tents of wickedness. Isaiah describes this situation in these terms:

> For every boot stamped with fierceness,
> And every cloak rolled in blood,
> Shall even be for burning, for fuel of fire. (9:5)

Fierceness is a good word, precise and true: for there is much in us that is full of fire and passion. Blood is also part of this description, for our body, our passions, are stained with blood. Again the prophet writes:

> For, O people that dwellest in Zion at Jerusalem,
> Thou shalt weep no more;
> He will surely be gracious unto thee at the voice of thy cry,
> When He shall hear, He shall answer thee.
> And though the Lord give you sparing bread and scant water,
> Yet shall not Thy teacher hide Himself any more,
> But thine ears shall hear thy Teacher;
> And thine ears shall hear a word behind thee, saying:
> 'This is the way, walk ye in it,
> When ye turn to the right hand, and when ye turn to the left.'
> (Isa. 30:19–21)

Which depicts today's situation: Those who reached Zion are now masters of Jerusalem.

"Christ's life is also a success: From the fortress of the soul it spreads all around and brings us peace. The same is true about the dwellers of Zion: They dwell in peace, tears have definitely stopped. Christ now lives in them, hears them, talks with them. Christ lives in them, gives them bread and water, body and spirit. It is not a pure blessing: Some bitterness is mixed with the honey. As St. Paul writes, 'For you have died and your life is hidden with Christ in God. When Christ, your life, shall appear, then you too will appear with him in glory.'

BOOK III

"Indeed, at that time Christ's growth inside our bodies will be complete, and we shall resuscitate from dust and become immortal and glorious, and reach the third and ultimate stage: Christ's presence in us will be total and will help us to overcome every weakness.

"A blinding light will then Christ be, one for all, and we shall all be true sons of God because of Christ's presence among us. The Son of God, the one and only Son of God, will make us all into true sons of God.

"Christ, we have seen, is born in many different ways. He is also called Son in the Scriptures in many different ways. Isaiah calls Him Ieled. David, in the second Psalm, calls Him Bar, in Psalm 71 he calls Him Nin. By David and Isaiah He is called Ben; Jacob in the blessing of his son Judah calls Him Sil. Born five times, He receives five names that mean Son, with slightly different meanings. For Ieled means 'generated'; Bar, 'raised, chosen'; Nin, 'the one who is growing'; Ben, 'the building'; Sil, 'the peaceful one' or 'the messenger.' All these qualities can be applied to a son, for a son is generated, raised, born, chosen by the mixture of his parents' bloods, he rises in their place when they die, upholding their name, he is like a building: In Spanish we call a family, especially thinking about sons and descendents, 'household' or 'house.' He is also a symbol of peace and harmony between his father and his mother.

"These names fit Christ especially: He was generated in an eternal birth, out of time, He was born to our world as a child and a man, He was chosen out of sin, cleansed from sin, He rose from the dead, He is like a building that contains the holy host, sending His grace to all of us through it, and through His condition of Son of God helps us all to get closer to God. For His Father knows that He is His only son, and at the same time wants to accept as His children all the human beings that have identified with Christ, and share His body, His soul and His spirit. The Father loves Christ in every creature that reflects Christ's virtues."

Juliano then stopped for a while, and finally said, "I did what you requested, dear Sabino, and I said all I knew about the subject. Perhaps I have bored you. Marcelo may talk now, and I am sure he will be more entertaining."

"I am sure," Marcelo said, "you did not bore Sabino. As for

me, I am certainly not bored but I am worried because I do not know how I can add anything to all the good things you have said."

Sabino was about to say something but was interrupted by something that took place in the woods near them.

As Juliano had proceeded with his speech, a small bird on top of a tree in the shore opposite our group seemed to listen with great attention and at times seemed to answer or comment with its song. The song was so sweet that more than once our friends looked and listened in that direction. As soon as Juliano stopped talking and Marcelo answered as we have mentioned above, before Sabino could speak, they heard a noise coming from the woods and when they looked they found the source of the noise: two big crows flying over the little bird, tracing circles around it, trying to hurt it with their beaks and sharp nails. At first the little bird tried to protect itself by sinking down among the thick branches of the tree. The attack continued, fiercer and more vicious every moment, until the little bird, at bay, desperate, plunged into the river, screaming, as if asking for help or mercy. The crows then flew to the river and, flying over the water surface, attacked it again and again until the little bird disappeared into the deep water and left no trace. Sabino screamed, "The poor little bird drowned!" The three friends became sad and silent. The crows departed full of the joy of victory. A short time elapsed. Juliano was trying to console Sabino, who cursed the crows and lamented the death of "his little bird," as he called it. Suddenly, near Marcelo, almost at his feet, the little bird's head emerged from the river and soon the bird was on the bank, wet and tired. Flying to a low branch, it spread its wings and shook off the drops of water from its feathers, then flapping its wings it rose on the air singing with greater sweetness than before. Upon hearing the singing many other birds like the small one came out of the grove, flew around the first one, and seemed to congratulate it on its success in surviving its enemies. Then all together and as in a triumphant march they made three or four wide circles in the air and flew upward and onward until they disappeared from sight.

Sabino was overjoyed. Marcelo's expression was intense, as if he was thinking deep thoughts. Raising his eyes to the heavens, with a sigh, he murmured, "Let us trust Jesus, our Savior."

After which he turned to Sabino and said, "I agree: it is now my turn to speak."

LAMB

"This name, 'lamb,' is so proper and typical of Christ that I hardly need to point it out. Who has not heard a thousand times, during mass, the words of St. John? 'Behold the lamb of God, who takes away the sin of the world!' And yet this is a name that hides a mystery which we must try to solve. 'Lamb' applied to Christ depicts three qualities in our Savior: meekness and sweetness in His character, purity and innocence in His behavior, and finally readiness for sacrifice, acceptance of sacrifice. St. Peter describes Christ thus: 'Who did no sin, neither was deceit found in his mouth. Who, when he was reviled, did not revile, when he suffered, did not threaten, but yielded himself to him who judged him unjustly; who himself bore our sins in his body upon the tree, that we, having died in sin, might live to justice' (1:22–24). A good summing-up of Christ's main traits.

"Let us now say something about the three qualities I have mentioned a moment ago. Meekness, sweetness, was typical of His behavior on earth and of the way He accepted to suffer. For He suffered much for us and is still doing so daily because of our sins. Isaiah was anticipating the sweet disposition of our Savior when he wrote,

> He shall not cry, nor lift up,
> Nor cause his voice to be heard on the street. (42:2)

And Christ said about Himself, 'Learn from me, for I am meek and humble of heart' (Matt. 11:29). Such was His behavior: With humble folks He was humble, His love was more intense toward those who were despised and held in low esteem, and He was sweetest toward the repentant sinners. The sweetness of our lamb saved the adulterous woman condemned by the law. When the sly Pharisees consulted Him about her and her penalty, He was unable to utter the word 'death' and managed to absolve her for lack of an accuser: Nor would He condemn her, but told her to go her way, and from then on sin no more. Meek and sweet was He toward the sinning yet penitent woman in the house of a Pharisee, as told by St. Luke: He let her anoint his head with oil and He forgave her sins, for she had loved much (7:36–50). Jesus was meek in trying to see and speak to the children that His disciples wanted to keep away from him, and in listening to the lengthy speech of the woman from Samaria: He never turned people away, listening to all with utmost patience.

"No wonder: He was then among us, but even afterward when reigning in the heavens, He accepted to come down once more and live among us in the shape of the Sacrament. Once more He has to accept with patience our boorish impertinence. There is no humble hamlet where we cannot find him in the host, dwelling in a modest church. And although we read in the gospels that Christ reprimanded verbally St. Peter once, and the Pharisees many times, and attacked physically the merchants at the temple, yet He never showed fierceness nor anger, but rather in each one of these occasions remained calm, serene, sweet. As God, He moves all yet is unmoved. As a man He can reproach without passion and criticize without anger. Even in his criticism He was always a model of loving concern. Let us listen to the words of his loving wife, according to the great love poem, the Song of Songs:

> His mouth is most sweet;
> Yes, he is altogether lovely.
> This is my beloved, and this is my friend,
> O daughters of Jerusalem. (Song of Songs 5:16)"

And then Marcelo said, "Such a voice, can you vouch for it, Sabino? Is it a sweet and lovely voice, do you think? Listen to it: 'His mouth is most sweet, Yes, he is altogether lovely' (Song of Songs 5:16).

And then Sabino: "Now let us think: when Christ says, 'Depart from me, accused ones, into the everlasting fire which was prepared for the devil and his angels' (Matt. 25:41), can you state that this sentence could be uttered without anger and heard without fear? Moreover, if Christ is as meek as you have said, how can He be described as a lion, as this is done in the Holy Scriptures?" (Apoc. 5:5).

"You are right," Marcelo answered, "and yet I think that

about your first objection the answer is clear: The wicked ones will be frightened to death by such a statement. Looking at the judge, at his acid and stern face, will be a harsh torture for them. Yet all of this will not change in the least Christ's soul. He will go on being meek, although He will torture with strong bellowings the ears of His enemies, and moreover, being sweet in His mind and His body, He will paralyze His friends and enemies by a powerful hypnotic stare. What irritates me most about sin is that it seems to place Christ's sweet meekness on the verge of bitter condemnation and violence. He, who became a man for the sake of His love for mankind, who suffered so much in order to save us, who delights in dealing with us, who, alive and dead, mortal and full of eternal glory, thinks mainly about our salvation, our health, our future, sometimes is compelled to explode in anger: Our strong affinity toward evil may change the lamb's attitude and voice. Usually God knows how to deal with wicked men: He hides His face from them and leaves them to their own devices; they soon destroy themselves. As the Prophet writes.

For Thou hast hid Thy face from us,
And hast consumed us by means of our iniquities. (Isa. 64:7)

Therefore sometimes the urgency to mete out a just punishment makes him into an angry avenger, bitter words in his mouth, sword in hand.

"Now with respect to what you, Sabino, said about the lion: Christ is both a lion and a lamb: There is no contradiction in this duality. For Christ is indeed a lion when the time comes to defend and protect our people, yes, and also our goods, our possessions, against our devilish enemies. First of all, it was Christ who delivered us from the demons and overthrew their empire. He laid waste their temples and turned against them the few peasants who still worshiped them. He threw them down into the deep dungeons of the earth's entrails and liberated a thousand prisoners. Then and now he is capable of defeating them. St. John knew all this when he called him lion when he said, 'Do not weep; behold, the lion of the tribe of Juda, the root of David, has overcome to open the scroll and its seven seals.' In the second place, we know no one dares take its prey from a lion's clutches. In the same way no one can take from Christ's embrace those beings that are beloved by Him. He states, 'My sheep hear my voice, and I know them and they follow me. And I give them everlasting life; and they shall never perish, neither shall anyone snatch them out of my hand' (Jn. 10:28).

"We read in Isaiah, along similar lines:

> For thus sayeth the Lord unto me,
> Like as the lion, or the young lion
>   Growling over his prey,
> Though a multitude of shepherds be
> Called against him
> Will not be dismayed at their voice
> Nor abase himself for the noise of them;
> So will the Lord of Hosts come down
> To fight upon Mount Zion, and
> Upon the hill thereof. (31:4)

In a way Christ is a lion because He was first, toward us, a loving and meek lamb; because of His infinite love for us He has to stand up fiercely against those who would harm us. He is meek toward us, cruel and fierce toward our enemies. Some men can accept meekly the rude behavior of other men yet do not accept their foul language. Others may accept bad words, curses, insults, and yet they cannot accept anyone laying their hand on them. Christ, our lamb, accepted our wordy insults, and also our cruel blows to His body, as a lamb before her shearers.

"Christ's sufferings out of His love for us were endless. Insults, false accusations, blows and slaps, whippings, a crown of thorns, nails, a cross. Yet He endured it all. St. Augustine remarks upon Christ's meekness and nonresistance to evil: His weapon is kindness and wisdom, and Christ is the best example of such behavior, since we can find no one else so abused yet so serene and victorious. He sought and helped those who abused and tortured Him, washed His enemies from their sins. A lamb for all of us, a lamb that fed both friends and enemies, for there was no part of His body that could not be reached by our knives and teeth: His breast, His feet, His hands, His holy head.

"A lamb once and forever, always trying to give us something even while we attacked and victimized Him. God's shining model had been, at first, Adam. Adam was ordered by God to work and till the soil, to bring forth fruits from the earth. And so Christ through His sweet meekness accepts us and our sins, works and tills our souls, disregarding our ingratitude. This is true now and then: In the past when He lived here among us, now when He dwells in the heavens as a king of the whole world. He sees us despise His blood and go against His example, and yet He keeps calling us, opening His arms to us through His deep sweet love for all of us.

"It is, in truth, an excess of love on His part that has helped bring in Him such a sweet meekness. For charity, as St. Paul explains (in Cor. 1:13; 4) is always allied to patience. Loving and suffering are closely related. Christ's love was and is so great that it explains by itself the extent of his meekness. Because he loves us he is patient and sweet with us. And he loves us also because he sees that His Father loves us. His Father loves us in such a deep and marvelous manner that He gave for the sake of our salvation the life of His only Son. As St. John expresses it, 'For God so loved the world that he gave his only-begotten Son, that those who believe in him may not perish' (3:16). And in this text 'to give' means 'to surrender unto death.' And Paul: 'He who has not spared even his own Son but has delivered him for us all, how can he fail to grant us also all things with him?' (Rom. 8:32).

"Because God's love, Christ's love, is boundless, His meekness is also boundless. Both feelings are, so to speak, twins. To think otherwise would be confusing: How could Christ be Lord of the world if it were otherwise? If such power had been given to an overbearing, arrogant, cruel being, the situation would soon become intolerable and we would all be lost. The very nature of human society requires that the greater the power entrusted to an individual, and the number of people ruled by him, the more this person should be meek and patient. This is why God, the Emperor of the whole universe, is the sweetest and meekest of all beings. This was explained by God to Moses: 'The Lord, the Lord, God, merciful and gracious, long-suffering, and abundant in goodness and truth; keeping mercy unto the thousandth generation' (Ex. 34:6–7). It also has been said that Moses, God's lieutenant on earth, was also very meek and patient (Num. 12:3). All of which brings us to the realization that Christ's lamblike meekness is without end. His power is also without end, requiring such meekness, and we can also see that He is more like God the Father than any other creature, and thus He imitates and follows God in this respect, as in every other trait.

"A lamb because of His meekness, He is also a lamb because of His innocence and purity. St. Peter puts it this way, 'You know that you were redeemed from the vain manner of life handed down from your fathers, not with perishable things, with silver or gold, but with the precious blood of Christ, as of a lamb without blemish and without spot' (I Pet. 1:18–19). St. Peter wants us to appreciate our redemption through the value and purity of Christ's sacrifice: We had our sins washed away by the purest of all bloods: We must not waste such sacrifice. St. James states that 'if anyone does not offend in word, he is a perfect man' (3:2). And St. Peter says about Christ that he was one 'who did no sin, neither was deceit found in his mouth' (I 2:22). It is true that what God loves and appreciates above all in His creatures is holiness and purity, for being pure means having accepted the law given to us by God, and we must above all adjust our behavior to our being, which is ruled by the law. God loves us especially when we follow His path. He is the being who is truly, and wants us to be true, to be like him, because what is false and deceitful does not have a true being. Purity means truth in being and acceptance of the law, and truth is what pleases most He who is pure being.

"If God loves above all the holy humanity of Christ, the obvious conclusion is that Christ's being is the holiest and purest of all creatures. Christ takes precedence. He is the son of God's love, the source of God's pleasure, the beloved for whose love both visible and invisible worlds were created. Both God's love and Christ's purity are beyond any comparison, as they are also beyond our understanding. The link that unites the Son and the Father cannot be fully comprehended by our minds. Whatever is close to the sun shines with clear light: and Christ, from the beginning plunged and submerged in such a source of pure light, of cleanness and purity, does shine with splendorous purity and blinding light. God sheds His rays everywhere. Yet He is closely linked to Christ as a man. Other creatures come closer to Him, or try to come closer, yet it is Christ that God holds in His bosom and embraces. The rays of God's light reverberate in other creatures, the same rays become a sun when coming close to Christ.

BOOK III

We read in Psalms (and the main subject is the heavens, the heavens that declare the glory of God) that

In them (the heavens) hath He set a tent for the sun,
Which is as a bridegroom coming out of his chamber,
And rejoiceth as a strong man to run his course. (19:4–6)

This is because the light of God found its dwelling place in Christ's human body, after which the body became much like the sun itself. Other things may sparkle with beauty, but Christ's body is a treasure of splendor. Other things receive from outside sources their purity and their innocence, but Christ's body is like a fountain and an abyss both together inside that body. Finally other things have to beg in order to receive the gift of virtue, while Christ's body is so rich in virtue, holiness, and wisdom that it can pour them all around and give them to others. Since everything that is saintly, pure, and innocent is born out of Christ's sanctity and purity, and whenever we find a particle of such virtues it is because Christ had put it there in the first place, we realize not only that Christ is more saintly, more pure, more innocent than all the other beings put together, but that He is the origin and the cause of such virtues and by that token the fountain and the abyss of any purity and innocence.

"Let us go one step forward. Christ is the universal principle of saintliness and of virtue, their source, and has enough saintliness so that He may sanctify every being created by God and an infinity of beings that might arise if God decided to continue His creation. As a sacrificial victim His sacrifice is enough to absolve and erase all the sins of the world and an infinity of sins in an infinity of worlds that God may create continually. We cannot talk about a degree of saintliness, a magnitude, a scale, since we are dealing with something infinite and boundless. As for sins, we see in Him a negative infinity with respect to them: There is no trace of sin in Him. There is not such an abyss between being and nonbeing, or between light and darkness, as the infinite distance and deep chasm that exists between Christ and any spark or glimpse of sin. For it is indispensable, and very much a law of nature, that whoever creates holiness should be holy, and whoever takes away our sins should be sinless and blameless. Nature has built our eyes, made to receive and see all colors and hues, devoid

317

of color and hue. If our organs of taste had been given a specific taste from the very beginning they would be incapable of detecting such a taste. In the same way Christ could not be a universal source of virtue and justice if He had not been free from any trace of guilt and if He did not concentrate in Himself all the treasures of virtue and justice.

"He came to erase evil from our souls, destroy wicked inclinations and desires: nothing crooked, dark, sleazy, could find a place in his soul. He endeavored to introduce order and harmony in our wandering imagination and our troubled intelligence: His mind perforce had to be like a serene sky full of harmony and light. Our will was sick and perverted: His had to be guided by justice and good health. Our senses were wild, full of fire, He was the only one capable of taming them: His senses had therefore to be a perfect example of moderation and temperance. Our bad inclinations were to be checked and finally uprooted by Him, which meant that He could not harbor a feeling or an inclination that was not inspired by lofty principles of justice. He came to cleanse us from original sin and to grant us forgiveness for our other mistakes: There could not be in His birth, in the activities of His life, in His soul, in His senses, in His body, in His whole being, any guilt nor traces of guilt. Since in the long run, when the dead would be raised, the virtue of His grace was bound to protect us completely from guilt and sin, it was necessary that Christ should be lacking in any kind of guilt, and that He should be impeccable from His very beginning. Since He had in him a remedy for all sins, for all men, for all times, and not only for just and fair-minded men but for all the rest, who are not just and are even incapable of being just when they want to be, and not only for those born in our earth but also for those who could be born in numberless other planets, it was basic that every kind of evil—original sin, imagined sin, real sin, inducements to sin, sins past, present, and future, the sins of countless unknown worlds, every shade and possibility of sin—should be as far from Christ as are the darkest hours of a gloomy night from the sun's brightest rays, as is truth from lies, as disease differs from a healing medicine.

"Jesus had to be a treasure of innocence and cleanliness because He was bound to become the one and only spring of inexhaustible innocence and purity. Look at the sun: No matter how hard you try to penetrate its surface you will see only a pure light, a splendor of fire and light. In the same way in Christ, our sun of justice, from whom comes every aspect of honesty and truth, you will not find, when you try to analyze Him and penetrate His surface, anything but a pure simplicity and a simple straightness, an eternally bubbling perfect kindness, a kindness that is part of soul, body, flesh, blood, bones, even to the marrow.

"Christ is body and soul, united by the grace of God and close to the Holy Spirit. Christ's body was well built from the very beginning. Other bodies are swayed by their humors, at times joyful, other times sad, elated or depressed. His body was well-balanced, handsome, beyond praise. It was a proof and a praise of the high qualities of the matter it was built from and also of the craftsman that built it. The matter was the pure and most holy blood of Mary, most exquisite and special. No cleaner blood could be found, no blood more in touch with the highest qualities and principles. A soul such as Mary's could turn each drop of Mary's blood into a holy and deep spring of purity. Her blood was unlike our blood, a blood as we have never seen before. The law of Moses—including its prohibition about eating certain foods, sacrifices, cleansing ceremonies, fastings, and so on—was a way of thinning our blood and our bodies, almost like distilling wine into brandy, until at a certain crucial moment a maiden could be endowed with a virginal blood which would be in extreme fashion clean and pure and could be the source and origin of Christ's pure body. The old texts in the Old Testament were very much like an alembic, a system to distill and bring out of an ancient, rich, and pure liquor, an even purer and refined liquor, until we reached the ultimate and most exquisite refined being, perfection itself.

"It is thus that the blood of Mary was the exquisite distillation of blood which became Christ's body. And thus, according to what we know about matter and physics, Christ was propelled from the start to do good and to be kindness itself. It was not only the virgin blood that created Christ in the sacred womb of Mary: After He was born, this blood sustained Him, turned into milk out of the holy breasts of Mary. This is why Mary, breast-feeding sweet Jesus, looking at her baby, being watched by the sweet eyes of Jesus, burning in chaste love for her baby, provided her milk in a moment, or an hour, of mystical, pure, kind love. Both beings, Mary and Jesus, communicated through their eyes, and both souls exchanged knowledge. A saintly milk communicated saintly wisdom to her son. Light is born out of the Father, who is in essence Light: So in the same way with respect to His body Jesus is born out of pure light.

"We have spoken about material elements. What can we say about the creative forces at work? For, as other human bodies are organized along lines of force determined by the basic factor of the father's blood, which the mother nurtures in her womb, when we think about the holy edifice of Christ's body, we must remember that the Holy Spirit was the one that replaced the sexual activity of the father, the male element, and it was the Holy Spirit that gave shape, without any one else's intervention, to such a holy body as the body of Jesus. And if we accept the fact that every work accomplished by God is intrinsically perfect, this one, this holy birth that He projected for so long, what is it? How can we define it? And if the wine that was miraculously created in Cana during a marriage feast was an excellent wine, for God made it out of water through His power, since matter obeys God in everything, what purity, what cleanliness, what holiness could we not find in the body that created Christ, infinitely holy, in such a holy way? Christ was born so exempt from vice or bad inclination that He was as close to spiritual perfection as was possible in a body that was to know suffering.

"A pure body inhabited by a pure soul. Scholastic philosophy teaches us, dear Juliano, that although all human souls belong to the same category, yet some are more perfect than others. They are bound to give shape to bodies in which they will dwell and through which they will act. Human bodies are not all the same, and the souls that inhabit them differ one from another. Each soul seems made to measure in order to fit the body it is going to inhabit. Since bodies differ, God gives to each body the soul best adjusted to it. Otherwise a body would not be the soul's dwelling place but rather its jail. In the same manner that a goldsmith adjusts a precious stone in the gold setting around it, God fashions souls and bodies in such a manner that they are adjusted one to the other. A body that is harsh and stiff and lacking in obedience cannot be married to a very virtuous soul. Body and soul should be at peace with each other.

"The shape and quality of animal bodies also determines that some will possess a more refined and sensitive soul than others: For instance, the soul of a mollusk is clumsier than the soul of a fish, the soul of birds is more sensitive than the souls of animals that live on land and inside water, the soul of a snake is higher than the soul of a snail or a worm. A dog's soul is more sophisticated than the soul of a mole. A horse's soul is more complex than the soul of an ox. The soul of a monkey is more complex and more sophisticated than the soul of any other animal. In human beings, in human bodies, we see so many differences between humors, complexions, body sizes, that even when we know that they belong to one species, one human race, still we doubt that they are all alike. We may say, and it stands to reason to say so, that their souls, with respect to the side of the soul that relates to the bodies, are built in special fashions, and that they can be graded and ranked: more or less perfect as givers of shapes to our bodies.

"If there is such a difference among human souls, Christ's soul, created by God in order to suit and fit the most perfect body, the body that could be most sensitive and most active, was endowed by principle and among other souls with a marvelous property, the sensitivity to holy principles and principles of greatness. There was nothing that could not be accomplished by such a soul. His body had been fashioned in such a way that nothing could scare or confuse it. The soul was of this same quality. It always looked toward excellence and perfection. A clean honest body was inhabited by a soul equally clean and honest. Humility was common to both. The body's humors created a climate of serenity, seriousness, balance. The soul, too, was well-balanced, and also generous, courageous. Their endeavor was to spread goodness and kindness: They reached for greatness, both of them, body and soul, and they, of course, managed to reach the utmost in all senses, all dimensions, all qualities.

"Moreover, if Christ's soul was already, by itself, from the beginning, so beautiful and refined, what can we say about it when we think about what divine grace may have added to it? Heavenly grace makes anything better. The seed of grace gives a crop, when falling upon good land, of one hundred for each grain of seed. Upon such exalted and superior soil, what could it do? We can think of no virtue, heroic effort, divine excellence and beauty that cannot be found to reside in such a soul. St. John expresses it this way: 'For he whom God has sent speaks the words of God, for not by measure does God give the Spirit. The Father loves the Son, and has given all good things into his hand' (3:34–36). We read in St. Paul that 'in him dwells all the fullness of the Godhead bodily, and in him who is the head of every Principality and Power you have received of that fullness' (Col. 2:9–10). And Isaiah, 'And the spirit of the Lord shall rest upon him' (11:2). And Psalm 45:

> Thou hast loved righteousness, and hated wickedness;
> Therefore God, thy God, hath anointed thee
> With the oil of gladness above thy fellows. (7)

There was, of course, good reason to give more to Christ than to anyone else, because all other human beings were bound to inherit from Him, and the crumbs that fell from His table would nourish us all. His grace and virtue were both outstanding and crucial: They were the source from which the grace and virtue of good people, of saints and just men, were to flow. There is no limit to the power of His source, since even if the number of human beings were to multiply into infinity, into an infinity of inhabited worlds, Christ could pour into each one the excellent message of virtue and justice that He carries in Himself as a bottomless pit of wisdom, knowledge, courage, kindness.

"The world which we see, and the world behind the one we see, are full to the brim with beings, values, individuals. Christ's soul, for whom the whole world was created, holds in itself everything that is good, perfect, beautiful, heroic, divine. In the same way that the divine Word is a clear and vivid image of the Father and holds in itself every perfection related to God, thus Christ's soul, so closely linked to God, surrounded by God's rays and mirror images, is a true portrait of God. There is no other image of God that can be said to be as faithful. By comparison the light that surrounds the cherubim is dark, gloomy, depressing.

"I do not know what to say about the link between the divine Word and Christ's soul, a link that is in and by itself a vast source of justice and power. Yet we must realize that when the divine Word united with such a happy soul, and through the soul with the body, not only God dwelled in such a place, but Christ as a man enjoyed the virtue and the very being of God, His wisdom, His mercy, His power. The link between Christ and God's qualities is so close that it is impossible to undo or cut or destroy it, and it is also equally impossible that while this strong link endures

Christ's life can ignore, or depart from, the great tradition, and the great perfection, of Justice. In the same fashion a piece of iron heated in the forge of an ironsmith, penetrated and possessed by fire, looks like fire, and while in the forge will look like fire and flames. In the same way when mankind is fired by God's presence, in God's abyss, penetrated by divine fire through each pore, forever and ever, this will mean that men will become like God, that they will have all of God's qualities and powers. Mankind is still far from this blessing because innocence, truth, and justice still have not found a perfect home in our souls.

"Our souls are a bridge between our bodies and God. God acts upon our bodies through our souls. A bridge is in contact with two shores and shares in the nature of these two shores. Christ's soul is both flesh and divine spirit and mind, created to be united with God and to receive in His physical and mystical body every aspect of divinity. Thus it was essential that Christ should mirror God and that Christ's soul should excel in kindness and justice all other beings put together. A source of charity and affection, a torch sending forth flames of justice, a light of lights, a splendor of splendors, a lake of beauty over an abyss of perfection. Surrounded by beauty, justice, innocence, meekness, our holy lamb became our only and perfect sacrificial lamb and accepted a cruel death on the cross in order to bring to us both justice and eternal life.

"When St. John says about our lamb that 'he takes away the sin of the world' (1:29) this means that He takes them over, He makes these sins his own, so that He can be punished for them, so that we can be freed from them. His sacrifice means that he has identified completely with mankind, and has assumed our burdens, while we in turn have identified with Him: When He suffers we do too. This is a marvelous thing: If we suffer on our own it would hurt more and be less useful for our salvation.

"Certain trees remain barren in the soil where they were born but give abundant fruit when transplanted. Thus mankind: Transplanted to Christ we can die without grief or regrets, death becomes a fruitful blessing. Our sin and guilt had made our souls sterile, barren. The only way out was to expiate our sins through a death sentence.

"This means that on the one hand we had to die, we had to accept and seek death, yet on the other hand death, as long as we were all alone, was useless to our salvation. It was therefore indispensable to have Christ die for us, and for us to identify with Him, with His kindness and justice, so that thorough links could be established and through Him our death became so meaningful that paradoxically it could give us a new life. The first thing our lamb did was, therefore, to get ready for His sacrifice. A sacrificial lamb, a scapegoat, was the device through which, according to the old Jewish law, the law of Moses, a priest would get his people rid of their sins (Lev. 16:21). Christ, acting like a priest, did the same— with His own life: He assumed our burdens, our guilt, concentrat- ed all of it in His soul, in an ineffable and mysterious gathering: We were part of it, and God linked into His Son's body and mind all of us who, according to our nature and because of our sins, were far away and out of reach. They became so close to Christ that they became close to each other and were able to communi- cate to each other their troubles, their victories, their moods. When Christ died we had perforce to die too. When our lamb suffered we too had to suffer. We had to expiate our sins, sins that the lamb had made His own. He called our crimes His, because He had taken them upon His shoulders, and because of them He was subjected to punishment, to whipping, to a death sentence decreed against Him from the heavens. He paid for what He could never have conceived or carried out. The strength of His love for us can only be compared to the intensity of His pain and grief. Love could join in Him justice and guilt. Grief was born in His clean soul when He saw himself deeply involved with guilt and crooked deeds. Perhaps this was one of His main sources of grief. Partly this is why He was plunged into agony and blood sweat in Gethsemane.

"Let us forget for a moment the army of tortures that He was going to face. What could be His feelings, His anguish, His nausea, when He, the essence of cleanliness and saintliness, who abhorred sin, who loved God with infinite love, saw His soul besieged by a crowd of sins, committed by mankind since the beginning of time, sins that came closer and closer, clumsy, gro- tesque, and horrible sins, sins that clung to Him and became part of His being and His memory without ever having been commit- ted by Him? Just like a leper, this is what He must have felt, He who could heal the sick and cure the lepers. Clad with injustice and evil, He who was the very essence of justice and kindness, He realized He had been wounded and whipped, and somehow He had been abandoned by God at the same time He was healing our wounds, how could He put all these things together, His innocence, our sins, His lofty goals, our vile ones?

"He was ready to be sacrificed as our lamb, to cleanse our sins in this way, to accept anguish, suffering, crucifixion, in order to achieve this purpose. Nailed to the cross, He suffered less from the wounds caused by nails and more from the many evil deeds, sins, evil people, that He carried on his shoulders. His infinite love for us pushed Him to assume such a burden, and on the other hand He wanted to flee these evil people, out of His own innocence and purity. He fought and burned in such contradictions, and in such burning fire He fought against His body and tried to protect His pure soul against corruption. His love for us pushed Him nearer to our corruption, His cleanliness and purity made Him more and more reluctant to come to our rescue. Burning in contradictions, He swayed in the winds of history. In such a fire our guilt was fired and burned and consumed. In His blood we as sinners bathed in blood. He died as a lamb and we died with Him. After all, Adam's apple was eaten by all of us, for we existed in him, and his sin became ours. He poisoned us all by poisoning himself. Thus it was only fair that when our lamb was sacrificed on the altar of the cross, when He was burned by the fire of death and destruction, such a fire would cleanse all of us, since we had become part of His being. This is, therefore, as I can see, the meaning of the word, lamb, which I have discussed for a while. Let us now go on to discuss another name given to Christ in the Bible, the name of 'well-beloved,' or simply the 'loved one,' as cherished by God with respect to his Son as the name of lamb."

Then Marcelo, realizing both of his friends were anxious to go on to the discussion of this new name, after a short pause, continued and said,

BELOVED

"My dear Sabino, you know quite well that I am never reluctant to pay attention to what you ask me to do. I do not want you to complain about any reluctance on my part. Juliano said that Christ was cherished by God above every other being. Yes, indeed, Christ is God's beloved, and ours, and the Scripture calls him by this name more than once."

"I am glad to see you so open-minded, Marcelo," Sabino commented, "but may I ask you to proceed, since you are on the right path."

"What I claim," Marcelo continued, "is that Christ is defined as the Beloved One for several reasons which I shall point out right away. For instance, in the Song of Songs the beloved wife gives her husband such a name, Beloved, many times. Isaiah, in chapter 5, speaking with him and about him, states,

> Let me sing of my well-beloved,
> A song of my beloved touching his vineyard. (5:1)

"And according to the same prophet, in chapter 26, we read,

> Like as a woman with child, that draweth near the time of her
> delivery,
> Is in pain and crieth out in her pangs;
> So have we been at Thy presence, O Lord. (26:17)

In an old Greek translation we read furthermore, 'Thus happened to us with our Beloved.' As Origen explains, this means that the Beloved One, that is to say, Christ, when conceived in our soul fills it with joy and light and is finally reborn in us, which creates pain and tension in our flesh, agony and moans of self-denial in our body. David calls his Psalm 44, in which he praises Christ and describes His betrothal, 'A Song of Love.' Paul calls Him 'beloved Son' in his Epistle to the Colossians (1:14), for the same reason. And our Heavenly Father, in the gospels, calls Him much the same way: 'And behold, the heavens were opened, and he saw the Spirit of God descending as a dove and coming upon him. And behold, a voice from the heavens said, "This is my beloved Son, in whom I am well pleased" ' (Matt. 3:17). 'Beloved' is therefore an important and significant name belonging fully to Christ.

"It does not mean merely that Christ is worthy of love or that He can captivate our souls in many ways. More than that, the Beloved One is the being that has been, is, and shall be the most loved and cherished among all other beings. Not only does He have the right to expect our love: He is truly loved by us in reality, in our everyday life. We shall never underline enough the importance of this relationship. Many deserve to be loved but are not, or are less loved than they deserve, but Christ has always been loved by mankind, perhaps not as much as He deserves but at least in any case as much as we are capable of loving. And if we look up toward the heavens we see that Christ is well loved by God, as much as he deserves, thus the name 'Beloved' or 'Well Loved' is appropriate, since no other being, nor all beings put together, are as deeply loved by God.

"Texts, prophecies, descriptions in our Holy Scriptures, all attest to what we have said.

"For instance, David in Psalm 72 prophesies about our love for Christ and states it in three ways. He sings first: 'The kings of Tarshish and of the isles shall render tribute' and then

> The kings of Sheba and Seba shall offer gifts.
> Yea, all kings shall prostrate themselves before him.

Finally,

> And blessed be His glorious name for ever;
> And let the whole earth be filled with His glory.
> Amen, and Amen. (Psalm 72:10, 19)

Such a deep love is rare enough. David expressed it powerfully and yet the truth is sometimes beyond words. Tribute, gifts, prostrated kings, glory that fills the whole earth, are only images and metaphors and however meaningful they still do not convey the fullness of mankind's love for Christ nor do they express the eternal love of the Father for His Son. We know that there is no blessing outside Christ, no good thing that is not connected with Christ, no true happiness or bright future far from Christ.

"Jacob, near death, spoke about our love for Christ when he announced to his son Joseph the good tidings to come:

> The blessings of thy father
> Are mighty beyond the blessings of my progenitors
> Unto the utmost bound of the everlasting hills. (Gen. 49:26)

327

"This meant that the blessings should go on and on through future generations, although it was implied that his blessing would last only until Christ was born and could spread it into the future. Judah when blessing his son also told him he would rule until Siloh arrived—Siloh, another name for Christ, the bringer of abundance and peace; Christ, everlasting and enduring as the hills endure. It is a pity that Jacob's heart was wounded in this process and that Jacob's sons reacted in a way that would prove detrimental to their lives.

"Love for Christ, desire of His presence: This is a feeling that is unique, and was prophesied about Him even before he was born: He was to be loved and desired more than any other being had been loved or desired before. The Prophet Haggai, talking about the second temple in Jerusalem, which was being built as he wrote, pointed out that such a temple would be better than the first:

> and I will shake the heavens and the earth, and the sea, and the dry land; and I will shake all nations, and the choicest things of all nations shall come, and I will fill this house with glory, saith the Lord of hosts. (2:6–7)

For indeed the common good depended on our Savior's coming to us, to our earth, and thus our cherishing Him is natural. He was desired by all of us. It had been so announced, and it became true.

"It is indeed a strong emotional attachment that brings us and Him together. Even before Christ was born, as soon as men and angels existed, the attachment began to form. When God introduced His Son to the world it was said, 'And let all the angels of God adore him,' (Paul's Epistle to the Hebrews 1:6), which means that the Father, from the very beginning of creation, wanted Jesus to be somehow present, as an heir. Jesus, the Savior, was to become our hope, our desire, the object of all our love.

"As old as the world, therefore, is our love for Jesus. We learned to love by loving Him. We learned to desire by looking at Him. St. John calls Him 'the lamb who has been slain from the foundation of the world' (Apoc. 13:8). We should also call Him 'well-loved,' 'desired,' from the very beginning of the world. He was present in spirit in all the sacrifices offered to God by men from the beginning of time, because all were an image, a foreshadowing, of the unique and great sacrifice of our lamb. And every image, every memory, increased our affection, our love for Christ. Those who love always want to carry with them a portrait of the loved one. In many ways men carried in their soul portraits of Christ and offered them to God as a sign of devotion.

"Our early love for Christ has lasted until the present and will go on until the end of time. There will always be souls in love with Christ. We thirst for Him, we sigh for Him. Love usually begins by a look at the loved one. Yet in this case both angels and men started to love Christ before they could look at Him, only after receiving news about Him. Rumors, vague images, shadow-like profiles, word of mouth: Such were the origins of our yearning, our love. The Song of Songs explains this reaction, our yearning, in this fashion:

Thine ointments have a goodly fragrance;
Thy name is as ointment poured forth;
Therefore do the maidens love thee. (1:3)

The very scent of Christ was capable of enticing our hearts. Isaiah puts it this way:

To Thy name and to Thy memorial is the desire of our soul.
With my soul have I desired Thee in the night. (26:8–9)

The night means, in this text, the very old time before human time, from the beginning of the world until Christ was born as a torch, as a new light, and even then He led our souls into feelings of hope, trust, joy.

"We can ask, how many souls? One, two, a few? It is a source of wonder to see how many true lovers Christ has and will have. A true friend is always hard to find. As the Sage states, a faithful friend is a strong protector: Whoever finds him finds a treasure. Christ found and will find a countless group of friends who love Him with such warmth and faith that they are called *faithful.* In every century, in every year, people were born, are born, who love Christ deeply. It is easier to imagine a darkened, lightless sun than to imagine a world where people do not love Christ. Such a love sustains the whole world, it prevents it from sinking down. It is our very reason to exist, to live, to act. Everything we see around us was created in order to give honor and glory to Christ. Without our attitude of love and reverence time itself, historic time, would come to an end, made useless by our coldness.

"Every time the sun turns around the earth new lovers of Christ are born. Although Aristotle asks himself (*Ethics*, Book 9, chapter 10) whether it is a good thing to have many friends, he concludes it is not such a positive thing. His reasoning, however, applies to our always somewhat imperfect earthly friendships. Yet our relationship with Christ is different: He makes us love Him as if we were one person in this relationship, we do not get in the way of each other, He is not compelled to respond to each one of us individually. Aristotle claims that few friends are enough because friendship is like the condiment we use with food: A little goes a long way and gives us all the taste and pleasure we need. This certainly does not apply to our relationship with Christ: The pleasure we obtain from it has no limit and can never be said to be excessive.

"Another drawback of having many friends is a practical one: If they are in need, all or most of them, we may have to spend all our fortune coming to their help. This does not apply either. Christ's power does not diminish when shared. Sharing does not exhaust such a relationship. Another problem when we have many friends: Unless they are friendly with each other we will run into trouble. Christ inspires love among those who love Him, He connects and warms our souls, our minds, He makes us feel friendly toward each other. We realize we have something important in common: our common love of Him.

"Finally, it is true, as Aristotle says, that it is often confusing to deal with many friends, some of whom are happy and merry at a certain moment, and at the same time others are sad and unhappy: How can we identify with both moods simultaneously? Yet Christ is different. Both our pleasure and our pain are in His hands: He can sort them out, organize everything, satisfy and please us all. He was born to be our beloved, and can achieve what we cannot: He can love many people with great intensity and attention to each. A true friendship can be so intense as to be exhausting—to us, not to Him. He can find strength to penetrate our souls, to uplift each one of us from the inside.

"In conclusion, Christ, born to love and to be loved, our

beloved, can and should have infinite friends and lovers, and this is indeed the case. We read in Solomon's Song of Songs,

> There are threescore queens,
> And fourscore concubines,
> And maidens without number. (6:8)

One of our Church hymns describes him walking among lilies, surrounded by choirs of dancing virgins. And in his Apocalypse (7:9) St. John describes an adoring crowd:

> After this I saw a great multitude which no man could number, out of all nations and tribes and peoples and tongues, standing before the throne and before the Lamb, clothed in white robes, and with palms in their hands.

"If so many human beings love Him, who could count the angels, closely attached to Him through love and a common purpose? There are countless millions of such heavenly creatures busy serving and helping God—and they all love Christ. It is something rare and beyond compare, to have someone so much loved by so many, to have the human nature of Christ so adored by the angels, to have such a perennial source of admiration and love among all of us.

"Even natural beings, dear Juliano, devoid of intelligence and of feelings, seem to respond to Christ's warmth and presence. Nature guides every being to seek what is best and more profitable to it, even without being aware of such a yearning. Things are guided by secret forces. They long to improve, to desire what can help them: They love Christ and are anxious to have Him come to them. As St. Paul writes in his Epistle to the Romans,

> The eager longing of creation awaits the revelation of the sons of God. For creation was made subject to vanity— not by its own will but by reason of him who made it subject—in hope, because creation itself also will be delivered from its slavery to corruption into the freedom of the glory of the sons of God. For we know that all creation groans and travails in pain until now. (8:19–22)

THE NAMES OF CHRIST

All of which expresses basically a hunger for Jesus Christ, the source of the freedom that St. Paul sings and everyone else desires. "In the Song of Songs the Shulamite states that

> King Solomon made himself a palanquin
> Of the wood of Lebanon.
> He made the pillars thereof of silver,
> The top thereof of gold,
> The seat of it of purple.
> The inside thereof being inlaid with love.
> From the daughters of Jerusalem. (3:9–10)

"Such a palanquin is an image for the high temple, in which Jesus dwells, and which was built by Solomon with great art and care: It is a palanquin because it carries forward the glory of its builder. The loving daughters of Jerusalem are also symbols, symbols of the love of every being, whether or not endowed with reason. Jerusalem is the city of peace, its daughters symbolize the children of peace, both men and angels. The palanquin and all its richly adorned sections is a symbol of another kind of being, a symbol for the natural beings, the beings without reason or voice yet attracted to Christ by a mysterious force going to the center as the spokes of a wheel converge toward the hub.

"Our love for Christ is a burning love, like the fire in a blazing log where only flames can be seen. Our hearts have been turned into burning logs. The number of those who love Him is vast, yet the quality is beyond and above the most important feature. Many people have captured the hearts of their fellow human beings, many leaders have been beloved by their followers, in politics and in religion many have excelled and won our hearts. Yet not one of them has been loved with the fervor and intensity we devote to our love for Him. It is very true that a loyal friend is better than a life-giving medicine, and it is easier to find such a friend for those who fear God. Those who love Christ also react to Christ's infinite love for God and try to imitate Him in this respect.

"A true, sincere, kind man is bound to find good friends. And someone who loves God and serves Him better than all the other creatures put together can hope to be loved by his friends in an exceptional way. Christ loved us in so many ways, with such passionate intense love, that we were to respond in a way that was both passionate and exceptional. For deep love seeks and desires only a similarly deep and true love. Christ fashions us into perfect friends of His.

"If men and angels loved Christ after their fashion, limited to their own vision and strength, which are somewhat limited, rough, and provincial, it could well be that their love turned out to be pale and weak. However, when we consider the inner source of such a love and we realize that its fire comes from an inspiration that reaches us from the Holy Spirit (and this is stated by St. Paul in his Epistle to the Romans: 'the charity of God is poured forth in our hearts by the Holy Spirit who has been given to us' [5:5]) we begin to understand. It is a love both exquisite and intense, lit up by God in the heart of men, inspired by the breath of the Holy Spirit. Only a love inspired by God is worthy of God and is made to resemble the heavenly spaces where the seraphim burn with loving intelligence. It is not possible that such a love, with such origins, should not be strong in its faithfulness, sweetest in its tender approach, everlasting and producing a bond of fusion, a tight embrace. There is no doubt, dear Sabino, that the love that unites one human being to another is, compared to the fire that burns in the bosom of those who love Christ, but a shadow, but an imperfect imitation. This is why Christ is called the Beloved: because God has inspired in us, toward Christ, a love which is different from other loves, much better than any similar feeling.

"Christ's Father, who loves Him as an only son can be loved by his father, had to try hard to create in us a similar love. Jesus, St. Paul writes, is God's beloved Son (in another version, his son of love) (Col. 1:13), in other words, God's love for Christ is deep and without boundaries. God naturally wants us to love Christ, if not with the same intensity, which is hardly possible, at least with the same kind of love—a love of a rare quality, truer and sweeter than any other earthly love. God wants us to love Christ not as a Lord but in order to find in Him the source of our values and our treasures. Our loving Him is an act of justice, of course, but it is more: Through our love we shall become one and the same with Him, will partake of His human and divine natures. Origen states that 'the flow of charity pours into the hearts of saints so that they may partake of God's nature, and that through this gift of the Holy Spirit the words of God may be fulfilled, That all may be one, even as thou, Father, in me and I in thee; that they also may be one in us. (John 17:21). That means, having them partake of our nature through the flow of abundant love communicated to them by the Holy Spirit' (*In Epist. at Romanos,* Migne, *Pt. Graeca,* 14, 997).

"I ask therefore, what kind of love can accomplish such a huge task? How can friendship lead to unity? How can a fire purify us from our vile instincts and turn dross into gold so that we come closer and closer to God? It is a very special love, abundant love as Origen writes, the love that is awakened in our hearts by the Holy Ghost. It produces the greatest of all miracles: It turns men into gods. It turns into the finest gold our lowly and vile mud. As a great alchemist, through the virtue of fire alone, might perhaps turn a fistful of earth into real gold, we see that such a special fire, endowed with such magic powers, must be indeed hotter, livelier, better than any earthly fire. Thus the love that unites us to Christ and that makes us like Him is better and more powerful than any other kind of love. We can no longer call it simply love, it is like hunger and thirst that leads us to embrace Christ and become part of Him: 'He who eats my flesh and drinks my blood has life everlasting' (John 6:54). We are asked, in so many words, to eat Christ. This is indeed the text: 'Amen, amen, I say unto you, unless you eat the flesh of the Son of Man, and drink his blood, you shall not have life in you' (John 6:53). In the Sacrament of the Holy Eucharist His body, present in the holy bread, is eaten by the faithful, and once inside their body it changes them into Him, and at the same time their hearts uplifted by the fires of love are brought closer to His spirit and bring it to themselves: Love here means hunger. Macharios expresses it this way: 'If the love born out of carnal knowledge separates us from our father, our mother, our brothers and sisters, it makes us cling to our wife, as it is written, Therefore shall a man leave his father and his mother, and shall cleave unto his wife, and they shall be one flesh (Gen 2:24). Thus, if carnal love so separates a man from all his other loves, how much more will those worthy to partake the amiable and celestial gifts of the spirit become free and separated from any earthly love? They will think everything on earth is superfluous and useless, for in their souls the desire to belong to heaven will have won the battle. This is what they will want, this shall always be in their thoughts, there shall they dwell, thereof will they speak: In heaven their soul will find abode, nothing shall remain in them save for the divine spiritual love lifting them to heaven and their links to the holy spirit' (*Homilia* 4, Migne, *Patr. Graeca*, 34, 483).

"We shall understand further the greatness of the love we are describing if we take into account the many and difficult steps that must be taken in order to preserve and increase it. There is no great merit in loving someone if in order to obtain and keep this person's warm friendship we must do only a few little things. A love is truly great and good as gold when it has to surmount great troubles in order to establish itself. The true lover is always ready for any sacrifice, ready to jump any barrier, always convinced that only his beloved is really worthy and good, and will think that if he attains the favors of his beloved anything else in the world is quite superfluous. All his other pleasures and whims can be forgotten, they are superseded by his feelings of love. He gets rid of everything in his body and mind in order to become pure love. This is what happens to Christ's true lovers.

"We see that in order to keep Christ's warm friendship it is necessary for us to keep the ten commandments; 'If anyone love me (Jesus says), he will keep my word' (John 14:23). This is not easy, it does not encompass merely one or two injunctions, but rather may plunge us in many troubles. It means to accept and obey what reason preaches, justice commands, fortitude asks for, prudence and moderation, with all other virtues, establish and ordain. It means to follow in every way the righteous and straight path, without deviating out of self-interest or without compromising out of fear, rejecting the siren song of pleasure, and the high sounds of personal pride and honor; it means we must go against the grain, against our senses. And we must keep His law on every occasion, no matter how hard we find it. We must deny ourselves, we must take the cross, place it upon our shoulders and follow Christ, that is to say, we must walk where He walked and place our feet over His footprints. Finally, we must reject what we see and despise what our senses offer us, we must reject what we know by experience is pleasant and sweet, we must lift our thoughts toward what cannot be seen or felt, we must desire only what has been promised us, what our faith tells us we must believe, we must trust everything to His word. Such a love, if capable of all this, is indeed powerful. No ocean of water is capable then of putting out its fire. As we read in the Song of Songs,

> Many waters cannot quench love,
> Neither can the floods drown it. (8:7)

And in St. Paul: 'Charity is patient, is kind; charity does not envy, is not pretentious, is not puffed up, is not ambitious, is not self-seeking, is not provoked; thinks no evil, does not rejoice over wickedness, but rejoices with the truth; bears with all things, believes all things, hopes all things, endures all things.' (I Cor 13:4–7).

"All of which means that the love that men feel for Christ is not a mere human love, a passing fancy, but a feeling that encompasses in itself everything that is great and pure, a virtue that gathers in itself all the other virtues, a fire that burns in every part of our body and soul and turns us into a flaming, yearning presence.

"If lightning falls into the sea it becomes harmless. The same applies to any crisis that strikes a soul in love with Christ: The impact seems to melt away and no harm takes place. A rock, a tower, a diamond, are adequate images for the resistance of our soul when Christ is inside us.

"Charity, according to St. Paul, is kind: This means that it is not simply biding time in order to take revenge. Our desire to imitate Christ precludes the thought of harming others. Turning the other cheek, returning good deeds for bad, is the norm. This is the meaning of the words of the Apostle: Charity is not pretentious or self-seeking. We do not think of ourselves, only try to think about others. Virtue, not fear, moves us, we are not stingy in our efforts. And we are not vain: Proud people are impossible to deal with, since everything seems to irritate them. True love is always humble with respect to the beloved. Our love for Christ spills out toward all of mankind, and thus makes us humble as part of all mankind.

"The loving heart endures all things. Our humility and charity protect us against any kind of snobbishness and make us friendly toward every human being.

"We cannot be provoked. This means that insult and injury that other people try to inflict on us will be disregarded by us, because we are humble and do not think about ourselves. More-over, there is no task, no work, no craft or office that we will reject as lowly or undignified if by it we can be of service to our Beloved and His projects.

"The basic reason for such a behavior is that we are not self-seeking and do not get angry: All our desire and purpose is to come closer to kindness and goodness, and therefore we cannot imagine harming other people. We rejoice over other people's happiness, lament their suffering. We obey the commands of our Lord, believe what He tells us, accept with bliss everything He sends us: We love truly only Him. When someone is ill with a fever he rejects any food or drink however delicious: The inner fire is too strong to allow him to think about food. Similarly whoever is prey to the secret fire of the spirit and burns in love for Christ will reject anything that others appreciate. Nothing on earth or in heaven will distract him from his love. As St. Paul puts it, 'Who shall separate us from the love of Christ?' (Rom. 8:35). And it is impossible to find the celestial spiritual love if we do not give up all that the secular world has to offer: We must liberate our souls from every earthly temptation so that they can concen-trate upon obeying all of God's commandments and so that they can devote themselves fully to the love of Jesus.

"Such a deep love uproots in our soul every possible desire that can become its rival and becomes then true and absolute lord of our soul. Its intense fire consumes and destroys anything that opposes it, exiling from our hearts our love for other creatures, and by replacing such bonds is also capable of creating new ones: In our love for Christ all the other beings are loved by us even better than before. For our love toward Jesus is never selfish but rather in it and by it we embrace all the other men and bring them into our bosom, with such pure affection that it can never be self-seeking or selfish, with so tender a bond that their hurts become ours, so full of care that we lose sleep over their fate, so unswerv-ing that we will not stop caring unless we stop caring for Christ. It is rare for a friend to risk his life for the sake of friendship: and yet those who love Christ are willing to do so not only for people who are their friends but even for strangers, even for those who hate and persecute them.

"Our Beloved is so well loved by us that through Him we come to love all of mankind. He is the source of every kindness and goodness that has been poured in our souls, and also the source of our love, which spreads around us in such a way that it creates countless bonds. Strangers get close to one another and form a family around this love. It is only fair for us to love the one who has helped shape and mold God with His own hands, one who, moreover, is trying to make gods out of us, one who makes possible the acceptance of every law, the victory over every obstacle, the strength to overcome every setback, the one who turns bitterness into honey, who brings peace and harmony, the one in whom the whole world is reconciled in a universal embrace.

"There is no need to go any further: Let us hear what some of the people who fell in love with Christ have to say to us. Through their words of fire shines their intense loving emotion. Thus St. Paul: 'Who shall separate us from the love of Christ? Shall tribulation, or distress, or persecution, or hunger, or nakedness, or danger, or the sword?' (Rom 8:35). And later: 'For I am sure that neither death, nor life, nor angels, nor principalities, nor things present, nor things to come, nor powers, nor height, nor depth, nor any other creature will be able to separate us from the love of God, which is in Christ Jesus our Lord' (Rom. 8:38). Such is the burning love that unites us with Christ.

"St. Ignatius of Antioch tells us:

I am writing all the faithful to let them know that I am dying for the sake of my love for God and that I am doing so full of joy. Please do not try to prevent it. Let me be devoured by wild beasts as a means to reach union with Christ. I am Christ's wheat and after being crushed and ground by the lions' teeth I shall become God's white bread. Instead of trying to scare the wild beasts I beg you to make them come, as I want them to devour me completely. Then I shall become a true disciple of Christ, when my body has totally disappeared from this world. Pray for me to the Lord so that I can be the willing victim of this sacrifice. I cannot send you messages such as those sent by Saint Peter or Saint Paul, for they were Christ's Apostles, and I am only an insignificant man; they were free even in their service of Christ, while I am still in bondage. But if I suffer as much as I wish I will be finally freed and I shall resuscitate in Jesus, free at last. Now, already captured by him, I am learning to reject anything and everything that belongs to this world, since it is all vanity. I am being sent from Syria to Rome, with the purpose of delivering me to the lions in a circus. I am traveling by land and by sea, tied up and surrounded by ten guards just as cruel as beasts. I do not mind in the least. I long for the wild beasts that await me, I long to be face to face with them. I will beg them not to spare me, as they spared other Christians thrown to them: They did not dare touch them. If they do not want to eat me up, I will force them to do so. Forgive me, my sons: I know what is truly good for me, for my salvation. I wish nothing from this world, I wish only to come closer to our Lord. Fire, the Cross, wild beasts, wounds, broken bones, anything the Devil may bring, let it all happen to me, provided I can get close to Christ. Better to die for him than to rule the world. He is the one I desire, the true son of God, the one who died and came back to life for us. Forgive me, my brethren, do not prevent life to flow on and on, for Jesus is life to his followers. Do not wish me to die, for indeed life without Christ is death and only death. (*Epist. ad Romanos*, Migne, Patr. Gr., V, 690–691)

"We should also listen to St. Gregory, the Theologian:

O light coming to us from the Father! O holy word, better than any other word! An infinite beam coming out of infinite light. Only child, you are an image of our Father, and a seal of what has no beginning, a splendor that shines with Him, the end of time, so clear and bright, giving of immense riches, sitting upon a high throne, celestial, all-powerful, infinitely worthy, ruler of the world, giving life strength to all creatures. You create everything, because you, or Christ, are in charge of the Sun in the heavens, with its mane of light, stealing light from other stars. Compared with your light the brightest spirits appear dark. Because of your will we see the moon, our night's illumination, grow light at times, then fade. Because of your will the zodiac circle and the dancing stars above order and regulate the year's seasons, each season bringing its harmony to the whole year. Both the stars and the comets are the heralds of your wisdom. Out of your light come the heavenly voices that sing the glory of our holy Trinity. Man, placed by you on the earth, also sings your power and glory. O great light, dimmed so as not to blind me! Light twice brought to life, my tongue speaks in thine honor. (*Hymnus ad Christum*, Migne, Patr. Gr., XXXVII, 1325).

"St. Augustine is also eloquent in his *Confessions:*

How will I manage, O Lord, to rest in thy bosom? How will I manage to have you come into my bosom and make me drunk with thy presence, and that I may forget my ailing and embrace thee, my beloved? Who are thou to me, or who am I to thee, so that thou can command me to love thee, and if I do not do so thou canst get angry at me and menace me with great trouble, as if not loving you were not trouble enough? Alas. Tell my soul, who art thou, tell it 'I am thy salvation' so that I can hear it. I shall run after this voice and I shall embrace it. My soul is a humble abode for thee: Make it bigger and better. It is falling apart: You can repair it. Some details may offend thine eyes, I know. Who can clean it, who can I ask for help, if not to thee? Clean me, O Lord, of my sins and errors, forgive thy servant his transgressions. (*Confessions*, I, ch. 5)

"This is a long, indeed an endless story, for the world will come to its end before we can give a complete account of all that the men and women who are in love with Christ tell Him as an expression of their love. Let us speak through the Shulamite and let her be our messenger: Her words express better than any other words the depth of our love. She says,

Let him kiss me with the kisses of his mouth—
For thy love is better than wine.

BOOK III

And then goes on, 'Draw me, we will run after thee,' and still,

>Tell me, O thou whom my soul loveth,
>Where thou feedest, where thou makest they flock to rest at
> noon

and still,

>My Beloved is unto me as a bag of myrrh,
>That lieth betwixt my breasts.

Later on, as her beloved praises her, she answers,

>Behold, thou art fair, my beloved, yea, pleasant;
>Also our couch is leafy.
>The beams of our houses are cedars,
>And our panels are cypresses. (Song of Songs I 1, 3, 6, 12:16–17)

She then compares him to an apple tree and says how delightful it was to sit under its shadow and to eat of its sweet fruit. She is fainting with love and asks to be refreshed with flowers and with apples, and asks to be embraced by her Beloved, explaining how he should do so. She adds that she sought him by night in her bed and did not find him: She got up, left her house, searched the city until she found him, managed to have him come back with her to her house. Another night she also came out in his search, calling his name out loud along the streets, but he did not hear her; the watchmen mistreated her. She spoke to those who could hear her,

>I adjure you, O daughters of Jerusalem,
>If ye find my Beloved,
>What will ye tell him?
>That I am love-sick. (5:8)

And a little later,

>Come, my Beloved, let us go forth into the field;
>Let us lodge in the villages.
>Let us get up early to the vineyards;
>Let us see whether the vine hath budded,

341

Whether the vine-blossom is opened,
And the pomegranates be in flower;
There will I give thee my love.
The mandrakes give forth fragrance,
And at our doors are all manner of precious fruits,
New and old,
Which I have laid up for thee, my Beloved. (7:11–13)

And finally, burning with love, she concludes,

O that thou wert as my brother,
That sucked the breasts of my mother!
When I should find thee without, I would kiss thee;
Yea, and none would despise me.
I would lead thee, and bring thee into my mother's house,
That thou mightest instruct me;
I would cause thee to drink of spiced wine,
Of the juice of my pomegranate.
Thy left hand should be under my head,
And thy right hand should embrace me. (8:1–3)

"Words are superfluous where deeds abound, for in love deeds are always better than words. There is not one man that can give to anyone the proofs of deep love that Christ's friends have given Him along the centuries. People have left their families, they have given up everything that can be seen or imagined. They have renounced to themselves, to their own lives, and this is something that is still taking place every day. If it is possible to be alienated from oneself, if a soul can be divided and separated from itself, something that only God's spirit can make possible, this also is taking place day after day, all for the love of Christ. He can turn poverty into riches, a desert into a paradise, torment into pleasure, persecutions into bliss. So that love can live in them, Christ's lovers choose to die to the world and its riches, and give up their own bodies, their own faces, becoming an 'I' without body or shape so that Christ's love becomes in them what gives them shape, life, being, becoming, acting, and ultimately so that everything in them resembles their beloved Christ. This shows without doubt how He is the only being that can be truly beloved in such a fashion.

BOOK III

"O greatness of love! O desire and goal of the best men! O sweet fire that burns our souls! For the sake of your love, O Lord, small children accepted to die, weak adolescent girls managed to find strength to walk upon fire. Your love grows even upon the desert. When we love you our body becomes like fire, like light: Bliss is what we become."

At that point Marcelo became silent. He paused for a while, and after a long time he lowered his eyes to the ground and said,

"It is too daring to express in words what God sends us as a message to the few chosen individuals who love His Child. What we should keep in mind is simple: All love comes from God. For us this love is essential: To us it is like the sun, a rain of honey, the target of God's love: God loves every being through Christ. God communicates with us through Christ's image, through His soul. His image has been projected into our soul: It makes us intelligent and beautiful and healthy, and His name is Jesus, a name which still needs our description."

Marcelo then became silent. After a long silence he spoke again, and while he did so he looked to Sabino:

JESUS

"My dear Sabino, I must state that the name of Jesus is Christ's true and proper name. The names that we have mentioned so far are also names that can be applied to Him, because they point to some of His qualities. Some names point to things that He has in common with others, while other names point to some outstanding and significant traits that are particular to Him. Jesus is a name reserved to Him, God named Him thus through an angel. It means to us the whole meaning, not a part of it, and we should pay attention to this message.

"And yet we should remember that Christ has two natures, two beings, two ways of relating to us, and also, correspondingly, two real names. One follows the divine nature according to which He is eternally born out of His Father. We call it the Word. Yet He has another name. We call and pronounce this second name, Jesus. Both names portray Him perfectly.

"Let us assume that one of these two names is the original one and the other name is a translation that brings it closer to us. The

343

original name is the name that was revealed by God to the prophets, and they wrote such a name in the language that they knew, whether Syrian or Hebrew. Thus, the very first name, which to us is the Word, was in the original language called Dabar. The name Jesus was in the original language Iehosuah. Translations tend to obscure these original words and the way they were written. We must go back to these original names. Dabar, for instance, I think also applies to Christ, because it means not one meaning, it means many things, it has many meanings especially if we consider its syllables and each one of the letters in this name.

"As for the first letter, the *D*, it works as an article, say the article *the* in English. An article is useful inasmuch as it helps us to relate to a noun; it points out the noun's quality, lineage, and so forth. This is of course related to the work of Christ among us, since He placed things before our eyes and explained their origin, their lineage, their hierarchy.

"The second letter, or rather the second consonant, is a *B*, and stands for building. Indeed Christ is our original building, through Christ our whole world has been built according to God's plan. Christ was the mason that worked hardest in this project. This is why he was called Tabernacle in the Holy Scriptures. Saint Gregory states, 'The Son of God is a Tabernacle, he holds in himself every thing created, and he made us into a tabernacle' (Migne, *Patr. Gr.*, XLIV, 382).

"The main argument that we want to state is this: Before existing every being had its dwelling in Him, and when they came out to light He helped them to do so and at the same time He found a way to be a part of them, to live with them. He was a dwelling, a house, and thus He became a house once more. He is our house because we live inside Him, and we are, in turn, His house, since He lives in us. Wheels within wheels, living creatures in the wheels, the wheels in the living creatures, as Ezekiel describes it (1:15–19). Both wheels are in Christ, because He is divine (through the Holy Spirit) and human through His having incarnated, and the vast diversity of all creatures is expressed in His existence.

"The third letter in Dabar is the *R*, a letter which according to St. Jerome means head, beginning. Christ is, in essence, beginning. He is called 'beginning' in the gospels because in Him our modern world began, and because He upholds, re-creates, and sustains all the created things that make up our world. He is also called beginning because in every family tree and every lineage we can see Him above everybody else: He is eminent, privileged, the fountainhead of grace and privilege. St. Paul has written that Christ is the origin of everything and that He arrives first everywhere. As far as creation of beings is concerned He is the fountainhead and origin of being for us. If we think about ways to improve our being He also is the leader and inspiration of every positive change. When it comes to life, He is the source of life, the life-giving spring of creative waters. He was the first to resuscitate His own flesh and body, and also the body of others. As for glory, He is the one in charge of it, He swims in oceans of glory. He is the king of kings, the priest of priests, the prince of angels, the Lord even of rebellious angels or men, to sum up, the beginning of everything, the first among all of us.

"The letter *R* means also, according to St. Jerome, the Spirit. This is a word that can apply to the three persons in the Trinity, and yet it has been applied especially to the Holy Spirit because it seems to define the way in which it acts and moves us. Yet Christ has been called Spirit for some special and specific reasons. As husband to the soul he takes the role of Spirit. The Soul is also Spirit, Christ is the Word and is in some way soul of the soul and spirit of the spirit. In His union with the soul He manages to keep the laws and the rules that are proper to the Spirit, blowing here and there without warning and without fixed schedules. St. Bernard describes this situation in a wonderful passage that I would like to share with you. He writes,

> I confess that the Word has visited me many times, although it may be unwise to admit it. He entered my soul several times, and yet I was never aware of the moment in which he carried out his entrance. I was aware that he was in me, I remember his stay, and once or twice I suspected his arrival. Yet I was never conscious of his entrance or of his exit from my soul. Even now I do not know whence he came from, when he came to me, or where he went, when departed from me. As it is written by Saint John, 'The wind blows where it will; and thou hearest its sound but dost not know where it

comes from or where it goes.' (3:8). There is no surprise
here, since he is the one of whom it is said, 'And Thy
footsteps were not known' (Ps. 77:20). Truly he did not
enter my soul through my eyes, since I did not see any
color or shape in front of me. He did not enter my soul
through my ears, since he made no noise, no sound. My
nose was not the point of entrance: He did not mix with
air or breath, nor was my mouth, since he is not drink-
able or edible. Or through my skin: The sense of touch
could not detect him. How did he then enter into me?
Perhaps he did not enter me, perhaps he was not outside
me. Yet he was not already inside me, because he is
entirely good, and there is nothing in me that is good. I
tried to climb to the summit of myself, only to find that
the Word was higher still. I plunged to the lowest areas
of my being and found that he had descended lower still.
Looking outside I found him further away. Looking inside I found him there too. Then I knew that what I had
read was true: 'For in him we live and move and have our
being' (Acts 17:28). Happy are those who live and move
in him. Yet someone may ask, If it is so difficult to reach
him and understand his actions, how do I know that he
was present in my soul? The answer is: Because this
Word is alive and acts powerfully: As soon as he entered
my slumbering soul he woke it up. My heart was hardened and sick: he moved it, softened, made it sensitive.
Then he started to tear down and clear away the debris
in my soul, and began to plant and rebuild and watered
the parched lands and shed his blinding light on every
dark recess. He straightened what was crooked and
turned mountains into straight roads. My heart and my
soul bless the Lord and his holy name. Yet when the
Beloved Word entered in me, as he did several times, he
never announced his arrival, either through his voice or
by showing himself or making his footsteps be heard.
Neither his movements nor my senses told me that he
had arrived and had penetrated in the recesses of my
bosom. As I have said, it was only because of my heart's
restlessness and sensitivity that I understood he had arrived in me. Because my vices fled from me and my

carnal desires ceased I understood the extent of his power. Because he brought to light my secrets, discussed
them and corrected my errors, I understood the depths of
his wisdom. I experienced his kindness and benevolence
through the change and amelioration in my behavior that
he brought about. The renewal of my soul and my spirit
let me catch a glimpse of his beauty. And the impression
that remained in my mind was one of greatness and
power without limit. Yet these feelings were not permanent. As it happens when a pot is taken away from the
fire, it then stops boiling, so with my soul: its feelings
soon began to weaken, to become cold and numb: I
understood then that my visitor had departed. My soul
then was plunged in sadness and would remain sad until
again my heart would stir once more and I would thus
become aware that my visitor had come back. (*Sermones in
cantica canticorum*, Migne, Patr. lat., CLXXXIII, 1141)

"Let us now go back to the name 'Dabar,' and we shall see
that each one of its letters stands for a trait in Christ, for one of
His qualities. The syllables of this word are especially significant:
'da' and 'Bar' which put together mean 'the son' or 'this is the son,'
which as Juliano has mentioned previously is an apt description of
Christ, and reminds us of what the Father said from the cloud
addressing the three disciples: 'This is my beloved Son, in whom I
am well pleased; hear him' (Matt. 17:5) which meant, 'he is Dabar,
he is the one who eternally and invisibly was born from me and is
now reborn in the flesh and made visible.' There are many other
words in Hebrew that mean 'son' but this one, 'bar,' is especially
meaningful. It originates from other words that mean 'to bring to
light' and 'to raise,' so that we can understand that the son
designated by such a name is also someone who can bring others
to light and can raise them, and in some way we are all his sons.

"And if we read the word backward it is also meaningful. For
'bar' read backwards is 'rab,' which means 'an abundance of
excellent qualities' which is also an apt description of Christ, both
as God and as a man. For in His divine nature we find the ideas
and causes of everything that is good, and in His human nature
the best qualities of all mankind, as we pointed out yesterday.

"Now let us examine the whole word, after our comments

about its parts: We will find that its meaning is no less important. 'Dabar' expresses, in the Holy Scriptures, many great things. The first meaning is, 'the word that conceives understanding in and by itself,' the word that depicts an image quite like the thing it represents. Christ is Dabar because the image that it projects is equal to the greatness of God the Father. Dabar means also 'the word that takes shape in the mouth,' which means the image of something that our mind would like to conceal. Christ is Dabar because He gives us an image of the Father that was hidden in the Father and had been reserved for His eyes. Now such an image is brought to light and impressed in every being created by God. Dabar means also 'law and reason, what is demanded by custom' and finally 'duty guiding our actions,' all of which fits Christ, who is the reason beings are created, the structure that orders them, the law that must apply to them (both in the natural and the supernatural worlds), and the duty that should guide every being that does not wish to perish, that is to say, the duty to model our life upon Christ's. Yet another meaning of Dabar is 'an important fact that has its source and origin in another fact.' Christ is the most important 'fact' that had its source in God, and through Christ we received fully God's message. A great deed, indeed, a bosom of pure light, wisdom born out of wisdom, the source of all knowledge, power, greatness, and excellence, life and immortality. Dabar means all of this, because it points to everything great, noble and wonderful that flows toward us from one being.

"It means also—and with this meaning I conclude—'any aspect of being' and by extension 'being itself and the reality of creation'—all of which fits Christ perfectly, because all aspects of being and reality are contained in His person, and we find in Him the source and the root from which all the creatures derive their being, their essence, their life, and their works.

"Let us now leave behind us the name Dabar and go back to the name Jesus, so fitting and adequate to the human side of Christ. Dabar connected Him with His divine origin, with the Father. Jesus expresses His human side better than any other name.

"I will not deal with the number and the meaning of each one of the Hebrew letters that make up this name, or about the numerical value of such letters, or about the number that results from adding all of these partial numbers, and the meaning hidden in this number. Other scholars have dealt with these details, and although I do not criticize or condemn their efforts, I still think these are mere details.

"One aspect seems important to me: The Hebrew word for Jesus is 'Jehosuah,' as has been mentioned before. And in it we find all the letters that go into the name of God in Hebrew, the so-called 'four letter name of God' or 'Tetragrammaton,' plus two letters more. As you know, the name of God with four letters is a name that is not uttered, because vowels are not pronounced, because we do not know what their real sound should be, or because of the respect due to God, or else, as I have suspected sometimes, because it is like the mumbling sounds that a dumb person utters as an expression of friendship, affection, love: without a clear pattern, shapeless, as if God wanted us men to use as a word to express His infinite being a clumsy word or sound that would make us understand that God is too large to be embraced or expressed in any clear way by our understanding and our tongue: Pronouncing such a name is tantamount to admitting that we are limited and dumb when we come face to face with God. Our confusion and mumbling are a hymn of praise, as David declared; the name of God is ineffable and unutterable. And yet in Jesus' name two letters have been added and the name can indeed be pronounced and said out loud with clear meaning. What happened with Christ also happened with Christ's name: It is the clear portrait of God. In Christ we see God joined to a man's soul and body. God's name, which could not be said, now has two more letters and it can be said, mysteries can be revealed, made visible, can be talked about. Christ is Jesus, that is to say, a combination of God and man, of a name that cannot be uttered and a name that can.

"We must now explain the meaning of the name Jesus, and why it is a fitting name for Christ.

"Jesus means 'salvation' or 'health.' Health, certainly, for us, since he has no need ot it, given his powers and his perfection. Ill health is, of course, our problem, and Jesus' excellent health is intended to be the cure and remedy of our poor health. If we reflect upon our diseases and troubles we will understand more clearly the importance of Jesus' health, and at the same time the importance of the meaning of this name, Jesus.

"Man is by nature restless, changeable. From his ancestors he inherited weaknesses and defects that afflict every part of his body and his soul. His mind is often cloudy, his will is weak, he is prey to many perverse yearnings and desires. He forgets easily. His senses lie to him, or else overheat his desire. His body decays and moves toward death, is at war with itself, is prey to countless diseases. These weaknesses are inherited from his parents, and mainly original sin is the source of these troubles, as it pulls us away from grace, makes us enemies of God, and turns us into allies of the Devil. To the general weaknesses and faults that we share with all mankind each one of us adds some specific, individual faults, sins, and troubles. We are, moreover, bad patients: We become the allies of our ailments and bring death nearer through our excesses. We are therefore condemned to be unhappy, because of our sins, our weakness, our poor choices, because of God's laws against sinning, and because of the Devil's tyranny over all those who sin. Our disease is not merely a disease: It is the sum total of every disease, every pain, every grief that the world has known.

"The only remedy to our sufferings is Christ: He delivers us from them in the ways that we mentioned yesterday and today, and because He is our physician, our medicine, our cure, He is called Jesus, that is to say, salvation and health. His health is infinite because our disease is infinite. The name Jesus is especially meaningful because since our disease can be found everywhere it is fitting to have Jesus everywhere, fighting our weakness and our ills in all fronts. We have mentioned previously the fact that Christ is also called 'bud': a new life, and the things that created this new life undoubtedly did so because they needed the healing powers of Jesus, the giver of health. When Isaiah asks the heavens to give birth to a savior, he cries out,

> Drop down, ye heavens, from above,
> And let the skies pour down righteousness

adding right away

> Let the earth open, that they (the heavens) may bring forth
> salvation (45:8)

"Moreover, if Christ is called 'faces of God' it is because He is our salvation, which will take place when we come closer to God and can see God's face, as Christ Himself states, 'Now this is everlasting life, that they may know thee, the only true God, and him whom thou hast sent, Jesus Christ.' (John 17:3). By the same token, if we name Him, 'way' or 'mountain,' He is our way because he is our guide, and He is mountain because He is our protection, our fortress. He would not be justly named Jesus if He were not our guide and our fortress, for one cannot reach health and salvation without a guide, or preserve it without a defense and a fortress.

"In the same manner He has been called 'father of the future century' because the health and salvation that mankind is trying to reach cannot be attained unless man is born again. Christ therefore would not be our Jesus, our salvation, if He were not first our generator, our father. He is also called 'arm' and 'king of God' and 'Prince of Peace': arm that fights for our freedom, king and prince that rule us wisely, all helpful to our health and salvation, fostering and preserving them. Something similar can be said about the name 'husband,' for health by itself is not enough: It is imperfect when not enjoyed in the company of the one we love. Christ, our Jesus, our salvation and health, is also our husband, for He delights our souls and His company is sweet, and in a chaste union He will engender in our souls the future men. All His names are thus linked and interdependent: because He is called Jesus we must also call him husband and king. Prince of Peace, arm, mountain, father, way, bud. And also, as we read in the Scriptures, shepherd, sheep, holy wafer, priest, lion, lamb, vine, gate, physician, light, truth, sun of justice, and other similar names.

"Indeed if He is our Jesus, our health and salvation, all the other names also belong to Him. If they did not He could not be fully our Jesus, our health and salvation. Given our ills, the power of the Devil, our sins, and God's wrath, our salvation and good health would be unattainable if Christ were not our shepherd guiding us to good pastures, our sheep feeding and clothing us, our holy wafer offered in sacrifice for our sins, our priest that could intercede for our sins with respect to the Father, our lion always ready to tear apart the lion of sin, our enemy; our lamb, carrying on His back the sins of the world; our vine giving us life-giving juice; our gate opening the way to heaven for all of us; our physician capable of healing a thousand wounds; our truth protecting us against error; our light showing us the way through our dark life; and finally our sun of justice shining on and on from the center of our souls free at last. This is why we say that the name Jesus is implied in all of the other names given to Christ because all of their meanings can be related to Christ being perfectly Jesus.

"St. Bernard expresses this thought clearly when he writes,

Isaiah states that Jesus will be called Admirable, Counselor, God, Strong, Father of the Future Century, Prince of Peace. It is true that these are great names, but what has become of the name that more than any other name is the appropriate name, the name of Jesus? No doubt we shall find this name in all the other names that I have previously mentioned, in some way spread out among them all, in the same way that the Shulamite says in the Song of Songs, 'Thy name is as ointment poured forth' (1:3). For a name appears as a result of the summing up of all the other names and their meanings, the name 'Jesus': It would not apply if the other names were absent. Can we not see when we think about the way he has changed our souls that we should also call him Admirable Christ? This is also the meaning of the name Jesus. The beginning of our health and our salvation starts when we begin to reject what we used to love, to lament what used to give us joy, to embrace what used to frighten us, to follow what we used to flee, to desire with passion what we used to despise. There is certainly much to admire in a being that accomplishes such wonders. We also need his advice on how to correct our faults and how to organize our life, for sometimes zeal and good will can go too far and rob us of all pleasure. We must also remember that as God he can forgive our past sins. Without such forgiveness there is no salvation, and it can come only from God. Nor is all of this enough to save us: He must also be strong in order to protect us against our evil enemy so as to keep at bay our old desires. Jesus has all of these qualities, they are implicit in his name, especially when we remember that he is also called 'Father of the Future Century' which means that he can and will resuscitate to eternal life those who have been given a limited lease on life, life in this world, in this century, by their earthly parents. Even all of this would not suffice if, as 'Prince of Peace,' he did not pacify his Father, to whom the Kingdom will be delivered.' (*In circumcissione Domini*, Sermo II, Migne, Patr. Latina, CLXXXIII, 136)

"From all of this St. Bernard concludes that the names given to Christ are all necessary so that He can be called justly and truly Jesus, for in order to deserve completely such a name it is necessary that Christ have the power that is implicit in all His other names and that He carry out the activities these names imply. Thus the name Jesus is the summing up of the other names and therefore the name that is most fitting to Christ. St. Bernard also remarks that it is not a name given to Him arbitrarily but rather a name that belongs to Him in essence and that is woven into His very being, because, as we will point out in detail later on, everything in Christ, every quality and action of his being and His life, is related to our spiritual health and our salvation. And to accept such a name, as Christ did, a name that relates to us, that has us in mind, is another token of His love for mankind. He could have chosen as a favorite name for Himself a thousand other names, names having to do with divine powers and riches, since as St. Paul points out they belong to Him, yet He chose a name that relates Him to us: Nothing in the world is as important to Him as our salvation. God related His name to us for the first time when talking to Moses in Exodus, 'Thus shalt thou say unto the children of Israel, The Lord God of your fathers, the God of Abraham, the God of Isaac, and the God of Jacob, hath sent me unto you: this is my name forever, and this is my memorial unto all generations' (3:15). He states that His name is 'the God of Abraham' because of all that He had done before and would continue to do in order to favor and protect the children of Abraham, all those who kept the faith: God had been present in Abraham's mind, had given him rules, defended him, multiplied his seed, helped, redeemed, blessed him: In a word, God had been 'Jesus' to Abraham, God had been his salvation.

"God states this is the name that belongs to him for all generations, which includes the rebirth of men in a world of eternal life, the victory of divine justice, all of which indicates the intervention of Christ Jesus, that is to say, as our Savior. When

THE NAMES OF CHRIST

Moses went up the mountain, when he saw the glory of God as he had been promised, God placed him upon a hollow in a rock, covered him with His hand, and everything that He showed Moses He defined with the following words, 'The Lord, the Lord God, merciful and gracious, long-suffering, and abundant in goodness and truth, keeping mercy for thousands' (Ex. 34:6–7), by which we understand that His essence is mercy, He wants to help us, to have mercy upon us, His being is full of love and sweet charity. When He appeared before our eyes, not because we went to the mountain but because God became man and came down to us, the main name He took for Himself was 'salvation,' 'Jesus.' This name expresses His being, His attitude, His works. Mercy, pity, salvation.

"This name 'health' or 'salvation' expresses not only one quality but many other qualities. When we are in good health we are strong, we can run fast, we are also good-looking and our voice is even and pleasant. Our mind works better, every sense, every muscle, every part of our body becomes more efficient. To be in good health is to enjoy every kind of pleasure and well-being. Because Christ gives to us everything that is good and enjoyable He fully deserves the name of Jesus. As God He is the source of all that is good, and as man He supplies us with the advice and the medicine that can heal all our diseases. There is no human being so just and perfect that he or she cannot benefit from Christ's grace, from his healing powers, from Jesus' power to give us perfect health both to our body and to our soul.

"Jesus helps each individual as such, and helps us all as a group, cleaning our sins away, freeing us from tyrants, rescuing us from hell, giving us His grace and His spirit, and finally giving power and glory to our senses and our bodies. David expresses this in a psalm that I interpreted yesterday in a certain way, and you, Juliano, gave us a translation that was somewhat different, and there is yet a third possible translation which I will give now. It is my version of Psalm 110.3

> Thy people shall feel noble
> In the day of thy power;
> Thy army shall feel noble surrounded by holy splendor
> More than the womb and more than the morning
> We find in thee the dew of youth.

BOOK III

My interpretation is as follows: The day that begins when the night of our dark century is over, truly a great day because it does not end in night and because in it truth shines, and thus it will be a day surrounded by holy splendors, since the splendor of just people, now hidden in their breasts, will come to light; then, upon that day, all the people of Christ will feel noble. We assume that the people of Christ will be composed by the just men and women only, because in the Holy Scripture they are the ones who are called 'people of God.' And the same group that is called 'people' is later on described as an 'army.' They are called thus not because they make Christ powerful through physical power and weapons but because they are the living proof of Christ's great power, and when I say power I mean especially the virtue and efficacy of His spirit, with which He has brought us out of our misery into happiness and a full life.

"The psalm states that Christ's people, Christ's army, shall feel noble, because Christ by giving them health has made them confident and imbued in them a feeling of superior power: The flags of victory can be seen in the highest towers of the castle. Christ was capable of such a feat because there was in him the dew of youth, and here by dew I understand the strength of His spirit, often symbolized by water in the Holy Scriptures. It is called dew of youth because it leads His faithful to be born to a new life in which they will be eternally young. More than the womb and more than the morning dawn: This underlines the power and abundance of such dew. Power, because it will bring us into a new life faster than the sun rises at dawn, faster than the baby is born from a pregnant mother whose womb clearly tells us birth is approaching. Abundance, because Christ has more life-giving dew than we can find water in springs and sources.

"Let us proceed. Health is based upon the harmony of forces and humors and can be compared to sweet music played by the body's humors. Christ also creates harmony, and this is one more reason why He was named Jesus. As God He creates harmony and proportion among all the beings in the world; as a man He establishes a system of relationships and harmonies in our everyday life. St. Paul writes in his Epistle to the Colossians, about Christ, as follows: 'For it pleased the Father that in him should all fullness dwell; and, having made peace through the blood of his cross, by him to reconcile all things unto himself; by him, I say, whether they be things in earth or things in heaven' (1:20). And elsewhere, in the Epistle to the Ephesians, he states that He managed to get rid of the division that had existed between men and God, and also the quarrels among men, Gentiles against Jews, for instance, and out of both groups He created one new nation. For the same reason in Psalm 118, lines 22–23:

> The stone which the builders refused
> is become the head stone of the corner.

"Because He reconciles the opposites, He is the knot that ties the visible and the invisible, reason and the senses. He is the sweet melody and its counterpoint, a music that soothes and gives serenity.

"The name Jesus explains what we can expect from Him, what we can ask from Him. For if we are ill we are not cured by the ointments and medicines applied to our skin, but rather by a realignment and a new balance of the humors that fight inside our body. Once this new order has been established deep inside us all the signs of good health appear in our face and body, since we are indeed cured. Christ gives us His help, His holy medicine, not visibly and externally, but by acting inside our bodies and souls. Not only our leaves and flowers, but our stems and roots, the stems and roots of our souls, are cleansed and healed. This is why Isaiah states:

> Cry out and shout, thou inhabitant of Zion:
> For great is the Holy One of Israel in the midst of thee. (12:6)

He does not say 'around thee,' but rather 'inside thee, in thy entrails, in the very core of thy soul.'

"Christ's main purpose is to establish harmony between the secret and innermost parts of our soul, to put them in touch with God and also create harmony in that relationship. By harmonizing the soul's humors, by refining the fire of passions and evil desires, this can be accomplished. Not face and body, not by performing the right ceremonies and rituals. For these can be holy and good if performed thinking about God, but what Christ does to us is indeed something different. He heals us from the inside: Ceremonies and rituals influence what we may call our outside life. They may make us look healthy, their purpose is to make us healthy, but they are not health itself and are less powerful than the internal means to reach health. Before Christ, and after Christ, many religious regulations and rituals were established, about our food and diet, about the way we should clean and wash ourselves and make use of ointments, the way to order our looks, our movements, our gestures. Yet no instruction of this kind could give us the source of inner health: Only Jesus could do it, and this is why we call Him Jesus.

"Macharios describes aptly this situation when he writes,

What is typical of Christianity has nothing to do with our appearance, our garments, the way we look. Some think this is so, and mistakenly want to be different from others in this external way, yet inside their souls they are troubled, insecure, anguished, just as the rest of mankind. Their looks may be different, some of their actions are acts of kindness and charity, yet their hearts and souls are still tied with earthly chains, and they cannot enjoy by themselves, lonely, alone, in secret, of the peace brought by God, of the heavenly serenity that rejoices the spirit, because they have not taken the trouble to ask for such high rewards and even because they do not believe that God will grant them such gifts and privileges. Indeed this new creature, this new man, in other words, the perfect Christian, the true Christian, differs from the other people who live today in the way he has renewed his spirit, in the serenity and peace that he has attained and also in his love for God, in his burning desire to attain the rewards of Heaven. Christ asked just this, he wanted that those who believe in him should receive such spiritual rewards. The Christian's goal, and his glory, is the beauty of the Heavens, and it can be attained only with hard work and sweat, and by undergoing many hard trials and tests, and, most of all, through the gift of divine Grace. (*Homily V*, Migne, *Patr. Graeca*, XXXIV, 498)

"This text describes Christ's doctrine, His path, and our goals. As for the doctrine and the path, we must accept that any advice that does not try to uproot our evil passions and create in our souls a climate of justice, moderation, and order, is not holy, even when the outside looks and appearance seem to be holy. It is unworthy of Christ's name, of salvation and Jesus. Christ's name, in Greek, means 'anointed,' and His function is to anoint us in a way that reaches deep inside, down to our bones. Other beings, other attitudes, are superficial: They do not go beyond our skin. Only Christ can subdue our passions: Other people are capable only of disguising them under a thin veneer of 'goodness.' They even aid and abet such passions. Thus only Jesus can give us true health."

And then Sabino commented: "It is possible, dear Marcelo, that today we cannot find in our Church a guidance of the quality that your words have suggested we are in need of."

"We agree on this point," Marcelo answered, "and yet there was such a guiding light in the Church in ancient times, and it can reappear in the future. This is why we should pay attention to this message."

"Yes, we should pay attention," Juliano added, "and we should remember that Christ also warned us, through the gospel, about the false prophets. They lead us astray, they point toward crooked and mistaken roads. They look like lambs and behave like wolves."

And then Marcelo, "We have witnessed sad situations where we were being misled. For instance, charity is a good thing in principle. Yet when you are advised to dress for it as for a parade, to announce your charity with drum and fife, to shoot your guns in the air, to boast and rival your neighbors in almsgiving, this is a way to increase our vanity, our pride, our need to be praised. Instead of correcting our sinful instincts this attitude encourages them, glossing them over and sanctifying them in the name of charity and good works. Our sickness worsens, just the opposite of what Jesus tries to accomplish in us.

"Our aim as Christians is to become one with Christ, to hold Christ in us while we become like Him. Christ is health. Health does not mean that we are going to be covered with bandages or with ointments: it means our body will recover its inner balance and harmony. Only then, when we are perfectly balanced inside, can we become like Him, like Jesus. We can do many things unsuccessfully. For instance, we can fast, we can keep silent for a long time, as in meditation. We can take part in every choir song and prayer. We can wear a hair shirt. We can walk on snow and ice with bare feet. We can beg our food and dress in rags. Yet if in the meantime we are burning with sinful passions inside, if the the old man is still alive in him, if wrath and pride, selfishness and cupidity are very much in evidence, if hatred, envy, vainglory, ambition are still in control, no matter how many gestures that seem virtuous he makes, the fact is that he has not reached the health and the salvation that we call Jesus. He should know that no one that has not been healed by this cure, by the health that Jesus exemplifies, can enter heaven and have a clear view of God. St. Paul puts it this way: 'Follow peace with all men, and holiness, without which no man shall see the Lord' (Heb. 12:14). Whoever falls in this description should wake up to this fact and try to come closer to Jesus. Let him ask for health from Jesus and, as St. Paul puts it, 'forgetting those things that are behind, and reaching forth to those things that are before, I press toward the mark for the prize of the high calling of God in Jesus Christ' (Phil. 3:13–14).

"Now, is fasting a bad thing? The hair shirt, ascetic sufferings, are they bad? No, they are good. Good, as medicines that can help us are good: Yet they are not health itself. These medicines are a witness to the fact that we are still in poor health. They are ways and means to reach justice, yet they are by themselves not justice itself. They are clues to the soul's harmony, but they are not harmony. Sometimes they become separated from their goal: Then they are only hypocrisy and lies. On the one hand we must reproach the heretics who condemn any show of external piety, since it can be beautiful and helpful, when it is born from inner beauty. Yet on the other hand we must warn the faithful that such external piety is not and cannot be a goal in itself, is not in and by itself the soul's treasure and salvation. It would be a pity if a soul in her journey toward God were to find herself frustrated, and went into a blind alley, looking for God yet embracing Solon, Pythagoras, at best Moses. For Jesus is health, and health is secret justice and harmony inside our soul: When this comes to pass it creates rays of wisdom that beautify the outside world and every aspect of our body.

"It is, as I have said, a mistake to despise and condemn the external forms of worship, and another error is to think that they can alone supply our soul with the strength it needs to reach salvation. Only Jesus is the right answer, and this is explained by St. Paul when he writes about Christ that He 'is the Son of God with power, according to the spirit of holiness, by the resurrection from the dead' (Rom. 1:4), which means that the main reason to believe that Jesus is the true Messiah, the Son of God promised by the Law (in the same way that a thing can be known by the definition of the noun that expresses it) is because Jesus carried out the work and the actions that were reserved to the Messiah by God, by the Scriptures, by the prophets. He has 'power.' How does He make use of it? According to the spirit of holiness. This is seen inasmuch as He makes holy His followers, not in a superficial way, through new life and a new spirit, which are celebrated in a special victory, the resurrection from the dead. In other words, they are celebrated in the fact that Christ resurrects His dead, that is to say, those who died with Him when He died on the cross: After He resuscitated He gave them new life. For the death that we suffered in our soul when He died is the reason our sin and guilt finally died. His resurrection was also our resurrection. And when sin and guilt die in us, the life of justice is born in our soul, as we pointed out yesterday.

"Let me repeat: To condemn external ceremonies is as much a mistake as it is to think that in them reside grace and justice. The means between these two extremes is the right solution: The ceremony is good when it serves and helps the true sanctification of the soul, for it can help us, and when it is born out of a holy inspiration it is better since it brings us closer to heaven, yet it is not the true living health that Christ brings to us—and that is why we call him Jesus.

"We do so not only because He brings us health but because He is health. Truly He does bring us justice and health through His grace, and beyond this, He brings us Himself, and through His spirit He joins our soul, heals and graces it. This presence is like a glowing light and by itself it brings health to us. St. Macharios puts it this way:

> When Christ realizes that you are seeking him and have put your hope in him, he comes to the rescue and gives you true charity, that is, he gives himself to you, and entering your soul, becomes everything: paradise, tree of life, precious pearl, crown, builder, tiller of the soil, man

of compassion, man free from all passion, man, God, wine, life, water, lamb, spouse, warrior and weapons of war, and, finally, Christ, who is everything in all of us. (Homily V, Migne, Patr. Graeca, 34, 498)

Thus he embraces our soul in His and clothes our soul with His presence, as St. Paul writes: 'But put ye on the Lord Jesus Christ' (Rom. 13:14). And when this happens he takes over our very soul.

"Let us remember that when we bake bread we deal with a huge amount of dough which by itself lacks leaven and salt, has no flavor, and this is why we need leaven. Leaven becomes fused to the dough, it becomes part of it: It acts upon it not from the outside, but by becoming fused with it. Mankind was like dough, a damaged and sick dough. God made Jesus, so that He could help us by bringing us a sort of health that would work from the inside. Thus he compares Himself to leaven (Matt. 13:33). Let us also think about iron being forged. Its being is iron, and also fire. Yet it looks like fire, not like iron. Thus Christ, united with me, become my Lord, can free me from my troubles, giving me so many new resources that I no longer resemble the sick man I was, I no longer am this sick man: I have become so healthy that I am the very image of health, that is to say, the very image of Jesus.

"O blessed health! O sweet Jesus worthy of every desire: Could I be entirely under your dominion. Could your health penetrate my soul and my body. Could you free me from all this dross, from my old age. I would like to become totally like you. There is nothing in me that I do not despise. Almost everything that is born in me is poverty, pain, imperfection, sickness, lack of health. It was written in the Book of Job,

So am I made to possess months of vanity,
And wearisome nights are appointed to me.
When I lie down, I say,
When shall I arise, and the night be gone?
And I am full of tossings to and fro unto the dawning of the
    day.
My flesh is clothed with worms and clods of dust;
My skin is broken, and become loathsome.
My days are swifter than a weaver's shuttle,
And are spent without hope.

THE NAMES OF CHRIST

O remember that my life is wind:
Mine eye shall no more see good.
The eye of him that hath seen me shall see no more:
Thine eyes are upon me, and I am not. (7:3–8)

As for myself, O Lord, I would like to flee from myself, so that having created a vacuum you should take over and become my life, my self, my health, my Jesus."

After saying this Marcelo ceased talking. His face was blushing. He sighed deeply several times, after which he continued, "It is not possible for a sick man to discuss health without mentioning how sad he is to be deprived of it. So please forgive me if my misery moved me and made me speak out."

After a silence he spoke again and said, "Christ and health are one and the same thing. A name means much: It means that the essence of the being can be found in the name. Virtue, health, are powerful names. Health can be described as health of the soul, health of the body, and in this last category we have to consider the different parts of the body: the head, the stomach, and so on. Christ as a giver of health provides help in two areas. On the first hand He preserves the health we already have. Yet further on He gives us back the health we lost. The basic idea is to bring useful strength to our body and at the same time to get rid of harmful interferences. Health food is of two kinds. It can make our body strong, and it can also purge it from harmful humors. The health that Jesus gives us has also these two functions: It preserves and strengthens the health we already have, and it restores it when we do not have it.

"Jesus is the bread of life, as He calls himself, and this bread has been made out of two substances, holiness, which makes us strong, and hard work, which purges and destroys our vices. This bread has been kneaded with poverty, with humility, suffering, anguish, insults, blows, thorns, the cross, death. Each ingredient is a remedy against a vice. Still other ingredients are God's grace, the wisdom of the heavens, holy justice, moral values, and all the other gifts from the Holy Spirit. With such ingredients it becomes a powerful life-giving medicine which, eaten with faith, uproots and destroys our vices with its bitter parts, and enhances our life with its holy ingredients. The thorns in it purge us from our pride. The whippings in it cleanse us from excessive softness and

362

love of pleasure. The cross fights selfishness, Christ's death puts an end to my vices, while other ingredients are equally active: When we eat in this bread God's justice, the spirit of justice grows in our soul. Holiness and grace act upon our body creating in us true holiness and grace. A portion of heaven is thus born in me when I become the son of God by eating in this bread the substance of God made man. We become then like him, dead to sin, living for justice, and true salvation, true Jesus, comes to us.

"Jesus means therefore all kinds of salvation, because Jesus is a being entirely made of the essence of salvation. His words increase our health, and so do His works, His life, even His death. What He did, what He thought, what He suffered, His afterlife, everything connected with Him gives us health and salvation. He heals us with His life experience, He gives us salvation through His experience with death. His grief and His pains diminish ours. Isaiah puts it briefly:

> But he was wounded for our transgressions,
> He was bruised for our iniquities:
> The chastisement of our peace was upon him;
> And with his stripes we are healed. (53:5)

His blisters are an ointment for our souls, His poured blood makes our virtue stronger. His example, as a model, wakes us up to purity, health, survival.

"He is like the tree described in Apocalypse or Revelation, a tree planted on either side of the river, a tree of life, near the pure water of life, proceeding out of the throne of God and of the lamb. The leaves of the tree, it is written, were for the healing of nations. Thus Jesus: Not one leaf in His tree that is not a source of life, for me, for us, for the nations and for the whole world.

"The tree of life described by St. John bore twelve manner of fruits, and yielded one fruit every month. Again the parallel applies, for Jesus brings us health not by healing one illness or by helping us during one season of the year but by protecting us against every serious accident, every mortal wound, every bleeding cancer. He heals our pride by showing us His reed as a scepter. The purple cloak, given to Him as an insult, can heal our ambition. His crown of thorns upon His head can heal our wicked love of empty pleasures. His bruised body wounded by the whip can get us rid of everything that is gross and clumsy. His naked-ness reminds us that our cupidity is wrong. His endurance tells us that we should not be rash. Our self-centered attitude weakens when we remember how He never put Himself in first place. The Church, inspired by the Holy Spirit, on the day and the hour that commemorate the crucifixion, knowing the meaning of such an event, asks something from Christ. In the first place, it asks health and salvation for our souls and our bodies. It asks such a mercy for the popes, the bishops, the priests, the kings and princes, for all the faithful. It asks that sinners should repent and do penance. The just people should persevere in their attitude. The poor should be helped and protected. Prisoners should be freed. Sick people should be healed. Pilgrims should be able to travel happily and come back to their homes without any mishap.

"Jesus means health and salvation even to heretics, unbeliev-ers, Jews. It is significant that in Solomon's Song of Songs the Shulamite calls her lover 'a cluster of camphire in the vineyards of En-gedi' (1:13). Perhaps it was God's idea that we should not be told what 'camphire' was, and so we did not know what kind of plant, what kind of bush or tree that name represented, and then we had to search for the word's etymology, and then learn that 'camphire' means 'forgiving of sins.' Then we realize how accu-rately the Shulamite calls her lover by this name. By this she points out that He does not free us from one single sin, but rather He is a cluster of mercies, of ways of forgiving us from our sins, an infinite salvation, a source of protection, a spring of life and health giving us its sweet waters for ever and ever.

"Now, at this point, dear Sabino, another subject, another doubt comes to my mind. It is as follows: do you think that the creatures of this world have been created out of nothing, out of nothingness?"

"I believe," Sabino answered, "that God created them out of His infinite power, without a matter or a mold that could help Him in any way."

"Therefore," Marcelo continued, "no one, no creature, no being, has in it, in its core, something that is durable, no being possesses by, and for itself, nor through some external help, the being that it has, that keeps him or her or it alive and active among us?"

"This is what I think," Sabino said.

BOOK III

"Well, then," Marcelo replied right away, "a building without foundations, or built upon sand, can it last for long?"

"No, it is not possible."

"We have stated that none of the creatures and beings in this world have a solid and permanent foundation that belongs to them. Therefore all of them, left to themselves, are in danger of falling down. They seem to walk or run toward their annihilation. They were born from nothing, or nothingness, and they travel toward their destruction and death: They find out that their origin was death and nothingness and they race toward their beginning. Job says about angels, and also about his servants in general,

> Behold, he put no trust in his servants;
> And his angels he charged them with folly:
> How much less in them that dwell in houses of clay,
> Whose foundation is in the dust,
> Which are crushed before the moth? (4:18–19)

And about the basic elements of the world, and about the heavens, David has this to say,

> Of old hast thou laid the foundations of the earth:
> And the heavens are the work of thy hands.
> They shall perish, but thou shalt endure:
> Yea, all of them shall wax old like a garment. (Ps. 102:25–26)

As we see in these texts the Holy Spirit seems to be condemning to destruction and death all the creatures, and the reason for such a harsh sentence is the weak foundation that cannot support us. If the very angels could be accused of folly it may have been because their being was not entirely founded upon a bedrock of reality and holiness. As for men, their feet and their foundations were made of clay. The heavens and the earth do grow old. How can this process be described? Just as cloth is attacked by moths our world is attacked and destroyed by evil, since it has such a weak foundation."

"This may be so, Marcelo," Sabino said, "but please tell us how to make sense out of what you have just said."

"Yes, I will, but first answer me, did we not agree yesterday

365

that God created all the living beings so that He could live in them and so that His kindness could shine through this new life?"

"Yes, we did agree about that," Sabino acquiesced.

"Then," Marcelo went on, "if the creatures, because of the basic disease at the very origin of their being, are always struggling to sink back into nothingness, always falling down, always becoming worse, and since God, who created them, had to find a way to heal and protect them: He thought about the Word, His son, and had the Word, who was the image and brief digest of all the creatures, come down to our world and take flesh by becoming a man. Jesus came into being, always in touch with eternity and with God, and He was to become our help, our medicine, our salvation. Many words describe him: In Hebrew the word is Dabar, in Greek it is Logos, in Spanish it is the Word, and they all mean Jesus; in Hebrew, and in Spanish the meaning is health and salvation.

"In Jesus Christ, as in a deep well, as in a vast ocean, we find a treasure of Being. We find the essence of the whole world. Moreover, when the world becomes damaged or sick, His son is the project, the plan, the image, the ways and means of creation that made possible the creation of so many beings. The Father had His son born again, as a man, whose name was Jesus, eternally alive and capable of restoring health to every creature. In Jesus we find condensed as in a vast ocean the whole being and substance of the world. Since much of this substance is fragile and can be easily damaged, Jesus, always available, can always come to the rescue: always the first, as Saint Paul states, always the alpha and the omega, the beginning and the end. He created beings, and He gave them health and salvation. The Word and Jesus are fused into one and the same person.

"Not only human beings, but angels dwelling in heaven recognize that their health is spelled Jesus, who brought back to life some people who were dead, and gave vigor to others so that they would not die. His cross and His blood embrace and make clean and pure the whole four elements and the earth and the heavens: He helps creatures who are endowed with reason, and He helps the other creatures, the ones devoid of a reasoning brain, to the point that they feel a part of the normal world. Yesterday we discussed this issue and concluded that all things, both those who are alive and who are sensitive, and those that are without senses, were created in order to bring to light this situation. Jesus is also called fruit and also bud: In this fashion the very holy person for whose embodiment as a man all things were created, was created, as in a fair game, a fair returning of values, in order that He could repair and heal the health and salvation of every other creature, and this is why He was given the name of Jesus.

"And now, dear Sabino, so that you can admire the wisdom of God, we must remember and consider that He did not help His Son become a man just to satisfy a whim, but rather this whole effort was carried out so that the created beings could be healed and recreated. The Word could carry out the task, and the power was His, yet in order for the Word to be also Jesus and salvation, He also had to become man. He was to create and re-create, and just as a sculptor carving a block of marble knows that he did not make that marble, it was made by nature and acquired by him, so too the Holy Spirit simply was confused and baffled. These beings came from God: The Word would have to become more powerful than God in order to effect any change in such a vast work. It was indispensable for the Spirit to become closer to the damaged parts in need of repairs. Everything had to be scaled down to the size of the patient. Then, putting together the patient, the creatures around the patient, the forces coming from inside the patient and from outside, coming down from outer space into our world, we could see that this ideal bridge, this giver of shapes and giver of reforming laws and principles, this symbol of life and of health, was, indeed, Jesus, our Jesus Christ.

"Just as in Paradise, the ideal place in which were placed our early parents Adam and Eve by God, there were two trees, one tree related to knowledge and the other one related to life, the first tree capable of giving fruits of science, the second giving nourishing fruit, and God wanted Adam and Eve to eat from the second tree, not from the first: Thus in this second stage God has prepared for us two wonderful trees, one having for its essence knowledge, that is to say, the Word, whose deep secrets are still forbidden to us, since it is written,

It is not good to eat much honey:
So for men to search their own glory is not glory. (Prov. 25:27)

THE NAMES OF CHRIST

There is yet another tree, a tree that restores, cures, heals, saves, gives eternal life, and its name is Jesus, and we shall eat from its fruit. It is not a forbidden fruit, rather it is highly recommended and even ordered that we should eat it. He states it himself quite clearly, 'Verily, verily, I say unto you, Except ye eat the flesh of the Son of man, and drink his blood, ye have no life in you' (John 6:54). The same way that we cannot see without the light from the sun, because the sun is our general source of light, we cannot enjoy health without Jesus, who by name and action is our general source of health: Without Jesus we shall become ill and die.

"He gives us health in our soul and our body, He gives health to our senses, our eyes, our tongue. No health without Jesus. Both in sickness and in health Jesus turns out to mean health and salvation. We are born without sin and related to God because of Jesus' help. Later on he cleanses our soul from the traces of old sins. We try to go on living, and find Him by our side: He stretches His health-giving hand and places it upon our body racked by disease, and His hand cools the infernal fires of our fever, and even more it almost turns our body into spirit. Finally, when death unravels our fabric, He does not abandon our ashes, but rather, close to them, He becomes our salvation: He makes our ashes rise to a new life, He clothes them with eternal life, with undying glory.

"I am certain that the prophet David when composing Psalm 103 was much aware of this divine health, for he feels so full of hope and happiness when thinking about the grace that pours down from heaven that he talks to his soul and incites it to praise the Lord: His soul is then asked to bless the Lord, to remember His benefits, since He is so kind (Ps 109). Become a living language and spend all your energy and time in praise of the Lord. Public and secret voices should speak to this goal. May your voice come out of the deepest part of your entrails, may the secrets in your heart sing out about all the favors granted by God, so that the memory of such favors will remain there as a precious heritage. You were turning into nothingness and death, and the Lord created a new order to give you back your being. You had become your own plague, your own poison, and the Lord gave you a new and powerful health, Jesus, who forgave all your sins and cured your aches. He became your relative, your brother, surrounding

368

your body and your life with care and affection. A giver of health, a health that can satisfy your desires, give you countless treasure, glorious jewels, a handsome new body, made young and strong, rid of its old weaknesses, as a young eagle gets rid of useless feathers and proceeds to soar to the sky.

"For, indeed, the Lord is an executor of righteousness and carries out acts of justice for all that are oppressed. He always takes pity on those who have been downtrodden, those who have been pillaged, and restores their rights. From the very beginning He stated to Moses and to the sons of His beloved Israel that He would favor them, and said that He was full of compassion and of clemency, His heart was full of love, He was patient and long-suffering, easy in forgiving, loath to quarrel with us.

"This is what the Lord stated, and this is what we see in fact: The Lord has not dealt with us according to our sins, He is not punishing us according to our transgressions. As far away from the earth is heaven as the Lord's charity towers above us and helps us. We occupy a plain, a lowland, and your charity and mercy are the heaven above it. We walk on parched fields but your benevolence comes down like rain. Mud is vile, heaven is divine. We perish in our dust, while your charity is eternal. Mists cover our horizon, while you are a ray of light shining far above us. We bend toward the center of gravity, your heavenly virtue soars and lightens every burden. You have separated and protected us from our guilt and our sins in such a radical way that we have to think about the distance from one star to another if we want to have a clear idea about such a change. We were born west of Eden, west of Adam, and you have placed us in your East, in your Orient, where your sun of justice shines. As a father anxious to help his sons, you became transformed into a merciful son in order to pour upon our heads your mercy and friendship as a father. Because, O Lord, you made us the way we are, and you know very well our ways, our strengths and weaknesses. You know that we are like dust. You know that our days are like spring grass: We are born, we grow, we flower, we wither fast. Like wild flowers, we seem to be something and are nothing; we promise much and are only flying pollen; a gust of wind comes and we perish leaving nothing behind us.

"Yet when we appear weaker and more perishable your mer-

cy, O Lord, shines brighter. We pass away but your mercy endures from one century to the next, and goes on forever. It comes
down to us, and from the fathers it passes on to the sons, and to
the sons of these sons, and so on. Your throne is in the heavens,
and from there your mercy flows down to us: Nothing will
change in your love for us.

"Let all creatures bless you, O Lord, since you are the salvation of all of us. Let your angels bless you, they who are ever
valiant executors of your orders, let your armies bless you, as well
as your ministers, always ready to follow your instructions. Let all
your created works praise you, all over the horizon, as far as your
empire stretches out, and together with them, let my soul praise
you too. It is said, in Psalm 96, at the very beginning, 'O sing unto
the Lord a new song,' and indeed your greatness is so special that
it deserves to be praised by a new language, a new music, a new
song. Your arm became our salvation, your Word became our
Jesus. Your very power, your right hand, your strong fortress and
castle, became for us a sweet and helpful medicine. You brought
your Son Jesus in front of all of us, as our salvation, and by it you
made your cause acceptable and accepted by everybody. No one
will complain that you let us fall in the past, since you helped so
much to retrieve and save us from such an ancient fall. There was
guilt, yet the medicine was all-powerful. We may even say that it
was a happy sin, since it brought for us the salvation of our Jesus.
And here ends my speech. You, Sabino, as usual, can give our
conversation a good ending."

And then he fell silent, at which Sabino said, "You have given
us the perfect ideas to end our meeting. What I can do myself is
only recite a few lines that I have composed, and here they are."

And then he spoke out loud,

O soul of mine, let us praise God
And all that's light in thee
Celebrate today His Holy Name,
His blessed memory.

An army of stars parades above,
Mankind unfolds her story,
And stars and men, made one at last,
Sing only of Thy glory.

BOOK III

And then he fell silent. And so ended the conversations of our three friends about the names of Christ, whose is the power and the glory for all centuries past, present, and future. Amen.

Select Bibliography

There are detailed bibliographies of primary and secondary texts in languages other than English in: Karl A. Kottman, *Law and Apocalypse: The Moral Thought of Luis de León (1527?–1591)* (The Hague: Martinus Nyhoff, 1972 and *De los nombres de Cristo,* ed. Cristobal Cuevas (Madrid, 1977).

TEXTS

Obras completas castillanas. Edited by Felix García. 2 vols. Madrid: Biblioteca de autores cristianos, 1957.

De los nombres de Cristo. Edited by Federico de Onís. 3 vols. Madrid, 1914–1921.

Louis de León: Les noms du Christ. Translated by Robert Picard. Paris: Etudes Augustiniennes, 1978.

Fray Luis de León. *De los nombres de Cristo.* Ed. de Cristóbal Cuevas. Madrid: Catedra, 1977.

SELECT STUDIES

Ashtor, Eliyahu. *The Jews of Moslem Spain.* 2 vols. Philadelphia: Jewish Publication Society, 1973, 1979.

Baer, Yetzhak. *A History of the Jews of Christian Spain.* 2 vols. Philadelphia: Jewish Publication Society, 1966.

Bell, Aubrey F. G. *Luis de León.* Oxford: Oxford University Press, 1925.

Castro, Americo. *The Spaniards: An Introduction to Their History.* Berkeley: University of California Press, 1971.

Durán, Manuel. *Luis de León.* New York: Twayne, 1971.

Fitzmaurice-Kelly, James. *Fray Luis de León.* Oxford: Oxford University Press, 1921.

BIBLIOGRAPHY

Green, Otis H. *Spain and the Western Tradition.* 4 vols. Madison: University of Wisconsin Press, 1963–1966.

Hamilton, Bernice. *Political Thought in Sixteenth Century Spain.* Oxford: Clarendon Press, 1963.

Netanyahu, B. *The Marranos of Spain.* N.p.: American Academy for Jewish Research, 1966.

O'Callaghan, Joseph F. *A History of Medieval Spain.* Ithaca: Cornell University Press, 1975.

Peers, E. Allison. *The Complete Works of Saint John of the Cross.* Wheathampstead: Anthony Clark, 1978.

———. *Studies of the Spanish Mystics.* 3 vols. London, 1927–1960.

Roth, Cecil. *A History of the Marranos.* New York: Meridian Books, 1959.

Scholem, Gershom. *Major Trends of Jewish Mysticism.* New York: Schocken Books, 1972.

Sufis of Andalusia. Translated by R. W. J. Austin. Berkeley: University of California Press, 1977.

The Unknown Light: The Poems of Fray Luis de León. Translated by Willis Barnstone. Albany: State University of New York Press, 1979.

The Wisdom of the Spanish Mystics. Selected by Stephen Clissold. New York: New Directions, 1977.

Welch, Robert J. *Introduction to the Spiritual Doctrine of Fray Luis de León.* Washington, D.C.: Augustinian Press, 1951.

Index to Preface, Foreword and Introduction

INDEX

INDEX

Index to Text

INDEX

INDEX

INDEX

INDEX

Other Volumes in this Series

Sharafuddin Maneri • THE HUNDRED LETTERS

Martin Luther • THEOLOGIA GERMANICA

Native Mesoamerican Spirituality • ANCIENT MYTHS, DISCOURSES, STORIES, DOCTRINES, HYMNS, POEMS FROM THE AZTEC, YUCATEC, QUICHE-MAYA AND OTHER SACRED TRADITIONS

Symeon the New Theologian • THE DISCOURSES

Ibn Al'-Arabī • THE BEZELS OF WISDOM

Hadewijch • THE COMPLETE WORKS

Philo of Alexandria • THE CONTEMPLATIVE LIFE, THE GIANTS, AND SELECTIONS

George Herbert • THE COUNTRY PARSON, THE TEMPLE

Unknown • THE CLOUD OF UNKNOWING

John and Charles Wesley • SELECTED WRITINGS AND HYMNS

Meister Eckhart • THE ESSENTIAL SERMONS, COMMENTARIES, TREATISES AND DEFENSE

Francisco de Osuna • THE THIRD SPIRITUAL ALPHABET

Jacopone da Todi • THE LAUDS

Fakhruddin 'Iraqi • DIVINE FLASHES

Menahem Nahum of Chernobyl • THE LIGHT OF THE EYES

Early Dominicans • SELECTED WRITINGS

John Climacus • THE LADDER OF DIVINE ASCENT

Francis and Clare • THE COMPLETE WORKS

Gregory Palamas • THE TRIADS

Pietists • SELECTED WRITINGS

The Shakers • TWO CENTURIES OF SPIRITUAL REFLECTION

Zohar • THE BOOK OF ENLIGHTENMENT